In Defense of
a Political Court

Terri Jennings Peretti

PRINCETON UNIVERSITY PRESS, PRINCETON, NEW JERSEY

Library of Congress Cataloging-in-Publication Data

Peretti, Terri Jennings, 1956–
In defense of a political court / Terri Jennings Peretti.
p.   cm.
Includes bibliographical references and index.
ISBN 0-691-00905-8 (cl. : alk. paper)
1. Judicial review—United States. 2. Political questions and judicial
power—United States. 3. Constitutional law—United States—
Interpretation and construction. I. Title.
KF4575.P466   1999   99–12206
342.73—dc21

This book has been composed in Baskerville

The paper used in this publication meets
the minimum requirements of
ANSI/NISO Z39.48-1992 (R 1997)
(*Permanence of Paper*)

http://pup.princeton.edu

Printed in the United States of America

10   9   8   7   6   5   4   3   2   1

In memory of
my parents, Jack and Lois Jennings,
and to Rachel

CONTENTS

· ·

ACKNOWLEDGMENTS

· ·

MANY friends and colleagues have been generous in sharing their ideas and their support throughout my academic career and in the writing of this book more particularly. However, I am especially indebted to Bob Kagan. His contribution as a careful and discerning critic on numerous drafts of this manuscript was simply immeasurable. He was especially helpful in sparking the development of the final and most painful chapter. Bob's comments were typically voluminous, but always on the mark—a truly wonderful balance of encouragement and helpful criticism. I cannot think of a scholar for whom I have more respect.

This book is much better as well for the extremely helpful comments of the scholars who reviewed it for Princeton University Press—Sanford Levinson and a second reviewer who remains unknown to me. I would also like to thank Nelson Polsby, for his faith in my abilities and academic future and, more particularly, for his early guidance in helping me to develop the book's theoretical focus. To Martin Shapiro, I owe a great intellectual debt. His pathbreaking work on the subject of judicial politics was an inspiration and a necessary precursor of my own work in the field. Like Nelson, he provided valuable feedback on the manuscript at several critical junctures. I would also like to thank Professors Judith Gruber and Patricia Boling for their helpful comments on individual chapters.

I also wish to thank my colleagues in the Santa Clara University political science department for their support and encouragement. Peter Minowitz, our department chair, has been especially generous to me in that regard and my thanks to him are deep and heartfelt. I am also grateful to Jane Curry and Leslie Bethard for their considerable support and assistance, professional and personal.

Finally, thanks go to Princeton University Press for their patience and assistance and to Cindy Crumrine for her careful copyediting.

In Defense of a Political Court

Introduction

We are under the Constitution, but the Constitution is
what the judges say it is.

Charles Evans Hughes[1]

THIS candid remark of Chief Justice Hughes has been frequently cited, often
accepted,[2] but never endorsed as an ideal state of affairs. This book comes
rather close to doing just that.[3] It provides more than a grudging acceptance
of the reality that the Constititution lacks determinate meaning apart from
that provided by Supreme Court justices and that the justices' personal political preferences strongly influence their interpretations of the Constitution.
It celebrates that reality and regards political motivation on the part of the
justices as critical to insuring that the Court exercises its power of judicial
review in a responsible, legitimate, and democratic manner.

This thesis runs directly counter to the view that has long dominated normative constitutional law scholarship. My effort here is not to create yet another "grand theory" of judicial review[4] to be placed alongside the others,
nor does it provide considerable new empirical evidence regarding the
Court. Its aim instead is to subject the underlying premise of most contemporary constitutional theories—the dangers of a political Court—to critical
analysis, employing the substantial empirical evidence already amassed by
social scientists.

The first three chapters comprising Part I examine a number of very different theories of judicial review. It concludes that it is the fear of politics
which pervades them and which leads, as the title of Part I indicates, to the
failure of contemporary constitutional theory.

The primary assumption of conventional constitutional theorists is that
judicial review is fundamentally at odds with democratic values and, thus, is
in need of a special or exceptional source of legitimacy. As chapter 1 dis-
cusses, the typical solution is to provide a method by which the Court can
derive and apply constitutional principles in a neutral and coherent manner;

these scholars further assert that the justices possess special skills and attributes appropriate to that task. Three such approaches—interpretivism, noninterpretivism, and process-oriented review—are examined. While there are significant differences among them, a common bond is the premise of "legal autonomy"—the belief that constitutional outcomes can be significantly determined and justified in an objective way, rather than by reference to the justice's personal values.[5]

With the help of Critical Legal Studies scholars, chapter 2 rejects that central premise. However, the Critics use their finding of constitutional indeterminacy and judicial subjectivity to denigrate all uses of judicial power as arbitrary and a tool of liberal-capitalist oppression, a situation necessitating radical reform in our law and our politics. Their prescriptions unfortunately provide no practical answers to the questions of the Court's proper role in American democracy or of how an indeterminate Constitution should be interpreted in the here and now.

A more moderate response, examined in chapter 3, is provided by the Skeptics, whose acceptance of judicial subjectivity and judicial fallibility leads them to view the Court's constitutional decisions as "provisional" and wisely subject to political checks imposed by the other branches. Yet, like many conventional theorists, the Skeptics insist that the Court's role remains the provision of moral guardianship and prophecy. Such an accommodation of judicial review with democratic theory, however, makes little sense. Why should the morally impoverished legislature be permitted to check the constitutional decisions of the morally superior Court?

Conventional scholars, the Critics, and the Skeptics are united by their fear of a political Court and political motivation in constitutional interpretation. For the conventional scholar, subjective and politically motivated decisionmaking is undemocratic: it permits unelected judges to impose their personal and idiosyncratic views in opposition to the desires of the people, who are then virtually powerless to alter the Court's judgments. For the Critical Legal Studies scholar, the judge inevitably imposes his own elitist views or is the servant of liberal-capitalist oppression. Despite their acceptance of judicial subjectivity and fallibility, the Skeptics cannot resist the temptation to transform the justices into Platonic Guardians. All of these scholars express a profound pessimism about the virtues of politics and the capacities of judges to be effective and responsible political leaders. Their pessimism and skepticism require that they invent a nobler role in order to distinguish the

Court from ordinary political institutions and the justices from mere politicians. The roles suggested—whether modern-day agent of the Framers, protector of the democratic process, moral prophet, or catalyst for a new political order—are paternalistic and fundamentally antidemocratic.

There is no need, Part II argues, to provide such a sharp distinction between the Court and other political institutions or to find an alternative to politically motivated constitutional decisionmaking. Chapters 4 and 5 advance that argument by demonstrating that there are many benefits which flow from political motivation in constitutional decisionmaking. For example, the empirical evidence is quite strong in support of the view that when a justice decides in accordance with her personal values, she is vindicating those values deliberately "planted" on the Court by a recently elected president and Senate. Thus, value-voting promotes political representation by the Court.

Evidence also supports the conclusion that, contrary to the conventional scholar's view, political checks on the Court are effective; furthermore, it is policy motivation on the part of the justices that activates those checks and renders them effective. Only a justice who cares deeply about the success of a particular decision—for example, regarding racial equality—will also care about the willingness of other branches to fund and enforce that policy or the possibility that sanctions will be imposed against the Court. Strategies developed by policy-motivated justices to enhance policy success, such as actively seeking support, avoiding political sanctions, or moderating the Court's stance, even through a temporary retreat, can be viewed as quite valuable consensus-building activities. Thus, rather than leading to judicial tyranny as conventional scholars charge, political motive in constitutional decisionmaking insures that the Court exercises its power in a politically responsible and democratically defensible manner.

Chapter 6 examines and rejects the often-made counterargument that a political Court necessarily jeopardizes its legitimacy and its power. Public opinion research clearly and consistently refutes that conventional wisdom. The public pays little attention to the Court and its decisions and does not hold the Court in particularly high regard. Furthermore, when the public does evaluate the Court's decisions, it is political factors, particularly agreement with the substance of those decisions, that dominate the public's calculation of support or opposition. Evidence from its history also shows that when the Court has encountered public and political hostility, the explanation has been the political unacceptability of its decisions rather than its refusal to stay out of the political fray or to base it decisions firmly on the constitutional text or the Framers' intentions. In any case, the Court's decisions are consistent with majority views more often than not; it simply does not need a special sort of public reverence in order to sustain its legitimacy and thus its capacity to play a countermajoritarian role.

The final charge against a political Court—its inconsistency with democratic values—is addressed in chapter 7. That charge, I argue, rests upon a fundamentally flawed understanding of American democracy, one that erroneously emphasizes majority rule and legislative supremacy. Pluralist theory, in contrast, offers a more empirically accurate characterization. The American political system is not in any way directed to the goal of majority rule; it is in virtually all respects an antimajoritarian system, including its *rejection* of legislative supremacy. The American system of government, instead, consists of numerous and diverse political institutions, none of which is hierarchically superior to another. This provides groups, especially minorities, with a variety of arenas in which to advance their interests and contest policies with which they disagree. In this pluralist system, judicial review is neither deviant nor illegitimate; rather, it is a quite normal expression of the pluralist principles of redundancy and diversity in political representation.

The concluding chapter addresses two questions that remain upon acceptance of this political view of the Court: Whither the Court and Constitution? Why bother with a Court or a Constitution if judicial decisionmaking is primarily driven by the personal political preferences of the justices and their judgments as to the political acceptability of those preferences?

Pluralist theory supplies the answer to the first question regarding the Court's purpose. The Court simply serves as another (and slightly different) step in the policy process, nothing less and nothing more. It provides yet another opportunity for the policy initiatives of other branches to be challenged and possibly altered or rejected. Accordingly, the chance that government policy will in the end prove more satisfactory to the diverse interests in our nation is increased, as is the stability of the system as a whole. Because the Court makes policy in the context of individual cases, it may also compensate for the over- and underinclusiveness of legislative policymaking. Thus, the Court's value in American democracy does not lie in the mystical and superior attributes of judges and the judicial process. Rather, the Court possesses *instrumental* value in terms of enhancing both the stability of the political system as a whole and the quality of the policymaking process, particularly regarding the breadth of interests represented.

The question of the Constitution's purpose, given its indeterminate nature and its "manipulation" by politically motivated justices, remains. Is it not possible that such a view would destroy the Constitution as a source of moral and political principle and would lead to a severe weakening of the public's sense of political obligation to regard the Constitution as "law" worthy of obedience? The small dose of realism offered here is not likely to produce such an outcome, nor should closer public scrutiny of the Constitution and the Court be regarded as an undesirable development in a democracy. There may indeed be value in weakening the sense that the Constitution is the sole (and determinate) source of our public values and that the Court is the sole (and neutral) expositor of its meaning. The alternative offered here is to regard the Constitution as providing a system of numerous and diverse political arenas in which an ongoing debate about our public values takes place, with the Court merely serving as one of those arenas. Such a conception is both more accurate and more democratic.

PART I

The Failure of Contemporary Constitutional Theory

• •

CHAPTER 1

Conventional Constitutional Theory: The Neutralist Approach

CONSTITUTIONAL theory attempts to resolve the question of the legitimacy of judicial review in a democracy. As Professor Siegan has simply stated the matter, "The United States Supreme Court is an unusual institution for a nation that proclaims its dedication to democratic processes."[1] Why, scholars ask, should we entrust power in a democracy to a deviant, undemocratic institution such as the Supreme Court? Its members are unelected, serve "during good behavior," typically for life, and can be removed from office only through the difficult and rarely employed impeachment process.[2] Additionally, the Court's decisions, made pursuant to its power of judicial review, can be reversed only by constitutional amendment, which has occurred only four times in our nation's history.[3] Yet we grant this institution tremendous power—the power to strike down or "veto" as unconstitutional the decisions and policies of the people's elected representatives. And it has exercised this power in a variety of policy areas: school desegregation, abortion, affirmative action, rights of the accused, the death penalty, reapportionment, school prayer, sex discrimination, libel, obscenity, and even campaign finance reform.

The reason for concern then is obvious: nine and often only five unelected, life-tenured judges have the power to tell the people, "No, you cannot have your way." In a democracy, that is both puzzling and troubling.

The self-perceived task for legal scholars is to resolve the two problems associated with the Court's power of judicial review. The first is the legitimacy problem—the problem of reconciling the Court's power with democratic values. What possibly legitimate role can an undemocratic institution perform in a democracy? What are the legitimate uses of judicial review and the limits on its use? The second problem is how to police or enforce those limits. How can we effectively constrain judicial power and guard against judicial abuse? How can we insure that these unelected, life-tenured judges do not exceed the limits on their power and interfere with and restrict the democratic process arbitrarily?

At a general level, conventional legal scholars are in agreement about how to solve these two related problems. With regard to the legitimacy question, the dilemma of justifying an undemocratic institution in a democracy, it is asserted that even in a democracy the majority may legitimately be told "No." This derives from the nature of a written constitution and a government of limited powers, as well as the clear fears of majority tyranny on the part of the Constitution's Framers.

It is argued that ordinary democratic means for resolving political issues, such as vote counting or interest-group pressure and bargaining, are on occasion inappropriate. For example, issues involving minority rights or fundamental constitutional rights, such as freedom of speech and the right to vote, are unlikely to receive fair treatment in the political arena.

It is further asserted that Supreme Court justices possess certain virtues—legal training and methods of reasoning, capacities for dealing with matters of principle and, in particular, insulation from political pressure—that make them uniquely well suited for resolving those sorts of issues. In other words, the special attributes of judges and the legal process give the Court a heightened capacity for serving as a principled check or restraint on ordinary political processes.

The problem remains, of course, of defining those boundaries between the apolitical judicial sphere, where the people can and should be told "No," and the democratic sphere, where the people should have free rein.[4] Those boundaries must be defined as clearly and precisely as possible in order to resolve the enforcement problem—how to police those limits effectively and prevent judicial invasion of the democratic sphere. The justices must be given clear guidelines to follow and legal scholars (and perhaps, by inference, the people as well) must be able to know when the Court is exceeding its legitimate authority.

These scholars are quick to point out that fears of judicial abuse are not merely theoretical. In fact, we need only look to *Lochner*,[5] a case representing to most constitutional law scholars the worst example of judicial abuse.[6] In the *Lochner* case, the Court struck down a New York statute regulating the hours of bakers, enacted as a health and safety measure.[7] The Court reasoned that the statute violated the bakers' "liberty of contract," their freedom to contract to work as many hours as they might choose or deem necessary to support themselves and their families. The *Lochner* case was not by itself terribly important, but is deemed representative of a series of decisions from the end of the nineteenth century through the early New Deal years. During this period, a conservative Court interpreted the Constitution as giving special protection to economic liberties and property rights and the Court's central role as vigorously protecting those constitutional rights. As a result, the federal and state governments were barred by the Court for four decades from enacting economic regulatory programs, including protective child labor laws, minimum wage legislation, and much of the New Deal agenda.

The Supreme Court's error, according to conventional wisdom, was in attempting to substitute its personal political judgment on economic matters for that of the people and with no constitutional authorization other than the vague due process clause. Accordingly, the Court had no business opposing the clear and overwhelming will of the people, at least not in an area, economic policy, clearly reserved for majorities. The Court invaded the democratic sphere arbitrarily, motivated only by a personal bias favoring laissez-faire capitalist values.

Not only was the Court wrong, but it paid dearly for its error. The severe public criticism and political attacks on it that ensued, particularly FDR's Court-packing plan, greatly damaged its reputation and authority. This, of course, was not the only price paid. The ideal and the reality of democratic government were lost, even if only temporarily.

The task then is to avoid a similar disaster in the future.[8] What is needed is a theory or method of constitutional decisionmaking that clearly, coherently, and objectively identifies the properly limited set of issues appropriate for judicial (rather than majoritarian) resolution. Such a theory must additionally be capable of generating outcomes independent of the personal values or ideology of the judge. The underlying assumption then is that there exists "out there" a decisionmaking source that the justices can discern and apply in a neutral manner while keeping their personal values or biases in check. (Accordingly, the term *neutralist* will often be used in place of the more cumbersome *conventional constitutional law scholar.*)

The neutralists' search is for an intellectually coherent and objective answer to the question of what qualifies as a "good enough reason" for the

Court to interfere with the democratic results of electoral and legislative processes. In Alexander Bickel's words, "Which values, among adequately neutral and general ones, qualify as sufficiently important or fundamental or whathaveyou to be vindicated by the Court against other values affirmed by legislative acts? And how is the Court to evolve and apply them?"[9] Once these questions are answered, scholars are then in a position to know when the Court is playing its proper role and when, alternatively, it is exceeding its legitimate authority.

Three Neutralist Approaches to Constitutional Interpretation

There are a variety of theories of constitutional interpretation, even within this neutralist approach, and explaining each is no easy task. However, there are three distinct categories into which most of them fall—interpretivism, noninterpretivism, and the process-perfecting approach.[10] To simplify, the interpretivists tell the Court it can legitimately advance, in opposition to majority will, only those values expressly stated or clearly implied in the constitutional text. Noninterpretivists wish the Court to advance "society's fundamental values" (variously defined) even if not clearly expressed in the Constitution. The most prominent process-perfecting approach is Ely's representation-reinforcing theory, in which the Court may intervene only to protect and enhance the "democraticness" of the political process itself.[11] Each approach will be explained and then applied to various Court decisions and doctrines.

Before I do so, however, a brief caveat is in order. In simplifying a stupefying variety of neutralist approaches to constitutional interpretation to only three categories, some are inevitably left out or fail to fit neatly into a single category.[12] Notably absent in (or more accurately cutting across) my classification scheme is the legal process school, which deserves a bit of discussion here. Rather than emphasizing the legitimacy of any particular source of constitutional decisionmaking or the correctness of any particular outcome, these theorists regard the *process* or methodology of legal decision-making as centrally important in reducing the tension between judicial power and democratic rule. In Philip Bobbitt's apt characterization of the legal process school motto, "It's not *what* judges do . . . it's *how* they do it."[13] Thus, judges should carefully and persuasively articulate the reasons supporting their decisions, speaking in terms of general principles that transcend the immediate case.[14]

In stark contrast to legislators, it is argued, judges possess a unique capacity to fulfill this role of reasoned elaboration of legal principle. Because judges are protected from political pressures, they can be impartial and dispassionate; they are free to entertain issues of principle, rather than relying on mere partisan preference or political expediency.[15] Furthermore, the legal process itself obligates the judge to listen to all parties, to make a decision, and to justify that decision according to law. Legitimacy results from the judge's adherence to this special process of "dialogue and independence"—in short, in behaving like a judge and not a legislator.[16] Thus, at the core of the legal process approach is the belief that "legitimacy is largely a point about institutional integrity."[17]

The primary reason for not including legal process as a separate category is that nearly all neutralists endorse its primary tenets. Conventional constitutional theorists do disagree with regard to the sources of constitutional decisionmaking they advance as legitimate. However, they are all quite optimistic about the ability of judges to discern and elaborate constitutional principles from that source (however defined) in a neutral and coherent manner. Legal process scholars distinguish themselves by the greater (and often exclusive) emphasis they place on process as the key to protecting the Court's legitimacy. Further, they tend either to ignore[18] or advance only vaguely[19] the source and substance of the principles that judges are then to apply in a general and neutral fashion. That, of course, was the most common complaint against Wechsler's call for neutral principles in constitutional adjudication—his failure to tell us, substantively and concretely, which values the Court should be principled about.[20]

Thus, the central issue of contention among neutralist scholars is not *whether* judges should be principled, but what is the proper source of constitutional values which the Court may legitimately advance in opposition to majority desires. It is to that disagreement—between interpretivists, noninterpretivists, and process-perfecters—that I now return.

Interpretivism

According to Professor Ely's definition, an interpretivist approach requires that "judges deciding constitutional issues should confine themselves to enforcing norms that are stated or clearly implicit in the written Constitution."[21] By implication, noninterpretivists would permit the judge to "go beyond that set of references and enforce norms that cannot be discovered within the four corners of the document."[22]

As Ely acknowledges, there is a sense in which we are all interpretivists. No scholar would attempt to advance the notion that the constitutional text is an irrelevant or illegitimate source of constitutional decisionmaking. As Ely notes, interpretivism fits our "ordinary notion of how law works: if your job is to enforce the Constitution, then the Constitution is what you should be enforcing, not whatever may happen to strike you as a good idea at the time. Thus stated, the conclusion possesses the unassailability of a truism, and if acceptance of *that* were all it took to make someone an interpretivist, no sane person could be anything else."[23]

What then is distinctive about interpretivism? First is the insistence that the Court is to enforce only those principles that are preexisting and discoverable in the constitutional text (supplemented if need be by the Framers' intentions). Second is the claim that interpretivism is the only method of constitutional interpretation that successfully reconciles judicial review with democratic values and effectively constrains judicial power.

No doubt the leading (or at least best known) interpretivist is former law professor, judge, and Supreme Court nominee Robert Bork.[24] In Bork's view, the Constitution "holds that we govern ourselves democratically, except on those occasions, few in number though critically important, when the Constitution places a topic beyond the reach of majorities."[25] As a nonpolitical institution, the Supreme Court plays a critical role in determining when such an occasion arises. Since the Constitution is law and defines those boundaries itself in a comprehensible way, that is where the judge must look for answers.

To Bork, "There is a historical Constitution that was understood by those who enacted it to have a meaning of its own. . . . It is that meaning the judges *ought* to utter."[26] That intended meaning or "original understanding" of a constitutional provision does not lie in the subjective intentions of the Framers themselves, but in "how the words used in the Constitution would have been understood at the time."[27] Thus, the judge looks not only to the words and phrases themselves, but also to secondary sources (convention debates, newspaper articles, dictionaries used at the time) to discover the provision's meaning *at the time of enactment.*

As Philip Bobbitt points out, Bork's "historicist" approach of enforcing the Framers' and ratifiers' intentions is not the only type or style of interpretivism.[28] For example, some interpretivists are "textualists," like former Supreme Court Justice Hugo Black. A textualist believes that the words in the text have a certain meaning that, using common sense, we can reasonably ascertain. Thus, there is no need to consult the history of a provision's enactment. There are also "structuralists," such as Charles Black, who look not to specific constitutional language or to the Framers' intentions, but to the logic and structure of the Constitution as a whole.[29]

Additional disagreement among interpretivists exists regarding the ability of the text or Framers' intent to constrain interpretive choice. For example, Raoul Berger, another historicist, is, in Sunstein's terms, a "hard originalist."[30] Berger believes that there is a clear, certain, and unassailable meaning to the Constitution.[31] Correct constitutional answers can in fact be discovered by a proper inquiry into what the Framers intended by and the historical circumstances surrounding the adoption of particular provisions. Thus, judicial discretion is all but eliminated.

A more moderate strand of interpretivism acknowledges that the Constitution necessarily speaks in terms of abstract, general principles that must be adapted to changing situations and contexts. Obvious examples include the due process and equal protection clauses, the Fourth Amendment's ban on "unreasonable" searches and seizures, and the Eighth Amendment's prohibition of "cruel and unusual" punishment. These interpretivists further argue that such a restrictive, "clause-bound" approach undermines the purpose of a Constitution intended, in Chief Justice John Marshall's words, "to endure for ages to come, and consequently to be adapted to the various crises of human affairs."[32]

The moderate interpretivists (or "soft originalists"),[33] thus, doubt that judicial discretion can be eliminated by a narrow, crabbed approach such as Berger's.[34] For example, even Bork acknowledges that we can rarely know the specific intentions of the Framers with sufficient certainty and particularity to resolve constitutional issues in an unequivocal manner.[35] Further, he admits that the application of general constitutional principles as then understood is no simple task; "two judges equally devoted to the original purpose may disagree about the reach or application of the principle at stake and so arrive at different results."[36] Thus, "The result of the search is never perfection; it is simply the best we can do; and the best we can do must be regarded as good enough."[37] Bork also admits that social and technological change, such as the advent of electronic surveillance, may require the judge to adapt a given constitutional principle to protect against a new threat, although he takes pains to distinguish this from the creation of new principle.[38]

Nonetheless, interpretivists claim a distinction from the noninterpretivists: "an insistence that the work of the political branches is to be invalidated only in accord with an inference whose starting point, whose underlying premise, is fairly discoverable in the Constitution."[39] Although not eliminated, judicial discretion is bounded. "Interpretivism will not always provide easy answers to difficult constitutional questions. The judicial role will always involve the exercise of discretion. The strength of interpretivism is that it channels and constrains this discretion in a manner consistent with the Constitution. While it does not necessarily insure a correct result, it does exclude from consideration entire ranges of improper judicial responses."[40]

Beyond this restriction on judicial discretion, the interpretivists urge caution and self-restraint. If the meaning of the Constitution cannot be discovered with reasonable certainty or if the Constitution is silent,[41] then the judge is left with no authoritative or principled reason for preferring one value (or "gratification")[42] to another. And "the judge who looks outside the historic Constitution always looks inside himself and nowhere else."[43] Thus, if the Constitution does not clearly and persuasively justify intervention, "judges must stand aside and let current democratic majorities rule. . . . Where the law stops, the judge must stop."[44]

For the interpretivists, the consequences of judges restricting majorities and the democratic process without clear constitutional authorization are quite severe. Such judicial overreaching represents a violation of the constitutional plan and the very notion of a written Constitution. The Constitution attempts to balance democratic rule with the need for individual freedom and minority rights. It does so structurally, through a careful division of authority among the various branches and levels of government and by providing specific individual protections and guarantees such as those contained in the Bill of Rights. When judges invest the Constitution with a new and unintended meaning, they threaten to destroy that balance, as well as the security and stability created and maintained by a written constitution. As Thomas Jefferson observed, "Our peculiar security is in the possession of a written constitution. Let us not make it a blank paper by construction."[45] Thus, "without adherence to the 'original intention,' the words employed by the framers are but 'empty shells' into which the Court may, and does, pour its own meaning. Then . . . are the 'chains of the Constitution' with which Jefferson hoped to bind down our delegates from mischief, reduced to ropes of sand. To thrust aside the 'dead hand' of the framers, therefore, is to thrust aside the Constitution."[46]

Furthermore, when the Court exceeds its constitutionally authorized powers, it necessarily does so at the expense of the democratic branches, at the *people's* expense. The people are denied their right to govern themselves as they wish. The result is "to substitute government-by-judiciary for government by the people, to act upon the discredited principle that the end justifies the means."[47] Even if judges might reach more just and enlightened decisions—and, of course, there is no such guarantee—"a benevolent judicial tyranny is nonetheless a tyranny."[48] If the Constitution produces unjust results or is in need of revision, the Constitution itself provides the proper remedy—amendment by the people. Resorting to a judicial quick fix is, in Chief Justice Rehnquist's words, "a formula for an end run around popular government."[49]

The danger of judicial activism extends further, to the possibility of weakening the democratic process itself, removing from the people the responsibilities attending self-government.

> [Judicial review,] even when unavoidable, is always attended with a serious evil, namely, that the correction of legislative mistakes comes from the outside, and the people thus lose the political experience, and the moral education and stimulus that comes from fighting the question out in the ordinary way, and correcting their own errors. The tendency of a common and easy resort to this great function, now lamentably too common, is to dwarf the political capacity of the people, and to deaden its sense of moral responsibility.[50]

Of course, the interpretivists do not deny the necessity or desirability of judicial review or its attendant dangers. However, an insistence that its use be restricted to clear constitutional authorization provides a more stable and enduring set of constraints on majorities, leaves ample room for the democratic process to operate, and reduces judicial discretion and the potential for abuse. Furthermore, those judicially imposed constraints can themselves be characterized as democratic in character.

> The noninterpretivist would have politically unaccountable judges select and define the values to be placed beyond majority control, but the interpretivist takes his values from the Constitution which means, since the Constitution itself was submitted for and received popular ratification, that they ultimately come from the people. Thus the judges do not check the people, the Constitution does, which means the people are ultimately checking themselves.[51]

Thus, "under the pure interpretive model . . . when a court strikes down a popular statute or practice as unconstitutional, it may also reply to the resulting public outcry: 'We didn't do it—you did.' "[52]

As in most neutralist approaches, legal scholars play a special role in supervising and enforcing judicial adherence to the interpretivist norm. Constitutional law scholars can judge whether the Court is remaining true to the constitutional text and its original meaning and employing appropriate modes of legal reasoning and justification. They can sound the alarm when judges fail to articulate sound constitutional reasons for their decisions, when there is suspicion that judges may be relying on some arbitrary basis such as personal political bias.

The appeal and power of the interprevist approach is obvious. It envisions a rather modest role for the Court. It leaves most public issues and concerns to the people, permitting the democratic process to operate freely and, thus, to flourish. The interpretivist model additionally restricts the opportunity for judicial discretion and arbitrariness. It is respectful of the purpose of a written Constitution and a constitutionally limited democracy. And it is on safer ground in democratic terms as well: the Court is only enforcing the more basic and fundamental wishes of the people as expressed in the Constitution itself.

Noninterpretivism

Noninterpretivists are willing to concede that the case for interpretivism is a powerful one. They also admit that a Court permitted to impose values not expressly found in the Constitution is also a Court more prone to abuses and to illegitimate forays into the democratic sphere. However, the noninterpre-

tivists believe that the cost of failing to make a persuasive case for noninterpretivism is great: a hollow Constitution lacking substantive moral meaning
and force.[53]

Richard Saphire is one such scholar critical of constitutional theorists'
"obsession" with the legitimacy question. He argues that this has led scholars
to proceed too cautiously.

> If the judicial process could not be purged completely of discretion—if it
> could not be rendered objectively pure—it could not be justified. As thus
> conceived, the animating purpose of constitutional theory has been to
> neutralize Constitutional doctrine of its moral content by restraining the
> range of judicial choices that could be regarded as legitimate. The success
> of its practitioners has been measured not so much by their ability to delin-
> eate the range and depth of values properly invocable in Constitutional
> argument, but by their ability to point to those that are not.[54]

By denying the moral content of the Constitution, we fail to recognize "the
Constitution as a vehicle for facilitating the evolution of moral growth in our
society, as well as . . . the ability of the Constitution to act as a legitimating
and stabilizing force."[55]

Professor Karst similarly observes a "substantive void" in constitutional law
and constitutional law commentary.[56] For example, equal protection cases
are resolved by the two-tier test of whether a "suspect class" or fundamental
interest is affected. If so, the Court applies strict scrutiny, under which the
legislation is nearly always ruled unconstitutional. If not, the rational basis
test is applied, under which virtually all legislation passes. This formalistic
approach is designed to restrict judicial intervention to carefully prescribed
cases and perhaps makes sense in those terms. However, as Karst notes, this
preoccupation with the "which standard of review shall be used?" question
limits or overshadows any inquiry into the *substantive* meaning of equal protection. The Court addresses fundamental moral issues regarding competing notions of equality and fairness in formal, theoretical and, ultimately,
meaningless terms.

Noninterpretivists agree that a narrow, literal approach to judicial review
unduly restricts the Constitution's substantive, moral content and, thus, its
moral power in our society. They agree too that judicial review may be justified "not by its method but by its result. Decisions are legitimate on this
view, because they are right."[57] Beyond this, however, the noninterpretivist

approach dissolves into a collection of rather individualistic theories of how the Court should determine and apply the Constitution's substantive meaning.

It is one thing to announce that the Court's duty is to discover and apply those values and moral principles deemed fundamental to a just society. It is quite another to instruct the Court clearly and precisely how it is to do so. To scholars such as Harry Wellington and, earlier in his career, Michael Perry, "conventional morality" should serve as the extraconstitutional source of values that the Court should enforce.[58] Others, such as Laurence Tribe, Kenneth Karst, and David Richards, believe that the Court should enforce "fundamental rights" that are in essence natural law and, thus, exist independently of conventional morality or social consensus. Such fundamental rights are variously defined. Tribe emphasizes "rights of privacy and personhood."[59] Richards speaks broadly of "human rights," particularly personal autonomy and an entitlement to equal concern and respect.[60] Rogers Smith (similarly to Sotirios Barber) advances the "preservation and enhancement of human capacities for understanding and reflective self-direction," which he refers to as "rational liberty."[61] Arthur Miller urges the Court to promote "a humane and ordered society that has human dignity for all as its central goal,"[62] a constitutional guide that former Supreme Court Justice William Brennan has also endorsed.[63] Ronald Dworkin argues for a fusion of constitutional law and moral philosophy, specifically inviting judges and scholars to examine John Rawls's theory of justice.[64] And Kenneth Karst advances the "principle of equal citizenship," which requires that "each individual is presumptively entitled to be treated by the organized society as a respected, responsible, and participating member."[65]

While many noninterpretivist theories advance egalitarian values, most emphasize personal autonomy. This is not surprising, given the extensive criticism scholars have given the Court for its privacy decisions, which are regarded as lacking persuasive constitutional authorization. An important motivation thus seems to be: if interpretivism requires "doing without privacy," then our constitutional theories are sorely in need of revision.[66] Noninterpretivism is the response.

An exception to the noninterpretivists' focus on personal autonomy is the approach offered by Stephen Macedo.[67] Professor Macedo criticizes the intentionalist approach of Berger and Bork as impractical and flatly at odds with the Constitution as well as with the Framers' own intentions regarding constitutional interpretation. However, he also criticizes the "selective activism" of the left, wherein the Court gives no protection to economic rights and vigorous protection to personal rights.[68] In its place, Macedo advocates a libertarian approach. According to Macedo, the Court should take seriously the numerous constitutional protections, both explicit and implicit, of personal *and* economic liberties. In short, the Court must conduct a searching and principled inquiry into each and every government intrusion into its citizens' liberty. He would require the government to "provide 'real and substantial' justification for restrictions on the full array of liberties protected by the Constitution's scheme of values."[69] Thus, the Court is given broad responsibility for insuring that government officials exercise their powers reasonably and constitutionally.

Few scholars make the argument that noninterpretive review is legitimate from a democratic standpoint.[70] Rather, their point is that our excessive concern with the "Court's legitimacy in a democracy" problem leads to a weakening of the Constitution as a source of moral guidance and moral legitimacy. They emphasize the myopia of legislatures in responding to immediate crises, momentary passions, and the narrow and selfish demands of wealthy and well-organized interest groups. We cannot expect moral guardianship and leadership from legislatures, but we can and should expect it from the Court. Thus, noninterpretivists claim not to have found a way to reconcile judicial review with democratic values. Rather, they have found the path to moral invigoration and growth if not moral perfection in our society. Noninterpretive review, democratic or not, thus serves a vital societal function.

Despite what seems to be rather fundamental differences between the noninterpretivists and interpretivists, there does exist some common ground. They shared a concern for delineating the justifiable grounds upon which the Court may interfere with the democratic process and tell the people's elected representatives what they may and may not do. They additionally assume that judicial intervention in the political process must be bounded and warranted by more than the personal beliefs and motivations of any existing majority of justices. For example, Laurence Tribe is a noninterpretivist accused by Bork of being a "constitutional revolutionary" whose theory of judicial review "departs drastically from all the usual criteria of constitutional adjudication" and "takes whatever form is necessary at the moment to reach a desired result."[71] However, Tribe quite strongly and specifically states his objection to those who would "use the language of the Constitution simply as a mirror to dress up their own political or moral preferences in the hallowed language of our most fundamental document."[72] He finds abhorrent the "idea of an empty, or an infinitely malleable, Constitution" and endeavors to "find principles of interpretation that can anchor the Constitution in some more secure, determinate, and external reality."[73]

Thus, for both interpretivists and noninterpretivists, the source of constitutional interpretation exists outside (or above) the collective (or summated) personal judgment of the justices. For noninterpretivists, society's fundamental values, natural law, or Rawls's theory of justice replace the Framers intentions as a coherent, objective, nonarbitrary source of constitutional decisionmaking. Although the content of constitutional principles elaborated in a noninterpretivist approach may be substantive and moral, the source of those principles exists apart from the personal, arbitrary biases of the justices and, thus, may be regarded as legitimate. In that sense, noninterpretivist review may be seen as fitting, along with interpretivism, within a neutralist perspective.

Professor Ely's Representation-Reinforcing Approach

John Hart Ely has developed a process-based theory of judicial review, one that borrows heavily from the Court's own *Carolene Products* approach.[74] Although other scholars have advanced similar theories,[75] Ely's is more thoroughly developed and has received the most attention. Ely argues that the Court's sole legitimate function is to correct malfunctions in the political process, thereby improving or perfecting representational processes.

Although he does criticize "clause-bound interpretivism" as being at odds with the Constitution's open-ended provisions,[76] Ely's primary target is the variety of noninterpretivist, fundamental values approaches to constitutional adjudication. Ely notes the impossibility of discovering either universal human principles or conventional morality in other than a highly abstract way, which is of little practical utility in constitutional decisionmaking (50–52, 54, 60, 64). He is further troubled by the elitist and undemocratic notion that judges are best suited to discover what is best for society or what the people truly desire (despite legislation to the contrary) (58–59, 67). Ely acknowledges that "the constitutional document itself . . . contains several provisions whose invitation to look beyond their four corners . . . cannot be construed away" (13). However, he believes that since there is no defensible, principled approach to interpreting these "open-textured" provisions, the Court must decline the invitation to noninterpretivism.

To Ely, the noninterpretivists ask the wrong question (and, in quoting Alexander Bickel, "No answer is what the wrong question begets.") (43, 72). Noninterpretivists ask, "Which source of values should the Court consult in discovering the substantive meaning of the Constitution? Which values may the Court legitimately impose in opposition to popular or majoritarian preferences?"

Ely's response is that neither democratic theory nor the Constitution itself grants the Court any such power to "impose values."

> Contrary to the standard characterization of the Constitution as "an enduring but evolving statement of general values," . . . in fact the selection and accommodation of substantive values is left almost entirely to the political process and instead the document is overwhelmingly concerned, on the one hand, with procedural fairness in the resolution of individual disputes . . . and on the other . . . with ensuring broad participation in the processes and distributions of government. (87)[77]

In part because of the Constitution's own emphasis on process, Ely argues that judicial intervention is legitimate only when the political process is "systematically malfunctioning."

> In a representative democracy value determinations are to be made by our elected representatives, and if in fact most of us disapprove we can vote them out of office. Malfunction occurs when the *process* is undeserving of trust, when (1) the ins are choking off the channels of political change to ensure that they will stay in and the outs will stay out, or (2) though no one is actually denied a voice or a vote, representatives beholden to an effective majority are systemically disadvantaging some minority out of simple hostility or a prejudiced refusal to recognize commonalities of interest, and thereby denying that minority the protection afforded other groups by a representative system.[78]

The Court, Ely elaborates, is peculiarly well suited to identifying and correcting such malfunctions.

> Obviously our elected representatives are the last persons we should trust with identification of either of these situations. Appointed judges, however, are comparative outsiders in our governmental system, and

need worry about continuance in office only very obliquely. This does not give them some special pipeline to the genuine values of the American people: in fact it goes far to ensure that they won't have one (103).

Thus, judges have the requisite objectivity to evaluate claims regarding systematic biases in representational and decisionmaking processes. In addition, they possess special expertise as lawyers in insuring that each party's claims receive a fair and full hearing (102).

According to Ely's theory of judicial review, the Court is to act only as a referee, intervening only to insure that there was a "fair fight," not because the policy results are unwise or different from what the justices might personally prefer. Thus, a statute is constitutional as long as the political process producing it is open and fair.

The appeal of Ely's theory is obvious. It allows courts "to perceive and portray themselves as servants of democracy even as they strike down the actions of supposedly democratic governments."[79] The Court avoids altogether substantive moral judgments regarding the wisdom of legislative policies. It is not substituting its personal preferences for those of the people. Rather, the Court is better enabling the people to express and enforce their own preferences.

Applying Conventional Constitutional Theories

Each of these scholars attempts to distill from the Constitution and from democratic theory a specialized judicial role or function. That role must be one which respects democratic values but which also justifies occasional judicial displacement of legislative decisions. The judicial role must also be defined precisely enough to serve as an effective constraint on judges' behavior. The role constraints specified are intended to operate "both directly, by the moral force it exerts on their work, and indirectly, by providing an agreed-upon standard against which their work can be measured."[80]

The value and the constraining force of constitutional theory then is demonstrated and revealed largely in its application. Any theory must provide a clear and objective way for scholars to determine when the Court is legitimately exercising its power and, alternatively, when the Court is exceeding its legitimate authority. The next step then is to examine how interpretivists, noninterpretivists, and process-perfecters apply their theories to praise or condemn specific uses by the Court of its power of judicial review.

Applying Interpretivism

Nearly one-third of Bork's *The Tempting of America* is devoted to evaluating the Court's performance in light of his theory of original understanding.[81] Chief Justice John Marshall receives most of the praise, the Warren Court most of the criticism.

Bork's consistent point of reference in his analysis is the Court's faithfulness to intervening only when the Constitution permits and then only in a manner consistent with its original meaning. Thus, Chief Justice Taney's creation of, in effect, a constitutional right to slave ownership in *Dred Scott* is "as blatant a distortion of the original understanding of the Constitution as one can find" and "was the first appearance in American constitutional law of the concept of 'substantive due process'"(30–31). Bork similarly criticizes the *Lochner*-era Court for its use of the judicially created "liberty of contract" to strike down minimum wage laws and legislation designed to insulate businesses from competition. The Court's policy judgments were probably correct in Bork's estimation; however, its constitutional judgments badly missed the mark: "Perhaps there ought to have been a constitutional provision invalidating those laws. But there was not, and the Court had no business striking them down" (47).

Bork regards *Brown* as "a great and correct decision . . . supported by a very weak opinion" (75). *Brown* rested in large part on modern social-scientific evidence of the harmful psychological effects on black children of state-sanctioned racial segregation in public education. However, "the inescapable fact is that those who ratified the amendment did not think it outlawed segregated education" and, in any case, "it is impossible to see how later studies on the baleful psychological effects of segregation could change that meaning" (75–76). In contrast to Chief Justice Warren's dismissal of original intent as inconclusive and largely irrelevant, Bork believes that "the result in *Brown* is consistent with, indeed is compelled by, the original understanding of the fourteenth amendment's equal protection clause" (76). In Bork's view, although the ratifiers of the Fourteenth Amendment intended equality under law, they probably did not perceive segregation as incompatible with that goal. However, by 1954, it was increasingly clear that the two were indeed

inconsistent. Thus, the Court's only choice was either to abandon the ratifiers' goal of equality and permit segregation or to ban segregation in order
to achieve equality. Since the latter option is consistent with both the language and intent of the equal protection clause, the Court was required to
choose equality over segregation (81–82).

According to Bork, *Brown* could have been, but was not, justified in terms
of that original understanding. However, the Court's ruling in *Bolling* v.
Sharpe, prohibiting segregation in the District of Columbia public schools,
could not be so rooted since the equal protection clause applies only to the
states. The Court, in Bork's view, should have resisted the temptation to
revise the Constitution in the name of consistency and "good results," and
instead should have allowed Congress to repeal the District's segregation
laws, which it "most certainly" would have done (83–84).

In addition to *Brown* and *Bolling*, Bork takes the Warren Court to task for
its one-person, one-vote reapportionment decision (84–90);[82] for striking
down state poll taxes (90–91)[83] and literacy tests (91–93);[84] and most particularly for its creation of a constitutional right of privacy in *Griswold* (95–100).[85]
According to Bork, the willingness to depart from the original meaning of
the historic Constitution continued unabated, even with the supposedly
more conservative Burger and Rehnquist Courts.[86] Examples include the
Court's approval of affirmative action (101–10),[87] its unprincipled extension
of the illegitimate right of privacy to abortion (111–16),[88] and near extension
to "homosexual sodomy" (116–26),[89] and its prohibition of laws criminalizing flag burning (127–28).[90]

To state the obvious, Bork finds the Court's performance in the modern
era lacking. It has abandoned the Constitution's original meaning with regu-
larity, instead illegitimately enacting into our constitutional law a liberal
agenda that has failed to gain approval through the democratic process.

While other interpretivists would generally agree, their application of the
interpretivist norm in particular cases and doctrinal areas often diverges. For
example, Bork, Berger, and Justice Black are all interpretivists; yet Black
played a major role in the Court's decision to enforce the Bill of Rights on
the states through incorporation, of which Berger is quite critical,[91] and Bork
surprisingly ambivalent.[92] Additionally, both Bork and Berger are his-
toricists, yet they disagree on *Brown*. For Bork, the result in *Brown* can be
justified as consistent with the core principle of equality the Framers and
ratifiers intended. For Berger, *Brown* was inconsistent with the Framers'

rather limited intent to incorporate the Civil Rights Act of 1866 into the Constitution.

Interpretivists are united, however, in their opposition to the right of privacy decisions, principally *Griswold* and *Roe*. In order to strike down a Connecticut statute making it a crime to use contraceptives, the Warren Court relied on a constitutional right of privacy, which it acknowledged was nowhere explicitly mentioned in the Constitution. Instead, the Court reasoned that privacy was constitutionally protected by the Fourteenth Amendment's concept of personal liberty and by the "penumbras" or zones of privacy guaranteed by a number of other amendments. For example, the Court mentioned the First Amendment's right of association, the Third Amendment's prohibition against peacetime quartering of soldiers, the Fourth Amendment's prohibition of unreasonable searches and seizures, the Fifth Amendment's self-incrimination protection, and the Ninth Amendment's reservation to the people of unenumerated rights. In its efforts to satisfy the interpretivist norm, the Court appeared to employ a shotgun approach. If no single constitutional provision clearly and specifically authorized judicial protection of a right to privacy, perhaps four or five or more vague constitutional provisions together would do the trick.

To interpretivists, the Burger Court then compounded the problem (to state it more mildly than they would) by extending the right of privacy to a woman's decision to choose to have an abortion. Justice Blackmun's majority opinion has been widely and thoroughly criticized.[93] As aptly stated by Mark Tushnet, Justice Blackmun's "innovation" in *Roe* was "the totally unreasoned judicial opinion."[94]

Blackmun reviewed with regard to abortion (and in painful detail) ancient attitudes, the Hippocratic Oath, common law, English statutory law, and American law. He additionally described the views of the American Medical Association, the American Public Health Association, and the American Bar Association. At last we get to Blackmun's constitutional analysis, in which he ever so briefly discussed the right of privacy (itself weakly rooted in terms of text and intent), to which he blithely tacked on a woman's right to choose abortion. He further divided the pregnancy into trimesters, based on medical developments regarding fetal viability and maternal health and safety, varying the level of judicial scrutiny accordingly.

For interpretivists, there are no better examples than *Griswold* and *Roe* of judges abandoning both the intended meaning of the Constitution and the requirement of reasoned elaboration. The inevitable result is judicial tyranny: unelected judges usurping legislative authority and substituting their own moral judgment for that of the people, who are powerless to overrule them.

Applying Noninterpretivist Theories

Illustrating how the noninterpretivists apply their theories to evalute the Court's decisions is particularly difficult. The theories themselves are numerous, diverse, and stated in rather abstract terms.

Perhaps one example will suffice. The starting point for most noninterpretivist theories is the assertion of a "core constitutional value," typically stated at an abstract level, that the Court should promote. Rogers Smith, for example, finds "rational liberty," or the enhancement of rational human self-direction, to be the core constitutional value the Court should protect.[95]

Following a defense of that value (typically in terms of its fundamental importance in our society, its existence as a "basic human right" or, occasionally, as a value rooted in the Framers' philosophical beliefs), the noninterpretivist fleshes out the principle and applies it to concrete cases or doctrinal areas. This is more often than not preceded by a warning, such as Smith's, that the suggested approach "claims only to direct the proper decision-makers to the proper questions . . . offers no fixed and timeless solutions to the constitutional problems of interpretation" and will require further elaboration.[96]

Smith's rational liberty approach requires the Court to intervene "when the community has unnecessarily infringed on conduct generally conceded to be essential to the rational self-governance of some persons."[97] Among the rights and liberties with which the Court should be especially concerned because they are "integral to the rational self-guidance of most persons" are: the right to live with one's family, the right to an education, the right to pursue one's preferred occupation, freedom of expression, the right to vote, the right to marry, the right to travel, and the right to fair treatment by the criminal justice system (237).

Smith accordingly approves of the Warren Court's "due process revolution" in the criminal justice area as consistent with rational liberty for all. For example, "Respect for the citizens' capacity for rational self-direction . . .

requires that they be informed of their rights, so they can make genuine choices about cooperating with the police," thus supporting *Miranda*; "that they be assisted in doing so by competent counsel," thus supporting *Gideon*; that "the courts avoid complicity in police conduct violative of civil liberties by excluding evidence thus obtained," supporting *Mapp*; and "that genuine opportunities for appeal be afforded to all to safeguard the system against error," supporting *Griffin* (231–32).[98] However, because the rational liberty approach does not rely so heavily on the privacy rights of the accused as did some Warren Court decisions, Smith believes it does not create an ethos that is "prone to be corrupted into a license for lawless behavior" (235).

A commitment to the rational liberty of all permits some restrictions on free speech, in Smith's view. For example, obscene and offensive speech that unquestionably and "overwhelmingly denies or disregards the capacities for rational self-direction of some persons or classes of persons" could be prohibited. Examples include "'snuff' pornography, visual child pornography . . . and some glamorizations of nonsexual violence" and "the wearing of swastikas in especially sensitive locales, such as the Jewish neighborhoods of Skokie, Illinois" (244). Regarding libel, Smith would provide more protection than the Court to "public" figures, such as entertainers, and more protection to the private conduct of "political" figures. Allowing "almost unlimited derogation of public figures" does little to enhance "society's powers of self-guidance," while potentially causing irreparable emotional and professional harm to the individual and thus her self-directing capacities (245–46). Additionally, regulation of campaign expenditures and corporate speech would be permitted, at least "in principle." Because those with greater wealth may enjoy an enhanced capacity to be heard, "community deliberation on public issues may be biased, and rational self-governance may therefore be impeded" (248).

Smith would also prefer the Court to be less deferential with regard to government restrictions on economic rights. For example, if the legislature interferes with the liberty to pursue one's occupation of choice, as the state did in *Williamson* v. *Lee Optical*, strict scrutiny should be triggered (255).[99] Since "meeting basic subsistence needs can obviously be assumed to be central to the liberty of all," Smith's theory additionally provides for "constitutional rights to welfare assistance and meaningful work, but only for those who are unable to provide for themselves, and only within the limits of economic feasibility, as decided chiefly by the political branches" (254). A rational liberty standard does not, on the other hand, necessitate strict scrutiny for *all* laws that may more greatly burden the poor. Some such inequalities may "promote material welfare for all" or may not "endanger any basic liberty interest"; however, "if a public measure exacerbates the significance of economic differences in ways that endanger the basic liberties of some, strict scrutiny is demanded" (256). Finally, in contrast to the Court, Smith believes that there is a constitutional right to education, since education is "essential to the development of capacities for rational self-guidance" (257). Thus, the property-tax financing system upheld by the Court in *Rodriguez* would be subjected to (and likely fail) strict scrutiny,[100] although not because of its disproportionate impact on the poor or because some students were relatively deprived, but because it so greatly endangered the ability of some districts to provide for a *minimally adequate* education.

Demonstrating how noninterpretivists apply their theories to actual issues and cases is difficult not only because the theories are so numerous and distinct, but because applications of seemingly similar theories often diverge as well. For example, in Paul Brest's examination of fundamental rights theorists, he finds that although they share the same basic approach and emphasize personal autonomy values, "Wilkinson would uphold sodomy laws, while White, Karst, Tribe and Richards would strike them down; both Wilkinson and White would uphold adultery laws, while Tribe finds them constitutionally doubtful."[101]

Additionally, the two "conventional morality" theorists discussed, Wellington and Perry, disagree in their analysis of *Roe*. For Wellington, the Court ventured beyond the existing moral consensus that abortion is permissible only if the mother's life is endangered or if the pregnancy is the result of rape.[102] For Perry, *Roe* reflects an accurate reading by the Court of conventional attitudes toward abortion. As evidence, Perry cites nonenforcement of abortion statutes and results of public opinion polls.[103]

As mentioned previously, noninterpretivists have generally taken up the cause of defending many of the Court's more controversial rulings, such as its equal protection and privacy decisions. Most do so by employing a Rawlsian approach emphasizing personal autonomy and egalitarian values. Insofar as the Court pursues those values, thereby promoting a free and just society, the Court is acting legitimately, even though such decisions may not be firmly rooted in the constitutional text.

Applying Ely's Process-Based Approach

Unlike the interpretivists, but similar to the noninterpretivists, Ely approves of much of the modern constitutional doctrine developed by the Court, particularly the Warren Court.[104] However, his reasons for doing so differ. For example, Ely regards the race discrimination cases as clearly legitimate matters for the Supreme Court. African Americans are, of course, a discrete and insular minority, suffering historical discrimination of the most egregious sort, including their systematic exclusion from the political process. However, far more significant for Ely is the likelihood of predominantly white legislatures continuing to act out of hostility and prejudice toward and with a general lack of understanding and concern for the interests of that minority group. Thus, the Court is quite justified in being highly suspicious of any law that draws lines on a racial basis; such laws are so likely to be the product of prejudice, bias, and neglect rather than the end result of a fair political fight.[105] However, affirmative action is a special case, in Ely's view. While the Court should be vigilant with regard to all racial classifications, "there is nothing constitutionally suspicious about a majority's discriminating against itself" (172).[106] After all, white legislators are unlikely to try to harm whites as a class out of prejudice or indifference.

Ely would also have the Court employ strict scrutiny for other "racelike" classifications, such as alienage (161–62) and sexual preference (162–63),[107] but stops short of recommending such a rigorous test for gender classifications. He argues that women are neither a minority nor discrete and insular (164). Furthermore, obstacles to political participation have been removed, enabling women to protect their interests without the special help of judges. Thus, except as regards those laws enacted before women were permitted to vote, we should not adopt the paternalistic attitude that women do not know and cannot adequately protect their own true interests. Rather, unless clearly proven otherwise, judges should adopt the view that "if women don't protect themselves from sex discrimination in the future, it won't be because they can't. It will rather be because for one reason or another—substantive disagreement or more likely the assignment of a low priority to the issue—they don't choose to" (169).[108]

Like the Court, Ely also does not regard every law, or even most laws, that disproportionately burden the poor as suspect. Such laws "do not generally result from a sadistic desire to keep the miserable in their state of misery, or a stereotypical generalization about their characteristics, but rather from a reluctance to raise the taxes needed to support such expenditures" (162).

Unlike interpretivists such as Bork and Berger, Ely strongly approves of the Warren Court's voting rights and reapportionment decisions. To Ely, "unblocking stoppages in the democratic process is what judicial review ought preeminently to be about, and denial of the vote seems the quintessential stoppage" (117). By enhancing access to the ballot box and equalizing legislative representation, the Court is not substituting its own value preferences or policy judgments for those of the legislature. Rather, it is merely correcting a malfunction in the political process.

The Court is also justified in giving vigorous protection to free speech and imposing a restrictive definition of libel (105–16). Both contribute to informed and open public debate and, thus, to a more robust democracy.

However, the Court's decision in *Roe* cannot be justified according to his representation-reinforcing approach.[109] Abortion statutes neither reflect a systematic bias or blockage in representational processes nor single out an insular minority for discriminatory treatment. In fact, Ely believes that the proper application of a *Carolene Products* approach would result in greater judicial protection of fetuses than of women since "although very few women sit in our legislatures . . . *no* fetuses sit in our legislatures" (933). Thus, the Court in *Roe* acted illegitimately; it intervened not to protect the integrity of the political process, but merely to substitute its moral beliefs regarding abortion for those of the people.

Conclusion

Despite the obvious differences among these three approaches to constitutional interpretation, there are some common themes that deserve reiteration and that justify the neutralist label. First, the problem to be addressed is agreed to be that of a politically irresponsible institution, free from popular reprisal, which necessarily frustrates the will of the people when it acts. A justification, an alternative source of legitimacy, must be found for this substantial deviation from a system premised on popular control. Justices who merely impose their own personal values, untested and irreversible in the electoral marketplace, will not suffice.

The common solution is to assert that there exists "out there" a value or decisionmaking source (whether the Framers' intent, Rawls's theory of justice, or democratic theory) that the justices can discern and apply in a neutral manner while keeping their personal values in check. By reducing if not eliminating judicial discretion and judicial subjectivity, the legitimacy problem is solved. In Bickel's words, the Court's legitimacy in a democracy is saved by "keeping the judicial function distinct from the legislative and thus capable of being justified."[110]

The neutralists believe that there exists an objective theory of constitutional interpretation, which (1) the justices *can* apply in a neutral manner, (2) the Court *must* apply in order to protect its legitimacy and insure its survival, (3) successfully reconciles judicial review with democratic values, and (4) enables the Court to play a beneficial "apolitical" role (i.e., protecting principles embodied in the constitutional text, advancing society's fundamental values, or perfecting the democratic process). As the following chapters will attempt to persuade, the neutralists are simply wrong on every count.

●●●●●●●●●●●●●●●●●●●●●●●●●●●●●●●●●●●●●●●

CHAPTER 2

Constitutional Indeterminacy and Judicial Subjectivity: Critical Legal Studies

THE present chapter will examine one of the most important of the neutralists' assumptions in their attempt to reconcile judicial review with democratic values. That assumption is the existence of a neutral or objective theory of constitutional interpretation that significantly constrains judicial choice and significantly inhibits the influence of the justices' personal values on constitutional decisions.

One type of evidence bearing on this assumption is the existence of "value-voting," in which the justices decide in accordance with their personal political attitudes and preferences. In other words, constitutional outcomes may be better explained, as an empirical matter, as the product of the political attitudes of the justices, rather than as the product of a coherent and neutral theory of constitutional interpretation.[1] However, that line of inquiry will not be pursued at this point for two reasons.[2]

First, some legal scholars grudgingly acknowledge that a justice's personal values play some role in constitutional decisionmaking. However, they continue to invoke neutral or objectively constrained constitutional interpretation as a normative ideal that judges should make every effort to achieve, even if the ideal is never completely realized. For example, Frederick Schauer argues that the "myth of linguistic certainty" or "literalism" is like that of Santa Claus, in the sense that the myth matters and affects our behavior, even though it is only a myth.[3] This hope for objectively constrained interpretation serves as "the conscience on the judicial shoulder. . . . Judges who think about the text, and who try to do what they think the text permits, are at least thinking in the right direction, whether or not the goal is attainable."[4] Thus, the assertion of value-voting as an empirical reality is not seen by conventional scholars as undermining their prescriptive ideal, nor does it prove that objectively and coherently constrained constitutional interpretation is an impossibility. Thus, the assumption of legal autonomy—that constitutional outcomes can be significantly determined and justified in an objective way, rather than by reference to the justice's personal values—must be addressed more directly. In other words, not only *do* the justices "vote their values"; *must* they always and inevitably vote their values? To this end, we turn to the Critical Legal Studies Movement. Critical Legal Studies scholars (the "Critics") have successfully undermined the conventional scholars' stubborn and puzzling adherence to the possibility of certainty and judicial neutrality in constitutional interpretation.

The arguments and evidence provided by the Critics will be presented and evaluated. The chapter's end then explores the implications of and possible responses to acknowledging constitutional indeterminacy and judicial subjectivity. Two responses—the traditional call for self-restraint and the Critics' resort to "utopian speculation"—are rejected as futile and impractical. A third response—strengthening political checks on the Court to guard against judicial error and abuse of power—is a promising if incomplete step in the right direction. This route is more fully examined in the next chapter.

Critical Legal Studies

The basic premise of conventional constitutional theory is legal autonomy. As defined by Phillip Johnson, legal autonomy is the notion "that there is a method of legal reasoning that can generate outcomes in controversial disputes independent of the political or economic ideology of the judge."[5] That assumption was first challenged by the Legal Realists and more recently by the Critical Legal Studies movement.

The view that it is a judge's personal preferences which determine his decisions was first promoted in academic circles by the Legal Realists, particularly Karl Llewellyn and Jerome Frank in the early 1930s.[6] In addition to expressing a general skepticism about moral absolutes and their role in the legal process, the Realists argued that judges base their decisions on intuitive hunches and subjective preferences and then manipulate legal precedent to justify the desired result. As such, the Realists challenged the dominant analytical and normative approach to judicial decisionmaking, which emphasized its formalistic, deductive properties and the central role of legal principle and precedent. Where the Legal Realists most clearly succeeded was in debunking the myth that judges neutrally and mechanically apply the law as written and as expressed in precedent.

Certainly in its most extreme form, the notion that judicial decisions are value free, nondiscretionary, and objective is no longer accepted. However, the belief in the existence of objective *constraints* on constitutional interpretation, as opposed to objectively *determined* constitutional outcomes, is still quite strong in conventional constitutional theory. The persistence of that belief has prompted a new intellectual movement, in essence a revised Legal Realism, referred to as Critical Legal Studies.[7]

The target of Critical Legal Studies is the assumption of legal autonomy that is at the heart of conventional constitutional theory. The Critics argue that constitutional decisions are incapable of being discovered and defended in a coherent and value-neutral manner. Instead, constitutional interpretation is inevitably subjective and colored by the interpreter's personal beliefs, by political context, and by shared social understandings. This is so because the law in general and the Constitution in particular are "radically and hopelessly indeterminate." The Constitution contains vague and conflicting provisions whose true meaning cannot be discovered or defended in any objective way. Consequently, neither the constitutional text nor any theory of constitutional interpretation is capable of constraining raw judicial power. Thus, "the controversy over the legitimacy of judicial review in a democratic polity—the historic obsession of normative constitutional law scholarship—is essentially incoherent and unresolvable."[8]

Leslie Friedman Goldstein correctly identifies two types of Critical Legal Studies critiques.[9] The first is represented by scholars such as Mark Tushnet and Paul Brest, who place constitutional theory in the broader context of modern liberal theory.

> Liberal political theory distinguishes between will and reason as the motivation for individual actions. In its political institutions, liberal society allocates will to the legislature and reason to the courts; but the courts are staffed by individuals who can be willful. Constitutional theory attempts to limit the willfulness of judges. . . . [However,] none of the current theories succeeds. . . . Reason cannot limit judges.[10]

Thus, it is "the contradictions of liberalism, not any peculiarity about judicial review, [which] lead to an impasse for constitutional theory."[11]

The scholars comprising the second group of Critics, in Goldstein's view,

> pose an even more radical critique. They move outside the discourse of the legal tradition and argue that every legal text, like every linguistic text and even every human experience (as in the phrase, "the social context")

is open to interpretation to a degree that is hopelessly indeterminate. . . . Rather than emphasizing alleged flaws in the "liberal tradition," these scholars focus squarely on the problem of the radical indeterminacy of all interpretation.[12]

Thus, apart from what liberal theory has to say, constitutional interpretation, like all forms of interpretation, is inevitably discretionary, subjective, and colored by social and political context.

The Critics seek to prove their argument by employing the same method that neutralist scholars use to criticize the Court and each other—exposing the inconsistencies and value biases of all purportedly neutral theories of constitutional interpretation. Their aim is to demonstrate that "every proffered constitutional theory can be shown to contain the possibility of directly contradictory resolutions of every problem in constitutional law."[13] Accordingly, constitutional interpretation can be more accurately perceived as inherently subjective, idiosyncratic, and value laden, rather than as the objective discovery of a set of enduring and coherent principles.

What follows is a sampling of this mode of criticism as applied to traditional neutralist theories. To the degree that each theory can be shown to require subjective value choices or generate different and even contradictory outcomes, the edifice of legal autonomy upon which conventional constitutional theories rest is greatly weakened.

Critical Legal Studies versus Interpretivism

Raoul Berger's strict intentionalist or originalist approach is no doubt one of the easiest targets.[14] In attempting to discover the Framers' intentions, there is first the problem of imputing a precise and unified intent to them, which often did not exist and regarding which definitive records may be lacking or inconclusive. In ascertaining the Framers' intentions, disagreement inevitably emerges over what counts as evidence, how that evidence is to be weighed, and which of several plausible conclusions the evidence supports.[15] There is, further, our limited ability to understand and, by necessity, to reconstruct the Framers' world. Implicit in Berger's belief in our ability to discover clear and certain answers is "an implausible claim about the ability to retrieve meaning across time."[16] Thus, Tushnet concludes, "originalism is not a satisfactory answer to people concerned about judicial tyranny. In resolving historical ambiguity, drawing inferences from limited evidence, and taking account of social change, originalist judges have as much room to maneuver as nonoriginalist ones."[17]

There is additionally the problem of the Framers' interpretive intentions, as distinct from their substantive intentions.[18] Did the Framers intend their personal views on particular issues to bind future generations or did they intend only to establish general principles to be elaborated through a conventional textualist approach? H. Jefferson Powell's well-respected historical study indicates that the Framers did not in fact intend their secret deliberations and notes to serve as an authoritative source for future interpreters.[19] According to Stephen Macedo, there simply was no "original consensus" with regard to how the Framers expected the Constitution to be interpreted.[20] Thus, Berger's admonition to adhere closely to the Framers' intentions requires that we in fact disregard their intentions with respect to how they wished the Constitution to be interpreted.

Brest does regard the moderate strands of textualism and originalism as more sensible alternatives, as they are better able "to handle the ambiguity, vagueness, and figurative usage that pervade natural languages."[21] The moderate approach "takes account of the open-textured quality of language and reads the language of provisions in their social and linguistic contexts," seeks to ascertain constitutional principles "at a relatively high level of generality," and looks to "what the adopters' purposes might plausibly have been."[22]

However, Brest argues, in the process of discovering those purposes in order to resolve particular cases, we are inevitably led to other sources, whether history, tradition, or conventional morality. Such an inquiry is necessary, given the opaqueness of the text and the variety of possible applications of the general purposes of the text.

There is additionally an unresolvable difficulty with the moderate textualists' suggestion to read the Constitution as representing broad principles, rather than narrow policy intentions. At what level of generality then are the Framers' aims to be articulated? For example, with regard to equal protection, Bork has advised the Court to choose "a general principle of equality that applies to all cases."[23] As Brest notes,

> The very adoption of such a principle, however, demands an arbitrary choice among levels of abstraction. Just what *is* "the general principle of equality that applies to all cases?" Is it the "core idea of *black* equality" that Bork finds in the original understanding (in which Alan Bakke did not

state a constitutionally cognizable claim), or a broader principle of "*racial equality*" (so that, depending on the precise content of the principle, Bakke might have a case after all), or is it a still broader principle of equality that encompasses discrimination on the basis of gender (or sexual orientation) as well?[24]

Because of the creative, subjective aspects of both ascertaining the Framers' broad purposes and then selecting the proper level of generality, "interpretivism reintroduces the discretion it was intended to eliminate."[25]

Owen Fiss has responded that there is an "interpretive community" that shares a consensus regarding the rules of interpretation. Those authoritative "disciplining rules" produce, if not objectively correct answers, at least an acceptable form of "bounded objectivity."[26] However, as pointed out by Stanley Fish (from whom Fiss borrowed the term *interpretive community*), the disciplining rules are themselves "texts" requiring interpretation and, thus, cannot constrain all interpreters in a uniform and objective manner.[27] Thus, despite the existence of at least a general consensus regarding canons of interpretation, there remains considerable disagreement over which interpretations are correct and authoritative and why; the range of plausible outcomes remains quite broad. In any case, Brest argues, the interpretive community consists mostly of white, wealthy, male professionals. Thus, acceptance of Fiss's notion of "bounded objectivity" has the effect of legitimating the power of a ruling elite to "articulate 'our' public values" and to do so free "from external scrutiny."[28]

Various sources are offered by interpretivists to constrain judicial choice— the text, the Framers' specific intentions, their general purposes, widely accepted rules of interpretation, and, in the case of Ackerman, the higher lawmaking choices of "We the People."[29] However, as the Critics demonstrate, each is subject to manipulation and capable of producing contradictory answers. Thus, interpretivism fails to limit the exercise of judicial review in a coherent and objective manner.[30]

Interpretivism can further be criticized as being at odds with the Constitution itself. After all, as Ely points out, the Constitution contains many broad and "open-textured" provisions such as the Eighth Amendment's ban on cruel and unusual punishment, the Fourteenth Amendment's privileges and immunities clause, and, most significantly, the Ninth Amendment's reservation of unenumerated rights to the people. To Ely, such "provisions

... are difficult to read responsibly as anything other than quite broad invitations to import into the constitutional decision process considerations that will not be found in the language of the amendment or the debates that led up to it."[31] Thus, interpretivists give judges contradictory advice: follow the Constitution, but ignore its open-ended provisions, such as the Ninth Amendment.

Critical Legal Studies versus Noninterpretivism

To the Critics, interpretivism is no more a restraint on judicial discretion and power than is noninterpretivism, which is to say it is no restraint at all. With regard to noninterpretive review, the Critics seem to be less concerned, apparently because they regard it as so hopelessly unable to limit judicial power. Judges are left with no guidance, such as the constitutional text or the Framers' intentions, and instead are free to impose their individualized notions of contemporary or fundamental values.

Tushnet identifies two problems with noninterpretivist approaches. The first is the problematical nature of discovering either moral truths or contemporary values. The second is the difficulty in arguing that judges possess both the legitimacy and a specialized capacity to discover and enforce them.[32]

The first problem in asking judges to search for constitutional answers in moral philosophy is deciding which or whose moral philosophy is "best." Ely hypothesizes that should the Court follow this advice, we could expect a Supreme Court opinion that reads, "We like Rawls, you like Nozick. We win six to three. Statute invalidated."[33] There is the further difficulty of applying highly abstract theories and principles in order to reach conclusions about particular cases.[34] Sound moral deliberation, Tushnet argues, is undermined by both the rule-oriented tradition of law and the necessity of assessing context, especially the highly particularized factual contexts found in individual cases.[35]

The suggestion that contemporary values or community morality might alternatively serve as a source of constitutional decisionmaking fares little better. Again, there is the problem of discovering "contemporary values." Which values and beliefs are indeed widely and deeply shared by Americans, and how are they to be discovered? One possibility is for the Court to consult public opinion polls. However, as Tushnet notes, the problems with polling—for example, variation in results due to the wording of questions—limit the ability of the Court to arrive at any definitive answers; again, that is particularly the case with regard to the highly particularized issues raised in individual cases.[36] Ely also points out the ambivalent and conflicting attitudes of the public toward a variety of issues, such as affirmative action and abortion. And, in quoting Garry Wills, Ely notes that "running men out of town on a rail is at least as much an American tradition as declaring unalienable rights."[37]

As with moderate textualism, the level-of-generality problem remains. How are judges to avoid the arbitrariness involved in choosing how specifically or abstractly to define the relevant tradition or consensus? The Court has itself wrestled with this problem. For example in *Michael H.*, the Court rejected the claim to parental rights of a natural father with regard to a daughter conceived in an adulterous affair.[38] Justice Scalia advanced historical tradition, defined at the most specific level of generality, as the appropriate guide.[39] Thus, the question for Scalia was whether the adulterous relationship between the mother and natural father had been treated as a protected family unit under the historic practices of our society. The obvious, preordained answer was "No." In contrast, Justice Brennan chose a higher level of generality; he asked whether "parenthood" has historically received our nation's attention and protection. The answer, as again dictated by the question and the level of generality chosen, was "Yes." Disagreement between the Court majority and the dissenters in *Hardwick* similarly revolved around whether the case involved "the fundamental right to engage in homosexual sodomy" or "the right of consenting adults to make intimate choices regarding sexual activity," or, even more generally, "the right to be left alone."[40] Thus, consulting tradition or a contemporary consensus remains as useless a pragmatic tool in constitutional decisionmaking as does moral philosophy.

The second difficulty lies in the view that judges can legitimately and more effectively ascertain and apply either moral truths or contemporary values. An initial reason to be skeptical is the fact that judges are similar to other government officials in terms of their demographic characteristics and political views, due to the partisan and political basis of their recruitment and selection.[41] Perhaps their protection from electoral retribution might theoretically enhance the capacity of judges to make sound moral decisions. However, as Tushnet notes, "on the big issues—racial and sexual equality, the distribution of wealth, and the like—and over the entire course of U.S. history courts and legislators have not been very different"; it is thus "difficult to conclude that [the quality of moral discourse in our public life] has been systematically higher in the courts than in legislatures."[42]

The argument that judges are better equipped to ascertain and enforce contemporary values is even weaker. Even if such values were capable of being discovered, there is no reason to expect that unelected judges would be *more* attuned to that consensus than popularly elected representatives would be. Judicial review would in fact be unnecessary, since the legislature would be so unlikely to violate a popular consensus or society's traditional beliefs.[43]

If there is no determinate, ascertainable consensus on either contemporary values or higher moral principles, judges are left free to fill in the blanks with their personal beliefs regarding what is good for society. That opportunity is likely to be used, Ely argues, to favor

> the values of the upper-middle, professional class from which most lawyers and judges, and for that matter most moral philosophers are drawn. . . . Thus the list of values the Court and the commentators have tended to enshrine as fundamental . . . [include] expression, association, education, academic freedom, the privacy of the home, personal autonomy, even the right not to be locked in a stereotypically female sex role and supported by one's husband. But watch most fundamental-rights theorists start edging toward the door when someone mentions jobs, food, or housing: those are important, sure, but they aren't fundamental.[44]

The various noninterpretivist approaches are highly idiosyncratic and infinitely manipulable. Thus, they too fail to constrain judicial discretion in any significant or objective way. Noninterpretivism instead permits judges to impose their own elitist notions about "the good society" against the people's own judgments.

Critical Legal Studies versus Process-Based Approaches

Process-based theories such as Ely's are the product of this skepticism regarding the fundamental-rights approach to constitutional interpretation.[45] These theorists believe that the Constitution is not capable of yielding decisions resting on such "fundamental rights" apart from the justices' own value preferences. Thus, they demand that judicial review be used exclusively to discover and correct, in an objective way, defects in the democratic process.

However, as with both interpretivist and noninterpetivist approaches, the objective nature of process-based theories and their promised ability to eliminate the influence of the justices' personal preferences on their decisions proves illusory. To Brest, Ely's approach "turns out to be a fundamental rights theory, albeit disguised" and thus suffers the same infirmities.[46] Similarly, Tribe argues that "the constitutional theme of perfecting the processes of governmental decision is radically indeterminate and fundamentally incomplete. The process theme by itself determines almost nothing unless its presuppositions are specified, and its content supplemented, by a full theory of substantive rights and values—the very sort of theory the process-perfecters are at such pains to avoid."[47]

The first difficulty with Ely's theory is that "its basic premise, that obstacles to political participation should be removed, is hardly value-free."[48] Ely argues that the Court is not to impose values at all, but merely to protect the integrity and fairness of the political process. He does acknowledge that "participation itself can obviously be regarded as a value."[49] However, he justifies judicial imposition of participational values, since those are the values "(1) with which our Constitution has preeminently and most successfully concerned itself, (2) whose 'imposition' is not incompatible with, but on the contrary supports, the American system of representative democracy, and (3) that courts set apart from the political process are uniquely suited to 'impose.' "[50]

However, that reading of the Constitution is directly contradicted by "the stubbornly substantive character of so many of the Constitution's most crucial commitments."[51] The substantive values protected by the Constitution range from the First Amendment's protection of religious liberty to the Eighth Amendment's ban on cruel and unusual punishment to its protection of private property (through the contracts clause, just compensation clause, and the protection of property alongside that of life and liberty in the Fifth and Fourteenth Amendments). The Thirteenth and Fourteenth Amendments as well embody a substantive antislavery and antidiscrimination commitment. Thus, the assertion that participation is constitutionally privileged and exclusively privileged is flatly at odds with the Constitution itself. After all, "the Constitution itself provides for countermajoritarian trumps, called 'rights,' that the Court may play in appropriate cases."[52] Ely is preferring process to substance for other than *constitutional* reasons.

More significantly, Ely's assertion that a representation-reinforcing approach reduces discretion and gets the Court out of the business of making value choices is easily disproven. The most basic political right is the right to vote and would seem to be capable of neutral judicial enforcement. Yet the Court is inevitably involved in a number of substantive concerns, regarding both who can vote and how voting power is to be apportioned. Is the franchise to be limited to citizens, residents, or property owners? Who can be legitimately excluded—minors, aliens, convicted criminals, District of Columbia residents—and on what grounds? Does the state have any legitimate interest in preventing political instability or insuring that voters possess adequate maturity or loyalty or information? And what about six-month residency requirements or voter registration rules? The Court has been asked to resolve such issues and obviously cannot do so by the mere incantation of the platitude that "the right to vote is fundamental in a democracy."

The Court must further decide the proper allocation of votes, the very form of representation a democracy demands. The Court's use of the one person–one vote rule has the obvious appeal of both fairness and simplicity. But certainly it cannot be defended, on *neutral* grounds, as the only legitimate form of representation in a democracy. (One only need look to the representation of state interests in the U.S. Senate.) Similarly, which form of representation is "more democratic"—that achieved through district elections or at-large elections? That question can be answered only by reference to one's preferences regarding the value of neighborhood interests versus "the community interest" and regarding which groups should be accorded more effective representation and more power. Even the one person–one vote rule requires the Court to decide how much deviation is permissible. Furthermore, a plan may be neutral on its face or respect equality of representation in a purely numerical sense, but still advantage a particular group, party, or outcome. For example, in *United Jewish Organizations* v. *Carey*, the Court had to decide whether to approve a reapportionment plan that increased the voting power of African Americans while diluting the voting power of Hasidic Jews.[53]

Thus, Ely fails to recognize that "political participation can have many meanings. The meaning we choose will invariably depend upon the goals or values we think participation should promote."[54] However, his theory neither advances nor defends any particular "meaning." It is of little help in resolving those vexing issues of "defining the relevant community" and "determining whose preferences are to count."[55] Thus, even in voting rights cases, Ely's purportedly neutral representation-reinforcing approach is capable of manipulation and requires the Court to make choices among competing values.[56]

There is additionally what Tribe refers to as "the quandary of whom to protect."[57] Like the Court, Ely must answer the terribly difficult question that the *Carolene Products* footnote raises: *Who* qualifies as a discrete and insular minority entitled to heightened judicial solicitude? Ely fares little better than the Court in this line-drawing endeavor (which is to say not very well).

The first problem lies in distinguishing between discrete and insular minorities who are "ordinary" losers in the political process, such as the opticians in *Lee Optical*, and illegitimate losers, such as the African American children in *Brown*. The critical difference, according to Ely, is the existence of prejudice. Prejudice may consist of widespread hostility and dislike ("first-degree prejudice") or an inability or unwillingness to evaluate a group's interests carefully and fully due to that group's social isolation or the absence of group members sitting in the legislature.[58]

While perhaps a reasonable distinction on its face, Ely's guide proves difficult to apply, as his own examples demonstrate. For example, as discussed in the previous chapter, Ely does not include gender in his list of "racelike" classifications subject to strict judicial scrutiny. Women are not a minority numerically and, in any case, they now enjoy effective opportunities for political participation.[59] However, many reasonable men and women would dispute that claim. At a minimum, Ely's judgment—that women now enjoy effective (and equal?) access to political power and need not fear indifference or stereotyping at the hands of mostly male legislatures—is open to debate. Ely's appraisal is quite simply a subjective one. For example, Bruce Ackerman has argued that if lack of effective political access and legislative indifference are the proper grounds for judicial protection, then he would choose new recipients: "the anonymous and diffuse victims of poverty and sexual discrimination, who find it most difficult to protect their fundamental interests through effective political organization."[60]

Furthermore, as Paul Brest points out, Ely's formulation does not prevent litigants or lawyers from translating their fundamental-rights claim into a representation-reinforcing claim in order to receive the special judicial protection they desire. Using Brest's example, males with long hair or those who smoke pot need not rely on personal autonomy arguments to challenge restrictive laws and regulations. They need only restate their claims in Ely's representation-reinforcing terms: such regulations "are suspect 'we-they' distinctions, for (even today) most legislators do not smoke pot, most male school administrators do not wear their hair at shoulder-length, and many of these officials and their constituents are hostile toward and prejudiced against those who engage in these practices."[61] Because lawyers and judges are quite free to choose whichever "alternative rhetorical tradition" they desire, arbitrary value choice remains.[62]

Ely further runs into difficulty in determining when legislative hostility and discrimination *is* legitimate. For example, he would permit discriminatory treatment of burglars, despite the fact that burglars are victims of widespread hostility, and no legislators (as far as we know) are themselves current or former burglars. The qualification Ely is then required to make is that a legislature may discriminate to satisfy its "moral beliefs" but not to satisfy the "majority's dislike" of a particular group. However, a further qualification is then required:

> This doesn't mean that simply by incanting "immorality" a state can be permitted successfully to defend a law that in fact was motivated by a desire simply to injure a disfavored group of persons. The legislature couldn't, for example, outlaw the wearing of yarmulkes or dashikis and defend on the ground that it regards such conduct as immoral. The question here thus reduces to whether the claim is credible that the prohibition in question was generated by a sincerely held moral objection to the act.[63]

Despite his belief that homosexuals are a suspect class, homosexual *conduct* may be punished, in Ely's view, if it is based on the legislature's sincere belief that such conduct is immoral. However, as Brest aptly point out, "Ely forgets that racial segregation and antimiscegenation laws, as well as stereotypical gender classifications, have often been based—perhaps often sincerely—on the supposed immorality of racial intermingling and intermarriage, or of women not fulfilling their missions as mothers and wives."[64]

What Brest refers to as Ely's "conscientious objection" exception for legislative discrimination fails as a neutral and nondiscretionary distinction and "subverts the very purpose of the representation-reinforcing mode."[65] Furthermore, this puts the Court in the dubious business of second-guessing legislative motives, determining whether discriminatory treatment is motivated by "moral beliefs" and, if so, whether they are "sincerely held."

In these criticisms of Ely's theory as manipulable and inviting further value choice, the Critics are joined by conventional scholars as different as Raoul Berger and Laurence Tribe.[66] However, the Critics are alone in this, their final attack: Ely's theory is nothing more than "a sophisticated apology for the truncated, systematically biased political life of our liberal welfare state."[67]

Underlying Ely's theory is the belief that, most of the time, the American political process works well and, thus, requires only occasional adjustments by the Court. However, that judgment is itself a subjective one. For example, Tushnet argues that "informal obstacles to representation are far more pervasive than the theory's adherents seem willing to admit," including low voter turnout, political inequalities, and a fragmented structure protecting the status quo.[68] Should a Tushnet or Parker ever reach the bench and faithfully apply Ely's edict to intervene "only to protect and improve the democratic process," we would see a Court-directed democratic reconstruction project of immense proportions, which no doubt Ely would not welcome.

In the end, Ely's theory falters on the same grounds as the theories he criticizes. The choice of protecting participation over other "substantive" rights also recognized in the Constitution represents an arbitrary, value choice of the sort Ely seeks to avoid.[69] Furthermore, the application of his theory, whether regarding the right to vote or the protection of minorities, "demands precisely the kinds of controversial substantive choices that the process proponents are so anxious to leave to the electorate and its representatives."[70]

Thus, as Estreicher notes, Ely's analogy regarding the Court as an impartial referee insuring that the political process operates fairly is quite misleading. "Unlike, say the umpire in a baseball game, Ely's judges decide whether groups are taking 'unfair advantage' of other groups not on the basis of a shared, well-understood set of norms, but rather on the basis of norms that the referees themselves fashion in the course of calling political balls and strikes."[71]

"The Critics against Themselves"

The self-perceived task of Critical Legal Studies is deconstructing and "trashing" the work of conventional legal theorists.[72] In that endeavor, they owe a great debt to constitutional theorists themselves. Although Critical Legal Studies scholars do add their own evaluation of various constitutional theories, that is hardly necessary. Conventional scholars provide the critics with quite sufficient ammunition. Thus, Tribe criticizes Ely, who criticizes Dworkin, who criticizes Bork, et cetera, always on the grounds that the theory in question is subjective and biased. And, of course, judges engage in precisely the same enterprise. The classic dissenter's line is that the majority opinion represents nothing more than personal preference and bias, reflects a lack of deference due the legislative branch, and lacks a principled constitutional basis.

The appropriate response, of course, is "You're all right." All existing theories of constitutional interpretation, whether from the Court or the commentators, "are vulnerable to similar criticisms based on their indeterminacy, manipulability, and, ultimately, their reliance on judicial value choices that cannot be 'objectively' derived from text, history, consensus, natural rights, or any other source. No theory of constitutional adjudication can defend itself against self-scrutiny."[73]

For the conventional neutralist scholar, it is human frailty (or "everyone else's" frailties) that impedes the development and proper application of a value-free and coherent constitutional theory. For the Critics, the inability of any scholar or judge to develop a coherent body of constitutional decisions generated in a value-neutral way serves as evidence of and reflects the fundamental truth about constitutional decisionmaking and conventional constitutional theory. Given the indeterminate nature of the constitutional text, particular interpretations can be chosen and defended only by recourse to the decisionmakers' personal values. Given that fact, all attempts to discover a coherent and objective theory of constitutional decisionmaking as a source of legitimacy for the Court must fail. In choosing among competing theories of constitutional interpretation, "no defensible criteria exist."[74]

Where the Critics succeed is in revealing the value biases, subjectivity, and idiosyncracies of existing theories of constitutional interpretation and of constitutional law doctrines as well. If objectively constrained constitutional interpretation exists, we have yet to see it, which casts substantial doubt on whether we are ever likely to see it. In their quest for coherent, principled, and objectively defensible constitutional law, the neutralists must be a frustrated lot.

While Critical Legal Studies scholars do not conclusively prove that objectivity and certainty in constitutional interpretation are impossible, they certainly succeed in giving us sufficient cause to be profoundly skeptical of that possibility. Rather than continuing this seemingly endless and ultimately futile debate, why not examine the *implications* of the Critics being correct? Where might recognition of constitutional indeterminacy and judicial subjectivity lead?

Utopian Speculation

To the Critics, the primary consequences of judicial subjectivity and constitutional indeterminacy are that all exercises of judicial review must be regarded as arbitrary and illegitimate, at least according to the conventional scholars' definition of legitimacy. Conventional scholars argue that the Court's decisions are legitimate only to the extent that they rest on some clear, objective basis. To the degree that the Court's decisions rest on a subjective basis, such as the justices' personal views, then the Court is exceeding its legitimate authority. To this, the Critics respond, "Then the Court always and inevitably exceeds its legitimate authority, since constitutional interpretation is always and inevitably subjective."

Although the immediate task of Critical Legal Studies is to destroy the premises underlying conventional theory, the larger purpose, often explicitly stated, is political. By destroying the claim to neutrality in legal decision-making, the Critics hope to awaken us to the uses of law and legal theory as tools for mystifying and legitimating oppression and elite domination.[75] Constitutional theories then are more appropriately viewed as rationalizations of and "covers" for the dominant political philosophy and economic order. For example, the constitutional philosophy of the *Lochner* Court was that the text and the Framers' intent require special constitutional and judicial protection for economic rights. (And, of course, they were correct.)[76]

However, that constitutional philosophy was quite clearly a politically dominant, laissez-faire economic philosophy as well. Ely's purportedly value-free constitutional theory was in fact invented by Franklin Roosevelt's New Deal Court. Not surprisingly, that theory has as its consequence the protection of New Deal allies (workers, minorities, the poor, and left-leaning intellectuals) at the expense of New Deal enemies (primarily business).[77]

However, once our eyes are opened to this reality, it is not clear where the Critics wish to take us. Phillip Johnson is right on the mark in his critique regarding the ultimate emptiness of Critical Legal Studies: "There is no mystery about what the Critical Legal Scholars are against: They are against capitalism, liberalism, and illegitimate hierarchy. It is much harder to say what they are for. In fact, Critical legal writing has practically nothing to suggest in the way of a positive political program. For a movement that claims to be political, this is truly an astonishing vacuum."[78]

Among the Critics' proposals cited by Johnson are Duncan Kennedy's general call for "utopian speculation"[79] and Roberto Unger's conclusion that any solution can be "fully worked out only with the help of a metaphysics we do not yet possess."[80] Peter Gabel envisions "a living milieu in which human labor is a creative social activity in which the production of material goods is purposely designed to satisfy real human needs, and in which each person recognizes the other as 'one-of-us' instead of 'other-than-me' irrespective of sex or skin color."[81] Paul Brest suggests that we might "work toward a genuine reconstitution of society—perhaps one in which the concept of freedom includes citizen participation in the community's public discourse and responsibility to shape its values and structure."[82] Richard Parker advises a return to "the classical conception of a republic, including its elements of relative equality, mobilization of the citizenry, and civic virtue."[83] And similarly, Mark Tushnet argues that "the task of constitutional theory ought no longer be to rationalize the real in one way or another. It should be to contribute to a political movement that may begin to bring about a society in which civic virtue may flourish."[84]

As Johnson notes, the Critics' "program is platitudinous. Racial and sexual equality, civic virtue, meaningful work, satisfaction of 'real human needs,' active citizen participation in public affairs—these could be the least controversial planks in the platform of any civic organization from the Chamber of Commerce to the League of Women Voters."[85] Johnson's conclusion that the message of Critical Legal Studies is ultimately conservative thus is quite appropriate.

This refusal to address the pragmatic issue—What is the Supreme Court to do, given that there are valid objections to any course of action?—is typical of Critical legal scholarship, and explains why this kind of writing is so unsatisfying to persons of a practical bent. If the Critical scholars are making the point that utopian fantasy is the only alternative to conventional legal thought, then they are making the strongest possible pragmatic argument for maintaining our conventions.[86]

Neither a complete denigration of all exercises of judicial power as arbitrary and oppressive nor the call for utopian speculation tells us what the Court should be doing here and now—how it should decide individual cases and how we are to evaluate its performance. The Critics provide no practical, meaningful advice regarding how to proceed once we recognize the impossibility of reconciling with democratic values the subjective and value-driven form of constitutional interpretation they so effectively reveal.

Judicial Restraint

The call for self-restraint is another response to acknowledging that the justices often do and perhaps must invest the Constitution's open-ended provisions with "meaning" that is drawn at least in part from their personal political views. Since judicial intervention is always attended with the danger of judges arbitrarily imposing their personal biases in opposition to the people's desires, then one solution is for judges to limit their intervention as much as possible.

However, the self-restraint principle is typically advanced in a general and ill-defined way. In other words, it does not tell us when the Court is to defer to the legislative will and under what rare circumstances it may legitimately intervene. Accordingly, we may lose precisely those benefits which the Court, as a nonelective institution, is uniquely capable of providing. As John Agresto points out, "Recognizing that the United States Senate is nonmajoritarian, since senators of small states have an equal voice with those from large states, few would demand that it therefore exercise restraint in the pursuit of those functions it is empowered to perform."[87]

Nor does self-restraint provide any guarantee that those reduced number of acts of judicial intervention will be wise and beneficial ones. After all, the Court exercised extraordinary restraint for the fifty years following *Marbury* v. *Madison.* Yet its next exercise of judicial review (with regard to national legislation) was the "self-inflicted wound" of *Dred Scott.*[88]

Additionally, should the Court persistently withhold its assistance to aggrieved litigants, it would find that few would continue to seek its help, and quite rationally so. Thus, self-restraint is, as a practical matter, a prescription for the Court to lose its relevance and thus its power in American politics. "Power cast aside without provision for its further exercise almost invariably destroys the abdicating power holder—as, for example, Shakespeare's King Lear found out when he improvidently abandoned his power and was promptly crushed."[89] In any case, demands for judicial restraint simply have not been and never will be heeded.

Recognition of judicial subjectivity and constitutional indeterminacy has led to demands for judicial self-restraint, blanket condemnations of all judicial power, and vague calls for utopian speculation and a new metaphysics. Such alternatives are of no practical value. The Court will continue to exercise considerable power. The people (i.e., litigants) will continue to request that it do so. And the justices will inevitably look beyond the text, perhaps to their personal values, in resolving controversial issues with necessarily vague and limited guidance from the text. The problem of reconciling discretionary and subjective constitutional interpretation with democratic values remains.

Provisional Review

Apparently out of their frustration with failed attempts to justify judicial review on textual or otherwise objective grounds, particularly noninterpretivist decisions like *Roe,* some scholars have resorted to a new and more fruitful approach: provisional review. To the degree that objective constraints either do not exist or cannot prevent occasional abuses or errors in judgment, perhaps *political* constraints on the Court can provide a way of checking and, therefore, reconciling the Court's power with democratic values. As the next chapter argues, provisional review represents a small but important step in the right direction.

• •

CHAPTER 3

The Skeptics and the Idea of
Provisional Review

AN interesting development in several recent theories of judicial review is the idea of "provisional review." Quite simply, provisional review would permit the political branches to check in some manner the constitutional decisions of the Supreme Court. This alternative type of review has been advocated by scholars such as Harry Wellington, Michael Perry, Paul Dimond, and John Agresto as a way to reconcile discretionary and subjective judicial review with democratic values.[1]

Provisional review places a normative stamp of approval on the conclusions of various empirical studies regarding the finality of Supreme Court decisions. In his often-cited 1957 article, Robert Dahl argued that largely because elected officials recruit and select Supreme Court justices and turnover is relatively frequent, "the Supreme Court is inevitably a part of the dominant national political alliance." As such, the Court has rarely opposed "national lawmaking majorities" and when it has done so, such policy opposition has not endured for long. In short, "lawmaking majorities generally have had their way."[2]

Judicial impact studies have additionally shown that compliance with Supreme Court decisions is neither automatic nor uniform. Because the Court lacks the power to enforce and fund its decisions, it is highly dependent on voluntary compliance, faithful application by lower court judges, and the active support of other branches and levels of government.[3]

Additionally, Supreme Court decisions are themselves overturned or limited in their scope by subsequent decisions. This most typically occurs as a result of the deliberate efforts of the other branches to alter the Court's policy direction, for example by proposing constitutional amendments, refusing to fund or enforce the Court's rulings, attempting to restrict the Court's appellate jurisdiction, and, most significantly and effectively, packing the Court with appointees whose views are more ideologically suitable.[4] Thus, constitutional law development is in fact an ongoing political process with many participants.[5]

The thrust of these various studies is that, as an empirical matter, the Supreme Court does not have the final say. That empirical observation has provided an opening, an opportunity, for constitutional theorists to reconcile judicial review with democratic values. "Judicial value determinations are inescapable. . . . They are also unexceptional. What is exceptional in judicial review is that value determinations in constitutional cases have the appearance of finality. . . . If it can be shown, however, that often there is less finality in a constitutional decision than meets the eye, . . . then perhaps we can accept more readily the legitimacy of judicial review."[6]

The theories of provisional judicial review offered by Michael Perry, Paul Dimond, and John Agresto will first be presented. Their common themes and common weaknesses will then be analyzed.

Provisional review, it will be argued, has several virtues—dispensing with notions of certainty and objectivity in constitutional decisionmaking, rejecting judicial supremacy, and recognizing the necessity of political constraints on unelected judges making highly significant and discretionary political decisions. However, provisional review, in its current form, is internally contradictory and fails to follow the implications of its own premise. As will be explained, these "Skeptics" leave one foot inexplicably planted in the neutralist tradition: they insist that while the Court must be subject to political checks, its central role is to serve as the apolitical moral guardian of American society. The conventional fear of politics and of a political Court remains. It is that fear which constitutes the misguided and unjustifed raison d'être of conventional constitutional theory and of the legitimacy question at its center.

Michael Perry's Defense of Noninterpretive Review

Professor Perry's lofty aim is to resolve the central problem of contemporary constitutional theory—"the legitimacy of constitutional policymaking by the Supreme Court, especially in the area of human rights."[7] He sets for himself two criteria that any such resolution must satisfy. Noninterpretive review must, first, uniquely serve a "crucial governmental function" and, second, must serve that function "in a manner that somehow accommodates the principle of electorally accountable policymaking."[8]

Perry begins by discussing the now familiar distinction between interpretivism and noninterpretivism. This distinction is especially critical in Perry's theory.[9] "The legitimacy of interpretive review is not a particularly difficult problem . . . [while the] legitimacy of noninterpretive review is the central problem of contemporary constitutional theory."[10] Furthermore, "the decisions in virtually all modern constitutional cases of consequence . . . cannot plausibly be explained except in terms of noninterpretive review" (11). Thus, Perry asserts, virtually every important decision made by the Court since and including *Brown* is of dubious legitimacy.

Perry's self-perceived task, then, is to rescue and provide a justification for those decisions that he obviously regards as valuable though of questionable constitutional and democratic legitimacy. His solution is a functional justification for noninterpretive review: "If noninterpretive review serves a crucial governmental function, perhaps even an indispensable one, that no other practice can realistically be expected to serve . . . that function constitutes the justification for the practice" (92–93).

In his search for the function of noninterpretive review in human rights cases, Perry examines what he refers to as "American self-understanding," particularly its "religious" aspects broadly conceived. Central to the religious self-understanding of the American people is their belief that they have been "'chosen' in the biblical sense of that word" and are obligated "among the nations of the world . . . to realize . . . a 'higher law'" and to strive for moral evolution and perfection (97). However, "even a chosen people fail in their responsibility and need to be called to judgment—provisional judgment—in the here and now. That is the task of prophecy" (98).

It is against this background that Perry identifies the function of noninterpretive review. "Judicial review represents the institutionalization of prophecy. The function of noninterpretive review in human rights cases is prophetic; it is to call the American people—actually the government, the representatives of the people—to provisional judgment" (98–99).

The Court, Perry argues, is much better suited to fulfill that function of moral guidance and prophecy than are the elective institutions, for whom incumbency is the highest priority. "As a matter of comparative institutional competence, the politically insulated federal judiciary is more likely, when the human rights issue is a deeply controversial one, to move us in the direction of a right answer . . . than is the political process left to its own devices, which tends to resolve such issues by reflexive, mechanical reference to established moral conventions" (102).

We have thus arrived at Perry's justification for noninterpretive review in human rights cases: "The practice of noninterpretive review has evolved as a way of remedying what would otherwise be a serious defect in American government—the absence of any policymaking institution that *regularly* deals with fundamental political-moral problems other than by mechanical reference to established moral conventions" (101).

Perry is not yet satisfied that he has fully answered the charge that noninterpretive review is illegitimate. After all, as *Lochner* and *Dred Scott* demonstrate, "the Court is a fallible institution. It is capable of giving false prophecy" (115). Perry responds that "noninterpretivist review has functioned, on balance, as an instrument of deepening moral insight and of moral growth" (118). However, as Perry acknowledges, that answer too is incomplete. In addition to the likelihood of an occasional error, that the Court may impede moral growth, is the observation that "unlike prophecy, noninterpretive review is coercive" (125). Furthermore, noninterpretive decisions are derived not from the text or the people, but from the justices' own values (125).

Thus, although Perry has found his functional justification for noninterpretive review, the task remains of reconciling it with the principle of electorally accountable policymaking, of insuring that "constitutional policymaking by the judiciary is subject to important control at the hands of electorally accountable officials" (126). Perry rejects the impeachment process, constitutional amendment, joint presidential-Senate appointment power, and congressional control over the Court's budget as providing that significant political control necessary to accommodate noninterpretive review with the principle of electorally accountable policymaking (127–28). Instead, Perry finds his answer in Congress's power to restrict the Court's appellate jurisdiction (128). Congress can use its "power to silence" as an effective political check on the Court's exercise of noninterpretive review.

The result, however, is neither legislative nor judicial dominance, but a dialectical relationship.

The electorally accountable political processes generate a policy choice, which typically reflects some fairly well established moral conventions. . . .

In exercising noninterpretive review, the Court evaluates that choice on political-moral grounds. . . . If the Court rejects a given policy choice, the political processes must respond, whether by embracing the Court's decision, by tolerating it, . . . by moderating or even by undoing it (112).

The result of this constitutional dialogue between the Court and the people's representatives "is a more self-critical political morality than would otherwise appear, and therefore likely a more mature political morality . . . that is moving (inching?) toward . . . right answers" (113).

Perry believes that noninterpretive review, as he conceives it, serves an important societal function and can be rendered compatible with democratic values through Congress's power to restrict the Court's jurisdiction. However, such review was neither anticipated nor authorized by the Framers. "In that sense, noninterpretive review is extraconstitutional—beyond any value judgment the framers constitutionalized" (114).

Paul Dimond and Provisional Review

Like Perry, Paul Dimond attempts to discover "how the Court can address substantive rights issues under open-ended constitutional provisions consistent with the nation's commitment to representative democracy."[11] Existing theories of judicial review falter on one of two grounds. First, they often fail to confront the "dilemma of judicial choice" (6)—the fact that the "Constitution in its generality does not provide a specific answer but authorizes a range of choices" (10).[12] Second, and even more frequently, such theories fail to reconcile the Court's discretionary choices, "understood as *final*," with democratic values (11).

The solution, in Dimond's view, is simply to stop perceiving and treating the Court's choices as final. Similarly to statutory interpretation and common law development, and consistently with the text and structure of the Constitution and historical practice, the Court's constitutional decisions should be regarded "not as final judgments forever binding on the people but as provisional rulings that initiate an ongoing dialogue with the people" (4).

According to Dimond's interpretation of the structure of the Constitution, the Court is empowered to serve as a "neutral, national forum" to referee disputes between the federal and state governments, and its decisions are binding on the states; Congress, however, possesses the final authority to resolve those disputes (61–66). For those concerned that his approach leaves the states with too little protection, Dimond responds that the states may initially win in the Court and, if they do not, they may still win their battle in Congress, where states are effectively represented (70–71).

The Fourteenth Amendment provides the Court with another significant source of power over the states. In Dimond's view, the amendment permits, but does not require, the privileges and immunities clause to be read as "a rather open-ended invitation to articulate national rights, while the due process clause may be interpreted to cover fair procedures and the equal protection clause to protect against caste discrimination" (68). Similarly to its resolution of federal-state disputes, the Court's interpretive choices regarding the Fourteenth Amendment are binding on the states, but only until that time when Congress chooses to revise or reverse them. Treating its decisions as provisional rather than final "frees the Court to look to a variety of sources for interpreting substantive national rights" (69). After all, "there is nothing wrong in having the Court, as a neutral national forum which is at least somewhat insulated from the heated passions of the moment, address such critical substantive issues" (69).

Following the Court's "plausible initial attempts to develop a common law of national rights" (70) Congress may respond by exercising its Fourteenth Amendment enforcement power and its general article I, section 8 powers "to enact alternative national policies to bind the states" (67). In revising the Court's judgments, however, Congress does not possess unlimited power. It, too, is subject to constitutional restrictions, most importantly the Bill of Rights. As Dimond explains, suppose that the Court initially ruled that a state law establishing Christianity as the official state religion violated the Fourteenth Amendment. Congress could not then respond by passing a law establishing Christianity as a national religion. That law too would be unconstitutional under the First Amendment (79–80).[13]

Dimond regards the Bill of Rights as imposing relatively few and narrow substantive restrictions (80). Instead, the constitutional restrictions on Congress that the Court may enforce, authoritatively and with finality, are mostly procedural in nature and consist of three types. The first set of "external limits" is intended to protect the integrity of representational processes, insuring that the people are free to express their views, vote their preferences, and have their votes count in an effective and fair manner (81–82). Second is the "anti-caste principle," protecting outgroups from being relegated to a subordinate caste by legislative hostility and prejudice (82–85). Third, Congress must clearly and directly address the merits of any issue affecting constitutional interests (85–87).[14]

To summarize Dimond's approach, the Court possesses broad authority and discretion in resolving both federalism and substantive rights issues, and its decisions are binding on the states. However, Congress may enter the political dialogue on such issues and override the Court's judgments. Consistent with democratic values, Congress is given the final say, but only if, in the Court's view, the lawmaking process was "in fact representative, free from caste-based defects, and visibly focused on the merits of these critical issues" (88). As a result of provisional review, "the dilemma of judicial choice in a representative democracy is substantially reduced if not entirely eliminated" (11).[15]

Like Ely, Dimond believes that granting the Court a final say over substantive issues violates democratic principles, although finality with respect to process issues does not violate democratic principles. However, unlike Ely, Dimond would permit the Court to participate in a dialogue with Congress over the determination of substantive rights. (Ely demands that the Court avoid substantive issues altogether.)[16]

Similarly to Perry, Dimond does not wish to deny the Court a significant role in determining the meaning and scope of substantive constitutional rights; yet both are troubled by the finality of Supreme Court interpretations that are not defensible in terms of the Constitution's text and history. Their solution is to permit a congressional check on the Court's interpretation of substantive rights. However, Dimond would permit congressional revision, while Perry permits only congressional "silencing" of the Court through jurisdictional control. In Dimond's view, jurisdictional control makes little sense in Perry's scheme: "For one who proclaims the functional need for reasoned moral dialogue by the Court, . . . such a purportedly democratic solution would serve only to silence the voice of the Court altogether."[17]

John Agresto: Political Checks on the Imperial Judiciary

Professor Agresto is deeply troubled by a Supreme Court that is in effect supreme and autonomous in all matters constitutional. He is also critical of scholars who attempt to develop theoretical justifications for the modern expansion of judicial power and for what amounts to judicial supremacy. Agresto believes that, consistent with the structure of our government and the Framers' intentions to provide for balanced government, we must reexamine and strengthen the political restraints on the Court's power. His goal is to return the Court to its proper role "as a partner in the shaping of constitutional law rather than as its final arbiter."[18]

Agresto begins with the now familiar criticism of the Court's "imperialism."

> The judiciary is imperial not because it is "active," which it is. It is imperial not because it is essentially unchecked, which it also is. It is imperial and exceedingly dangerous because it is active and unchecked in its ability to be the creator, the designer, of new social policy. . . . Rather than acting as a check on precipitous social change—the "sober second thought" of an older constitutional understanding—the courts are now themselves the agents of social change, with no candidates for the role of sober second thinkers in sight. We know how to check our legislatures; we do not know how to check our legislative judiciary.[19]

Scholars have responded poorly to this crisis, according to Agresto. Some have tried, and failed, to develop theoretical justifications for the Court's imperialism. (He targets Professors Ely and Choper.)[20] In response, Agresto provides historical and theoretical support for his alternative conception of American government and the Court's role in it:

> Constitutional interpretation is not and was never intended to be solely within the province of the Court, for constitutional government implies that the ultimate interpeter of our fundamental law is not an autonomous judiciary but the interactive understanding of the people, their representatives, and their judges together. We should see the American political system not as a pyramid, with the Court at the top as the ultimate authority, but rather as an interlocking system of mutual oversight, mutual checking, and combined interpretation (10).

Scholars have also responded to charges of judicial imperialism by calling for judicial restraint. Agresto, however, regards such demands as futile and therefore useless (114–15). More significantly, "self-restraint deprive[s] the whole nation of potentially valuable judicial contributions" (166).

What then *is* the nature of the Court's contribution? Agresto finds two beneficial roles for the Court to play—"as the legal check on political excess and as the mediator of our principles" (55). The first role, checking political power, particularly legislative power, is hardly unusual or controversial. The second is the more complex yet, to Agresto, the more important and dynamic role for the Court.

> The highest and most complex attribute of judicial review is its potential ability to help the nation as a whole govern itself and direct its progress in the light of constitutional principles: not only principles that might need to be applied to new circumstances, but principles that . . . might grow, develop, and expand. Its justification, if one is to be found, must be in that original American desire to be bound by and to live according to certain ideas and principles of just social conduct embodied in the words of a constitutional text. The underlying promise of judicial review is that with it we may bring our philosophy, our principles, to bear on our actions, and thus work out our present and our future in terms of our inheritance from the past (54–55).

Thus, the Court "adds a dimension to public life that might otherwise be absent" (143). When we ask the Court to be passive or restrained, we lose "the Court's potentially most positive contribution: the ability to discern, articulate, and develop, with us, our still living fundamental constitutional principles" (143).

Agresto does, however, recognize that judicial power holds both "promise and perils" (139–67). "The impetus that propels the Court to be a check also demands that no branch, not even the judiciary, become autonomous or unchecked itself; and the desire to live by stated principles means that no branch, not even the Court, can reform or shape those values freely or at will" (55). Both "the dangers of judicial supremacy" and "the potential fallibility of the Court" require that "the Court must itself be part of, and not above, the dynamic interaction of American politics" (97–98). In short, the Court too must be subject to checks enforced against it by the other branches.

Agresto's search is for ways for the people, through their elected representatives, "to reverse a ruling by the judiciary and to make the process of constitutional adjudication and interpretation a shared endeavor of the polity as a whole, and not the final prerogative of the Court" (119). Agresto examines and rejects a variety of checks on the Court. Impeachment, congressional denial of jurisdiction, and alteration of the size of the Court are regarded as "too heavy or too blunt a set of instruments to use against the Court. . . . All are more or less severe attacks on the Court's ability to function as an institution" (125).

A more effective and proper way for Congress to check the Court's decisions is to force the Court to reconsider its decisions and thereby to conduct a dialogue with the Court regarding its judgment as to the meaning of the Constitution. Congress may do this by reenacting or revising voided legislation, as it often does (125–30). Congress may also limit the impact of the Court's decisions, for example, as it has done with the prohibition of Medicaid funds for nearly all abortions (130–31). Yet another possibility, similar to Dimond's suggestion, is to regard the Fourteenth Amendment as an important source of congressional power to define national rights (131–33).[21]

As with both Perry and Dimond, Agresto believes that "judicial interpretations do not settle for the political branches the permanent meaning of the Constitution's text or its principles" (129). Rather, the Court's decisions are a vehicle for initiating and furthering "a 'continuing colloquy with the political institutions and with society at large' " (166).[22] By restoring the Court to its proper partnership role in the development of constitutional principle, we may begin to "see judicial review not primarily as a restriction on democratic life, but as a positive invitation to a democratic response" (166).

Why Provisional Review Fails

There are some common themes and common problems with these theories of provisional review. First, their proponents share a skepticism regarding the existence of objective constraints on constitutional interpretation, such as text and history. Additionally, they assume or expect judicial fallibility—that the justices will occasionally make "mistakes" in making value judgments "in the Constitution's name." And at least Perry and Wellington are more accepting of the view that the justices inevitably make subjective value determinations, even judgments influenced by personal belief and conscience. Accordingly, permitting the Court's decisions to be final and binding is to permit the justices' highly discretionary and occasionally mistaken judgments as to the meaning of the Constitution to rule society, to be unchallenged and unchallengeable. That is by definition judicial tyranny.

The solution is provisional review. Provisional review provides that the Court's constitutional decisions are not always final and binding; they do not represent "the supreme law of the land." Instead, those decisions are provisional judgments subject to a democratic response and possibly democratic revision. Instead of being the final and exclusive expositor of fundamental constitutional values, the Court is an equal partner in an ongoing political-moral dialogue.

The Skeptics have wisely abandoned the central task of conventional constitutional theory—the discovery and elaboration of objective and coherent constraints on constitutional interpretation. (Or in the language of the Critics, they have "abandoned liberal premises.")[23] They have replaced objective constraints with political constraints, which ease the tension between judicial review and democratic values in both a normative and practical sense.

The primary virtue of the provisional review approach is its revision of the legitimacy question. We are no longer permitted to justify judicial review on the basis of infallible judges neutrally applying an objectively correct theory of constitutional interpretation. Nor do we continue to confront the unresolvable problem of how to reconcile judicial *supremacy* with democratic values. However, the Skeptics do not follow the implications of their recognition of constitutional indeterminacy and judicial fallibility (or at least they do so only partially in the form of sometimes permitting political checks on constitutional decisionmaking). Those implications should include abandoning all pretenses as to the apolitical function of the Court and its "special" role in American democracy. It is the Skeptics' failure to do so that ultimately creates problems for and undermines their theories, as the following analysis demonstrates.

The first problem facing the Skeptics is determining *when* it is necessary or desirable that the Court be checked. While they acknowledge the possibility of judicial error and of judicial overreaching, they fail to provide a clear and objective way for scholars or the Court or Congress to identify those decisions requiring correction. Perry and Dimond both confront this problem directly and both fail to solve it, while Agresto ducks the issue entirely.

For Perry and Dimond, the notion that Congress may silence or overrule *every* constitutional judgment made by the Court is itself anticonstitutional.

That is a prescription for legislative tyranny and in effect rewrites the Constitution, in particular eliminating its restrictions on majorities and legislative powers. The problem then is providing an objective, principled way for determining when the Court's judgments are final and when they are merely provisional and subject to congressional silencing or revision.

Perry's solution rests on the interpretivist-noninterpretivist distinction. Interpretivist decisions, in which the Court enforces "value judgments constitutionalized by the Framers," are final and not subject to Congress's jurisdiction-limiting power. Noninterpretivist decisions are only provisional, and the Court may accordingly be "silenced" by Congress. The obvious problem is that Perry assumes that it is in fact possible to distinguish clearly and unequivocally between the Court's interpretive and noninterpretive decisions in order to determine whether they are to be regarded as final or provisional.[24]

Perry's casual and inadequate response is that we need not be concerned since "in very few consequential human rights cases of the modern period can the Court's decisions *even plausibly* be explained as products of interpretive review."[25] That judgment is *itself* subject to dispute. Telford Taylor is one of many who find Perry's view of what constitutes an interpretivist decision "implausibly narrow."[26] Similarly, Larry Alexander argues that "Perry has . . . entered the interpretivism-noninterpretivism fray, as so many others have done, without a cogent theory of interpretation. Because his justification for judicial review treats interpretive and noninterpretive decisions fundamentally differently, it is doomed to failure in the absence of such a theory."[27]

Dimond rests his distinction between provisional and final judicial judgment on a similarly indeterminate and manipulable basis. The Court's decisions are final (with respect to Congress only) when it invokes the "largely" procedural, representational restrictions of the Bill of Rights. However, as discussed in the previous chapter, Laurence Tribe, Paul Brest, and others have demonstrated that process-based approaches do not, as promised, deny the Court the opportunity to make substantive value judgments.[28] The distinction between procedural and substantive restraints imposed by the Court is not crystal clear, as Dimond assumes.

Dimond and Perry both distinguish between provisional judgments and final judgments in ways that are subject to manipulation. Thus, the question becomes who decides whether the Court's decisions are binding or merely provisional—the Court or Congress? Each is quite likely to have a different view, yet we have no objective way to determine who is correct, even assuming there might be some way to enforce it. As Larry Alexander notes with regard to Perry's distinction, that is not an insignificant problem.

> Where Congress reacts hostilely to a Supreme Court decision, it will be just as strongly disposed to view that decision as "noninterpretive" and thus subject to an article III "silencing." The Court on the other hand, faced with a congressional threat to overturn its decision, will be just as strongly disposed to view the decision as "interpretive" and thus not vulnerable to such a response. Consequently, Perry's democratic check on noninterpretive decisions may fail because of the Court's (or Congress') overly expansive view of interpretation; or, if the Court is acquiescent when Congress silences it, the democratic check may succeed too well, repealing interpretive decisions along with noninterpretive ones.[29]

Perry has, in fact, since acknowledged this problem (although in a footnote) and abandoned his reliance on the interpretivist-noninterpretivist distinction. "If the Court ever concedes such a [jurisdiction-restricting] power to Congress, as a practical matter the power will have to cover all judicial review, and not just 'nonoriginalist' review. The distinction between an originalist and nonoriginalist decision is not so easily administered that it can be the linchpin in judicial review of particular jurisdiction-limiting legislation."[30]

A similar problem occurs with Dimond's approach, in which the finality of the Court's decisions rests on the distinction between procedural and substantive restrictions. The Court, no doubt, is likely to characterize most of its decisions as procedural and thus binding, rather than substantive and thus subject to congressional revision. Dimond even admits that "how the Court chooses to interpret these limits on Congressional power will determine the extent to which Congress may substitute its policy preferences for those of the Court."[31] Thus, he leaves open the possibility that the Court will interpret the Bill of Rights expansively to insure judicial supremacy. He further consistently points out the indeterminate nature of the Constitution and the "dilemma of judicial choice" thereby created; yet he rests his theory on the assumption that the Court will read the Bill of Rights narrowly, especially the Fifth Amendment's due process clause, and will ignore the Ninth Amendment.[32] Perry and Dimond both fail to solve the problem of clearly, coherently, and objectively determining who has the final say.[33]

Agresto and Wellington at first glance successfully handle the issue of determining the proper spheres for judicial as opposed to legislative finality. Agresto's response is the empirical answer political scientists typically offer: neither the Court nor the Congress does have or should have the final say. "When we look at the various branches of national power we should see that the answer to the question 'Who governs?' must remain '*They* govern. All of them.'"[34]

Wellington similarly responds that we need not be so concerned regarding the finality of the Court's constitutional decisions since

> the process has its own built-in dynamic of evaluation. Of course Justices are fallible. But when they make mistakes, they hear about them: signals are sent, groups are formed, legislation is proposed, and the public forum is heavily used. New cases will afford the Court strong opportunities for reevaluation. The doctrine of stare decisis is not strong in the constitutional realm.[35]

Agresto and Wellington appear to be content to allow the process to run its course, to have the branches battle it out over all political and constitutional issues. Such a resolution of the finality question accordingly resolves the legitimacy question, at least in part. If the Court's constitutional judgments are in fact subject to continual political revision by elected officials, we need not be overly concerned about the tyranny of unelected, life-tenured judges. However, the notion of submitting constitutional decisions to an ongoing political process (an idea I support) is at odds with the role these Skeptics assign to the Court—providing moral insight and prophecy.

Given their skeptical view as to both the availability of objective constraints on constitutional interpretation and the likelihood of occasional judicial error, it is surprising to see the Skeptics defend the Court and define its role in such lofty terms. For Wellington, courts generally "are better suited to derive and articulate the community's moral ideals."[36] For Perry, only Supreme Court justices can deal with issues such as "distributive justice and the role of government, freedom of political dissent, racism and sexism, the death penalty, human sexuality . . . in a way that is faithful to the notion of moral evolution."[37] Agresto is especially given to exalted praise of the Court's role and special capacities. He believes we have properly entrusted to the Court questions of political and moral philosophy, since it is, "at its core, philosophic, devoted to reasoned inquiry and reasonable analysis. . . . It is this potential for the Court to be the institutionalized theoretician of the nation that gives meaning to the Madisonian dictum that, after separating the branches of power, we should then 'collect the wisdom of its several parts.' "[38] Further, the Court "grapples with our deepest thoughts," quite rightly has the power "to elucidate and nourish" our national ideals, and, as such, is "the most politically important and pivotal institution in the land."[39]

It is here that we find the internal contradiction in these theories of provisional review that is their undoing. If the Court is better equipped institutionally to provide moral guidance and prophecy, then why allow its judgments to be second-guessed by a political body, the U.S. Congress, which is by all accounts its moral inferior?[40]

The reasons the Skeptics offer are inadequate. One reason for political oversight is the possibility of judicial error. As Agresto argues, "Because legislative mistakes and shortcomings are possible, judicial review has merit. Because *judicial* mistakes are possible, political interaction with the decisions of the Court is a necessity."[41] However, why subject all of the Court's constitutional decisions to congressional checks if the Court's judgments are, for the most part, morally superior to those of the Congress? Of course, the same criticism applies to Perry, who asserts that "noninterpretive review has functioned, on balance, as an instrument of deepening moral insight and of moral growth."[42]

It is more sensible to permit only the Court's "mistakes" to be revised or reversed by the political branches. However, to do so requires having available a theory of constitutional interpretation that can clearly and objectively identify such interpretive errors. None is currently available and, if the Critics are right, none will ever be available. Agresto apparently has his own, as implied by his personal judgment regarding examples of the Court's "serious errors."

> The racial cases of the 1880s, the economic decisions of the earlier part of this century, and the crisis of constitutional adjudication in the first years of the New Deal are obvious candidates for the title of serious constitutional mistakes. . . . More recently the Court's abortion decision in *Roe* v. *Wade* is a transparent attempt to impose a constitutionally unfounded policy preference on the unwilling words of the Constitution. And insofar as

the Court's affirmative action decisions have reestablished race as a legitimate criterion for preference or reward, the Court has not expanded our highest constitutional principles but twisted them.[43]

Agresto's judgments regarding when the Court has "elucidated and expanded" our principles and when it has "twisted" them is, at best, open to debate and, at worst, highly idiosyncratic.

The other reason for political review of the Court's judgments is the need to complete the central task of conventional constitutional theory—reconciling judicial review with democratic values. The Skeptics may have reached some sort of accommodation of the tension between judicial review and democratic values, but it is one that is nonsensical, at least in light of the function they assign to the Court. Taylor is right on the mark in wondering, "If the courts are superior in this area [human rights issues], what reason is there, other than empty worship of the word 'democracy,' to subject them to a legislative review?"[44]

As evidence that this is in fact the case, Perry seems to hope that Congress never follows his advice. He notes the tension between, on the one hand, the superiority of judicial human-rights policymaking yet its undemocraticness and, on the other, the democraticness of legislative human rights policymaking yet its inferiority. However, as Taylor notes, this tension

> plunges Perry into a sea of ambivalence. He ruefully acknowledges that he is "not happy conceding such a broad jurisdiction-limiting power to Congress," and that he "would be most unhappy were any of the jurisdiction-limiting bills now pending in Congress to become law." But his treatment of the subject reveals no awareness on his part that those bills have generated . . . a torrid debate in Congress, in the press, at the bar and in the groves of Academe about the power of Congress to use its jurisdiction-withdrawing power as a means of overriding the Court's constitutional decisions. I would not fault Perry for concluding one way or the other on this much-mooted matter, but the lamentably sketchy teatment he has given it, followed by saurian tears, impels me to the conclusion that he has taken this position not out of firm conviction that it is right, but rather to use it as a dialectical prop for the capstone of his theory.[45]

Where the Skeptics err is in their insistence that the Court's moral judgment is superior to that of the people and their elected representatives. Of course, there is the initial problem of why we would then grant to the people and their representatives the task of choosing their moral prophets.[46] There is also the not insignificant problem of proving in some persuasive way (e.g., logically, empirically) that the assumption of judicial superiority is a valid one and is something more than an elitist preference for oligarchical rule by judges.[47] Judicial review that is premised on the moral superiority of its practitioners simply can never be successfully reconciled with democratic values. In any case, if we can be assured that judges will, most if not all of the time, issue more enlightened and morally correct judgments, then why bother with democracy? In the end, provisional review fails to resolve *sensibly* the Court's discretionary power of judicial review with democratic values.

Constitutional Theory and the Fear of Politics

These first chapters comprising Part I have identified and examined three distinct approaches or strands of thought in constitutional theory—the conventional neutralist approach, Critical Legal Studies, and the Skeptics' theory of provisional review. Despite their diverse prescriptive solutions, their focus remains on the problem of the legitimacy of the undemocratic power of judicial review. Their shared inability to solve that problem is a product of their unjustified skepticism about politics and their fears of a political Court.

The traditional answer to the legitimacy question is that the Court's power is justified to the degree that the Court acts as an apolitical check on the excesses of democracy. Thus, the Court may legitimately intervene in the political process when necessary to check its weaknesses or malfunctions. For example, the political branches may stray from the Constitution's clear instructions and the Framers' original intentions. The political branches may give insufficient attention to or lack the institutional capacity to deal with moral issues in a thoughtful, principled way. At the behest of overbearing and impassioned majorities, they may ride roughshod over individual and minority rights. Or the "ins," those in power, may try to rig the democratic process in a way to benefit themselves and their supporters. Each of these situations in the political sphere has been suggested as qualifying as a "good enough reason," as legitimate grounds, for the invocation of the power of judicial review.

Furthermore, when the Court does intervene, it must decide in a way dictated by something other than the personal preferences of the justices. The Court must decide in an objectively correct way, according to some scholars. For example, Berger believes that it is possible to determine accurately the precise intentions of the Framers in order to resolve current constitutional conflicts.[48] Others believe constitutional answers can be if not objectively determined then objectively constrained, whether by the language of the text, authoritative rules of interpretation, contemporary values, or the application of given moral principles or theories. The legitimacy of judicial review rests on the degree to which judicial intervention and constitutional decisions are objectively and coherently derived, rather than subjectively and arbitrarily generated from the justices' personal values.

In their ability to challenge each available theory on the grounds of manipulability and value bias, Critical Legal Studies scholars cast substantial doubt on this endeavor. If each interpretive theory is capable of producing a broad range of even contradictory constitutional answers, judicial discretion is not bounded and the opportunity remains for personal political bias to influence or even dictate when and how the Court intervenes under constitutional auspices.

The proponents of provisional review seem to have taken the Critics' charges seriously. The Skeptics doubt the existence of objective constraints on constitutional interpretation and accordingly doubt the legitimacy of permitting the subjective judgments of fallible justices as to the Constitution's meaning to be final and binding on the people and their elected representatives. Instead, the Court's judgments should be regarded as provisional and legitimately subject to a political response and political revision. Thus, judicial review is less problematic from a democratic standpoint. However, their insistence that the morally superior judgments of the Court are subject to revision or even rejection by the morally impoverished legislature simply makes no sense.

Advocates of provisional review should have taken their skepticism more seriously or perhaps taken it a step further. They doubt the existence of objective constraints on constitutional interpretation and worry about judicial fallibility. They recognize the empirical fact that the Court's decisions are not truly final and find that fact comforting from a normative, democratic theory point of view. Their skepticism and their confrontation with the empirical world, however, do not extend to permitting Supreme Court justices to be who they are or to do what they do. Why is it necessary to transform the Court into Learned Hand's "bevy of Platonic Guardians?"[49] Why is it that the justices are not permitted to be ordinary former politicians rendering ordinary political judgments as to what they personally and perhaps idiosyncratically believe to be best for society?[50] (If this were the case, then provisional review *would* make sense.)

The reason is the traditional neutralist fear of a political Court and politically motivated justices. To the neutralists and Skeptics, and to the Critics as well, permitting the justices merely to "vote their values," to express their personal political beliefs in their interpretations of the Constitution, is the very definition of judicial tyranny. As expressed by Agresto, "Judicial activism understood as the liberty of judges to act on their own desires and personal views is unquestionably indefensible."[51] For the conventional scholar, subjective and politically motivated judicial decisionmaking permits unelected judges to impose their personal views, not subject to popular validation or reversal, against the people's will, for example as occurred during the *Lochner* era. For the Critical Legal Studies scholar, the judge necessarily imposes his or her own elitist views or is the servant of liberal-capitalist oppression.

Both views express a profound and unjustified skepticism about the virtues of politics, the capacity of judges to be effective and responsible political leaders, and, particularly, the capacity of elected officials to deal with substantive, moral issues in a principled manner.[52] If politics is regarded as nothing more than crass utilitarianism, interest group power struggles, or class domination, then why would we want the Court to be part of the political process? The denigration and rejection of politics requires inventing a nobler role for the Court to play, as an apolitical check on the excesses of democracy, as a moral prophet, or as the catalyst for a new economic and political order. Such alternatives are not only illusory and utopian, but paternalistic and patently undemocratic as well. They are also, fortunately, unnecessary in order to "solve the Court's legitimacy problem."

The desire to create this noble role arises out of the perceived need to distinguish the Court from ordinary political institutions. However, the Court need not be so distinguished to save its legitimacy in a democracy. In short, there is nothing wrong with a political Court or with political motive in constitutional adjudication. The task of the remaining chapters is to develop and defend that thesis.

• •

PART II

In Defense of a Political Court

Introduction

THE persistent search for neutral or principled grounds as the only legitimate bases for constitutional decisions is driven by the rejection of political motive in constitutional decisionmaking. Traditional theories of judicial review seek to exorcise, to the greatest degree possible, subjectivity, discretion, and personal political preference from constitutional interpretation. Critical Legal Studies scholars attempt to reveal the subjective and politically biased nature of all ostensibly neutral and coherent constitutional decisionmaking, but for the overriding purpose of denigrating it as arbitrary and oppressive. Provisional review proponents (or at least Wellington and Perry)[1] permit Court's constitutional judgments to be influenced by the justices' values, but assuage their doubts as to their resulting legitimacy, first, by pretending the Court's judgments are morally superior and, second, by nonsensically denying that they are or should be treated as final. Each approach rests upon and is necessitated by the rejection of the legitimacy of personal political preference as a significant or controlling factor in constitutional decisionmaking. However, the chapters that follow argue that there is nothing harmful or illegitimate in such "value-voting" and, in fact, there are many benefits to be obtained from the practice.

The Charges against a Political Court

Before I defend value-voting and political motive as both necessary and legitimate ingredients in constitutional decisionmaking, it is necessary to review (briefly at this point) the nature of the practice and the indictment against it. Politically motivated constitutional decisionmaking is quite simply decisionmaking motivated by a variety of political considerations—personal political preference (for particular policies and/or case outcomes), partisan or interest group loyalties, or political feasibility. "What seem to be emphasized are not the impartial, disinterested, law-applying functions of a court which are traditionally and rather vaguely subsumed under the labels 'law' and 'justice,' but the activist, law-making, policy-making, personal preference, and public pressure-oriented functions which the term 'politics' suggests."[2]

The indictment against an activist, political Court consists of several charges. First is the familiar claim of inconsistency with democratic principles. Second is the argument that a political Court is more vulnerable to political attack and is likely to lose its legitimacy, the primary source of its power. Third, the loss of its power means the loss of the Court's ability to carry out its specialized and valuable role, particularly protecting the ideal of the rule of law and the triumph of reason over mere will or force.[3]

The chapters that follow seek to rebut those charges and advance political motivation in constitutional decisionmaking as legitimate and democratically defensible. Chapters 4 and 5 argue that these scholars mischaracterize politically motivated decisionmaking, needlessly casting it in a negative light. They further ignore the democratic benefits that flow from value-voting and political sensitivity in constitutional adjudication, such as enhancing political representation by the Court and strengthening the effectiveness of political checks on the Court.

Chapter 6 examines and rejects the argument that a political Court jeopardizes its legitimacy and power. Empirical evidence, from public opinion surveys and the Court's history, simply does not support this view. The persistence of the "legitimacy crisis" argument, despite its lack of empirical grounding, can be attributed to its normative and rhetorical value to advocates of both judicial restraint and judicial activism.

Chapter 7 addresses the claim that personal preference as a source of constitutional decisionmaking clashes with democratic values. It will be argued that this charge rests on a fundamentally flawed understanding of American democracy, one that erroneously emphasizes majority rule and legislative supremacy. Pluralist theory better reflects the normative ideals and empirical features of American democracy. A pluralist perspective alternatively emphasizes the dispersal of governmental power into numerous, diverse, and nonhierarchically arranged institutions, and the importance of that dispersal for enhanced group access, greater political stability, and reduced opportunities for tyranny, whether by officials, a majority, or a minority. With this *pluralist* system of governance, an activist political Court *can* be reconciled.

The concluding chapter addresses the obvious question that remains upon acceptance of this political view and role of the Court: "Whither the Court and Constitution?" In short, why have a Court *or* a Constitution if judicial decisionmaking is permitted to consist of the personal and perhaps idiosyncratic views of nine and often only five unelected, life-tenured individuals? What consequences of value to American democracy result from having a Court composed of individuals seeking to advance their personal policy agenda, and what do these imply about how we should evaluate the Court?

• •

The Virtues of Political Motive in Constitutional Decisionmaking: Political Representation

LEGITIMATE doubts exist regarding our ability to eliminate, or minimize even significantly, the need for subjective value judgments in constitutional decisionmaking. Yet the traditional scholar clings to that hope, due to the horror with which they regard the alternative—a political Court. This chapter and the next will argue that politically motivated constitutional decision-making is mischaracterized by traditional scholars and its virtues are over-looked. As will be demonstrated, value-voting and policy motivation on the part of the justices serve a number of democratic ends. First, value-voting facilitates political representation by the Court. Second, policy motivation is essential to the effectiveness of political checks on the Court. And, third, a policy motivated justice is induced to engage in certain behaviors that constitute a form of consensus-building, a function of great value in a fragmented political system such as exists in the United States.

The Politician versus the Judge

The language and tone employed by scholars in their discussions of a "political Court" are overwhelmingly negative and alarmist. There is apparently no evil worse than a "politician" or a "political judge." However, political motive in judicial decisionmaking is denigrated more by definition and labeling than by discussion, analysis, or provision of evidentiary support.

A Court that is driven by policy motivation, political loyalties, or political pragmatism reaches decisions typically labeled as arbitrary, idiosyncratic, or ad hoc. Such decisions constitute "personal fiat" or "whim" rather than reason, "the dictate of nine individuals" rather than "the law." A Court that pursues its policy goals while it is at the same time mindful of professional or scholarly expectations of neutrality and reasoned elaboration (as advised by Martin Shapiro)[1] is a "manipulative" Court, according to Archibald Cox.[2] To defend this political Court is to be "content simply with a Court that grinds whatever political ax it prefers on a particular day."[3] According to Professor Ely, elevating the recognition that judges *may* vote their values to the normative view that they *should* do so is the "fallacy of transformed realism": it is like arguing that because people have always been tempted to steal, that is what they should be doing.[4]

In contrast to this vision of the political judge as merely a self-interested, shortsighted politician, we are given an idealized picture of the apolitical judge. She possesses "integrity," judges by "disinterested and objective standards," and pursues the goal of "impartial justice *under law*."[5] These right-thinking judges steeped in the legal tradition "epitomize reason rather than emotion in helping seek justice."[6] To perform their duties requires that judges possess the "strength of character" and "intellectual power" necessary for "that breadth of vision, that capacity for disinterested judgment which the task demands."[7] These various attributes are apparently incompatible with the traits of the political judge (or perhaps with those of politicians generally).

Why is it necessary to distinguish so sharply between the politician and the judge and to do so by denigrating the former and ennobling the latter? It is seen by constitutional law scholars as the key to saving the Court's legitimacy. "The political branches are the forums where group-interests are served, coalitions are built, loyalties are formed, and obligations respected. The function of the Court . . . is illuminated *by contrast with* the political branches. Its decisions are legitimate only when it seeks to dissociate itself from individual or group interests, and to judge by disinterested and more objective standards."[8] However, in carrying out this task of distinguishing judges from mere politicians, these scholars fatally overstate their case. Their attack on the political Court simply sweeps too broadly.

The typical empirical referent for the negative characterizations of politically motivated decisionmaking is either the conservative *Lochner*-era Court or the liberal-activist Warren Court. Chief Justice Warren, in particular, was severely criticized for his unwillingness to adhere to professional norms of legal reasoning and craftsmanship. Scholars typically faulted the Warren Court for its failure to articulate fully and clearly the reasons underlying its decisions, to explain them honestly and coherently in terms of text and precedent, to give proper respect to precedent, and to address and rebut the objections of dissenting members.[9] However, as Professor Shapiro notes, "So far so good. Everyone is against sin and for a good argument. Not even the most rigorous legal realist prefers a badly written, illogical, incomplete opinion to a clear and learned discourse."[10]

Additionally, scholars have long urged the Court to base its decisions on enduring and objective principles transcending the immediate case, rather than deciding arbitrarily according to preexisting political loyalties or a predisposition toward one party over another. Shapiro correctly responds that "again there can be little objection. Not even Justice Frankfurter's famous khadi dispensing justice under a tree would be performing satisfactorily if he always decided for the pretty blond and against the wizened crone."[11]

The capacity to provide well-reasoned, principled, and intellectually honest and coherent opinions simply has little to do with whether judges seek to promote their moral beliefs and policy views. Norms of legal craftsmanship can be satisfied irrespective of the outcome of any particular case. One only need look at the justices' opinions and law review articles to note the amazing variety of constitutional interpretations, most of which are reasonable and persuasive and which *do* in fact satisfy traditional norms of legal reasoning and argumentation.[12] Similarly, for those finding Justice Blackmun's opinion and rationale in *Roe* weak and unpersuasive (in other words, for all of us), one need only look to Justice Douglas's concurring opinion in *Roe* or Blackmun's dissenting opinion in *Hardwick* for a more coherent and persuasive presentation of the existence and reach of a constitutional right of privacy.[13]

The political judge does not *necessarily* issue decisions that lack consistency or coherence. The political judge need not be biased and arbitrary in the treatment of litigants or important legal issues. Nor does a political Court necessarily "proceed from sympathy" or mere emotion, or go about its business arbitrarily choosing winners and losers.[14] The political judge can be characterized more favorably, just as the apolitical judge can be cast in a less favorable light.

A political judge can alternatively be viewed as a political leader who has demonstrated his commitment to public service and who has strong moral and political beliefs and a deep abiding conviction in them. Of course we know that most justices have had political experience prior to their appointments. In fact, until recently, that seems to have been a prerequisite.[15] However, that does not necessarily imply an incoherence or capriciousness in their subsequent decisionmaking. Such a judge may instead believe strongly in his convictions and seek to persuade others, in an intelligent and coherent manner, as to the rightness or value of those considerations.

The impartial, disinterested legal craftsman, on the other hand, may be criticized as interested only in the logical consistency or intellectual purity of a decision, and as one who is callous and indifferent to the issues of fairness and justice, or to potentially harmful human and political consequences. (Robert Bork's assertion that he wished to serve on the Court because it would be an "intellectual feast" comes to mind.)[16] J. Braxton Craven describes the practitioner of this sort of "sterile intellectualism" as concerned only with "legal problems" and the logic of the law: "It is a delight to him to construct painstakingly, with adequate display of erudition, an edifice of logic and precedent upon which justice may be sacrificed."[17] And further, should the results be unjust, that is "to him simply proof in full measure of his dedication to law."[18]

Before appraising the virtues or vices of the political judge, we must distinguish the issue of political motivation in constitutional decisionmaking from that of intellectual rigor and legal craftsmanship in opinion writing. They are two entirely separate and separable facets of constitutional decisionmaking, and they are not necessarily incompatible. The notion of the arbitrary political judge deciding by fiat and whim rather than according to law and reason is nothing more than a useful stereotype (as is the callous and indifferent legal craftsman).

It is time to dispense with such stereotypes and examine the consequences of political motivation on the part of Supreme Court justices as dictated by logic and as supported by empirical evidence. As noted in this chapter's introduction, there are three such consequences deserving special notice. First, policy motivation and value-voting constitute a form of political representation. Second, policy motivation activates political checks on the Court and renders them effective. Third, as a consequence of those checks being made effective, the policy-motivated justice is induced to engage in consensus-building activities. Thus, judicial review, conceived as politically motivated constitutional decisionmaking, is not simply "reconcilable" with democratic values; such review contributes in a significant and positive way to the democratic process.

Political Representation

Policy motivation, particularly in the form of value-voting, serves as the primary vehicle by which the Court performs an important representation function. Representation occurs when the justices decide in accordance with their political views, which have been consciously and deliberately sanctioned by elected officials competing for political control of the Court through the selection process. Rather than acting arbitrarily, the justices are merely carrying out the "policy premises" of their appointments. Although not enforced via direct election, the link between the value premises of a justice's selection and then the value premises of her subsequent decisions is significant and consequential and constitutes an indirect form of political representation.

The effectiveness of value-voting as a vehicle of political representation is, however, dependent on two preexisting conditions. The first is the prominent use by the president and Senate of ideological and policy considerations in their recruitment and selection of Supreme Court justices. The second is competition and a relative balance of power between the president and Senate in their efforts to use the selection process to control the Court's composition and ideological makeup. The degree to which such conditions typically prevail will be examined shortly.

As Sheldon Goldman notes, a correspondence between the views and preferences of the people and those of Supreme Court justices is certainly a logical consequence of a politicized judicial selection process. "Judges chosen by a democratically elected president can be expected in a general sense to reflect the values and policy outlook of the appointing administration and in turn the majority that elected the president. Senators, also democratically elected, represent, in theory, further links between the judiciary and public opinion."[19] These connections are supported by more than logic, however. The empirical evidence is very strong and widely accepted, at least among social scientists.[20]

Most of this chapter is devoted to examining such evidence in order to test and validate this model of political representation empirically. Are political considerations in fact paramount in the recruitment and selection of Supreme Court justices? Is there indeed competition and a relative balance of power between the president and Senate in the selection process? And finally, as the last step in the causal chain, do Supreme Court justices "vote their values," thereby enacting into law the policy premises of their appointments?

Political Considerations in Judicial Selection

Although some may find it abhorrent, the process by which federal judges, especially Supreme Court justices, are recruited and selected is highly political. Judges are not recruited and chosen through a civil service system emphasizing merit, as in some European legal systems, but through a political process controlled by politicians and emphasizing partisanship and ideology.[21]

Numerous studies confirm the importance of political motivation in the president's selection of judicial nominees. Henry Abraham's exhaustive historical review of Supreme Court appointments led him to conclude that "political and ideological compatibility . . . has arguably been *the* controlling factor" in the nomination decisions of presidents, outweighing other considerations such as objective merit, personal friendship, and symbolic representation.[22] Hulbary and Walker examined presidential motivations in eighty-four Supreme Court nominations and similarly concluded that "presidents are almost always [in 93 percent of the cases] motivated by the potential nominee's political philosophy."[23]

Sheldon Goldman, a well-respected student of judicial selection, believes that "political party credentials," especially a "background of previous party activity," have been the most important factor in the president's selection of judicial nominees and that "in general, political party considerations have taken priority over the ideological or policy views of the candidates, which in turn have tended to be more important than their legal scholarship."[24] David O'Brien similarly concludes that "partisan politics dominates the selection of judges," despite the "myth . . . that judges should be selected strictly on the basis of merit."[25] The importance of party affiliation is verified by the fact that, on average, about 90 percent of a president's appointments to the federal bench generally and the Supreme Court more particularly are from the president's own party.[26] Furthermore, when presidents have broken with tradition and appointed an individual to the Court who does not belong to the president's party, "the nominee usually has been ideologically close to the president"[27] or the nomination provides him with significant symbolic benefits.[28]

Goldman asserts that "judicial appointments have always been linked to a presidential agenda," whether a partisan agenda to enhance political support for the president and his party or a policy agenda to achieve substantive policy goals.[29] It is modern presidents who are especially likely to emphasize the achievement of policy goals through their judicial appointments.[30] (These conclusions are also supported by Solomon's study of presidential motivations in courts of appeals appointments.)[31] Goldman's evidence, furthermore, shows that whether the president pursues a partisan agenda or a policy agenda is related to party system changes; when the party system is undergoing significant change (i.e., during "realignments"),[32] presidents are more likely to make policy-oriented appointments, and during periods of stability partisan appointments are more likely.[33]

Walter Murphy agrees that "most presidents have looked on judgeships" as patronage, as "grand political plums,"[34] and similarly finds that partisan and ideological considerations have been historically dominant.[35] A nominee's "intelligence, integrity, and competence" are important as well, but only instrumentally—as a tool to enhance the president's popularity and prestige[36] and to insure the *effective* enactment of the president's policy agenda.

Also verifying the importance of political considerations in the president's selection of Supreme Court nominees is a study of twenty-four Supreme Court nominees (from Earl Warren to Anthony Kennedy) by Cameron, Cover, and Segal. The empirical evidence supported their model of the rational president who chooses nominees to the Supreme Court either to maximize popularity or to achieve policy change.[37]

Presidents have, of course, varied in the emphasis they place on particular criteria.[38] For example, Truman was especially prone to "crony" appointments, emphasizing personal friendship and political loyalty over ideology per se.[39] President Ford, similarly to Eisenhower, "placed a premium on professional considerations, and likewise relied heavily on his attorney general in selecting a nominee whose professional reputation put him outside the place of partisan political controversy."[40] Nonetheless, 95 percent of Eisenhower's judicial appointees were Republicans.[41] President Ford did in fact appoint a significantly lower percentage of Republicans to the federal bench than had other Republican presidents—81 percent, thus perhaps verifying his relatively greater concern with merit and professionalism.[42] However, Ford was constrained in pursuing a more political agenda due to his "accidental presidency," a Democratic majority in Congress further strengthened by the "Watergate babies,"[43] and the perceived need to restore public faith in government in the post-Watergate era.[44] Although much was made of President Carter's stated desire to emphasize merit and affirmative action in his judicial appointments, 90 percent of his appointees in fact belonged to the Democratic Party.[45] Gottschall, thus, more accurately characterizes Carter's overriding goal as "merit selection among Democrats."[46] Nominees' policy views were critical in the judicial appointment decisions of FDR, Johnson, Nixon, and Reagan.[47] And with regard to Reagan, the consensus is that his "administration elevated ideology and legal policy to the highest concern" and "instituted a systematic screening process unprecedented in American history."[48] Similar to Reagan's, President Bush's appointees were overwhelmingly Republicans possessing a conservative judicial philosophy, a majority of whom had a history of party activism.[49] Particularly as compared to Reagan's approach, President Clinton's judicial appointees and the manner in which they were screened and selected have been nonideological.[50] Furthermore, "unlike administrations dating back at least as far as Richard Nixon's, judgeships did not take center stage in the president's domestic policy agenda."[51] Nonetheless, Clinton has displayed an extraordinary degree of partisanship in his judicial appointments. For example, the proportion of Clinton's same-party appointees is similar to that of his three predecessors (approximately 90 percent); however, the percentage of opposition-party appointees is the smallest of all four administrations.[52] The Clinton administration can be further distinguished by the record number of female and minority appointments made to the federal bench.[53]

Numerous studies, thus, consistently confirm that political factors, particularly partisanship, are paramount and persistent in the president's recruitment and selection of judicial nominees.[54] Additional empirical studies prove that political considerations are important to the Senate as well in its confirmation role.

Abraham suggests that, historically, the "more prominent reasons" for Senate rejections of Supreme Court nominees include: opposition to the nominating president, the incumbent Court, or the nominee's political philosophy; the president's failure to respect senatorial courtesy; the nominee's lack of qualifications; interest group opposition to the nominee; and fears regarding a nominee's dramatic impact on the Court's ideological balance.[55]

Although the particular mix of factors explaining Senate rejections varies in individual cases, three have emerged as the most significant: partisanship, presidential clout, and ideological opposition to the nominee.

Several studies have substantiated the impact of partisanship on Senate confirmation voting. For example, Segal found that the Senate confirmation rate for Supreme Court nominees was significantly lower when the Senate was controlled by the opposition party (59 percent) as compared to when the Senate was controlled by the president's party (89 percent).[56] According to Ruckman's study, nominations that attempt to replace a Democratic justice with a Republican justice (or vice versa) double the Senate rejection rate; in fact, "almost 60% of all unsuccessful nominations have involved attempted opposite party replacement."[57] Furthermore, "critical" nominations that attempt both "opposite party replacement" and a critical alteration of the partisan balance on the Court produce a 42 percent rejection rate, compared to a 15 percent rejection rate for noncritical nominations.[58] The Felice and Weisberg study of nine recent controversial nominations also demonstrated the considerable influence of party affiliation on confirmation voting— Republican senators voted to confirm Republican presidents' nominees 86 percent of the time compared to 44 percent by Democratic senators.[59] Senate votes on the Bork and Thomas nominations were clearly party based: 96 percent of Democrats voted against Bork, while 87 percent of Republicans voted for him, and 81 percent of Democrats opposed Thomas, while 95 percent of Republicans supported him.[60] Other studies have also confirmed that partisanship is a critical factor: senators belonging to the president's party are more likely to vote to confirm the nominee,[61] and the probability of a nominee's confirmation is critically affected by whether the Senate is politically aligned with the president.[62]

The president's lame-duck status also affects confirmation voting. Nominations made in the last year of a president's term are significantly more likely to result in Senate rejection. For example, Segal found that 88 percent of the nominations put forward in the president's first three years of office were confirmed, compared to 54 percent for nominations occurring in the president's fourth year.[63] Several other studies have confirmed the significant influence of lame-duck status on confirmation success.[64] Presidential clout or political strength, a function of both party control in the Senate and lame-duck status, is thus an important determinant of confirmation success.[65] As expressed by Palmer, "A President whose party controls 60 percent of the Senate and who has three years left in his term has about a 90 percent chance of having his nominee confirmed. However, a President whose party controls 40 percent of the Senate and who has one year left in his term has about a 52 percent chance."[66] As further evidence of "antipresidential motivations" in Senate confirmation voting, Segal and Spaeth note that "nominees politically close to the President fare especially poorly: 29 percent of current cabinet members have been rejected versus only 17 percent of non-cabinet nominees."[67]

Particularly important for the purpose here, of defending value-voting by the justices as a form of political representation, is the consistent finding that ideology plays a decisive role in Senate confirmation voting. For example, Sulfridge concluded that although "ideological opposition alone is not sufficient to make a nomination highly controversial . . . once a nomination becomes controversial, the ideological position of a senator is a major factor in determining how he will vote."[68] Similarly, analysis of the 2,054 confirmation votes from Earl Warren to Anthony Kennedy by Cameron, Cover, and Segal revealed that "confirmation voting is decisively affected by the ideological distance between Senators and nominees."[69] Additionally, simple correlations between senators' liberalism and their confirmation votes were quite high for several recent controversial nominations: Abe Fortas (+.79), Clement Haynsworth (−.84), G. Harrold Carswell (−.84), Robert Bork (−.83) and Clarence Thomas (−.81).[70]

Most importantly, several studies have demonstrated that the influence of ideology on confirmation voting is independent of partisanship. For example, Rohde and Spaeth examined the Fortas chief justice nomination, and the Haynsworth, Carswell, and Rehnquist nominations and concluded that it was senators' liberalism, rather than their party affiliation, that influenced their confirmation votes.[71] Similarly, Songer found that policy disagreement with the nominee was "the major cause of most votes against confirmation" for the fourteen controversial nominations that he studied; furthermore, that relationship between policy views and confirmation votes was independent of both senators' party affiliations and their views of the ethical issues concerning the nominees.[72] The Felice and Weisberg study is especially significant here, finding that "only . . . ideology . . . had a consistently large effect on all of the [nine controversial] confirmation votes. Region and party each affected only a few nominations, and presidential support was even less of a factor."[73] The importance of ideology persisted despite controls for

these other factors, leading the authors to conclude that "the voting of senators in the past three decades on controversial Supreme Court nominations
is largely compatible with an ideological interpretation. . . . Ideology is an
important cue for individual senators on nomination voting."[74]

Despite the urging of many scholars,[75] "objective merit" does not appear
to be nearly as important a criterion in the Senate's decision as the afore-
mentioned political factors. Halper has noted that the nominee's lack of
qualifications, while commonly advanced by senators as explaining their
negative confirmation vote, is merely "the most easily defended voting rationale."[76] His examination of Senate rejections from 1794 to 1970 led him to
conclude that "in the overwhelming number of instances objective qualifications are not decisive (and often are not even important) in influencing the
chamber's actions"; instead, "value considerations" and presidential
strength were key determinants.[77] In further support of his conclusion regarding the lack of importance of merit, Halper notes that historians Charles
Warren and Henry Abraham found "only four instances in which charges of
lack of qualifications played a decisive part in rejection," with the Senate's
rejection of G. Harrold Carswell increasing the number to five.[78]

However, in contrast to this consensus among scholars regarding the relative unimportance of a nominee's qualifications is the conclusion of the
Cameron, Cover, and Segal study. Their analysis of Senate confirmation
votes from Earl Warren to Anthony Kennedy did indeed find ideology to be
a critical factor in Senate voting, as previously noted. Nonetheless "equally
important . . . are the qualifications of the nominee."[79] Thus,

> Senators, even opposition senators, serving with a weak president, will vote
> for a poorly qualified nominee if the nominee is ideologically close (e.g.,
> Southern Democrats for Clement Haynsworth). They will vote for an ideo-
> logically distant nominee if the nominee is highly qualified (e.g., liberal
> Democrats for Anthony Kennedy). Ideological distance, however, be-
> comes paramount for nominees with even moderate questions concern-
> ing their qualifications. Alternatively, we could say that qualifications be-
> come paramount for nominees of even moderate ideological distance
> from senators.[80]

The consensus remains, nonetheless, that Senate confirmation voting is
primarily determined by political factors. Partisanship, presidential strength,

and ideology are the primary determinants of whether senators vote to confirm or reject presidential nominees to the Court.[81]

Notably absent from this account of political influence in the Supreme Court selection process is the role of constituency and interest group pressure. This is not an oversight, but a reflection of the limited attention it has traditionally received from scholars.[82] One does find occasional references in the literature to interest group influence, most notably in the Senate rejections of Parker, Carswell, and Bork.[83] However, constituency and interest group mobilization have only begun to be incorporated into judicial selection models and tested empirically.[84]

According to Caldeira, this inattention to the impact of grass-roots and interest group activities is due only in part to the difficulties in measuring that impact; it is due as well to the widely shared assumption that judicial selection is an elite-dominated process.[85] However, that perception may no longer be accurate.[86] For example, the Bork and Thomas confirmation hearings seem to represent, in Caldeira and Smith's words, "the advent of battles so pitched and public as to be more in keeping with an electoral campaign than the traditional quietude of federal judicial selection."[87] Interest group participation and the mobilization of senatorial constituencies, most notably evident in the defeat of Bork, have transformed "fights over controversial nominations to the federal courts . . . [into] constituency-driven events."[88] Furthermore, as a result of the existence of over four hundred organizations committed to involving themselves in federal judicial nominations, "organized group mobilization and pressure on controversial judicial nominations has become a permanent feature of our political landscape. . . . This conflict has become institutionalized."[89]

Segal and Spaeth have provided empirical support for the existence of interest group influence in the selection process. For example, they found that interest group *opposition* does in fact significantly affect Senate confirmation voting, while interest group *support* for a nominee has only a slight effect.[90]

Several recent studies further suggest that (unorganized) constituency influence on Senate confirmation voting is indeed significant and deserving of more research. Segal, Cameron, and Cover found that "confirmation voting is decisively affected by the ideological distance between senators' constituents and nominees" to the Supreme Court.[91] Segal and Spaeth's analysis of 2,153 confirmation votes from the nomination of Earl Warren through the nomination of David Souter revealed that "overall, senators voted almost 99 percent of the time for nominees who were close to the average views of their constituuents, 83 percent of the time for nominees who were a moderate distance from their constituents, and but 67 percent of the time for nominees who were distant from their constituents. . . . Senators are much less likely to vote for nominees who are distant from their constituents."[92]

A study of confirmation voting in the Clarence Thomas nomination found that senators facing reelection and representing a large African American population were more likely to vote to confirm, consistent with strong majority support for Thomas among African Americans.[93] However, while the relationship was significant, it was much smaller than the effects of party affiliation and ideology. Nonetheless, the authors correctly note that even a small "constituency effect" can play a critical role in close votes, such as the four-vote margin of victory for Thomas.[94]

Should future research continue to verify the existence of significant interest group and constituency influence in Senate confirmation voting, this would represent a further politicization of the process and, especially significant here, an increase in popular input.[95] In short, the claim for the Court's representativeness would be further bolstered.

As a final note, the participation of the American Bar Association in the judicial selection process does not represent an apolitical influence or a much-needed focus on merit and professional qualifications.[96] For example, Grossman's examination of the ABA's Standing Committee on Federal Judiciary during the Kennedy years revealed the dominant role of wealthy, conservative, corporate lawyers in evaluating judicial nominees.[97] After much criticism, the ABA did in fact increase the diversity of those requested to evaluate nominees and added women and minorities to its committee. Nonetheless, Slotnick's 1983 study found that, out of numerous possible correlates of high ABA ratings, the most significant was "the candidate's white male status."[98] He concluded that the ABA does not "approach the judicial selection process in a political vacuum. Rather, like all groups active in the political process, the ABA and its standing committee are composed of individuals responding to political events from a value structure and perceptions of self and societal interests not necessarily shared by all interested parties in the political arena."[99] Ironically, the ABA committee has more recently been accused by conservative groups of being too liberal and overly political in its evaluations of Reagan and Bush nominees.[100]

In conclusion, the first condition for the effectiveness of value-voting in enhancing the representational quality of the Court has been met. There is no question that political considerations, particularly partisanship and ideology, dominate the recruitment, nomination, and confirmation of Supreme Court justices.

A Balance of Power?

Yet another condition that would further enhance the representativeness of the Court is competition and a relative balance of power between the president and Senate in attempting to control the Court's membership and ideological composition. The Senate might fail to inject its political and constitutional preferences into the selection process in an independent, aggressive, and consistent manner. Value-voting by the justices would then advance only presidential desires, rather than the consensual and, therefore, more fully representative preferences of both the president and Senate. Thus, it is important to know not only the determinants of Senate confirmation voting, but the frequency with which the Senate challenges or rejects presidential nominees to the Court.

Many scholars believe that senators perceive opposition to the president's judicial nominations as costly, time-consuming, and typically weak in terms of an electoral payoff. Thus, absent a compelling reason, they argue, such opposition is quite unlikely.[101] However, this overly generalized view fails to recognize an important development in the twentieth century—a significant and undesirable shift in the competition to control the Court in the president's favor.[102]

In his 1985 book arguing for more rigorous and ideology-based Senate review of Supreme Court nominees, Laurence Tribe noted that nearly one in five Supreme Court nominations have failed to win confirmation.[103] Based on this figure and his brief historical review of Senate rejections, he concluded that the Senate has hardly been "spineless" in its advice-and-consent role. Rather than merely rubber stamping presidential nominations, "the upper house of Congress has been scrutinizing Supreme Court nominees and rejecting them on the basis of their political, judicial, and economic philosophies ever since George Washington was President."[104]

Tribe is correct that a 20 percent rejection rate is indeed significant. In fact, the rejection rate for nominees to the Supreme Court is the highest of all offices requiring Senate approval.[105] However, Tribe fails to note that only five Supreme Court nominations have failed to win Senate confirmation in the twentieth century.[106] This includes a seventy-five year span, from 1894 to 1968, in which only one nomination was rejected. Additionally, only six Supreme Court nominations since the end of World War II have produced more than twenty-five negative Senate votes.[107] The one in five rejection rate cited by Tribe masks the far greater one in three rejection record established by the Senate in the nineteenth century.[108] In contrast, only one in ten nominations has failed to receive confirmation in the twentieth century.[109] This sharp difference has been noted by several scholars, including Sulfridge, who asserts that since 1894 there has existed a "Senate presumption in favor of confirmation,"[110] and Friedman, who similarly remarks that the "confirmation process has, for the most part, become routine."[111] According to Richard Friedman, the primary cause of this dramatic change in the Senate's response to Supreme Court nominations was the elevation of the Court's status and apolitical reputation. In the first half of the nineteenth century and especially during Reconstruction, "the Supreme Court was at a low point in prestige and was regarded much like a political institution, the membership of which, senators believed, should be geographically dispersed and politically reliable."[112] As a result, Senate opposition to nominations based on partisan and patronage grounds was "politically reputable."[113]

By the end of the nineteenth century, however, momentous changes had occurred. Sectional and partisan rivalries had dissipated, and the workload and reputation of judges in general, and in the Supreme Court in particular, had vastly improved. As a result, "political interference in the selection process was generally scorned" and "confirmation of qualified justices was perceived as a welcome expression of nationalism and nonpartisanship."[114]

The twentieth-century norm of judicial independence has worked to the distinct advantage of the president, as the initiator of the appointment process. Court-packing attempts by presidents are easy to mask. They need only employ the proper terminology and pay tribute to normative expectations regarding the judicial role. Thus, the nominee is inevitably intelligent and open-minded, would interpret the Constitution rather than legislate from the bench, and possesses the requisite integrity and judicial temperament.[115] While Court-packing attempts by the president are typically disguised and tolerated, politically motivated rejection by the Senate is regarded as improper interference with the independence of the Court.

The sharply contrasting nineteenth- and twentieth-century rates of rejecting nominees, buttressed by Friedman's account, make a strong case for the conclusion that the Senate has become "the President's compliant servant" with regard to Supreme Court appointments.[116] However, others have argued that such a stark conclusion is not empirically supported. For example, Segal found that a nomination occurring in the twentieth century increased the probability of confirmation by 12 percent.[117] While quite significant, it is not as great as one would expect; nor was this "twentieth-century effect" as large as other factors, such as whether the president's party controlled the Senate or whether the nomination occurred in the fourth year of the president's term.[118]

As Scigliano has suggested, and as Segal has verified, the relationship between the twentieth century and confirmation success is, in part, spurious. A higher proportion of nominations occurring since 1900 simply "lack those characteristics associated with rejection. In fact, while 24% of the appointments prior to 1900 were made during the fourth year [of the president's term], only 6% of those made in the twentieth century occurred under the same circumstance."[119] Baum similarly notes that "the relative success of twentieth-century presidents in obtaining confirmation for their nominees stems in part from the infrequency of unfavorable circumstances," particularly fewer instances of nominations occurring in election years or at times of divided party control between the president and Senate.[120]

Neubauer also seeks to revise the conventional wisdom that Supreme Court confirmation has become routine in the twentieth century. He does acknowledge that "most nominations sail smoothly through the confirmation process," and that only one nomination from 1900 through 1967 failed to win confirmation.[121] However, Neubauer believes that "since 1967, the pendulum has swung back," noting that four nominations have been defeated and Rehnquist's two nominations generated significant opposition" (as did the nomination of Clarence Thomas).[122]

Baum similarly regards the low Senate rejection rate in the twentieth century as misleading. He finds two periods—1910 to 1930, and 1949 to the present—in which "a high proportion of nominees have faced serious opposition."[123] Additionally, in recent years, "Senate care in scrutinizing nominations, as indicated by such measures as the length of time spent in hearings, has increased markedly. Although nominations usually have been successful even during these periods, clearly the Senate has not adopted a policy of automatic confirmation for nominees."[124]

In addition, Senate rejection rates and anticonfirmation votes do not tell the whole story regarding the balance of power between the president and Senate in controlling the Court's membership. Presidents may take great care in selecting their nominees so as not to arouse Senate opposition. Thus, Senate influence may operate indirectly, with the president anticipating Senate reaction and selecting a less preferred, but also less contentious, candidate in order to secure confirmation. A recent example is President Clinton's nomination of Stephen Breyer to the Supreme Court, rather than his preferred candidate, Interior Secretary Bruce Babbitt. Clinton sought to avoid a difficult fight with (and an uncertain outcome in) the Senate; of particular concern were western Republican senators (including Judiciary Committee Chair Orrin Hatch), who were angered by Babbitt's attempts to raise grazing fees. "The effect of avoiding controversy," as Watson and Stookey correctly note, "is to empower one's opposition"—in this case, the Senate in its confirmation role.[125]

A study by Cameron, Cover, and Segal provides further empirical confirmation of this model of "popularity maximizing" presidents who act rationally by "anticipat[ing] the spatial logic of legislative decisionmaking and adjust[ing] their proposed nominees accordingly," thereby avoiding confrontations with the Senate and preserving their popularity and power.[126] The Clinton administration has been unusual in the degree to which it has followed this nonconfrontational approach, even consulting with and accommodating the Republican-controlled Senate, especially Judiciary Committee Chair Orrin Hatch.[127]

The Senate has, on several occasions, chosen to exercise its power to advise presidents in advance with regard to their Supreme Court nominations. In 1869, Congress submitted a petition to President Grant, signed by a majority of members in both the House and Senate, urging him to nominate Edwin Stanton. Having seen his first nominee rejected, Grant acceded to congressional wishes.[128] Upon the retirement of Oliver Wendell Holmes, President Hoover abandoned his desire to nominate a "noncontroversial western Republican" in response to the Senate Judiciary Committee's stated preference for another progressive and to Senate Foreign Relations Committee Chairman Borah's insistence on Benjamin Cardozo.[129] The subsequent easy confirmation of both nominees can hardly be characterized as demonstrating the Senate's weakness as a player in the judicial selection process.

A more recent example of a president altering his selection of judicial nominees occurred during the Reagan administration. When conservative Republican Senator Strom Thurmond chaired the Judiciary Committee and Ed Meese took the reins at the Justice Department, the Reagan administration made its most controversial lower court judicial appointments, as indicated in part by lower American Bar Association ratings.[130] However, the Democrats regained control of the Senate in the 1986 elections, and new Committee Chair Joseph Biden took a more aggressive posture—for example, reducing the committee's size (resulting in the ouster of Thurmond) and strengthening the committee's investigative staff. The response of the Reagan administration was predictable and rational: "The administration in turn was slow to fill vacancies and named fewer controversial conservatives. Officials in the Justice Department perceived that the kinds of conservatives approved by Thurmond's committee were not as likely to win confirmation, hence not always worth the trouble of nominating."[131] There is some evidence then that suggests that Senate power in the appointment of Supreme Court justices cannot simply be measured by formal rejection rates.

At least thus far the evidence is somewhat mixed with regard to Senate opposition to and rejection of presidential nominees to the Court. Senate rejections have decreased dramatically in the twentieth century. However, this is at least in part attributable to the reduced frequency of unfavorable confirmation conditions. Additionally, Baum and Neubauer suggest that we are witnessing a resurgence of Senate verve and vigor.

According to this account, however, one would have expected far more Senate opposition to Reagan's nomination of Anthony Kennedy and Bush's nomination of David Souter than actually occurred. The Democrats retained their majority status in both the House and Senate, and party polarization and party-line voting in Congress increased during the Reagan-Bush years. At the time of the Kennedy nomination, Reagan was lame-duck and politically weakened, due to the Iran-Contra scandal. Tensions between Congress and the Court continued to escalate, spurred by several Court decisions regarding civil rights, executive power, and abortion. Additionally, Anthony Kennedy was to replace the less conservative Powell and, even more of a watershed, David Souter would be taking the seat vacated by William Brennan, no doubt the strongest and most effective voice for the Court's liberal wing. Given these many factors predisposing the Senate to reject, why did it not respond more vigorously to or even reject the Kennedy and Souter nominations?

The Senate's failure to reject Clarence Thomas is similarly puzzling. Thomas possessed limited experience, had been severely criticized for his performance as chairman of the Equal Employment Opportunity Commission, received the lowest American Bar Association rating of any previously confirmed nominee, and was vigorously opposed by civil rights and women's rights groups, particularly as a replacement for the liberal civil rights crusader Justice Thurgood Marshall. Thomas also attempted to distance himself from numerous controversial statements regarding the uses of natural law for conservative purposes and incredibly asserted that he had never expressed nor formulated an opinion, not even in private, regarding the Court's *Roe* v. *Wade* abortion decision. Even serious charges of sexual harassment made by a credible witness, Professor Anita Hill, were insufficient to produce majority opposition in the Senate.[132]

Presidential skill and popularity in part account for this heightened spinelessness on the part of the Senate. Presidents Reagan and Bush used their built-in advantage in Court packing with exceptional skill. They raised (or lowered, depending on one's view) the art of screening judicial candidates and waging an effective confirmation campaign on their behalf to a new level.[133]

In addition, Reagan and Bush learned an important lesson from the Bork debacle. A conservative Republican president can choose one of two strategies to win support from a Democratic Senate for conservative judicial nominees.[134] The first is to fight—to employ all the tools of persuasion and power available to the president and try to bludgeon the Senate into acceptance. As the Bork nomination proved, that is a risky strategy. Alternatively, the president can resort to subterfuge by employing the strategy, now proven successful, of nominating individuals whose primary virtue is anonymity.[135] Thomas and the enigmatic Souter both possessed slim credentials and minimal experience to qualify for a seat on the Supreme Court. More importantly, they had spoken or written little on the burning constitutional issues of the day, thus making the Senate's search for a "legitimate" basis for rejection more difficult. Unfortunately for the Senate, the nominees possessed no controversial paper trail, and the Senate itself no longer possessed the nineteenth-century luxury of rejecting the president's nominees to the Court virtually at will.

These recent appointments suggest that the Senate lacks the will and the power to defeat Supreme Court nominees it would prefer to reject. Had the views and subsequent decisions of Kennedy, Souter, and Thomas been presented to the Congress in the form of statutory initiatives or constitutional amendment proposals, they would no doubt have been rejected.[136] However, when such "proposals" are hidden or disguised in the form of a Supreme Court nominee (especially a "stealth" nominee like Souter), and when they are put forward by a popular and skillful president, the Senate is far more constrained.

The twentieth-century rate of Senate rejections has significantly declined, and the Senate acquiesced in the Reagan-Bush transformation of the Court far more than the conventional wisdom would have led us to expect. Also relevant is the fact that Congress has greatly reduced its use of constitutionally provided Court-curbing and Court-influencing tools, particularly alteration of the Court's size for political purposes.[137] These three pieces of evidence all point in the same direction: the interbranch competition for control of the Court's membership and ideological composition has declined, and the president now holds a decided advantage.[138] Unless the president mistakenly nominates an individual who is obviously unqualified and ill-suited for the Court like G. Harrold Carswell,[139] or out of the mainstream like Robert Bork,[140] it is unlikely that the Senate will challenge or reject the president's nominees.[141] While the president does not yet possess complete power to "build the Court of his dreams,"[142] Senate-imposed constraints or boundaries within which presidents must operate in selecting their nominees have broadened considerably.

How well then have the two conditions for a representative Court been met? Historically and typically, Supreme Court appointments have been the product of partisan and ideological battles among the president, the Senate, and interest groups over political control of the Court and its future policy direction. However, the competition between the Senate and president has not, in recent years, been as vigorous or as balanced as it should be to insure the Court's representativeness.[143] The Senate is a significant, though too unreliable, political check on the president's power to shape the Court.[144] This weakens, but does not invalidate, the claim being made here for the representativeness of the Court: the values, constitutional policy views, and inter-est group loyalties of Supreme Court justices are actively and deliberately chosen by elected officials and, indirectly, by the voters and groups they represent. When the justices "vote their values," they are advancing presiden-tial desires and often, though not always, Senate desires as well.[145]

A Representative Court?

Supreme Court justices are selected by the president and Senate—elected officials—primarily because of their partisan loyalties and political beliefs. Thus, the values held by the justices and represented on the Court are highly likely to reflect the values currently (or at a minimum recently) dominant in the society and in the government. This is insured by not only the dominance of political considerations in the selection process, but also by turnover on the Court, making for a *dynamically* representative membership. This aspect of the Court's membership is not typically given sufficient significance, per-haps because of the common and misleading observation that Supreme Court justices "serve for life." Despite the "old saw" that "judges seldom die and never retire,"[146] turnover on the Court inevitably and regularly occurs. On average, a vacancy on the Court occurs every 1.82 years, giving a single-term president 2.2 appointments and a two-term president 4.4 appointments.[147]

Given turnover on the Court and a membership that has passed the parti-san and ideological litmus test applied by elected officials, it can be con-cluded that the values of the justices mirror and certainly lie within the range of those values currently or recently receiving official representation in other branches of government. It is the existence of this phenomenon, the inter-play of turnover and a politically controlled, ideology-dominated selection process, that results in and permits recognition of the particular political identity of various Courts over time, for example, the early Federalist Courts, the pro-business and pro-laissez faire Courts of the late-nineteenth and early-twentieth centuries, FDR's New Deal Court, the liberal Warren Court, and the conservative Rehnquist Court. Particularly when a new public philosophy is strong and relatively enduring, the Court inevitably comes to share that philosophy as well.[148]

The politically controlled and ideology-infused selection process, com-bined with turnover, will typically operate to produce a membership that is representative in terms of its political outlook. However, the more important question here is whether that "representativeness"[149] is of consequence for the decisions the Court makes. Given that Supreme Court justices are not subject to reelection or easily removed from office, there is certainly a theoretical possibility that the justices could abandon the implicit ideological or otherwise representative basis of their appointments and decide on an alternative and arbitrary basis. Additionally, the nature of the institution, its traditions and norms, for example *stare decisis*, may influence the justices and the way in which they decide, perhaps also leading the justices to abandon or set aside their personal beliefs and biases.

Thus, the critical issue is whether political representation on the Court effectively translates into political responsiveness via the Court's decisions. In other words, do the people and their elected representatives, in selecting Supreme Court justices, also select or influence the value premises of the justices' decisions? Mishler and Sheehan's study suggests that is indeed the case.[150] Their time-series analysis found that the Court's decisions followed the public mood (after a brief time lag) from 1956 to 1981; the key explanation was the politically motivated use of the appointment process.[151] Their empirical tests supported a model in which the party of the president and the ideological composition of Congress influenced the ideological composition of the Court (with the party of the president being the significantly stronger influence), which in turn influenced the liberalness of the Court's decisions. Several subsequent studies, though differing as to the length of the time lag, provide further empirical verification of the model.[152]

The question of whether the people, through their elected officials, select the value premises of the justices' decisions, thereby promoting political responsiveness, can be examined in two additional ways. First, we can examine the general relationship between a justice's political attitudes and his decisions; that is, is value-voting an empirical reality? The second approach examines the more specific issue of whether the justices, through their decisions, fulfill or satisfy the expectations of those who have appointed them, particularly the expectations of the president.

Value-Voting

With regard to whether a justice's personal political views influence her decisions, Part I has argued that there is quite simply no alternative available. Conventional constitutional theory fails to limit significantly the necessity of discretionary and subjective value choice in constitutional decision-making or to deny justices the opportunity to decide in accordance with their personal beliefs. Additionally, as Segal and Spaeth emphasize, members of the Supreme Court "lack electoral or political accountability, ambition for higher office, and comprise a court of last resort that controls its jurisdiction [which] . . . enables the justices to vote as they individually see fit."[153]

Although the justices have the opportunity to vote their values, do they as an empirical matter? As the following examination of the judicial behavior research will demonstrate, "overall, the evidence is compelling that policy making on the Supreme Court is a reflection of the ideological preferences of the justices, that such attitudes are formed before justices are appointed to the Court, and that justices are highly consistent in casting ideologically oriented votes in most types of cases and from term to term of the Supreme Court."[154]

Certainly the existence of a strong and direct relationship between a justice's personal values and his decisions has long been an assumption or operating principle of the many actors involved in selecting Supreme Court justices. However, it was not perceived by students of the Court as a sound and productive theoretical assumption worthy of empirical investigation until the mid-twentieth century.

Goldman and Sarat find the "intellectual origins" of contemporary judicial behavior research "in the political behavioralism and legal realism movements of the 1920s and 1930s."[155] However, a great debt is owed as well to the Court itself. Beginning in the early 1940s, the Court was increasingly divided, with unanimous opinions becoming less and less frequent. While an average of 8.5 dissenting opinions were written per 100 majority opinions prior to 1941, an astounding 73 dissents per 100 majority opinions have on average been filed since.[156] As Walker, Epstein, and Dixon explain, this "radically changed the way scholars viewed the judiciary. Prior to 1941, traditional legal approaches provided satisfactory explanations for a Supreme Court whose institutional practices led to consensus decisions. . . . [However,] after 1941 there were huge variations in judicial voting behavior begging to be explained."[157]

C. Herman Pritchett was the first to attempt to do so and is quite properly regarded as the father of modern judicial behavior research. His study of the

Roosevelt Court was novel both in its emphasis on the justices' attitudes as a potentially powerful explanatory variable for their decisionmaking behavior and in its use of statistical devices and quantitative measures for analyzing a large sample of case data.[158] From his observations of voting patterns, Pritchett inferred that the justices' voting and opinion behavior could be explained by differences in the attitudes of individual justices toward particular policy issues, such as labor, freedom of speech and religion, criminal justice, and economic regulation. He additionally found considerable stability in the voting alignments among the justices along traditional liberal and conservative lines.

It is Sheldon Goldman who next provided in early judicial behavior research the most significant methodological and theoretical advances.[159] He assumed that the justices' attitudes (ideal or i-points) and case stimuli (j-points) could be ideologically scaled in multidimensional space. According to his "psychometric" model, "the decision of the Court in any case will depend upon whether the case dominates, or is dominated by, a majority of i-points."[160] Goldman and other scholars found that most justices (on the Vinson and Warren Courts) exhibited a high degree of ideological consistency in their votes across different clusters of issues and that groups of justices sharing similar views tended to vote together.[161]

Rohde and Spaeth also developed a multidimensional attitudinal model and found a high degree of ideological consistency within three categories of cases implicating three distinct values—freedom, equality, and New Dealism. These three values explained more than 85 percent of the decisionmaking variance in the Warren and Burger Court periods studied.[162]

More recent research continues to find voting patterns that appear to be attitudinally based. There is a high degree of ideological variability in voting among different justices and a high degree of ideological consistency and stability "within" each individual justice. For example, Justice Douglas voted the liberal position in 91.5 percent of all civil liberties cases formally decided by the Court from the 1953 to 1991 terms; very high percentages of liberal votes were reported as well for Chief Justice Warren and Justices Brennan, Marshall, Goldberg, Fortas, and Black.[163] On the other hand, Rehnquist (both as associate and chief justice) voted for the liberal outcome in only 20.4 percent of the civil liberties cases; strongly conservative voting patterns were also reported for Chief Justice Burger and Justices Reed, O'Connor, Kennedy, Souter, Scalia, and Thomas.[164] Other studies similarly report what appear to be ideology-based voting patterns.[165] For example, Rehnquist voted in favor of the criminal defendant in only 10 percent of the eighty-two nonunanimous criminal rights cases decided between 1986 and 1988, while Marshall did so 93 percent of the time.[166] Segal and Spaeth also found that Justice Douglas dissented from liberal decisions in civil liberties cases only 1.3 percent of the time, compared to 77.7 percent of the time for conservative decisions; while on the Burger Court, Justice Rehnquist dissented in 54.8 percent of the liberal civil liberties decisions, but in only 0.9 percent of the conservative decisions.[167] Variation in judicial attitudes is the highly likely explanation for such substantial variation in voting.

Patterns of interagreement among justices also comport with an ideological explanation of Supreme Court decisionmaking. Justices with similar political views tend to vote together and join each other's opinions. For example, Justices Douglas and Goldberg voted together over 90 percent of the time in civil rights and First Amendment cases.[168] In the 1988 term, Rehnquist, Kennedy, and O'Connor had an interagreement rate of 90 to 93 percent, and Justices Brennan and Marshall voted together 94 percent of the time (and "were nearly inseparable on the three courts on which they served together")[169]. In the 1994 term, Justices Thomas and Scalia voted together 88 percent of the time, and Justices Ginsburg and Breyer voted together 83 percent of the time.[170] In the 1986 through 1989 terms, Marshall joined 81 percent of Brennan's special opinions (concurrences and dissents) but none of Rehnquist's special opinions.[171] Empirical tests conducted by Segal and Spaeth suggest that these patterns are not due to the exercise of influence; rather interagreement is a function of "like-mindedness."[172]

Further evidence that the justices' values make a difference is seen when examining the impact of new justices on Supreme Court decisionmaking. For example, Segal and Spaeth found that "the resignations of Earl Warren and Abe Fortas had a strong and immediate impact on the Court's civil liberties decisions"; the percentage of liberal decisions rendered by the Court fell from 80.3 percent in the 1968 term to 54.5 percent in the 1969 term.[173] The impact of Nixon and Reagan appointees is especially apparent. Fifty-five percent of the civil liberties decisions of the early Warren Court (1953–60) were liberal, rising to nearly 77 percent from 1961 through 1968. However, only 41.8 percent of the Burger Court's decisions in civil liberties cases (1969–85) can be characterized as liberal, and in four years (1976, 1980, 1983, 1985) the percentage fell below 40 percent.[174] Several other studies verify that decisionmaking change on the Court is primarily caused by membership change.[175] Sheehan, Mishler, and Songer also found that the changing ideological composition of the Court had a significant impact on litigant success, especially in comparison to the conventional explanations of differential litigant success—litigant resources and experience.[176]

The results of these and other studies are consistent with an ideological explanation of Supreme Court decisionmaking.[177] However, they do not decisively prove, particularly the earlier studies, the existence of a *causal* link between judicial attitudes and judicial decisions. This is due to a basic research design in which attitudes are inferred from consistency in voting patterns, rather than measured independently. As a result, it is impossible to attribute causation to judicial attitudes or, as Gibson notes, "to determine the *degree to which* behavior reflects atittudes, whether the relationship is direct, indirect, conditional, or curvilinear, and whether attitudes [are] better predictors of behavior than other independent variables."[178] In addition, because many studies relied on only the subset of nonunanimous decisions (where one finds the required variance in voting behavior), differences in voting patterns are necessarily exaggerated. Insofar as factors other than attitudinal differences (including legal factors) might be at work in producing unanimous decisions, these studies excluded important evidence contrary to the presumed direct, unilinear attitude-behavior relationship. Thus, all that can be concluded from many studies is that for the subset of nonunanimous decisions,[179] clear and predictable voting patterns can be readily observed that are consistent with and do not disprove the theory that judicial attitudes "cause" judicial decisionmaking outcomes.

Such methodological problems are increasingly being solved, however. Alternative statistical techniques permit the inclusion of unanimous decisions, and studies have found the influence of ideology even in unanimous decisions.[180] For example, 88.7 percent of the Warren Court's unanimous civil liberties and economic decisions (from 1961 to 1968) were liberal, while only 52.2 percent of the Burger Court's unanimous decisions were liberal following the appointments of Powell and Rehnquist.[181]

More significantly, efforts have been made to develop independent measures of judicial attitudes. This permits a more direct and definitive empirical test of the explanatory and predictive power of attitudinal variables with respect to judicial outcomes. In the first such effort, David Danelski "measured" the attitudes of Justices Brandeis and Butler by analyzing their speeches prior to their appointments to the Court. He then found a correspondence between support or opposition to laissez-faire (independently discovered) and the direction of the justices' solo dissents in cases involving economic issues.[182] While this represents an innovative approach, extending it to more than a handful of justices would require a substantial research investment.

A more promising approach has been developed by Jeffrey Segal and Albert Cover.[183] To determine where to place each justice on an ideological scale from liberal to conservative, they conducted a content analysis of editorials from the nation's leading newspapers regarding justices from Earl Warren to Anthony Kennedy,[184] from the time of the president's nomination to the Senate's confirmation vote. The correlation between the justices' perceived ideology and their votes in all civil liberties cases (from 1953 through 1987) was quite high, at .80.[185] Segal and Spaeth replicated and extended the Segal-Cover analysis through 1989, with similarly high correlations.[186] Mishler and Sheehan also found great congruence (.77) between the ideological composition of the Court (independently determined using the Segal-Cover approach) and the liberalism of the Court's decisions (covering the period 1956–89).[187] And finally, a 1995 study extending the Segal-Cover approach to economic issues and to FDR and Truman appointees produced weaker though still very significant results; the results for Bush's appointees (Souter and Thomas) were very strong and close to the earlier marks of .80 (for both economic and civil liberties issues).[188]

Alternative empirical tests conducted by Segal and Spaeth also avoid the circularity problem of earlier studies. One such approach uses past voting behavior to predict future voting behavior.[189] Using Burger Court justices' past votes in death penalty cases (and, for Justices Scalia and Kennedy, newspaper editorials, off-the-bench speeches and writings, and lower court decisions), the authors correctly predicted the voting alignment of Rehnquist Court justices in nineteen of the twenty-three death penalty cases decided from the 1986 through 1990 terms.[190] In yet another test, Segal and Spaeth correctly predicted 74 percent of the individual votes in search and seizure cases from 1962 through 1989, combining facts (case stimuli)[191] with criminal justice attitudes (measured by content analysis of newspaper editorials, the justice's party affiliation, and judicial ideology of the appointing president).[192] The attitudinal variable was more significant than the fact-based variable in increasing the prediction rate.[193]

Social background studies also avoid the problem of relying on judges' decisions to infer attitudes, but have proven only moderately successful at best. These studies assume that certain attributes or background characteristics (religion, education, occupational experience, region) represent socializing experiences that affect political attitudes, which in turn affect decisionmaking behavior. For example, John Schmidhauser found highly consistent voting patterns in the pre–Civil War period relating to party affiliation and region in slavery and economic regulation cases.[194] However, with two exceptions (to be discussed shortly), the background-behavior studies have met with limited success. The only variable which consistently correlates with voting behavior is political party affiliation, and the correlation is typically small.[195]

The two exceptions to the largely unsuccessful social background approach are C. Neal Tate's 1981 study and the more recent effort of Tate and Handberg.[196] Tate tested the relationship between twenty-one personal attribute variables and the voting behavior of the twenty-five justices serving between 1946 and 1978. He found that four factors correlated strongly with liberal voting on economic and civil rights and civil liberties cases: Democratic party affiliation, appointment by a president other than Nixon and Truman, judicial as opposed to prosecutorial experience, and lengthy prior tenure as a judge. Overall, Tate accounted for 72 percent of the variance in nonunanimous economic regulation decisions and 87 percent of the variance in civil liberties decisions.[197]

Tate and Handberg were able to explain about half of the variance in nonunanimous economic and civil rights and civil liberties decisions (from 1916 to 1988) with a model that included partisanship, appointing president's ideological intentions,[198] region, agricultural origins, religion, family origins, and career experience. Especially significant, the strongest and most consistent effects on decisionmaking were exerted by partisanship, appointing president's intentions, and southern and agricultural origins.

As Segal and Spaeth correctly point out, the label employed in these two studies—"personal attribute" model—is a misnomer. It is more accurate to describe party affiliation and appointing president's intentions, the two most significant "attribute" variables, as surrogates for political attitudes, rather than as attributes or antecedent causes of those attitudes. For example, Justice Scalia did not become a conservative *because* he was Republican or *because* President Reagan appointed him.[199]

The various Segal-Cover studies, the empirical tests of Segal and Spaeth, and the significance of party affiliation and appointing president[200] in explaining judicial outcomes strongly support the existence of a causal link between the attitudes of Supreme Court justices and their decisions across a broad range of issues. Together, they augment and strengthen the more inferential empirical evidence reviewed earlier regarding distinctive ideology-based voting patterns of individual justices, blocs of justices, and different Courts over time.

Evidence also exists that political attitudes influence not only the decision on the merits, but the decision to accept cases for review as well. The decision to grant review is in fact a complex one, influenced by more than judicial attitudes.[201] For example, the presence of the U.S. government, either as a party or as amicus curiae, greatly increases the likelihood that the Court will grant review.[202] Also increasing a certiorari petition's chances is the existence of conflict in the lower courts[203] and the presence of an amicus curiae brief.[204]

However, considerable evidence exists that ideological and strategic considerations play a decisive role in the justices' decision to accept a case for review.[205] For example, numerous studies have shown that votes to grant certiorari are related to subsequent votes on the merits.[206] For example, justices voting to review a case are more likely to vote to reverse the lower court's decision.[207] Indeed, the affirmance rate for certiorari cases with full opinions was only 32 percent in 1986,[208] 26 percent in 1988,[209] and 33 percent in 1994.[210] More particularly, justices are more likely to vote to review cases in which the lower court decision was in conflict with their personal political views.[211] In short, "liberals usually want to review conservative decisions, while conservatives want to review liberal decisions."[212] For example, Armstrong and Johnson found that the Warren Court pursued an "error correction" strategy with regard to economic cases, accepting conservative lower court decisions (i.e., "politically incorrect" decisions) for review more frequently; the Burger Court was consistently more likely to accept liberal lower court decisions in both economic and civil liberties cases.[213] Because of the growing conservatism of the Supreme Court in the 1970s and 1980s, it was more likely to accept liberal lower court decisions for review.[214] This was especially evident in criminal cases; the Burger and Rehnquist Courts were considerably more likely to grant review to criminal cases filed by prosecutors than the Warren Court had been and considerably less likely to do so for petitions filed by criminal defendants.[215] More generally, as Pacelle's study shows, changes in the Court's agenda over time are strongly influenced by membership change and the resulting alteration in the policy preferences dominant on the Court.[216]

Certiorari votes are also strategic. They are related to the justice's calculation regarding the likely outcome on the merits; justices believing the Court will decide in accordance with their preferences will vote to accept review, while those fearing an "unfavorable" decision will vote against review.[217] Finally, evidence exists that political attitudes influence decisions regarding access to the federal courts generally. Studies have found correlations between justices' votes regarding access and their rankings on a liberal-conservative scale.[218] As Segal and Spaeth characterize the relationship, "liberals vote to open access; conservatives to close it."[219]

Attitudinal influences also extend to opinion assignment decisions. The chief justice is empowered to assign the majority opinion when voting with the majority[220] and, in fact, makes most (over 80 percent) of the opinion assignments.[221] To maintain harmony on the Court, equality in opinion assignments is an important norm, which chief justices have closely observed.[222] However, as Segal and Spaeth argue, this practice has not operated as a bar to the achievement of ideological goals. Data show that, first, the "opinion assigner" disproportionately self-assigns important cases[223] and, second, disproportionately assigns opinions to justices who are closest ideologically.[224] Although there is some issue specialization on the Court (for example, Justice Brennan was the First Amendment specialist), the practice of assigning relatively more opinions to the "Court expert"[225] is again not inconsistent with ideologically motivated opinion assignment; specialists who receive a disproportionate share of opinions are also (uncoincidentally) ideological allies of the chief justice.[226] Finally, there is evidence that in close decisions, the "marginal" justice (the justice in the majority who is closest to the dissenters) is more likely to receive the opinion assignment, presumably to keep the small and precarious majority together.[227] The empirical evidence strongly supports the conclusion that ideology and policy motivation influence all three stages of the decisionmaking process—case selection, the decision on the merits, and opinion assignment.

Finally, there is "negative" evidence that supports the attitudinal model of Supreme Court decisionmaking In 1968, Professor Howard asserted that there is considerable "fluidity" in Supreme Court decisionmaking—that is, frequent changes in the original and final votes on the merits. He argued that this undermined the validity of the attitudinal model, first, by posing intervening variables relating to collegial or small group influences between attitudes and behavior and, second, by casting doubt on the reliability of the final vote as an indicator of political attitudes.[228] However, subsequent studies cast serious doubt on Howard's conclusions. For example, Brenner found that Vinson Court justices voted the same way in the final vote and the original vote 86 percent of the time, with vote changes producing a change in the outcome (a minority becoming a majority or a tie vote becoming a majority) in only 8.6 percent of the cases.[229] Additional studies have shown that when voting shifts do occur, they are consistent with an attitudinal explanation, rather than a "small group influence" or other nonattitudinal explanation.[230] Thus, "individual policy preferences appear to be considerably more important than group processes in shaping the Court's decisions."[231] Scalia and Rehnquist provide anecdotal evidence verifying that view, with their criticism of the lack of meaningful dialogue and interchange during conference "discussions"; Scalia, for example, characterized the conference as consisting of the "statement of the views of each of the nine Justices, after which the totals are added and the case is assigned."[232]

Additional negative evidence comes from Segal and Spaeth, who test for nonattitudinal factors that might provide an alternative or supplementary explanation of Supreme Court decisionmaking. For example, they find that judicial role orientations—normative expectations that "judges should behave like judges" by adhering closely to text, precedent, and the ideal of judicial restraint—have virtually no impact on Supreme Court decisionmaking.[233] Additionally, Segal and Spaeth failed to uncover evidence of the principled exercise of judicial restraint (conducting several different tests, across different issue areas), even for the justice with the greatest reputation for it, Felix Frankfurter.[234] They conclude that, with the exception of Rehnquist with regard to federalism issues, restraint and activism are used "as a means to rationalize, support, and justify their substantive policy concerns."[235]

A final piece of negative evidence reinforcing the consensus that policy considerations are paramount in Supreme Court decisionmaking is Brenner and Spaeth's study of *stare decisis*. Their empirical study of the Court's alteration and reversal of precedent from 1948 to 1991 led them to conclude that *stare decisis* has virtually no impact on the justices' decisions.[236] Segal and Spaeth's follow-up study produced similar results: except for Stewart's and

Powell's, the justices' support for *stare decisis* was "clearly idiosyncratic," leading them to conclude that "modern Supreme Court justices . . . virtually
never subjugate their preferences to the norms of *stare decisis.*"[237] These two
studies are not without their critics; nonetheless, even they are able to find
only limited influence for the norm of *stare decisis*—only in some cases, for
some justices, and possibly in structuring choice.[238]

This issue of the influence of nonattitudinal factors is by no means settled.
Additionally, there is *some* competing evidence, though limited, that suggests
that legal rules matter[239] and that judges may be driven by a multiplicity of
goals.[240] However, the consensus among judicial behavior scholars, as stated
by Songer and Lindquist, remains undisturbed: "A half century of empirical
scholarship has now firmly established that the ideological values and the
policy preferences of Supreme Court justices have a profound impact on
their decisions in many cases."[241]

Such a conclusion is, of course, anathema to the neutralists. For the
Court's members simply to vote their values is regarded as an illegitimate
form of decisionmaking and an arbitrary exercise of their power, given that
the justices are unelected and not easily removed from office. However, the
justices' policy preferences can themselves constitute a coherent source of
decisionmaking. More significantly, to the degree that the justices' ideological and policy views that serve as the premise of their decisions are consciously evaluated and chosen by elected officials (and, through them, voters
and interest groups), then value-voting is neither arbitrary nor illegitimate.
Indeed, a justice's personal values may be regarded as a decisionmaking
proxy that is representative or democratic in nature.

There is another more direct way to examine the degree to which there is
a significant policy link between a president's selection of a Supreme Court
justice and that justice's subsequent decisions. We can examine the degree
to which justices in fact fulfill or satisfy, through their decisions, the president's ideological or policy expectations.

Presidential Expectations and Judicial Performance

Scholars and presidents alike have offered their version of what Laurence
Tribe refers to as "the myth of the surprised president."[242] Thus, the eminent
Court historian Charles Warren asserts that "nothing is more striking in the
history of the Court than the manner in which the hopes of those who

expected a judge to follow the political views of the President appointing him are disappointed."[243] Alexander Bickel has expressed his agreement with this view that the ability of a president to predict judicial performance is necessarily limited: "You shoot an arrow into a far distant future when you appoint a Justice and not the man himself can tell you what he will think about some of the problems that he will face."[244] Professor Ely goes so far as to assert that "one sometimes wonders whether the appointee who turns out differently from the way the President who appointed him expected is not the rule rather then [*sic*] the exception."[245]

A number of former presidents have joined the chorus. President Truman declared that "packing the Supreme Court simply can't be done. . . . I've tried it and it won't work. . . . Whenever you put a man on the Supreme Court he ceases to be your friend. I'm sure of that."[246] Truman also offered as his answer to the question of his "biggest mistake as president" that "[Supreme Court justice] Tom Clark was my biggest mistake. No question about it. . . . He hasn't made one right decision that I can think of."[247] Similarly, President Eisenhower expressed his annoyance with the consistently liberal decisions of two of his appointees, Earl Warren and William Brennan. When asked if he had made any mistakes while president, Eisenhower replied, "Yes, two, and they are both sitting on the Supreme Court."[248]

Not surprisingly, Supreme Court justices themselves also do not endorse the notion that their decisions are so easily predicted by appointing presidents. Justice Frankfurter's response to the question of whether a person changes when he puts on the judicial gown was, "If he is any good he does."[249] Former Chief Justice Earl Warren similarly observed that he did not "see how a man could be on the Court, and not change his views substantially over a period of years . . . for change you must if you are to do your duty on the Supreme Court."[250] And in a speech shortly before the 1984 presidential election, (then Associate Justice) Rehnquist, perhaps seeking to lay to rest any concern that President Reagan, if reelected, would pack the Court with his conservative allies, argued that presidents can generally do so only with "partial success."[251]

As Watson and Stookey point out, "there are good reasons why presidents may fail to predict how their appointees will perform on the Court," including miscalculations by presidents and their advisers, the emergence of issues on the Court's docket unanticipated by the president, and changes in a justice's political and jurisprudential views over time.[252] Furthermore, studies by

Baum and by Hensley and Smith reveal that collective decisionmaking change on the Court is not exclusively caused by membership change, the vehicle of presidential appointment effects; also influential are issue change and changes in the voting behavior of "continuing" members.[253]

Nonetheless, the evidence rather clearly and consistently supports the conclusion that there is a strong and direct relationship between presidential expectations and judicial decisionmaking. According to the consensus among scholars, presidents historically and on average have enjoyed a 75 percent "success rate." In other words, most presidents most of the time succeed in predicting the future ideological course pursued by their Supreme Court appointees. Thus, Tribe is correct when he asserts that the myth of the surprised president is precisely that—a myth.

One approach to testing the presidential expectations–judicial performance hypothesis is simply to conduct a chronological historical review and count the number of instances of presidential success and failure. Rather than replicating the efforts of other scholars who have conducted either full or partial historical reviews of presidential appointments to the Court, I will summarize their conclusions.[254]

Scigliano and Tribe both specifically address the issue of whether justices satisfy presidential expectations with their subsequent decisions on the Court. Scigliano's conclusion that "most justices, most of the time live up to Presidential expectations" is amply supported by his historical survey of presidential appointments (ending with President Lyndon Johnson).[255] He further concludes that "about three-fourths of those justices for whom an evaluation could be made conformed to the expectations of the Presidents who appointed them to the Supreme Court."[256]

Tribe provides no comprehensive or systematic review of the historical evidence, instead highlighting a number of examples in which presidents clearly succeeded in shaping the Court's future decisions as they had intended with their appointments (for example, Presidents Washington, Jackson, Lincoln, FDR, and Nixon). He also examines the few cases of failed presidential expectations (e.g., Wilson's appointment of McReynolds, Ike's appointments of Brennan and Warren) and concludes that presidential failures are typically attributable to the president himself rather than to an unexpected judicial metamorphosis. Accordingly, Tribe concludes that "for the most part, and especially in areas of particular and known concern to a President, Justices have been loyal to the ideals and perspectives of the men who have nominated them."[257] He further concludes that the historical evidence is instructive regarding the *potential* for presidential influence on the Court's decisions through his appointments: "a determined President who takes the trouble to pick his Justices with care, who selects them with an eye to their demonstrated views on subjects of concern to him, and who has several opportunities to make appointments . . . can, with fair success, build the Court of his dreams."[258]

Richard Friedman, in his critique of Tribe's analysis, asserts that "most Justices fit at least very roughly the expectations that Presidents and Senators have at the time of nomination. But . . . there have been a substantial number of surprises."[259] He goes on to find twenty-two such surprises.[260]

In conducting my own survey of presidential successes and failures, based on existing historical reviews of presidential appointments, I found that close to two-thirds of the appointees can be regarded as clear successes, while 18 percent of the total can be categorized as cases of presidential failure, with the remainder providing a mixed or unclear record.[261] While this is similar to what other scholars have found, there are some significant differences, for example between my list of presidential failures and Friedman's list of presidential surprises.[262] Additionally, Scigliano concludes that 25 percent of the justices represent failures, whereas my own determination is that only about 18 percent should be categorized as failures. Part of the difference here is due to the fact that Scigliano's analysis stops with Johnson and thus excludes the largely successful presidents since. However, there is more to it than that.

In the end, I was left with strong reservations about this enterprise, due not only to the subjectivity of making such determinations, but to the existence of methodological difficulties as well. Problems include attributing specific appointment intentions to each president and accounting for the reality that presidents possess complex and competing motivations. Additionally, should one count presidential *surprises* (when a president truly could not have anticipated a justice changing ideological stripes, e.g., Blackmun), or presidential *mistakes* (when a president should have known that the appointee would decide contrary to presidential wishes, e.g., Brennan), or presidential *failures* (i.e., both surprises and mistakes)? What if a justice decides in accordance with presidential desires on some issues, but not on others (e.g., White, Frankfurter, Reed)? Should we defer to the president's judgment that he was strongly disappointed with a justice's performance, as Wilson expressed with regard to Holmes, or should we independently judge that Wilson "should have been" largely satisfied (as Tribe did but Friedman did not)?

Certainly, all of the historical accounts point in the same direction: the number of justices who satisfactorily fulfilled the ideological or policy expectations of their appointing presidents far exceeds the number of justices who failed to do so. However, the problems of methodology and subjectivity should lead us to test the proposition in alternative ways.

One such effort, by Rohde and Spaeth, tested the degree to which the voting records of all justices appointed from 1909 to 1971 (classified as liberal, moderate, or conservative) conformed to the liberal or conservative tendencies of their appointing presidents, as determined by their party affiliation, admittedly a rather simplistic test.[263] Consistent with the conclusions of other studies, they found that fewer than one-fourth of the nominees generally voted contrary to the views of their appointing president. However, where a nominee had a record of judicial experience, from which Rohde and Spaeth infer that the president was afforded a dependable indicator of his future voting behavior, only two justices were found to have deviated from predicted presidential desires; however, as the authors note, both justices (Cardozo and Brennan) were chosen more in spite of their views than because of them. The authors additionally examined the votes of Nixon appointees in criminal cases, in light of President Nixon's special concern with "law and order" and his strong objections to liberal Warren Court criminal justice decisions. They found that the Nixon appointees were indeed quite conservative on this high-priority presidential issue.

Improving on this approach, Heck and Shull used the public statements of presidents, rather than party affiliation, as an indicator of their attentiveness to and policy views regarding civil rights.[264] The authors then compared the civil rights support scores of Presidents Eisenhower to Ford with the percentage of their appointees' votes supportive of civil rights claims in racial equality cases. They found that only 64 percent (nine of the fourteen justices) voted in accordance with their appointing president's views, fewer than the 75 percent other scholars have found. The evidence, at first blush, seems to support their conclusion that "recent presidents have been only moderately successful in appointing justices who would later take positions consistent with the appointing president's public statements on civil rights."[265] However, three of the five justices who failed to reflect their appointing president's views were Eisenhower appointees—Harlan, Whittaker, and Stewart.

As Heck and Shull acknowledge, racial equality was not a highly salient issue for Eisenhower generally, nor did he care much about his nominees' views on civil rights issues. That inattentiveness is then reflected in the great variation in his appointees' support for civil rights in their decisions, ranging from a low of 60 percent for Whittaker to a high of 93.3 percent for Warren. (Interestingly, Heck and Shull classify Warren and Brennan as correctly representing their appointing president's liberal views, while most scholars, and Eisenhower himself, regard the two as presidential mistakes.) President Johnson was the most attentive to civil rights and the most supportive; his appointees, Fortas and Marshall, were, not surprisingly, highly supportive of civil rights claims, with scores of 85.7 and 94.0 respectively. Nixon was relatively attentive to civil rights, but much more conservative; his appointees were similarly much less likely to support civil rights claims—doing so as a group only 50 percent of the time (and for Rehnquist, only 33.3 percent of the time).[266] It is clear from these results that presidential success is highly dependent on the president's *attentiveness* to civil rights; the appointees of presidents who cared greatly about the issue, particularly Johnson, were much more likely to reflect their appointing president's preferences. The more accurate conclusion comes at the article's end: "Our study suggests that a determined president with an adequate number of appointments can take major steps toward reshaping the Court in his own image.' "[267]

Gates and Cohen also evaluated presidential success in appointing like-minded justices in the area of racial equality, but found higher levels of success, largely due to improvements in their measures of presidential preferences.[268] A president's party affiliation, consistent with the Rohde and Spaeth study, did in fact prove to be a significant predictor of the justice's votes. However, predictive success was significantly improved when using the "degree of liberalness" of the president's racial equality statements, instead of party affiliation, and was further improved by adding two more aspects of presidential policy preferences—attentiveness to the racial equality issue and concern with judicial policymaking on racial equality matters. The authors aptly conclude that "presidential appointment appears to guarantee long-term representation of the unique policy perspectives of presidents" and, thus, "holds strong potential as an efficient political control over the Supreme Court, given appointment opportunities."[269] Surprisingly, and in contrast to the findings of Rohde and Spaeth, prior judicial experience did not enhance presidential success in appointing like-minded justices.

Using a different approach, Jeffrey Segal also documented a connection between presidential ideology and the decisionmaking record of Supreme Court appointees. In his unpublished study, Segal correlated the domestic policy liberalism of presidents from FDR to Reagan (computed from a survey of political scientists) with the votes of those presidents' appointees in civil liberties cases. He found a .64 correlation overall.[270]

A study by Sue Davis provides "negative" evidence of the impact of presidential appointments on Supreme Court decisionmaking. She examined the growing conservatism of the Court after Rehnquist became chief justice and found no empirical support for the contention that it was due to Rehnquist's leadership or strategic behavior. Thus, she argues (consistently with the conventional wisdom), this conservative Court is better characterized as "Reagan's rather than Rehnquist's."[271]

More directly supporting the conclusion that presidents can predict and in a sense dictate the ideological orientations of their judicial appointees are numerous studies documenting the influence of appointing president on judicial decisionmaking. For example, as previously discussed, Tate found appointing president to be a significant predictor of the liberal or conservative voting tendencies of twenty-five postwar Supreme Court justices.[272] Tate and Handberg also found that appointing president's ideological intentions exerted a significant and consistent influence on appointees' economic and civil rights and civil liberties decisions.[273] In addition, Marshall and Ignagni found that the number of GOP-appointed justices on the Court strongly (and conservatively) influenced the Court's decisions in cases involving "rights claims."[274]

Scholars have repeatedly confirmed the existence of presidential appointment effects on judicial decisionmaking for lower federal court judges as well. For example, studies have found that Carter appointees were much more likely than Reagan appointees to vote the liberal position in cases involving criminal justice,[275] labor and economic regulation issues,[276] abortion,[277] civil rights,[278] and standing to sue in the federal courts.[279] However, differences between the two groups of judges were slight in areas providing fewer opportunities for judicial discretion (i.e., where the law is more clear, precise, and stable), such as voting rights[280] and certain economic regulation matters.[281]

A more extensive study (covering eleven presidents, from Wilson through Ford) also found appointing president (and, less strongly, partisan affiliation) to be a significant predictor of the liberalism or conservatism of district court judges' decisions.[282] Thus, for example, Lyndon Johnson's appointees to the federal district courts rendered significantly more liberal decisions than did Nixon's appointees. Similar results were found in another study of the percentage of liberal decisions rendered by district court appointees of Presidents Wilson through Reagan. The liberalism scores of appointees of Presidents Wilson, Johnson, and Carter were highest (51, 52, and 54, respectively) and in sharp contrast to the liberalism scores of Nixon, Reagan, and Bush appointees (38, 36, and 34, respectively).[283]

In yet another important study, Gottschall found significant presidential effects in the decisions of federal appellate court judges. For example, in nonunanimous cases involving civil rights and civil liberties, the Kennedy/Johnson judges voted in favor of the liberal outcome 61 percent of the time, Nixon/Ford appointees 26 percent of the time, Carter judges 63 percent of the time, and Reagan judges only 26 percent of the time.[284] Such differences were consistent and strong across a number of issue areas, such as criminal justice, race discrimination, First Amendment, labor, and welfare.[285] Nonetheless, it should be noted that only 17 percent of the cases studied were nonunanimous. Furthermore, Carter and Reagan appointees agreed in 74 percent of the cases in which they participated jointly; however, in the 26 percent of cases in which they disagreed, Carter's judges voted the liberal position 95 percent of the time, compared to only 5 percent for Reagan's judges. Other studies have reported similar results: in the minority of cases in which federal appellate court judges disagree (no doubt when the law is unclear or unsettled), considerable ideological differences in voting exist, based on the presidential appointment cohort to which judges belong.

This survey of the relevant empirical studies supports the generalization that a president can and usually does satisfactorily predict the future decisionmaking performance of his Supreme Court appointees (and lower court appointees as well).[286] Such a finding is additionally to be expected given the fact that most presidents place a high priority on partisan and ideological considerations in selecting their Supreme Court nominees.

The evidence that presidents fail, perhaps up to 25 percent of the time, is certainly significant, however. This finding may be seen as seriously weakening the argument advanced here—that "value-voting" is legitimate since those values are in fact chosen by the appointing president.

However, the argument has not been so baldly asserted and in fact cannot be so defended. As will be discussed (later in this chapter and in the next), the legitimacy of policy motivation and value-voting rests in large part, but not exclusively, on the connection between the value premises of a justice's decisions and the values the president believes he is promoting by placing that individual on the Court.

In any case, all that is necessary, in light of the conventional scholar's penchant for describing value-voting as arbitrary, idiosyncratic, and lacking *any* legitimate basis, is to show a strong, substantial, and consistent relationship. Obviously, there is generally and typically a substantial connection between a president's political views and the decisions of the justices he appoints. To discover that there is not a perfect and comprehensive correspondence between the views of a president and his appointees is not of great consequence. As Tribe states, "if that is all that the myth [of the surprised president] means—that Justices are not mere minions of the Presidents who nominated them—then we can conclude its undeniable truth because it is also irrefutably trivial."[287]

Furthermore, when we examine the various reasons for failed presidential expectations, we find that they do not undermine the legitimacy of value-voting. Nor are they fatal to the thesis that the value premises of a justices' decisions can be and largely are consciously chosen by elected representatives through the selection process.

The previously cited Carp and Rowland study of the influence of appointing president on the liberalism of federal district court judges is instructive.[288] The authors found that intuitive and anecdotal information regarding the appointment experiences of the presidents studied served to explain the variation in presidential success in predicting (or "dictating") the future liberal-conservative decisionmaking tendencies of their judicial appointees. In general, the authors suggest that presidents whose ideological impact on the lower courts was greatest were those who demonstrated a strong interest in and commitment to ideology-based appointments,[289] who had the opportunity to appoint a large number of judges, who enjoyed considerable popularity and political clout (with party leaders and with the Senate and its Judiciary Committee), and whose appointees found a judicial climate already favorable to their political views.

Thus, the finding that Truman's appointees were not as liberal as might be expected is less surprising given the knowledge that Truman paid little attention to his judicial appointments generally, relied on partisan and personal loyalty over purely ideological criteria, and additionally lacked strong popular support and a cooperative Senate. Similarly, Eisenhower's comparable lack of interest in ideology-based judicial appointments and the fact that his appointees were placed in an overwhelmingly Democratic federal bench under an increasingly liberal Warren Court provides an explanation for the only limited conservative impact of Eisenhower on his appointees' performance. Kennedy similarly did not enjoy great success in packing the federal courts with like-minded liberals, as the voting record of his appointees demonstrates; yet this conforms with our knowledge that Kennedy experienced great difficulties in his appointments with the Judiciary Committee, dominated by conservative southern Democrats, and with local Democratic party bosses. Both Nixon and Johnson were politically powerful presidents who demonstrated their personal commitment and skill in using their appointments to advance their policy objectives, and the appointees of each additionally found a receptive judicial climate (with the Warren and Burger Courts, respectively). Not surprisingly, the voting patterns of each group of judges provide a dramatic contrast in terms of their liberal-conservative tendencies.

The Carp and Rowland study and similar studies of the appointments of Presidents Bush and Clinton confirm the general argument that presidents can and do shape the liberal-conservative decisionmaking orientations of the federal courts through their appointments.[290] However, they further suggest that presidential success in doing so is a function of a president's personal commitment and skill in making ideology-based appointments, the degree to which his views are actively supported and widely shared by others (especially other political leaders), and the degree to which there exists an ideologically favorable judicial climate.[291]

It is these factors that in fact explain nearly all of the instances of failed presidential expectations with regard to Supreme Court justices. The cause is rarely, as the conventional explanation goes, an unpredictable, inexplicable, and therefore arbitrary judicial metamorphosis. In fact, the most common source of presidential failure in "programming" the Court is the president himself; either he has not taken sufficient care in evaluating his nominees or he lacks the political support necessary to win Senate confirmation of his preferred nominee.

The many instances in which justices have in fact fulfilled the policy expectations of their appointing presidents share a common factor: presidents who perceived their Supreme Court appointments as an opportunity to extend their influence by placing justices on the Court who held similar political views and who exploited that opportunity skillfully and to its fullest. Thus, both Presidents George Washington and John Adams were careful to appoint ardent Federalists to the Court, and they both got exactly what they wanted—a Federalist Court that consistently upheld the broad powers of the national government, particularly in commerce, and that struck down state laws which conflicted or interfered with those powers.[292] President Andrew Jackson and his Democratic successors also enjoyed a large measure of success in their Supreme Court appointments in the form of the states' rights and anticorporation orientation of the Taney Court. Abraham Lincoln carefully evaluated the views of his Supreme Court appointees on the issues of slavery and the war and was amply rewarded by their subsequent decisions. Thus, the Court consistently upheld Lincoln's expansive view of his war powers, retreating only after the Civil War's end in ruling unconstitutional some of Lincoln's more questionable executive actions.

Both Presidents Grover Cleveland and Benjamin Harrison selected their eight appointees (four apiece) for their antipopulist, pro-business, and pro-property rights views. Their concern regarding the political views of their appointees then paid off in terms of decisions by the Court that interpreted the Constitution as prohibiting a variety of governmental restraints on property and economic activities. With his nine appointments, FDR was given the opportunity to remake the Court according to his desires, and he used that opportunity wisely and skillfully. Roosevelt sought candidates absolutely loyal to his New Deal programs, and none of his appointees disappointed him in this respect.

In his four appointments to the Court, President Nixon shifted the Court away from the previous liberal path of the Warren Court.[293] He followed through on his campaign pledge to restore law and order to the country by appointing judges who would protect the "peace forces" against the "criminal forces."[294] Nixon's appointees have remained true to the law and order views for which they were selected. Although Justice Blackmun moved to the liberal wing of the Court (and is, in my view, one of the very few *true* cases of presidential surprise),[295] he has in fact charted a more moderate path in criminal procedure cases.[296]

To the dismay of their liberal critics, Presidents Reagan and Bush pursued a strongly conservative agenda in making their judicial appointments at all levels of the federal judiciary. With their six appointments to the Court

(O'Connor, Scalia, Kennedy, the elevation of Rehnquist to Chief Justice, Souter and Thomas), their efforts have proven quite successful.[297] The Court has been considerably and consistently more conservative in a variety of areas, most notably race discrimination, abortion, and criminal justice; it was also, during the Reagan and Bush administrations, more likely to defer to conservative executive branch interpretations of congressional statutes.

There are certainly other notable instances of presidential success in predicting future judicial performance, such as those of Presidents Wilson, Taft, and Johnson. However, the examples provided above are noteworthy for the clarity of purpose and the skill demonstrated by these presidents in selecting their Supreme Court appointees and for the clear and direct payoff in terms of decisions by those justices that corresponded to the specific policy desires of their appointing presidents.[298]

It should not be surprising that this rule cuts both ways: Presidents who fail to evaluate a nominee's political views carefully are more likely to be disappointed with their appointee's subsequent performance on the Court. Although such instances are normally counted as "presidential failures," it is clear that they do not constitute cases of true presidential *surprise*, where a justice unexpectedly deviates from presidential desires. For example, the appointments of Jefferson's three Democratic-Republican successors (Madison, Monroe, and John Quincy Adams) are typically regarded as failures in that their appointees did not reverse the Marshall Court's Federalist policies. However, these presidents did not share Jefferson's overwhelming concern with using their appointments to achieve that goal of reversing the Court's Federalist course. Additionally, President Madison appointed Joseph Story to the Court, despite the warnings of many (especially Jefferson) that Story was a Federalist in Democrat-Republican garb. Story's subsequent performance proved those warnings to be correct; according to Henry Abraham, Story "out-Marshalled Marshall."[299] Like Madison, John Quincy Adams was forewarned of Robert Trimble's Federalist tendencies, despite his nominal party membership, but appointed him anyway.

President Jackson's appointment of John McLean is similarly regarded as a failure, due to McLean's wild unpredictability on the Court and his support for the Federalist position on a number of issues of concern to Jackson. However, it is not so clear that McLean truly surprised the president with his performance. Jackson did not trust the ambitious and chameleonlike McLean, but felt compelled to appoint him due to his nominee's great popularity in the West and the desire to rid himself and his party of a trouble-some cabinet member. The view that McLean's political loyalty was suspect was confirmed both by his decisions on the Court and by no fewer than four attempts to run for president, under four different party labels, while serving on the Court. Under such circumstances, Justice McLean does not represent a true case of presidential surprise.

Another often-cited example of the inability of presidents to predict future judicial performance is Woodrow Wilson's appointment of James McReynolds, who is justifiably regarded as the most reactionary justice in the Court's history. While on the Court, McReynolds never failed to vote against the Wilsonian position on important cases involving the government's economic regulatory powers. However, there have been suggestions that Wilson was aware of McReynolds's latent reactionary tendencies and that he additionally sought to rid himself of this most obnoxious and abrasive member of his cabinet. Additionally, Wilson apparently relied on his nominee's record as an ardent trustbuster as sufficient evidence that McReynolds was at heart a political progressive, perhaps failing to recognize the strong conservative, procompetition case for trustbusting. This is not then such a clear-cut case of presidential surprise. Like the example of Jackson's appointment of McLean, the legitimacy of Wilson's subsequent claim of disappointment with McReynolds is suspect.

Eisenhower's appointments of Earl Warren and William Brennan, both liberal activists on the Court, are typically portrayed as modern-day reminders of the inability of presidents to predict future judicial performance. Yet, as a general matter, Eisenhower did not share with other "successful" presidents a fierce dedication to using ideological criteria in his judicial appointments. Additionally, it is generally believed that his appointment of the eastern, Catholic, and Democratic Brennan was intended to retain Democratic support in the upcoming election. Thus, Ike's subsequent dismay with Brennan's liberal decisions on the Court, which could have been predicted from his record as a New Jersey judge, can hardly be regarded as legitimate. (However, it is less clear that Eisenhower's disappointment with Chief Justice Earl Warren was his own fault.)[300]

These examples demonstrate that presidential carelessness or inattention, or a willingness to abandon ideological compatibility in the service of other goals, will often explain the instances of a president's disappointment with his appointee's decisions. Rather than providing evidence regarding the inability of a president to appoint justices who will faithfully adhere to a particular ideological course, these examples merely reinforce the generalization that presidents who consciously and skillfully select justices for their demonstrated political views will be rewarded in terms of those justices' future decisions on the Court.

Another set of factors influencing presidential success in using judicial appointments to advance his views on the Court is external in nature, having to do with the political climate in which the president operates. Thus, to the degree that a president is confronted with a Senate that is opposition controlled or generally hostile to his views, the president's freedom of choice in his appointments is accordingly restricted. The president's personal popularity, the unity and support of his party, and the existence of powerful interest groups who are supportive of his policies will also affect his appointment choices. Thus, a president who enjoys strong and broadly based support will have greater freedom in employing ideological criteria of his own choosing than will the president who is required to compromise his own political views in order to appease voters, interest group and Senate opposition, sectional demands for representation, or recalcitrant factions within his own party. Thus, the overwhelming success of such presidents as Washington, Lincoln, and FDR is attributable not only to their commitment and skill in making ideology-based appointments, but also to the considerable leeway in selecting their appointees afforded them by their great popularity and their political clout and standing with other political leaders.

A number of instances of failed presidential expectations can also be explained not as examples of an unpredictable judicial metamorphosis, but as the consequence of constraints on a president requiring that he sublimate his own ideological desires in his Supreme Court appointments in order to satisfy the demands of others that alternative ideological criteria be used. For example, President Jackson's appointments of both Justices McLean and Wayne are regarded as examples of failed presidential expectations. Yet Jackson appointed McLean in part because of the nominee's great popularity in the West, and in the case of Justice Wayne, Jackson was attempting to placate the Whigs. Similarly, President Jefferson's claim to being surprised or disappointed with the decisions of his appointee Thomas Todd is less justifiable when it is recognized that Todd's appointment was motivated in part by geographical considerations and by the need for fence-mending with Congress. As previously discussed, the appointment of William Brennan was part of

Eisenhower's election strategy to win over Democratic voters in the East. Accordingly, his disappointment with Brennan's liberal activism (it could hardly be called "surprise") was entirely predictable and can be regarded as a cost that Eisenhower seemed willing to bear, at least ex ante.

President Hoover's appointment of Benjamin Cardozo represents a clear example of this phenomenon, wherein presidential disappointment is the product of selection criteria different from the president's preferred ideological criteria being imposed by others. Hoover fully expected Cardozo to pursue liberal-progressive policies once on the Court, which is why the president would not have appointed him but for the overwhelming and broadly based pressure exerted by interest group leaders, the organized bar, the legal academic community, and a large number of congressional members and leaders. Again, it is difficult to characterize this example as a true case of failed presidential expectations or as evidence that presidents are unable to predict or consequently to shape future judicial performance.

Recognition of the limits imposed by other political leaders or by the political climate generally upon a president's ability to choose his nominees freely on the basis of ideological compatibility thus helps to account for a number of presidential failures. It also helps to explain those instances where a president enjoyed only moderate success or where it is difficult even to determine presidential motivations with regard to particular appointments. For example, the pre–Civil War presidents established a still unchallenged record for Senate rejections of their Supreme Court nominations. Five of President Tyler's six nominees were rejected, and three of the four nominations of President Fillmore failed. Of course, both Tyler and Fillmore suffered for their status as unelected presidents, their running mates having died soon after reaching office. However, this period was in any case one of bitter interparty and intraparty disputes and of political stalemate, with no consensus on issues or, as a result, on acceptable candidates for the Court. The consequence of importance here is that our ability to test the degree to which these appointees' decisions conform to presidential expectations is significantly impaired under those circumstances.

Determining precisely what a president intended with a particular nomination is made more difficult when we recognize that the president must respond to demands imposed by the Senate (or other political or interest group elites). Additionally, the typical form of that influence is indirect, unlike the direct pressure and arm-twisting Hoover received regarding

Cardozo; such influence is furthermore constant rather than intermittent. A president must, of necessity, anticipate the probable political support or opposition to his potential nominees and adjust his nomination choices accordingly. As previously discussed, studies demonstrate that this is particularly true for unpopular and politically weak (e.g., lame-duck) presidents, who are significantly more likely to see their Supreme Court nominees rejected by the Senate.

When presidents appoint justices for reasons other than purely ideological ones, such as accommodating Senate opposition, the likelihood of presidential "failure" increases. Yet, this evidence does not lead us to conclude as a result that future judicial performance cannot be predicted; we can conclude only that the president is not always free to act on those predictions and his personal desire for such a future decisionmaking course. And, of course, this increases rather than decreases the likelihood that the Court's membership will be "representative."

Two important consequences must be noted regarding the existence of this limitation on presidential discretion and influence in his appointments to the Court. The first is methodological. Testing the degree to which the Court's decisions are politically responsive or "democratic" by examining their correspondence to the expectations of appointing presidents certainly has the advantage of analytical manageability. Yet it excludes a significant domain of data—the representation of the views of other actors involved in the selection process. A more appropriate formulation, although one not without its practical difficulties, is to test the degree to which Supreme Court justices put into effect the ideological or policy intentions of those actors (not only the president) responsible for their appointments.[301]

There is another important consequence of acknowledging that a president's freedom of choice in selecting ideologically compatible justices is a function of his general popularity and political support. Further insuring the acceptability or representativeness of a justice's ideological orientation is the additional litmus test imposed by other participants in the selection process—the Senate, interest groups, and, more indirectly, the citizens they represent. Thus, when a justice fails to satisfy presidential expectations, democratic standards of representativeness and responsiveness may still be satisfied. In other words, for a president whose views do not find widespread popularity or widespread expression in other political institutions, the claim that presidential desires *deserve* preeminence in Supreme Court appointments is accordingly more tenuous.

To reiterate, although other political leaders may limit the ability of a president to "produce" Supreme Court decisions which he desires, that does not invalidate the proposition that a justice's future decisionmaking course is predictable or that the personal-value premises of a justice's decisions are simultaneously an effective democratic constraint on their decisions since elected representatives have sanctioned those value premises. Rather, this evidence indicates only that elected officials other than the president also engage in the prediction of future judicial performance and also inject their ideological desires into the selection process and, consequently, into the judicial decisionmaking process as well.

Other limitations upon presidential influence on Supreme Court decisionmaking through the appointment process are those which Walter Murphy describes in *Elements of Judicial Strategy* (and which will be examined more fully in the next chapter).[302] A justice who wishes to carry out her policy goals (and by inference, the president's policy goals) must go beyond mere value-voting. To the degree that actual policy success is preferred to ideological purity for its own sake, a justice must build sufficient support for her preferred policies among other justices, lower court judges, and other political leaders. This may and typically does require some degree of moderation of those views, including compromise and bargaining.

Certainly, efforts to accommodate the views of other justices are an absolute necessity if the Court is to reach any sort of agreement at all.[303] Accordingly, collegiality as a facet of Supreme Court decisionmaking could also weaken or interfere with judicial fulfillment of presidential desires. The internal dynamics of the Court—the relationships among the justices, the leadership and consensus-building abilities of individual members—also influence a justice's decisions.[304]

This sort of influence is typically offered as the explanation for the failure of President Jefferson and his Democratic-Republican successors to overturn the Court's Federalist policies through their appointments. (Of the twenty justices I classified as clear examples of failed presidential expectations, seven are the appointees of these four presidents.) The traditional explanation for these presidential failures is that their appointees "were either mesmerized or overwhelmed"[305] by the towering intellect and persuasive powers of the Federalist Chief Justice John Marshall and "succcumbed to his spell, notwithstanding generic political differences."[306] The abilities of Chief Justice Warren and Justice Brennan to marshal majority support for the Court's new and far-reaching judicial doctrines may also explain the occasional disappointment Eisenhower most likely felt with his other typically moderate appointees (Harlan, Stewart, and Whittaker). As an explanation of Stone's liberal shift on the Court, Walter Murphy cites his growing social ties and consequently growing doctrinal ties with Holmes and Brandeis, as well as Stone's increasing personal animosity toward McReynolds.[307] Similarly, Smith and Hensley attribute the occasional departure of Kennedy and O'Connor from the Rehnquist Court's conservative voting bloc to the combative and confrontational style of Justices Scalia and Thomas.[308] To Smith and Beuger, it is the failure of Scalia and Thomas "to participate in persuasion and compromise" that partially explains why the Court has not been as conservative (or as consistently conservative) as Reagan and Bush hoped to make it with their appointments.[309] These various examples suggest that the influence of other justices and the dynamics of collegial decisionmaking may lead a justice to abandon or subordinate his or her personal values as a primary decisionmaking guide.

A justice is not immune from the influences of other members of the Court, nor are the justices immune from the influence of the larger political environment. This is so, as Murphy notes, to the degree that a justice cares about insuring political support sufficient for both policy success and institutional survival. Thus, an appraisal of the potential popular and elite support and opposition is a necessary and important part of the justices' decisionmaking calculus. However, that appraisal may in some cases lead justices to abandon their personal views, which have served as the central premise of their appointments. In other words, presidential expectations regarding a justice's future decisions may be sacrificed to the Court's need for policy success and for institutional legitimacy and survival as dictated by a changing political environment.

The apparent changes of heart of Chief Justice Hughes and especially Justice Roberts, which can as a result be regarded as examples of presidential failure, occurred under precisely those circumstances. The Court was facing considerable opposition to and criticism of its rulings striking down major New Deal programs. This opposition culminated in FDR's Court-packing plan, in which another justice would be added to the Court for every justice over seventy years of age, thereby giving FDR six new appointments and control of the Court. Roberts and Hughes had in fact already begun to weaken and withdraw their opposition to governmental regulatory efforts prior to FDR's plan (in response to the strong political backlash, according to most scholars).[310] Nonetheless, that shifting of views is typically referred to as "the switch in time that saved nine" (i.e., mooting the issue of whether FDR should be permitted to pack the Court.)

This explanation may also be appropriate for the unexpected decision-making course charted by Justice Stone, appointed by President Coolidge in 1925. Despite being considered a safe and solid Republican, Stone joined the liberal Justices Holmes and Brandeis and wholeheartedly supported the New Deal, leading FDR to promote him to the chief justice's seat. It is admittedly difficult to impute clear intentions to Presidents Coolidge and Hoover in their appointments regarding the desirability of emergency New Deal legislation and, thus, to label Stone, Hughes, and Roberts as clear presidential failures (although I did so). Yet it is possible, especially for Hughes and Roberts, to identify a change in their positions on the constitutionality of New Deal legislation after popular and political opposition mounted and became a real threat to the Court. The evidence strongly suggests that this judicial reversal was in response to the increasing political dangers attending continued invalidation of New Deal legislation. The ideological commitment represented by the appointments of Roberts and Hughes no longer commanded sufficient popular and elite support and, therefore, was abandoned in order to protect the power and legitimacy of the Court.

It should be noted that the "switch in time" represents an unusually clear example of a justice abandoning his personal beliefs in order to respond to changing requirements for the Court's continued power and legitimacy. That situation was highly unusual in that turnover on the Court was not following the typical rate; FDR had not had the opportunity to appoint a single justice during his first term. Additionally, there was simultaneously a major change, represented by overwhelming electoral victories for FDR and the Democratic Party in Congress, in the political values receiving popular support and political elite expression. The processes by which the Court comes to share the dominant values held by the people and expressed by their representatives simply did not operate as quickly or as smoothly as is typically the case, thus precipitating the crisis exemplified by FDR's Court-packing plan. Both because of turnover on the Court and because of presidential and Senate control of the selection process, such a clear and substantial conflict between the justice's personal values and the values or desires of the people and their representatives is unusual and unlikely. Adjustment of the Court's decisions to a changing political climate is ordinarily insured through turnover and the selection process, and only under exceptional circumstances requires that justices abandon or significantly moderate their personal views to achieve that end.

Yet it remains true that the justice's views, which the president has intentionally placed on the bench, will continue to serve as an effective decisionmaking constraint only insofar as those views retain their political viability. Accordingly, this represents another check or limitation, but an entirely legitimate one, on a president's ability to predict and shape the future decisions of his Supreme Court appointees.

Presidential Expectations and Judicial Performance: A Reassessment

A number of conclusions have been supported regarding the relationship between a president's ideological and policy intentions in appointing a Supreme Court justice and the decisionmaking course then pursued by that appointee. Most importantly, that relationship generally holds: most justices, most of the time, satisfy the ideological and policy expectations of their appointing presidents. This is to be expected given the great care with which most presidents evaluate the ideological credentials of their Supreme Court nominees and given the high degree of ideological consistency that most justices exhibit in their decisionmaking.

Evidence that presidents fail perhaps up to 25 percent of the time is, of course, significant. Yet, the cause of most of those failures is not, as the traditional expanation goes, an unpredictable and inexplicable judicial metamorphosis. In other words, these presidential failures cannot be used to invalidate the assertion that a justice's future decisionmaking performance is capable of being predicted. Nor can it be used to delegitimize value-voting as a mechanism for carrying out the value premises of a justice's appointment, premises that have been selected by the president and sanctioned by the Senate. For example, it was found that presidential success is a function of presidential commitment and skill in selecting ideologically-compatible appointees,[311] and presidential freedom to do so is a function of his popularity and political power. Additionally, presidential expectations expressed in Supreme Court appointments are more likely to be fulfilled when the judicial environment and larger political environment in which a justice makes his or her decisions is supportive of or conducive to a justice deciding in accordance with his personal (and, by inference, presidential) desires.

These sorts of deviations from presidential desires are not necessarily arbitrary or illegitimate on democratic grounds. For example, they are not to the degree that a justice responds not to presidential expectations but to the expectations of other politically responsible actors involved in her selection or to altered standards of politically acceptable judicial decisions. In other words, presidential intentions are a primary source, but not the exclusive source, of judicial decisions that may be regarded as legitimate or democratic.

Conclusion

The purpose of this chapter has been to demonstrate that democratic ends—political representation and responsiveness—are served by value-voting. There exists a substantial connection between a justice's personal values that guide his decisions and the values a president and Senate actively choose and sanction in the process of nominating and confirming that justice. The judicial selection process is controlled by elected officials, influenced by interest groups, and dominated by partisan and ideological considerations. When combined with turnover, this process produces a Court whose members are dynamically representative in political outlook. The justices will reflect or represent the political values and policy views currently (or at a minimum recently) receiving official expression and representation in other branches of government and, by inference, receiving a significant measure of popular support.

The fact that this representation takes a different form from that in other political institutions does not make it any less significant or any less legitimate. In fact, redundancy and diversity in the nature and forms of political representation is a hallmark of American democracy. Accordingly, there is no reason to denigrate and devalue the Court's representativeness simply by invoking a rigid and restrictive definition of "representation."[312]

Value-voting, an amply documented empirical reality, then fulfills the promise of a politically controlled and ideology-infused selection process.

Supreme Court justices carry out the democratically selected value premises of their appointments by voting their personal preferences—a democratic proxy of sorts. Most typically that means carrying out the policy desires or appointment intentions of the president. In fact, most justices have fulfilled the ideological intentions of the president appointing them. Of course, there are the largely legitimate limitations on the president's ability to "program" the Supreme Court through his nominations; for example, the Senate may on occasion constrain or reject the president's preferred choice. However, it remains true that through commitment and skill in selecting an appointee, the president provides an ideological anchor for a justice's future decisionmaking. Contrary to the conventional view that it is arbitrary, idiosyncratic, and illegitimate, value-voting may instead be regarded as a source of coherence, predictability, and democratic legitimacy: the personal ideology guiding the decisions of Supreme Court justices is simultaneously an ideological constraint imposed by the people and their elected representatives.

• •

The Virtues of Political Motive in Constitutional Decisionmaking: A Constrained and Consensus-Seeking Court

VALUE-VOTING is not merely the arbitrary expression of a justice's idiosyncratic views. Rather, it is the expression and vindication of those political views deliberately "planted" on the Court by an ideology-conscious and politically accountable president and Senate. Thus, value-voting promotes political representation.

However, additional democratic benefits flow from policy motivation on the part of Supreme Court justices. Policy-motivated justices must do more than merely vote their personal political preferences. They must be attentive as well to political checks on the Court and the political conditions necessary for policy success. Thus, as this chapter will argue, two additional and interrelated benefits attend policy motivation on the part of Supreme Court justices. First, policy motivation activates and makes effective a variety of political checks on the Court, thereby helping to reconcile discretionary constitutional decisionmaking with democratic values. Second, the activities and behaviors that a policy-motivated justice is required to perform constitute a form of consensus building, a valuable democratic function.

The Behavioral Consequences of Policy Motivation

Let us look more carefully at how a policy-motivated justice might behave and evaluate the legitimacy and desirability of such behavior. Fortunately, we need not begin this endeavor with a clean slate. Walter Murphy has written the classic analysis of policy motivation on the part of a Supreme Court justice and its behavioral consequences.[1] Because of the importance of his conceptual framework for this chapter, it will first be explained.

Murphy employs an approach he labels *capability analysis,* in which the task is to address the question, "How can a Justice of the Supreme Court most efficiently utilize his resources, official and personal, to achieve a particular set of policy objectives?"[2] Murphy's mode of analysis is to develop and examine the logical behavioral consequences of a justice's policy motivation, supporting them with historical examples drawn from the unpublished papers of a number of former justices.[3]

The most distinctive feature of Murphy's effort is its appreciation of the political context in which Supreme Court decisionmaking takes place. In the conventional scholar's world, the policy-motivated justice is single-minded and self-interested, picking winners and losers in a political and moral vacuum, arbitrarily and with finality. In contrast, Murphy gives us a justice with strong policy views, who pursues them in a complex and dynamic political world offering both opportunities for and constraints on policy influence. That difference is *critical* in vindicating policy-motivated judicial behavior.

In the strange and isolated apolitical world in which legal scholars place the Court, constitutional decisionmaking based purely on personal political preference would indeed be arbitrary and illegitimate. In that world, a policy-motivated justice simply votes her values and sees them immediately translated into "the supreme law of the land." Accordingly, there is no incentive to give much thought or consideration to any decision, to develop persuasive and intellectually coherent reasons in its support, or to consider the viability, intellectually or politically, of any such choice. There are, in short, no considerations other than the personal, arbitrary choices of that single unelected and life-tenured judge. It is not difficult to regard such behavior as unreasonable, irresponsible and, thus, illegitimate.

Fortunately, Supreme Court justices do not enjoy complete freedom to impose, arbitrarily and without thought or justification, their idiosyncratic views on a nation that is then powerless to reverse them.[4] In the real world, a Supreme Court justice wishing to achieve a particular policy goal cannot simply state his preference for that goal and expect it to become the law of the land. Instead, the policy-oriented justice operates within "the framework of judicial power":

> The American system of government bestows a "stupendous magnitude" of power on Supreme Court Justices. That same system imposes significant limitations as well. The Justices are subject to political, legal, institutional,

social, ideological, and ethical restraints. Any Justice who wishes to do good—or evil, for that matter—will have to take into account not only the scope and sources of his power and the instruments available to him, but also the restrictions on his power and the points at which those restraints could be most damagingly applied.[5]

As Murphy explains, a justice seeking to achieve a policy objective must be cognizant of and successfully employ the sources of judicial power (e.g., prestige, legal authority, the power to legitimate contested policies) and the instruments of judicial power (e.g., decisionmaking choice, opinion writing, jurisdictional control, enhancement of respect for the Court's decisions as "law" (12–19). The policy-oriented justice must additionally recognize the many constraints on the use of judicial power. Such constraints include public opinion, technical law–court restrictions (e.g., standing, justiciability, *stare decisis*), institutional restraints (e.g., the need for four other votes, reliance on lower courts to interpret and apply the Court's doctrines), political checks (e.g., impeachment, regulation of the Court's size and appellate jurisdiction, refusals to obey and implement the Court's policies, the selection process), and self-restraint (constitutional, political, and legal restrictions) (19–31). Further complicating the situation, these constraints are "limitations not absolute bars to the exercise of Supreme Court power" (29). Additionally, the "policy-oriented Justice would have to make frequent and careful appraisals of this power framework, since it is dynamic, not static" (31).

The individual justice seeking to achieve her policy goals within this framework of power must marshal the support of other justices, federal and state judges, the public, and other political leaders who can both assist the Court in achieving policy success and impose sanctions against it. As Murphy's numerous examples illustrate, there are many ways in which a justice may act to garner the support of this diverse array of actors. However, all fall under the headings of persuasion, negotiation, and accommodation.

Within the Court, the policy-motivated justice must devise "a strategic plan to secure a majority within the Court . . . [including] efforts to persuade on the merits of his policy choice, to capitalize on personal regard, to bargain, to threaten, and if possible to have a voice in the selection of new personnel" (43). Given that lower court judges enjoy significant discretion in interpreting and applying Supreme Court doctrine, the Court must also overcome the resistance of and, more affirmatively, secure the obedience of lower court judges. This can be accomplished through "intellectual or emotional persuasion, through personal or professional esteem, through threats or uses of sanctions, or through selection of new personnel, but he may also appeal to his authority . . . since he and his tribunal are at the highest level of the judicial hierarchy" (92).

The policy-oriented justice must also "secure positive action" from the legislative and executive branches while "preventing or minimizing hostile action" from them with regard to both the desired policies and the Court itself. The justice may choose the somewhat passive strategy of "anticipated reaction," in which she attempts to accommodate the contrary views of the political opposition. This constitutes a subtle form of bargaining or compromise. There are, however, more active and aggressive strategies. As Murphy notes, there are a variety of tools for attempting to persuade friends and foes alike as to the rightness of a justice's policy preferences: intellectually and emotionally persuasive opinion writing, the creative use of dicta, public speeches and writings, and personal contact and lobbying, either directly or indirectly through emissaries. The target of these efforts at persuasion may be members of Congress or the president. A justice may alternatively target the public or interest groups, who in turn pressure Congress and the executive branch. The policy-motivated justice might react to legislative or executive opposition by standing firm and hoping for the Court's prestige to carry it through. However, it may be necessary to limit the further extension of an unpopular doctrine or to execute a "tactical withdrawal" or perhaps a "massive retreat."

Murphy's book is replete with examples of such behaviors on the part of the Court's members (some of which will be discussed later in the chapter). Many scholars would likely find such activities inappropriate, if not downright tawdry. However, to denigrate the "political machinations" of various justices on behalf of their desired policies or on behalf of the Court itself is unfair. As Murphy argues, the Court must do so as a product of the competing roles and expectations to which it is subject and the political environment from which it comes and in which it operates:

> Justices are expected to act like statesmen yet be aloof from all considerations of policy; at the same time they are selected through a blatantly political process, frequently for manifestly political purposes, and are

asked to decide cases fraught with some of the most controversial of current public-policy issues. . . . The Justices are expected to operate on a much higher plane than elected officials, on a plane where compromise and devious stratagems have no place. To a great extent judges do operate on this higher plane. . . . And to a greater extent than legislators or administrators, Justices must and do publish statements justifying their compromises in terms of fundamental principles of jurisprudence. But as rulers, judges who wish to see their policy choices become operative cannot always escape the necessity of negotiation or resort to devious stratagems. . . . By giving judges the responsibilities of statesmen we have also imposed on them the burdens of politicians. (209)

Even though the Court's political activities—from accommodation and compromise to bargaining and even lobbying—may be a necessary consequence of their policymaking role and the political environment in which they operate, we need not go to great extremes apologizing for them. Such activities are not only necessary and appropriate, they are also democratically valuable. By moderating her policy preferences, actively seeking policy support, and avoiding political sanctions, the policy-motivated justice is responding to and fulfilling the purpose of political checks on the Court's power while also performing a consensus-building function.

Policy Motivation and the Effectiveness of Political Checks

The Supreme Court is subject to a number of political constraints on the exercise of its powers. These constraints consist of two types: formal checks, deriving from specific constitutional provisions, and informal checks, deriving from the nature of the judicial process and from the general structure of American government in which the Court possesses only a portion of all governmental powers. The following discussion explains how those checks work, how frequently they are used, and with what degree of effectiveness.[6]

Formal Checks on the Court

The Constitution provides a variety of formal political checks on the Court and its exercise of power. The most significant and effective control, as previously discussed, is the manner in which the Court's members are selected—

nomination by the president, with the advice and consent of the Senate. However, there are supplemental checks, although their effectiveness varies greatly, as will be seen.

Congress possesses the most impressive set of formal powers over the Court. Congress can impeach Supreme Court justices, limit the Court's appellate jurisdiction, alter the size of its membership, and propose constitutional amendments. Congress is also empowered to fix the terms of the Court, control the Court's budget and staff, and set (although it cannot lower) judicial salaries. The president's most significant formal power over the Court is his power to nominate Supreme Court justices. However, the president may also encourage Congress to use its checking powers against the Court.

Impeachment

The weakest of all formal political controls is Congress's power to remove Supreme Court justices from office via the impeachment process. No justice has ever been forced from office by impeachment, no doubt because it is such an extreme measure. Although Justice Samuel Chase was impeached by the House of Representatives in 1804, the Senate failed to convict by the required two-thirds vote, and he served out his term.[7] Efforts were made to impeach Chief Justice Earl Warren and Justice Douglas, but neither aroused serious support in Congress. Impeachment remains an ineffective mechanism of political control, but a potential tool to remove justices engaging in serious misconduct.

Altering the Size of the Court

Congress changed the size of the Court several times in the nineteenth century, primarily as a way to enhance or restrict the president's opportunities to alter the ideological composition of the Court.[8] For example, lame-duck president John Adams and the outgoing Federalists in Congress passed the Judiciary Act in 1801, which reduced the number of justices from six to five (effective with the next vacancy) in order to restrict Jefferson's future appointment opportunities. (However, the new Congress quickly responded by repealing the 1801 act and even postponed the Court's next term to insure that it could not hear an upcoming challenge to the repealing legislation.)

Congress has altered the size of the Court to secure a particular membership and ideological bent at other times as well. The number of associate justices was increased from six to eight in the final days of Andrew Jackson's administration. After a close five-to-four decision upholding the blockade of the Confederacy,[9] the size of the Court was increased to ten, thereby affording Lincoln a more secure pro-Union majority on the Court. To prevent President Andrew Johnson from appointing justices who might fail to uphold its Reconstruction program, the powerful Republican Congress reduced the Court's size, as each vacancy occurred, from ten to seven justices. The embattled Johnson was never permitted an appointment to the Court, and the existing majority of Lincoln appointees remained secure. After Ulysses Grant's election, Congress again expanded the size of the Court, this time to nine, where it remains to this day. President Grant promptly used the new vacancies to engineer a reversal of the *Hepburn* decision, which had denied Congress the power to authorize the use of paper currency.[10]

As I have argued elsewhere, Congress's power to alter the size of the Court for political purposes has unfortunately fallen into disuse.[11] There is no more clear and certain evidence of this than Franklin Roosevelt's failed attempt to secure congressional permission to expand the Court, in effect, by six members.[12] Fresh from their decisive electoral victory in 1936, both Roosevelt and his Democratic Congress were eager to proceed with their New Deal agenda and were united in their antagonism toward the obstructionist majority on the Court. However, Congress would not consent to a proposal that was seen as too direct and radical an assault on the judiciary, and one that had been foisted upon them by the impatient Roosevelt.[13] Altering the size of the Court remains a potential, but unlikely, tool of political control by Congress.

Jurisdictional Control

Congress is empowered by the Constitution to regulate and make exceptions to the Court's appellate jurisdiction. There is only one instance in which Congress succeeded in restricting the Court's jurisdiction. Congress eliminated the Court's appellate jurisdiction over the Habeas Corpus Act in order to prevent the Court from hearing a case challenging a military conviction under Reconstruction legislation. (Congress feared that the Court would strike down the Reconstruction Acts.) The Court upheld Congress's power to do so in *Ex parte McCardle*,[14] not surprisingly given the Court's politically vulnerable position in the post–Civil War era.[15]

There were serious jurisdictional restriction attempts by Congress in the late 1950s in response to the Court's protection of alleged communists.[16] The Court issued several decisions, particularly during the 1956 term, that greatly angered Congress. In *Pennsylvania* v. *Nelson*,[17] the Court ruled, contrary to the clear and specific intent of Congress, that the Smith Act preempted the states' authority to regulate subversive activity. In *Watkins* v. *United States*,[18] the Court directly challenged the authority of the House Un-American Activities Committee (HUAC) by overturning a conviction based on the refusal to testify. And in *Yates* v. *U.S.*,[19] the Court overturned the convictions of fourteen defendants and severely restricted the government's ability to obtain future convictions under the Smith Act.

Congress responded swiftly with legislation attempting to overturn these decisions and additionally sought to limit the Court's jurisdiction over matters relating to subversive activities. Although the Jenner Bill restricting the Court's jurisdiction was defeated in the Senate (by only a 41 to 49 vote), the fierce congressional reaction appears to have had its desired effect. In 1959, the Court upheld HUAC authority in *Barenblatt* v. *U.S.*[20] and state authority to investigate subversive activities in *Uphaus* v. *Wyman*[21]. What Walter Murphy terms a "tactical withdrawal" is further substantiated by a 20 percent increase in the rate at which the Court rejected civil liberties claims from the 1956 to the 1958 term.[22] Congressional attacks on the Court ceased. As Segal notes, this turnabout "helped reduce the pressure to attack the Court, much as Owen Robert's switch had in 1937."[23]

Proposals to strip the Court of jurisdiction have been a common congressional response to judicial decisions with which it disagrees. Between 1789 and 1959, 165 Court-curbing bills were introduced in Congress, with the highest rates occurring after periods in which the Court was especially active in striking down federal laws and during periods in which different parties dominated Congress and the Court.[24] Warren Court activism (and liberalism) in the areas of national security, school desegregation, criminal procedure, and school prayer resulted in over 60 jurisdiction-stripping bills being introduced in Congress from 1953 to 1968.[25] Unpopular Burger Court decisions on abortion and school busing produced another flurry of such bills in the late 1970s.[26] Although few of these bills received serious consideration in Congress, the Helms Amendment, which would have denied the Supreme Court (and lower federal courts) jurisdiction over the issue of voluntary school prayer, passed the Senate in 1979. Despite the infrequency with which Court-curbing bills are passed, it is important to acknowledge that "even failed attempts may lead to self-imposed limits on judicial policy making," as illustrated by the Court's response to congressional attacks in the 1950s.[27]

Constitutional Amendment

Congress may seek to reverse Supreme Court decisions directly by proposing a constitutional amendment, which must be approved by two-thirds of each house of Congress and then ratified by three-fourths of the states.[28] Four such attempts have succeeded. The Eleventh Amendment reversed *Chisholm* v. *Georgia*,[29] in which the Court had permitted federal courts to hear suits against a state by citizens of another state. The Fourteenth Amendment reversed the Court's decision in *Dred Scott* v. *Sandford*,[30] that slaves were not citizens. The Sixteenth Amendment permitted Congress to enact an income tax, which the Court had prohibited in *Pollock* v. *Farmers' Loan and Trust Co.*[31] And the Twenty-sixth Amendment reversed the Court's decision in *Oregon* v. *Mitchell*,[32] in which the Court had ruled that Congress could not grant by statute the right of eighteen-year-olds to vote in state elections.

In the last four decades, conservatives have sought to reverse a number of the Court's controversial rulings, especially regarding school prayer and abortion. Proposals to amend the Constitution to permit school prayer passed by simple majorities in both houses of Congress in 1966 and 1971.[33] President Reagan proposed a constitutional amendment in 1982 authorizing prayer in the public schools, which fell eleven votes short of the required two-thirds support in the Senate.[34] A 1983 "human life" amendment providing constitutional protection to fetuses at the "moment of fertilization" was defeated, as was a 1981 amendment proposal providing concurrent power to Congress and the states to restrict abortions.[35]

A more recent effort to overturn a Court decision was a proposed constitutional amendment providing that "Congress and the states shall have the power to prohibit the physical desecration of the flag of the United States." This was in response to two Supreme Court decisions—the 1989 *Texas* v.

Johnson[36] decision, striking down a state flag desecration statute, and the 1990 ruling in *United States* v. *Eichman*[37] that Congress's flag desecration statute, an attempt to reverse the *Johnson* ruling, was unconstitutional. The amendment received majority support, but fell 34 votes short of the two-thirds requirement in the House (254–177), and 15 votes short in the Senate (51–48).[38]

As with bills attempting to restrict the Court's jurisdiction, constitutional amendment proposals typically fail. However, again as with Court-curbing bills, they may have an impact nonetheless, though we are often left with only conjecture. For example, Baum points to two Court rulings that were favorable to government support of religious activities (upholding the use of legislative chaplains in *Marsh* v. *Chambers*,[39] and permitting a government-sponsored nativity scene in *Lynch* v. *Donnelly*[40]) and suggests that they may have been influenced by ongoing congressional opposition to its rulings against prayer in the public schools: "Presumably by coincidence, [the *Lynch*] decision was announced on the day that the Senate began debate on a constitutional amendment to allow school prayer exercises; a decision in the opposite direction probably would have increased interest in attacking the Court on church-state issues through support of the amendment."[41]

Statutory Reversals

Congress may also try to reverse the Court's decisions by ordinary legislation.[42] Of course, Congress is free to redraft legislation when it feels the Court has provided an overly broad or overly narrow interpretation. For example, the Civil Rights Act of 1991 overturned several conservative Court interpretations of existing civil rights statutes in the area of employment discrimination.[43]

Of more interest here is when Congress attempts to reverse the Court's constitutional decisions by statute. For example, in 1978 the Court ruled that the Fourth Amendment did not prohibit police from searching the offices of a newspaper if they had a search warrant.[44] Two years later, Congress afforded newspapers greater protection, requiring police to obtain a subpoena and additionally permitting a presearch challenge to its validity. Prior to its efforts at a constitutional amendment, Congress attempted to overturn the Court's *Texas* v. *Johnson* flag desecration ruling by statute, though the Court ruled it unconstitutional.[45]

The Court's *Roe* v. *Wade* decision prompted an avalanche of statutory responses by Congress. As Fisher and Devins note, in the decade prior to *Roe*, only ten abortion-related bills were introduced in Congress, while in the ten years after *Roe*, five hundred abortion bills were introduced.[46] Most sought to limit the impact of the Court's decisions, for example, by restricting federal abortion funding and prohibiting abortions at military hospitals and federal prisons. However, a bill introduced by Senator Jesse Helms and Congressman Henry Hyde sought to, in effect, reverse *Roe* statutorily. The Human Life Statute, declaring that "human life shall be deemed to exist from conception," was defeated in committee.[47]

Statutory revisions to and reversals of the Court's decisions are more frequent and successful than have been constitutional amendments or jurisdictional restrictions. For example, as Wasby explains, Court decisions were revised fifty times from 1944 to 1960, including thirty-four instances in which the Court had overturned sixty statutes. Additionally, 176 bills responding to Supreme Court decisions were introduced between 1950 and 1978, although only 13 percent received any serious consideration, and only one-third of those were enacted.[48]

Several studies have examined the factors that increase the likelihood that Congress will attempt to reverse, and then succeed in reversing, a Supreme Court decision. Not surprisingly, majority and interest group opposition to the Court's initial decision was consistently found to be the most important causal factor.[49]

Control of Judicial Salaries, Budget, and Staff

Control over the Supreme Court's budget may provide another opportunity for Congress to influence the Court. Congress can punish or reward the Court for its decisions by changing its annual budget (for judicial salaries, staff, and operating expenses). For example, Congress communicated its displeasure with the liberal Warren Court in 1964 by increasing the annual salary of federal judges by $7,500 while providing the justices with only a $4,500 increase. According to Warren, Congress was quite stingy as well regarding staffing for his Court, refusing at one point to fund even a library messenger.[50] More clear in impact was congressional action in 1937 extending full pay to Supreme Court justices choosing to retire. Although the bill was initially introduced two years prior to FDR's Court-packing plan, the reintroduced bill was debated simultaneously with FDR's proposal. It is clear from congressional debate that the retirement bill was seen as an alternate way, and to many a more palatable one, to change the composition and doctrinal approach of the Court. Its passage was intended to and appeared to hasten the retirement of several justices, thus affording FDR the Court-packing opportunities he desired, albeit in different form.[51]

Toma's empirical study supplements the anecdotal evidence, finding that Congress clearly "signals its overall approval or disapproval of the Court's direction through budgetary allocations."[52] At least during the 1946–77 period covered by the study, Congress rewarded the Court for its conservative decisions with budget increases and punished the Court for its liberal decisions with budget reductions. Although a direct response by the Court is difficult to document (and Toma's test does not do the trick),[53] Toma does conclude that "the budget appears to be a mechanism which, at the margin, allows Congress to exert political influence over Supreme Court decision making."[54]

The President

The president's power to nominate Supreme Court justices is his most potent formal weapon of control. Beyond this, he may pressure Congress to use its formal checking mechanisms, as did FDR regarding enlarging the Court's size and Ronald Reagan regarding a constitutional amendment permitting school prayer. Or presidents may lead the way in proposing legislation designed to reverse or limit the Court's decisions, as President Nixon did with regard to the Crime Control and Safe Streets Act of 1968, a legislative attempt to undercut several of the Court's criminal procedure rulings, including *Miranda*.[55] The Reagan and Bush administrations were quite vigorous in their attacks on the Court's *Roe* v. *Wade* decision. They "launched varied and numerous rhetorical attacks against abortion, including speeches, legislative proposals, and Surgeon General reports."[56] Additionally, by executive order, fetal tissue research was prohibited, as was abortion counseling at federally funded family planning clinics. (Both policies were then reversed by executive order by President Clinton promptly upon assuming office.) President Bush also used his veto power to maintain strict restrictions on federal funding of abortions.

As the above discussion illustrates, there is a broad array of tools that the other branches possess to communicate their displeasure with the Court, to reverse or alter the Court's decisions, to punish the Court, and to alter the Court's ideological composition. However, questions still remain as to their effectiveness. Conventional legal scholars are quick to point out that formal sanctions are in fact rarely imposed against the Court.[57] They are correct that no Supreme Court justice has ever been removed from office via Congress's impeachment power. It is also true that on only one occasion did Congress succeed in withdrawing an issue from the Court's appellate jurisdiction. The Court's decisions have been reversed by constitutional amendment only four times in its history. And Congress has not altered the size of the Court since 1869. Thus, they argue, such controls are ineffective as tools to check arbitrary judicial power.

However, this argument misses the mark in a number of respects. First, it sweeps too broadly, failing to acknowledge that political checks vary in effectiveness (with impeachment being the weakest) and with regard to the frequency of their use over time (for example, with Congress's power to alter the Court's size falling into disuse).

The argument against the effectiveness of formal political checks also fails to understand that such checks are intended to supplement the appointment process and complement one another, rather than each to stand alone as a complete and effective check in and of itself. Additionally, the politicized selection process, combined with turnover, normally insures that the Court is quite unlikely to be greatly and consistently out of step with the political views dominant in the other branches. As the next chapter demonstrates, the Court's countermajoritarian reputation is in fact greatly exaggerated; the Court simply does not need substantial and persistent "checking" by the other branches.

More importantly, the measure of the effectiveness of political sanctions is not simply the number of times they are actively and successfully applied. The "rule of anticipated reactions" is the typical manner in which political checks operate.[58] The Court is certainly aware of the political reactions to its decisions. It may avoid a decision it feels will provoke too much opposition, or may moderate its unpopular decisions to avoid a potentially successful and crippling political attack. Conventional scholars fail to examine the possibility that it is the Court's generally responsive and responsible behavior which obviates the need for the other branches to invoke formal sanctions against the Court.

In any case, scholars either ignore or downplay the not insignificant number of instances in which the Court has in fact executed a tactical retreat or withdrawal in the face of political opposition or attack. Certainly the most obvious example is the Court's shift, clearly evident in 1937, from opposing to supporting major New Deal programs and state economic regulations. Although FDR's Court-packing scheme no doubt played some role, the Court could not have been unaware of the depth and breadth of popular and elite opposition to its obstructionist policies. The resulting doctrinal shift was thus an unusually clear and direct response to a grave political threat to the Court's power and independence.[59] This episode represents nothing less than the forced abdication of a traditional field of constitutional decisionmaking—protecting economic rights.[60] It also should teach us that supplemental checks can and do work when the primary political control—the appointment process—temporarily falters.[61]

There are examples other than this most obvious judicial retreat. For example, Chief Justice Marshall, Baum notes, appeared to be motivated by a desire to avoid conflict with Congress, being "careful to limit the occasions on which the Court reached decisions that would further anger its opponents."[62] After the Civil War, the Court was at a low point in terms of power and prestige.[63] From a practical point of view, it wisely lay low and let the Radical Republican Congress run its course. This included permitting Congress to withdraw from its jurisdiction a critical case challenging the constitutionality of Reconstruction legislation. In both world wars and during the McCarthy era, the Court again knew better than to flout the spirit of the times; it consistently refused to come to the aid of political dissidents, antiwar activists, and real or imagined Communists. Even when the Warren Court began to restrict the government's power to investigate and prosecute subversives, it was forced by powerful congressional opponents to retreat temporarily.

Conflict between the Court and the other branches has not abated; its decisions regarding school prayer, abortion, criminal procedure, busing, and flag burning have generated much opposition and activity in Congress and the executive branch. However, in the areas of school prayer and flag burning, we have not witnessed a retreat by the Court in response. This does demonstrate that the Court possesses relatively greater freedom than the other branches do to withstand political opposition and attack. Nonetheless, the Court has become much more conservative, particularly in the criminal justice field, due to the appointments of Nixon, Reagan, and Bush.

The final blow against the claim that political checks on the Court are ineffective is Rosenberg's empirical test of the existence of "judicial independence," defined as the degree to which the Court's "decision-making is free from domination by the preferences of elected officials."[64] Rosenberg examined the Court's decisional reactions following nine periods of "intense congressional hostility." He found that in six of those periods, "the Court either acquiesced to the Congress and reversed decisions, or backed-off to some extent to mollify congressional opposition," supporting his conclusion that the judicial independence hypothesis must be rejected.[65] Not surprisingly, success in bringing the Court to heel was a function of the size, intensity, and electoral success of the opposition. Additionally, acquiescence or reversal by the Court in response to congressional opposition was not simply a function of membership change on the Court. Especially significant is Rosenberg's conclusion that "*enactment* of Court-curbing bills is not necessary to curb the Court. Arousing substantial opposition to the Court may be enough to dominate it."[66]

Informal Checks on the Court

The appointment process remains a primary tool of political control over the Court. However, it is supplemented and buttressed by formal political checks that can be quite effective. In addition, the Court's power is checked *informally* in two ways: first, by the influence of interest groups and the solicitor general at the agenda-setting stage and, second, as a result of Congress's legislative and budgetary powers and the president's enforcement powers, which may be used to support, limit, or even defeat the Court's policies.

Because of the nature of the judicial process and the system of separation of powers, the Court lacks the ability to initiate, administer, fund, or enforce its own policy decisions. This operates as a powerful constraint. The Court cannot simply create a new policy whenever the mood strikes, nor can it expect that policy to be immediately and fully implemented.

As is often noted, the Court is not "self-starting." It can only make policy decisions in the context of lawsuits, which do not simply "arrive at the Supreme Court's doorstep like abandoned orphans in the night."[67] Rather, cases must be brought by others—private individuals and, more typically, interest groups. In the late 1960s, Nathan Hakman challenged the idea that interest groups play an important role in Supreme Court litigation, going so far as to term it "scholarly folklore."[68] However, research since has consistently revealed that "the vast majority of court cases attract group participation" and that "group presence in the judicial process has reached an all-time high."[69] Lee Epstein's examination of the Court's 1987 term revealed that "organized interests represented appellants in 38.2 percent of the cases and appellees in 44.2 percent. . . . Fully 80 percent included the presence of at least one amicus curiae brief filed by organized or governmental interests. . . . All in all, during the term the justices received nearly 460 amicus curiae briefs onto which more than 1,600 groups and governmental interests signed!"[70] Some cases attract great interest group attention and activity; for example, some 400 groups participated in the *Webster* abortion case, with 78 amicus curiae briefs filed.[71] (The specter of a reversal of *Roe* in *Webster* also prompted an extraordinary demonstration in Washington, D.C., with over 300,000 people marching from the White House to the Supreme Court, as well as full-page newspaper ads.)

In addition to the high frequency of interest group participation, we now know that it is not only disadvantaged (typically liberal) groups who seek judicial aid out of necessity, as Cortner argued;[72] a broad range of groups, including advantaged and conservative groups do so as well.[73] Finally, interest group activity is not confined to the decision on the merits. Groups also try to influence the certiorari decisionmaking process by filing amicus briefs; thus, organized interests play an important agenda-setting role,[74] particularly in the civil liberties area, in which group sponsorship is critical.[75]

The interest group character of much Supreme Court litigation has important consequences. The policy-motivated justice, at the initial stage, requires a case that can serve as an appropriate vehicle for the policy she desires. Thus, she is dependent upon the existence of parties, primarily interest groups, who wish to initiate and are capable of sponsoring appropriate litigation. In other words, the policy-motivated justice can pursue her policy goals only in the context of, and is therefore constrained to that degree by, interest group demands and support. Of course, the Court does possess considerable discretion in case selection and, thus, considerable power to shape its own agenda. Nonetheless, the needs of both interest groups and policy-motivated justices create a relationship of mutual dependence. That interest group litigants "need" the assistance of the Court (and adapt to its changing membership and changing decisions)[76] is obvious. But does the Court in fact "need," react to, and rely upon interest groups?

The evidence is limited, difficult to acquire, and rather mixed; a number of studies support the conclusion that interest group sponsorship "matters" to the Court, while some dispute it. For example, the Court must give permission to third parties to file amicus briefs if the parties to the suit refuse to give their consent. According to one study, the Court does so far more often than not (89 percent of the time between 1969 and 1981).[77] More importantly, the presence of an amicus curiae brief significantly increases the likelihood that the Court will agree to hear a case.[78] In addition, Court opinions often directly cite and frequently parallel legal arguments in amicus briefs.[79] A number of case studies strongly suggest that group sponsorship increases the likelihood of success on the merits at the appellate level,[80] although as Epstein and Rowland note, this may be due to the fact that interest group failures in the courts do not attract the attention of researchers.[81] Epstein's examination of discrimination cases in the Court's 1987 term revealed that "group defendants of discrimination won 50 percent of their cases while all defendants of discrimination won 30.8 percent."[82] An empirical study of obscenity cases found that the *number* of amicus curiae briefs filed increased the likelihood of winning in the Supreme Court.[83] However, a study that covered a much broader range of Supreme Court cases found virtually no such amicus impact.[84] Group sponsorship increased the likelihood of success in conscientious objector cases in the federal district courts,[85] but an examination of a larger number of cases in the district courts casts doubt on the thesis that interest groups are "invincible."[86] Finally, other research suggests that interest group success is largely dependent on the ideological makeup of the Court.[87] Overall, it appears that interest group involvement is, certainly at the certiorari phase and less clearly so at the decision-on-the-merits phase, a significant factor to which the Court responds.

One "interest" frequently appearing before the Court deserves special mention—the executive branch. The solicitor general represents the executive branch before the Court and is overwhelmingly successful there, as numerous studies have demonstrated.[88] When the federal government appeals a case in which it was the losing party, the Court grants review 70 percent of the time, compared to 8 percent of the time for other parties.[89] The United States wins a strong majority of cases in which it is a party: 62 percent from 1801 to 1958,[90] and 63 percent from 1953 through 1991.[91] The federal government wins an even larger proportion as amicus curiae, 74 percent.[92] Solicitor general success holds even when controlling for other factors, such as the facts of the case,[93] the existence of lower court conflict (with regard to certiorari decisions)[94] and the ideological direction of the brief.[95] For example, the government (not surprisingly) won 91 percent of their "liberal briefs" before the Warren Court, but (surprisingly) won 75 percent of their conservative briefs as well.[96]

Clearly, the presence of the solicitor general in a case has a great impact on the likelihood of success, with regard to both the decision to grant review and the decision on the merits. In an initial effort to discover the cause of the solicitor general's great success, Segal found only weak support for the traditional explanations, such as strategic case selection by the Solicitor General's Office, the high quality of the legal arguments, or the president's influence in the appointment process.[97] Instead, "deference to the executive is a stronger explanation for the solicitor's success."[98] However, the neutrality and credibility of the office also appears to play a role, with a noticeable decline in its success during the Reagan administration, during which the solicitor general's role was politicized.[99]

A Supreme Court justice cannot simply announce his preferred policy position at will. And as the evidence indicates, neither does he ignore the existence of interest group or executive branch involvement. Both interest groups and the solicitor general play a significant role in the agenda-setting stage and thus shape and constrain the efforts of the policy-motivated justice.

Yet another informal check on the Court derives from the fact that its decisions are not self-executing. Because the Court lacks any means of enforcement or implementation, its decisions typically require a large measure of voluntary compliance on the part of the recipients of its orders. The Court further requires the active assistance of other government officials who possess the *discretionary* power to fund and implement the Court's decisions. Again, interest groups must be willing and able to monitor compliance with the Court's orders, initiate the often required follow-up litigation, and pressure other leaders for enforcement and funding support.

As Gerald Rosenberg's study demonstrates, the Court does not simply issue commands that are immediately followed; at least when it acts as an engine of (rather than a brake on) social change, the Court is quite ineffective.[100] The reality the Court hopes to create requires more than a legal decision. It requires broad-based political support and translation of that support by other government officials into highly effective compliance mechanisms. For example, as Rosenberg notes, ten years after the *Brown* decision, only 1.2 percent of black schoolchildren attended school with whites in the South (52). However, desegregation occurred rapidly in the South after Congress and the executive branch joined the battle, particularly by threatening school districts not in compliance with *Brown* with a loss of federal education funds (representing millions of dollars after the 1965 Elementary and Secondary Education Act). By the end of 1967, 16.9 percent of black children attended southern schools with whites; by the end of 1969, that figure had risen to 32 percent; and by 1972, 91.3 percent of black children attended school with whites in the South (50–52). Similarly, the most significant increases in voter registration among African Americans in the South can be attributed to the actions of Congress and the Justice Department, not to the decisions of the Supreme Court (57–63). The impact of the Court's 1973 *Roe* v. *Wade* decision is also suspect, according to Rosenberg. The number of legal abortions increased more sharply prior to *Roe* than after; many states had already begun liberalization efforts; and the Court may even have provoked an unintended counterresponse in the form of a vigorous pro-life movement. Additionally, whatever "success" the Court enjoyed in *Roe* derived not from its authority and power, but from the existence of a market incentive for compliance—the ability of abortion clinics to earn a profit from the Court's decision (175–201).

The empirical evidence that Rosenberg amasses is formidable and persuasive; it demonstrates that the Court, acting alone, cannot achieve significant social change.[101] The effectiveness of the Court's decisions is crucially dependent upon the existence of compliance mechanisms, either already available in the marketplace, as in the case of abortion, or created by a cooperative Congress and executive branch, as in the case of civil rights. For those concerned about "the imperial judiciary," Rosenberg and numerous judicial impact studies provide welcome news:[102] precisely as the Framers intended, the Court cannot unilaterally impose its reform agenda on a nation powerless to stop it; the Court is politically checked in a variety of effective ways, and its power is accordingly limited.

Political Checks and the Policy-Motivated Justice

Of what significance are these political checks for the policy-motivated justice? Only a Court composed of policy-motivated justices would care about and thus render effective these various checks on its power. If logical consistency and strict adherence to precedent and norms of legal reasoning were the only concerns of a justice (i.e., the approval of law professors and "first-rate lawyers"), then it would matter little if there existed supportive interest groups and political leaders or a powerful opposition willing to thwart the Court's policies and perhaps curb the Court as well. Perhaps that was the greatest failure of the anti–New Deal Court—its unwillingness or inability to assess accurately the degree of political opposition and hostility to its laissez-faire economic policy course.

To the degree that a justice cares deeply about her policy goals, she will be quite attentive to the degree of support and opposition among interest groups and political leaders for those goals. She will be aware of the resources (e.g., commitment, wealth, legitimacy) that the relevant interest groups possess who bear the burden of both carrying forward the appropriate litigation necessary for policy success and for pressuring the other branches for full and effective implementation. Only the policy-motivated justice will care about the willingness of other government officials to comply with the Court's decisions or carry them out effectively. And only the policy-motivated justice will care about avoiding the application of political sanctions against the Court that might foreclose all future policy options.

The school desegregation cases illustrate these points quite nicely. The Court could not pursue the goal of racial integration and racial equality until there was an organized and highly regarded interest group such as the National Association for the Advancement of Colored People willing and able to help. The Court further was required to protect that group from political attack, as it did in *NAACP* v. *Alabama*[103] and *NAACP* v. *Button*.[104] Avoidance of other decisions that might harm its desegregation efforts was also deemed necessary. Thus, the Court had legal doctrine available to void antimiscegenation statutes, but refused to do so on two occasions.[105] (Murphy notes that one justice was said to remark upon leaving the conference discussion, "One bombshell at a time is enough."[106]) The Court additionally softened the blow by adopting its "deliberate speed" implementation formula. Even so, the Court still needed the active cooperation of a broad range of government officials, in all branches and at all levels of government, in order to carry out its decisions effectively. Thus, significant progress in racial integration in the southern schools did not in fact occur until Congress and the Department of Health, Education, and Welfare decided to act. The Court further had to consider whether the political opposition that it knew would ensue would be sufficient to result in sanctions against the Court, such as withdrawal of jurisdiction or impeachment. These considerations arose *only* in the process of caring deeply about the policy goal at hand—racial equality in public education. They were not a by-product of caring only about the logical or precedential consistency of an opinion or of worrying only about deriving a decision from the Framers' intentions.

Political checks on the Court do exist, and they can be effective, if the Court possesses the requisite policy motivation and political sensitivity and if it is consequently willing to pay attention to the political reactions to its decisions. These checks can help to insure that the Court's decisions do not exceed the limits of what the people and their elected representatives regard as politically acceptable. They can provide the Court with forewarning of major political opposition or of a major assault on the Court as an institution. However, they can do none of these things without that key motivator: the justices' strong desire to pursue their policy goals.

Policy Motivation and Consensus Building

A justice who cares about both achieving his policy goals and the continued power of the Court as a vehicle of policymaking will listen to and, if need be, respond to those groups and government officials who possess the power both to affect policy success and to impose sanctions against the Court. The activities these political constraints put into motion—a justice anticipating and accommodating political opposition—constitute a form of consensus building and political coordination.

As chapter 7 will discuss more fully, building a political consensus on most issues in the United States is tremendously difficult. This is so due to the ambiguity, diversity, and complexity of policy preferences in the United States. Additionally, our political parties lack the strength and discipline necessary to organize those diverse preferences into any meaningful (i.e., coherent and comprehensive) policy-preference groupings. Finally, policymaking power is widely dispersed in our government to many different officials with different constituencies and interests; each possesses sufficient power to halt, alter, or in some way damage the policy initiatives of others. Thus, discovering, acting upon, and achieving a clear, final, and stable consensus on any major policy issue is a gargantuan task.

Because a policy consensus rarely exists either in some natural state or as a result of political party mobilization, the task of discovering and forging such a consensus falls to our government leaders.[107] They must develop policy initiatives that they believe or hope will command such a consensus. And they can attempt to mobilize policy support more directly, for example, through publicity,[108] speechmaking, and more active persuasion and bargaining. This is true for all policymakers, including the Court.

There are, of course, some differences between Supreme Court justices and other government officials with regard to the tools available for the task of anticipating and mobilizing a political consensus. Unlike legislators, Supreme Court justices do not regularly consult the polls, constituents, and campaign contributors. However, the justices certainly can read newspapers and journals, and consult informally with friends and contacts, and they are no doubt aware of the rumblings of opposition to their decisions.[109] Furthermore, in appraising the political support and opposition to their possible policy decisions, the justices can examine the interest-group sponsorship of the many briefs that are submitted in significant, controversial cases. Briefs submitted by the solicitor general (and state attorneys general) provide additional valuable information as to the interest and position of critically placed political leaders. A policy-motivated justice would be quite interested in obtaining as much of such information as possible in order to predict accurately the nature of political support and opposition that exist. That information is critical to insuring that sufficient political support will exist to make the justice's policy goal a *political* reality, rather than merely the expression of a personal opinion.

The policy-motivated justice would also take great care in case selection, waiting for the most favorable set of facts. For example, Baum notes that the justices and their clerks exercised great patience in searching for the "best" case in which to declare that indigents had a constitutional right to a state-provided attorney in felony cases. Clarence Gideon's petition was accepted because it was regarded as "ideal for the Court's purposes, in part because it involved the relatively minor felony of breaking and entering a poolroom with intent to commit a misdemeanor. A reversal of Gideon's conviction would arouse less public wrath than would the reversal of a conviction for a violent offense."[110]

In addition to choosing the best case-vehicle for the desired policy statement, the policy-motivated justice would attempt to build political support for and attract powerful allies to her cause. That might be accomplished by persuasive opinion writing, speechmaking, public writings (in law review articles, if the target is the legal-academic community), providing access to interest group allies, and by direct or indirect persuasion of key government decisionmakers.

In a similar vein, the policy-motivated justice would need to be concerned with the nature and strength of the opposition. In particular, she would have to appraise the necessity of responding to opponents, if they should represent a real threat to either policy success or an attack upon the Court. Such "responses" would need not be a clear and direct policy shift. Rather, the justice might diffuse or blunt the opposition or attempt to persuade them through careful opinion writing or, again, by strengthening the Court's allies (in the interest group, academic or governmental community). A justice might in fact decide to "ride out" the opposition, hoping the Court's prestige could carry it through. For those situations in which a justice believes the opposition is strong enough to threaten the policy goal or the Court, there are varying degrees of policy accommodation or moderation that can be pursued. Avoidance of the particular issue that threatens the opposition is another easy and often-used option.

These activities—anticipating political reaction, building political support and, if need be, accommodating the demands of the opposition—are nothing less than building a political consensus behind the justice's policy goal. The *desire* to do so, to predict and mobilize a consensus for a particular policy, is commensurate with the degree of commitment a justice has to that policy. The *ability* to do so, to engage successfully in that consensus-building task, is a function of the justices' political experience and instincts, as well as the quality of political information they are able to obtain.[111]

The school desegregation cases can again be used to illustrate these points. The Court, throughout the 1940s and 1950s, was forced by NAACP-sponsored lawsuits to consider the very real consequences for African Americans, particularly in higher education, of *Plessy*'s separate but equal doctrine.[112] Certainly the Court was then considering overturning *Plessy* as one such option. The political consequences of doing so were of paramount concern, particularly if such a decision was rendered by a divided Court. The desire for unanimity did not come out of a desire for the clear and uniform exposition of the law. Rather, the concern was with a political strategy to give the opposition as few weapons as possible, thus increasing the chances for ultimate victory on the issue of desegregation and educational opportunity for African Americans.[113]

When the *Brown* decision was rendered, the Court made every effort to present a united front. Additionally, the decision was read in full from the bench. To the chagrin of law school professors, the opinion did not provide a thorough or well-reasoned exposition of the legal principles deduced from the text or the Framers' intentions. Rather, it was much more in the style of a social science essay, preaching about the importance of public education and the psychological harm done to young black children forced by law to be educated separately from presumably superior white children. This too was a conscious choice made by Chief Justice Earl Warren. With regard to two such strategic choices, Warren wrote in his memoirs that,

> In my public career, I have never seen a group of men more conscious of the seriousness of a situation, more intent upon resolving it with as little disruption as possible, or with a greater desire for unanimity. To show how desirous we all were to present a united front, Justice Robert Jackson, who had been in the hospital for a month or so as the result of a heart attack, surprised us all by insisting on dressing and coming to the Court for the announcement. . . . It was not a long opinion, for I had written it so it could be published in the daily press throughout the nation without taking too much space. This enabled the public to have our entire reasoning instead of a few excerpts from a lengthier document.[114]

The Court continued to be sensitive to the grave political consequences that might ensue and that could undermine the success of its school desegregation efforts. Both its "deliberate speed" implementation formula and its virtual withdrawal in the early implementation phase can be seen as conscious choices to allow the conflict to develop and play itself out. The Court additionally refused to strike down Alabama's pupil placement law, even though "it was designed to insure that 'no brick will ever be removed from [the state's] segregation wall.' "[115]

This strategy of allowing the dust to settle—allowing the NAACP to mobilize more support, allowing southerners to vent their anger, transferring the primary conflicts to federal district courts, hoping for support from other political leaders—may be seen as unjustifiable as a matter of legal principle. However, as a matter of political prudence, they are sensible and, therefore, defensible.

The Court's commitment to desegregation also required, at least in its own judgment, that it temporarily avoid the neutral, uniform application of the antidiscrimination principle it had developed in the educational area. The application of this given legal principle was selective and political— avoiding its application to more sensitive areas of social relations, like interracial marriage, which might activate even more serious political opposition. Similarly, the Court refused to overturn trespass convictions against African Americans for using a segregated public golf course, relying on a rather questionable legal technicality.[116] The Court apparently reasoned that placing its general antidiscrimination effort in political jeopardy was not worth the value that might have come from a more principled, evenhanded and, thus, *legally* defensible approach to race relations.

Finally, the Court wisely gave federal court judges wide latitude in their desegregation efforts.[117] Accordingly, sensitivity to local needs and political realities was permitted to influence judicial implementation of desegregation. The use by federal district court judges of "special masters" in school and residential desegregation cases was a recognition of the *political* need for community-outreach efforts and for a "judicial" representative to ascertain and help to build a political consensus as to the appropriate desegregation strategy.[118]

In summary, the Court's policy commitment to desegregation particularly and racial equality more generally led it to adopt certain political strategies, such as the selective application of legal principle and a go-slow implementation approach. These strategies are not defensible in terms of conventional legal criteria. However, they are quite legitimate in terms of the Court taking care to insure policy success—building political support, blunting the political opposition, and, where necessary, temporarily acceding to opposition views and demands.

Two final points remain to be made regarding the Court's consensus-building activities. The first is that legislators and executive officials operate in this politically constrained environment no less than Supreme Court justices do. Other policymakers take into account the likely reactions of the Court and may choose to accommodate judicial opposition as well. In other words, the policymaking process is one of *mutual* adjustment between all of the political actors involved.

We regard this as acceptable for the political branches. As the Framers believed, when government officials are required to take into account the views of other leaders (and, by inference, the interests of other groups and constituencies), then policy in the end is likely to reflect a more stable and durable consensus. Certainly this is true as compared to a governmental system in which a single leader controls policy and, therefore, possesses little incentive to consider or act upon the diverse views and interests in society.

So too with regard to Supreme Court justices. Their policy choices, if made without regard to the views of other leaders and groups, are more likely to be arbitrary and restrictive with respect to other interests and views. Political failure is, thus, more likely. However, by forcing the Court to operate in a politically constrained environment, the justices too must anticipate and accommodate political opposition to their preferred policies. The benefits are the same—policy that is likely to attract more allies and embrace more interests. In short, policy motivation combined with political constraints lead the Court *away* from the type of selfish and arbitrary decision-making that legal scholars expect from a political Court.

The final point to be made is that policy motivation does not mean that the Court will always accurately predict that political consensus.[119] Certainly the Court in the 1930s did not correctly assess the degree of political opposition to its anti–New Deal policies until almost too late. And perhaps the Warren Court did not accurately anticipate the degree or range of opposition to its varied policies in its quest for equality in many aspects of American life. However, the point to be made is that such efforts will not be made at all without policy commitment on the part of the justices.

Additionally, a policy retreat by the Court or a corresponding ideological change in the Court's membership need not be regarded as a judicial failure. Rather, it in fact represents a triumph for democratic government. As noted, there are difficulties in ascertaining any clear and specific political consensus on any given issue in the United States. The value in the justices acting both on their personal policy preference and their expectations of policy support comes not only from their successes but from their failures. In the end, we have discovered more about the limits of what policies are politically acceptable and politically unacceptable. Policy motivation and the consensus-building activities they produce, like those of other political actors, are intrinsically valuable.

Conclusion

The conventional constitutional theorist views policy motive and sensitivity to political consequences as a great evil. Such political motivations transform the justices into mere politicians and the Court into just another political agency. It further has dangerous consequences for the Court's legitimacy and power (discussed in chapter 6) and for democratic government (discussed in chapter 7).

Before addressing these two charges, it has been necessary to examine the stereotypical image of politically motivated judicial decisionmaking. Conventional scholars (and the Critics as well) portray the politically motivated justice as engaging in a crass, ad hoc, and unprincipled form of decisionmaking; a Court composed of such members necessarily "grinds whatever political ax it prefers on a particular day."[120]

However, there is an unnecessary confusion here over the issue of intellectual rigor and coherence in constitutional decisionmaking and the issue of political motive in constitutional decisionmaking. These two qualities are in fact separate and not necessarily incompatible. A politically motivated justice can provide a coherent, well-reasoned, and well-crafted legal opinion; in fact, a justice who truly cares about seeing her policies prevail will make every effort to develop such an opinion.

Not only do conventional scholars mischaracterize and needlessly denigrate politically motivated constitutional decisionmaking; they overlook its benefits. Policy motivation and value-voting constitute a valuable form of political representation. When a justice votes in accordance with his personal political preferences, he is in fact carrying out the values premises of his appointment as determined by the president and Senate through the selection process.

The justices' commitment to particular policy goals additionally activates various political controls on the Court and makes them more effective. Only a justice who cares deeply about policy success will care about whether other government leaders will lend their policy assistance to the Court or whether the Court's policy pursuits might activate political sanctions to be threatened or used against the Court. By paying attention to the political reactions its policies provoke, the Court is insuring that the various political checks are effective, even if that means in the main insuring that the other branches rarely need to invoke those sanctions formally. (Nonetheless, as the previous analysis has shown, political checks against the Court are frequently threatened, sometimes employed, and often respected and responded to by the Court.)

This process of anticipating political reactions, developing political support, and accommodating the opposition can be likened to consensus building, a function of great value in our large, diverse society and in our highly fragmented government. Consensus building may in fact be performed in part merely by value-voting. A justice's personal values, having been recently approved by a president and cooperating Senate, may be a reliable indicator of those values that in fact are likely to command a political consensus.

However, a justice's policy commitment requires a supplemental evaluation. A policy-motivated justice must in turn assess the political support and opposition that is likely to ensue following the Court's pronouncement. If necessary, additional efforts can be made to increase political support by strengthening the hand of political supporters or by weakening or blunting the opposition's efforts. A final option is to accommodate the opposition by moderating the Court's policies.

The conventional scholar overlooks the positive consequences of policy motivation and political sensitivity. That error is a function of assuming that the justices operate in a political vacuum. They fail to recognize the consequences of the fact that Supreme Court justices operate not in political isolation, but in a dynamic political environment filled with many opportunities for and many constraints upon the exercise of policymaking power. It is *precisely* those political constraints which insure that the justices cannot decide arbitrarily or capriciously but instead must anticipate and create political support for their policies. Political checks on the Court and the constraints to which it is subject are the key to its legitimacy and the political responsibility that attends its policymaking activities.

CHAPTER 6

A Political Court and the "Crisis of Legitimacy"

ONE OF the primary arguments that conventional scholars invoke against the idea of political Court and policy-motivated justices is the "legitimacy crisis" that they believe will ensue. They argue that a political Court is more vulnerable to political attack and is likely to lose its legitimacy, the primary source of its power. The loss of its power in turn means the loss of the Court's ability to carry out its specialized and valuable role. No longer will the Court be able to protect constitutional rights and liberties and politically vulnerable minorities from majoritarian attack. And no longer can the Court promote and protect the ideal of the "rule of law" and the triumph of reason over mere will or force.

This chapter will address the empirical issue of whether, in fact, public support for the Court is a function of whether it restricts itself to an impartial, law-interpreting functions and accordingly behaves in an apolitical manner. Empirical evidence from the Court's history and from public opinion research simply does not support this view.

The idea that the Court's legitimacy is uniquely dependent on public esteem and reverence and will, therefore, be destroyed if the Court is too political persists despite strong evidence to the contrary. Accounting for that persistence is the value of the legitimacy crisis myth to conventional constitutional theorists wishing to advance their particular vision of the Court's appropriate role in American democracy.

The Crisis of Legitimacy Argument

Conventional legal scholars believe that a Court must neither confront political issues too readily nor dispose of them with regard to personal political preference or political calculation. If the Court fails to play its properly limited role or fails to issue opinions that represent careful, thorough, and persuasive expositions of the law, it risks self-destruction. This is so, they argue, because the Court's power is primarily if not exclusively dependent on its legitimacy; it is dependent on the regard of the public and the public's need to be convinced that the Court is in fact interpreting the law rather than arbitrarily remaking it.[1] The Court, thus, must be mindful of those public expectations regarding its role as well as the manner in which that role is carried out.

Should the Court lose its legitimacy and, consequently, its power, we in turn lose the benefits that only the Court can provide. Vitally important constitutional rights and liberties, as well as minority groups, would be unprotected and would likely suffer at the hands of an indifferent or hostile majority. An additional loss of paramount importance is the ideal and the reality of the rule of law. All government action would be reduced to arbitrary will and force, rather than being justified according to reason and, thus, rendered legitimate. The consequences of the Court losing its legitimacy and the ability to play its specialized role, if we are to believe Philip Kurland, are horrible indeed.

> [The Supreme Court's] function is to help maintain a society dedicated to the notion that law must be the choice over force as the means of resolving the conflicts that burden society. It must epitomize reason rather than emotion in helping seek justice. Above all it must emphasize individual interests against the stamp of governmental paternalism and conformity. At the same time it must retain the confidence of the American people. . . . The Court can survive without performing these functions. Courts have survived in other societies that have rejected the concept of law based on reason. They survived in Hitler's Germany, in Stalin's Russia, and in the Union of South Africa. It is not the survival of the Court that is at stake, but the survival of the primacy of individual liberty that is in question. And these values will remain viable only so long as the Court makes its appropriate contributions toward their maintenance.[2]

What must the Court do to be able to make this contribution? According to Kurland, the Court must avoid being "political." He advised the Warren Court in particular that it "will probably have to retreat from its political stance."[3] And, for the long term, it means taking care to select future Supreme Court justices with "strength of character," "intellectual power," and "that breadth of vision, that capacity for disinterested judgment which the task demands."[4]

The Warren Court is one of the typical empirical referents for this concern of legal scholars with overly activist and overly political Courts.[5] The Warren Court certainly expanded the range of social and political issues receiving judicial attention. And what is equally certain, the Warren Court was less concerned than other Courts with persuasively elucidating the legal principles underlying its decisions or with winning the support of law professors and the organized bar. What is not certain, however, is whether such behavior exacted significant costs in terms of lost respect for the Court.

That empirical issue then is the first task in addressing the argument that a political Court jeopardizes and may sacrifice its legitimacy and power in service of its political goals. What do the Court's history and public opinion research tell us about the empirical validity of this cause-effect relationship between a political Court and the Court's legitimacy?

Public Support for the Court: Public Opinion Research

As a matter of logic, the Court does indeed seem to lack any obvious sources of power and legitimacy. As Mondak and Smithey simply state the matter, "The Supreme Court is an inherently weak institution."[6] This weakness derives from the fact that the Court can rely on neither an electoral connection nor funding and enforcement mechanisms for insuring compliance and ongoing political support. Why is it then that the Court is permitted to endure as a significant national policymaker, particularly when it often acts against the desires of the majority and other powerful institutions?

The traditional answer offered is the special status of the Court in the public mind. As Adamany and Grossman explain, "Legal Realists and political scientists in the 1930s argued that public reverence for the Constitution is rooted in psychological needs for stability and security in human affairs and in the powerful hold that constitutional symbolism has on the American mind. This reverence in turn transferred to the justices of the Supreme Court, as interpreters and protectors of the sacred Constitution."[7]

This "judicial symbolism" or "sancrosanctity proposition"[8] thus argues that public support for the Court, even for its unpopular decisions, is insured by its connection to a powerful symbol, the Constitution. Public support is further assured by expectations of judicial infallibility and impartiality. These expectations arise from the lack of electioneering or partisan campaigning on the part of judges and by the outward symbols of judicial decisionmaking (e.g., the robes, the grandeur of the courtroom, secrecy), which inspire awe and respect.

To conventional legal scholars, certain normative implications follow. To the extent that the Court fulfills those "mythic" expectations, it will continue to receive the public support and confidence necessary for carrying out its often unpopular role of enforcing reason and the rule of law against the arbitrary will of the majority.

Some initial support for the belief that the Court is "revered and deified" came in the seminal socialization study conducted by Easton and Dennis.[9] Based on a survey of over ten thousand white middle-class children in grades two through eight, Easton and Dennis argued that children's images of the Supreme Court are of a "very special sort."[10] According to their evidence, children perceived the Court to be more knowledgeable and more powerful than other governmental institutions. Its "importance," according to the children in the sample, was surpassed only by the president's. The Court was also regarded as the political authority least likely to "make mistakes." Easton and Dennis concluded that the Court is held in very high regard by children. They further speculated that such "youthful idealization" may carry over into adulthood, thus explaining general tolerance for the Court's power and even for its unpopular decisions.

However, subsequent studies regarding the attitudes of both children and adults toward the Court have not produced any evidence of the type of reverence that Easton and Dennis found. In fact, further research has consistently revealed that: public awareness of the Court and its decisions is quite limited; public support for the Court is generally weak and shallow; the public is quite critical of the Court's specific decisions; and patterns of support for the Court's decisions are best explained by political variables, such as partisan affiliation, ideology, and value orientations.

Public Awareness of the Court and Its Decisions

In an attempt to test Easton and Dennis's "youthful idealization" thesis, Caldeira employed open-ended questions (rather than Easton and Dennis's close-ended approach) to discover children's perceptions of the Court and other major political institutions.[11] In contrast to the earlier study, Caldeira found that most of the children in his sample had very little awareness or knowledge of the Court, did not express any idealization or positive affect toward it, and were more indifferent toward the Court than toward other institutions. He concluded that "even in comparative terms . . . the Court does not command a large reservoir of support among children that might affect their attitude and behavior as adults. . . . Thus the 'youthful idealization' explanation of diffuse support for the Supreme Court seems to have little empirical basis."[12]

A number of other studies involving adult samples have yielded similar results. As the following survey of these studies illustrates, public awareness and knowledge regarding the Court, its personnel, and its decisions are quite limited.

In 1964, 59 percent of a national sample answered "no" to the question "Have you had time to pay attention to what the Supreme Court of the United States has been doing in the past few years?"[13] The 41 percent who had "paid attention" were then invited to comment further. Fifty-seven percent made only one comment, and only 1 percent made more than three.[14] Additionally, 60 percent of the "attentive" respondents could recall only one subject of the Court's decisions, and only 9 percent could recall three or more.[15]

Similarly, 21 percent of a Seattle sample in 1965 were unable to provide *any* response to the question "Speaking generally, how would you describe your own feelings about the Supreme Court?"[16] Two-thirds of these respondents admitted they lacked sufficient information to form an opinion.[17] Among those who did express an opinion regarding the Court, 54 percent expressed approval of the Court; however, 27 percent of those respondents "were not specific in their discussions."[18]

A 1945 national survey found that 60 percent could not correctly name the number of justices on the Supreme Court, and 17 percent could not name "the nation's highest court."[19] National surveys in 1964 and 1966 revealed that fewer than half of the public could name one or more decisions of the Court, and only 24 percent could name more than one decision they liked or disliked.[20] In 1966, only 49 percent of a national sample could name at least one Supreme Court justice (with Earl Warren being the typical response).[21]

A survey by Dolbeare and Hammond of Wisconsin adults also indicated low levels of knowledge about the Court. Of the 79 percent who offered an opinion about the Court, only 19 percent noted any specific case or the subject matter of a decision that had affected their opinion.[22] As with the

1964 Survey Research Center survey, the most frequently mentioned decisions were in the area of civil rights and school prayer.[23]

Even when more structured, close-ended questions were asked, the public continued to demonstrate its ignorance of the Court's decisionmaking activities. Respondents were asked whether the Court had made any decisions recently in eight specified subjects; the Court had in fact rendered decisions in only four of the eight subject areas. Despite the fact that respondents were not required to give the content of the decisions, only whether the Court had made any decision, 50 percent gave two or fewer correct answers, 36 percent gave three or four correct answers, and only 15 percent were correct more than half of the time.[24]

In another structured survey conducted by Liane Kosaki in 1989, St. Louis residents were surveyed by telephone regarding their awareness of several recent Supreme Court decisions.[25] The interviewer would briefly and generally discuss the issue, such as flag burning or the death penalty for minors, and then ask respondents if they were aware of any recent Supreme Court action on the issue. Instead of the expected uniformly low rates of awareness, Kosaki found considerable variation. For example, only 22.1 percent were aware of the Court's decision regarding "dial-a-porn,"[26] and 31.5 percent regarding its decision on the death penalty for minors.[27] However, 71.7 percent of the respondents were aware of Court action with regard to flag burning,[28] and 83.5 percent were aware of recent Court activity regarding abortion rights.[29] This study thus suggests that "the public is neither universally ignorant nor universally informed about Court decisions."[30] (However, as Kosaki acknowledges, the most significant bias in the sample was the "extremely high level of education," which we know affects political awareness, both generally and with regard to the Court.)[31] Another study, by Franklin and Kosaki, similarly suggests that public awareness of the Court's decisions is not always low; it may be higher shortly following the Court's decisions (i.e., in the very short term).[32]

More typical, however, is a Wisconsin survey conducted in 1976, which reveals the public's lack of specific knowledge of the Court's decisionmaking activities. When asked if they liked or disliked anything the Court had done, 62 percent could not name a single decision they liked or disliked.[33] Similarly, in a series of surveys conducted from 1964 to 1976, the majority of respondents in each sample could not name any decision by the Court that they liked or disliked.[34]

More recent surveys tell a similar story. As Thomas Marshall reports, only 41 percent of the respondents in a 1982 nationwide poll correctly understood that the Supreme Court permitted first-trimester abortions in *Roe* v. *Wade*, with 10 percent believing the Court banned such abortions, and nearly half offering no opinion as to *Roe*'s meaning.[35] In the same poll, 57 percent correctly understood that the Court's rulings prohibited school prayer, while 35 percent could provide no opinion, and 8 percent incorrectly believed that the Court allowed prayer in the public schools.[36] In 1989, the *Washington Post* conducted a national poll in which only 9 percent could name William Rehnquist as the chief justice, while 54 percent correctly named Judge Wapner as the judge on the television show *The People's Court*.[37] In the midst of the heated controversy over President Reagan's nomination of Robert Bork to the Supreme Court, 55 percent of Americans had neither heard nor read about his nomination.[38] Finally, in a 1990 survey, "less than one-fourth of the respondents knew how many justices there are, and nearly two-thirds of them could not name a single member of the Court."[39]

Clearly the Supreme Court lacks salience for most Americans. Its members are quite unfamiliar to them and, especially significant, "many (and probably nearly all) Supreme Court decisions pass by virtually unnoticed by most Americans—either because the decision receives little press attention, or because many Americans pay little attention to the Court itself."[40]

Of course, it should be noted that limited public awareness of the Court and its decisions reflects the low level of political awareness and political knowledge of Americans generally. For example, "only one-fourth [of Americans] can name their two senators, and only one-third can name their U.S. representative. More than one-third do not know the party of their representative, and 40% do not know which party controls Congress."[41] Furthermore, "misperception regarding government policies is widespread."[42] Not surprisingly, those with limited awareness of the Court and its decisions also displayed limited awareness of their representatives in Congress and current issues and candidates, both of which are a function of educational level.[43]

Public Perceptions and Evaluations of the Court

Research indicates that not only is the public's knowledge about the Court quite limited, its support for the Court is rather weak as well. In addition, the public does not perceive or evaluate the Court in unique or exalted terms, nor do most Americans strongly believe that the Court is politically neutral or impartial.

Dolbeare and Hammond examined national surveys over a thirty-year period (1937–66) and concluded that while support for the Court was widespread, those positive feelings were weakly held and lacked strong informational content.[44] Similarly, the 1965 Seattle survey revealed that while more respondents expressed a favorable attitude toward the Court, those attitudes were not strongly held, particularly compared to those who were critical of the Court. Again, informational support for those attitudes expressed by respondents was quite limited.[45]

When public support for the Court is tested in terms of "confidence" in the Court and its members, surveys reveal that the Court is not held in particularly high regard. In fact, in some studies, the Court has lagged behind other national political institutions.[46] For example, a 1964 national survey asked respondents to rank each branch in terms of trust and confidence on a scale of 1 to 10. The president received an average rating of 7.43, with Congress at 7.23, while the Court's rating was 6.89.[47] Similarly, Wisconsin respondents were least likely to express confidence in the Court (28 percent) as compared to the president (35 percent) and Congress (50 percent).[48]

Analysis by Adamany and Grossman of a 1976 Wisconsin survey also revealed that public support for the Court was not particularly high. Regarding its overall performance, the Court received a "very good" or "good" rating from 42 percent and a "fair" or "poor" rating from 46 percent of the sample.[49] Furthermore, when rated on a "confidence" scale, the Court scored lower than the presidency, the military, and local government and about the same as Congress, state government, and national elections; the respondents expressed more confidence in the Court only as compared to poorly regarded interest groups, political parties, and the bureaucracy.[50]

National polls have consistently revealed that "only a third to a half of Americans have held clearly favorable views of the Court."[51] As Marshall reports,[52] from 1963 to 1967, an average of 39 percent of Americans rated the Court's performance as "excellent" or "good," while 49 percent (from 1963 to 1973) gave the Court "only fair" or "poor" ratings. Gallup polls also found that from 1973 to 1986 and on average, 47 percent of Americans expressed a "great deal" or "quite a lot" of confidence in the Court, while 46 percent stated they had "only some," "very little," or "no confidence." In National Opinion Research Center polls conducted from 1973 to 1986, the percentage of Americans expressing "a great deal" of confidence in the Supreme Court never exceeded 35 percent and averaged 31 percent;[53] in addition, an average of 65 percent reported having "only some" or "hardly any" confidence in the Court. Unlike the previous surveys cited, the Court, at least since the 1970s, has received somewhat greater public support (about 15 percent higher) than Congress or the executive branch.[54] (However, this may be due to greatly declining rates of public support for the other branches, rather than greatly increasing rates of support for the Court.)

In addition to receiving only lukewarm support from the public, the Court is not widely perceived as playing a special or exalted role in the government, according to most studies. Recognition of the Court's Constitution-interpreting and law-interpreting functions ranges from only 30 to 45 percent of the public.[55] Additionally, in Casey's survey of Missouri adults, only 16.6 percent of the responses to an open-ended question regarding the Court's "main job in government" mentioned the Constitution.[56]

In any case, studies by Larry Baas cast doubt on the notion that the Constitution itself is so highly revered that the Court benefits by its constitutional connection. For example, he found that many Americans do indeed grant mythical qualities to the Constitution. However, some regarded it as a failure or viewed it in a "realistic" way, recognizing both its strengths and weaknesses.[57] Baas further suggests that the reverence for the Court and Constitution that does exist may be more the product of negative feelings of fear or vulnerability rather than positive ones of respect and awe.[58]

Casey did find some evidence of myth-related beliefs about the Court in his survey of Missouri adults. Among the 74.4 percent who provided a response to the question of the Court's "main job in government," a majority (60 percent) "freely [gave] expression to some manifestation of the judicial myth," for example, connecting it to the Constitution, law, judicial functions, or rights and freedoms.[59] Disproportionately represented among the myth-holders were the "more advantaged strata of society—socially, politically, and educationally."[60] Most important for our purposes here, however, Casey found that "neither the mass public nor elites seem disturbed by the purported conflict between judicial activism and retention of the myth. . . . It is much less vulnerable to court entanglement in controversial matters than [many scholars] have contended."[61] In a similar vein, Caldeira and Gibson found that very few Americans (15 percent of African Americans and 8 percent of whites) agreed that the Court should be "done away with altogether" (admittedly a strong statement) if it "continually made decisions that the people disagree with."[62]

Although a significant portion of the attentive public may connect the Court to symbolic or mythical aspects of its role and although large majorities (especially among whites) do not favor drastic institutional change,[63] there is not overwhelming public support for the belief that the Court makes its decisions in a neutral or nonpolitical manner. Only bare majorities or sizable minorities believe the Court is unbiased[64] or believe that judges decide according to a mechanical jurisprudence model.[65] For example, a 1991 survey found that 47 percent of Americans believe that the Court's decisions are based on political pressures or the justices' personal political beliefs, with 44 percent believing that they are based on facts and law.[66] This "realism" about the political influences on the Court's decisions does not appear to be a recent development. For example, 43 percent of the respondents in a 1946 poll agreed with the statement that the Court "decides many questions largely on the basis of politics."[67]

Studies have also revealed that the public's attitudes toward *specific* decisions of the Court are quite negative. Murphy and Tanenhaus report that respondents to a national survey in 1966 offered three times more negative comments than positive ones.[68] This ratio of dislikes to likes declined only slightly over the ten-year course of their study.[69] Similarly, when asked if they liked or disliked anything the Court had done, only 7.6 percent of a 1976 Wisconsin survey sample cited only decisions they liked, while three times as many, 20.7 percent, named only specific decisions they disliked.[70] At least two-thirds of all such responses to specific decisions in these various surveys are negative in nature.[71] As Caldeira puts it, "On the visible issues of the day, however one couches the issues, most people find fault with the choices the Court makes."[72]

The Court as "Legitimator"

Both Charles Black and Robert Dahl have given great importance to the Court's "legitimating" role—its capacity to confer constitutional legitimacy to disputed laws and policies.[73] However, as numerous scholars have observed, the conditions necessary for the Court to play such a role are notably absent: the public pays little attention to the Court, is not knowledgeable about most of its decisions, does not hold the Court in particularly high regard, and only since the 1970s has the public given higher marks (and then only moderately so) to the Court as compared to the other branches. The Court simply lacks sufficient public salience and regard to be able to confer legitimacy on the decisions of the other branches (or even on its own decisions).[74]

Thomas Marshall's analysis is especially to the point. He compared the eighteen Court decisions from 1935 to 1986 in which there was pre- and postdecision poll data. The Court's impact on public opinion was typically small, and the "direction" of impact varied—the public shifted in favor of the Court's position in only six of the eighteen instances, away from the Court's position in nine instances, and in three instances there was no shift at all.[75] Additionally, larger poll shifts in the direction of supporting the Court's position were more likely when the Court issued a liberal or activist decision (contrary to conventional expectations) or when there was a longer time lag between the Court's decision and the postdecision poll.[76] Overall, however, the evidence supporting the Court's legitimating capacity was rather slim; as Marshall concludes, "Supreme Court decisions seldom greatly influence American public opinion either over the short term or the long term."[77]

Rosenberg similarly found that the Court's decisions in the areas of race discrimination, sex discrimination, and abortion lacked salience both for the general public and for the groups targeted by and benefiting from those decisions. Nor did those decisions prompt greater media attention, provide added impetus to the civil rights and women's rights movements, or change public attitudes. Rosenberg simply found no evidence to support the hypothesis that the Court can achieve social change indirectly by serving as a catalyst in the form of raising public consciousness and altering public attitudes.[78]

Some contrary evidence exists, however, and is worthy of mention. For example, two studies conclude that Rosenberg undervalues the Court's influence on public opinion, at least with regard to its ability to draw media and public attention to issues with which the Court is concerned.[79] Johnson and Martin find that the Court can affect public opinion, but only under certain conditions—for example, when the Court has made an initial ruling on a salient issue rather than a subsequent revision to an existing ruling.[80] Caldeira also offers evidence of the Court's impact on public opinion in his study of changing public opposition to President Roosevelt's 1937 Court-packing plan. Two Court actions—its decision to uphold the Wagner Act in *NLRB* v. *Jones and Laughlin Steel*[81] and the resignation decision of a powerful

New Deal opponent, Justice Van Devanter—succeeded in decreasing support for FDR's plan by almost 10 percent.[82] Through its own initiative and actions, according to Caldeira, the Court affected public opinion and thus "outmaneuvered the president."[83] Although based on skimpier evidence, a second study, by Wlezien and Goggin, attributed growing public support in the 1980s for "current abortion policy" to media reports that Supreme Court decisions and nominations would lead to greater restrictions on abortion access.[84] In this case then, the Court may have shifted public opinion away from its own more conservative policy path.

Most studies, however, support the view that the Court has a very limited capacity to enhance public support for and confer legitimacy upon contested government policies. For example, Baas and Thomas conducted several experiments in which college students were asked their opinions on controversial policy statements, half of which were unattributed and half of which were identified by source, including in some cases the Court and the Constitution. Contrary to the legitimation thesis, there was no evidence that Court endorsement enhanced acceptance of any of the controversial policy views.[85] However, a similar study conducted by Mondak did find evidence of the Court's "persuasive force," but only under certain conditions, for example, when the issue lacked personal relevance or when the Court's credibility was substantially greater than other attributed sources (such as high school principals or city police).[86] Furthermore, the Court's influence, though significant according to another study by Mondak, is nonetheless "minor," "incremental," and "confined to the margins of public opinion."[87]

A study by Franklin and Kosaki regarding the impact of *Roe* v. *Wade* on public attitudes toward abortion suggests that the Court may influence public opinion, but in unexpected and unintended ways.[88] *Roe* did increase public support for abortion involving "hard" reasons, for example, in the case of fetal defect or when the health of the mother is endangered. However, with regard to public support for discretionary abortions (i.e., for "soft" reasons, such as being unmarried, poor, or not wanting more children), *Roe* had the effect of *polarizing* public opinion, increasing the opposition of prolife advocates and the support of prochoice advocates, with overall approval changing not at all.[89] Similarly, Rosenberg argues that the Court may have unwittingly given impetus to the antiabortion movement with its *Roe* decision.[90]

Although somewhat mixed, the evidence fails to support "the Court as legitimator" hypothesis. Most of the studies support the view that the Court has virtually *no* capacity to influence public opinion (particularly in the direction it desires), whether in support of its own policies or those of other branches.[91] And the few studies that do find Court impact on public opinion regard that influence as limited and conditional.

Explaining Patterns of Public Support for the Court

A final body of evidence relevant to this inquiry concerns explanations of patterns of public support for the Court and its decisions. Studies have found that support for the Court is primarily determined by broadly defined political values, ideology, partisanship, and specific policy views. While demographic variables (race, age, education, and region) also influence support for the Court, "beliefs about proper public policy tend to overwhelm demographic influences."[92]

Several studies have documented racial differences in attitudes toward the Court. A 1964 survey found blacks to be twice as favorable toward the Court compared to whites.[93] In their 1966 study, Murphy and Tanenhaus found both race and region to be important predictors of levels of support for the Court.[94] Not surprisingly, African Americans tended to support the Court, which had aggressively protected civil rights, while southern whites disapproved of the Court and its decisions. (Southern whites continue to be less supportive of the Court than whites are generally.)[95] And finally, several studies have documented the significant role of race in public support for the Clarence Thomas nomination.[96]

Subsequent studies have shown that the higher levels of support for the Court among African Americans in the 1960s had declined by the 1970s and completely disappeared by the decade's end,[97] coinciding with declining support given to civil rights by an increasingly conservative Court. Gibson and Caldeira found in their 1987 survey that diffuse support, in the form of opposing fundamental changes in the Court, was significantly lower for blacks than for whites; however, blacks who saw the Court as "too conservative" unexpectedly accorded it *higher* levels of diffuse support than did blacks who believed the Court was "too liberal" or "about right in its decisions."[98] This anomalous finding is explained by the existence of a "Warren Court cohort" consisting of African Americans whose attitudes toward the Court were positively shaped during their early adult years by the Warren Court's pro–civil rights decisions.

Studies have consistently found that political factors—partisanship and political views—are strong predictors of public support for the Court and, further, outperform demographic variables such as race and educational level.[99] Dolbeare and Hammond found political factors, specifically partisan affiliation and support for the president, to be important predictors of support for the Court. For example, Gallup polls in 1937 revealed substantial support among Democrats for "some kind of change . . . regarding the Court," including FDR's Court-packing plan, while Republican support for change in the Court was minimal.[100] Dolbeare and Hammond concluded that "the Court's leverage within the political system depends more on the general public's ignorance of specific decisions and consequent reliance on party-based confidence in institutional competence. . . . It appears to be not so much awe or reverence, or even non-partisan neutrality, that supports the Court, but rather the fact that one's political party controls the White House!"[101] Partisanship and support for the president, thus, explain Democratic opposition to the Court in 1937 and Democratic support for it after 1941; those variables additionally explain Republican hostility to the Court after 1941, excepting their approval during Republican administrations in the 1950s.

Murphy, Tanenhaus, and Kastner examined a variety of possible explanations of diffuse support for the Court.[102] They tested variables such as "absence of concern about federal power, youthful idealization, political partisanship, a view of government as a monolith, sympathy for the underdog, liberalism, and agreement with particular decisions."[103] The authors concluded that attitudes toward public policy were the best predictors of support for the Court at that time: conservatives expressed disapproval of the Court's policies while liberals approved of them.

Most studies have similarly concluded that diffuse support for the Court (typically defined as broad and enduring "institutional goodwill")[104] is primarily a function of ideology and "specific" support (defined as agreement with and support for the Court's policy decisions).[105] Like the Kastner, Murphy, and Tanenhaus study mentioned above, Murphy and Tanenhaus found a substantial connection between diffuse support for the Court among the mass public and partisanship, ideology, and agreement with the Court's policies (with correlations ranging from .45 to .55); the correlations were even higher (up to .80) for elites.[106] As William Daniels concluded from his review of much of this research, "In broad perspective, reactions to the Court were policy-oriented. That is, the public tended not to react to the niceties of the decisionmaking process, but to what the Court in fact decided."[107]

However, the important recent work of Caldeira and Gibson is the first to cast doubt on this conventional wisdom. In their 1987 survey of white Americans, they found that ideology exerted virtually no influence on diffuse support (measured as opposition to fundamental changes in the Court, or "institutional commitment").[108] Attitudes toward specific issues, in most cases, did not influence diffuse support, at least among the mass public. Although those expressing liberal views regarding abortion and residential racial segregation were more supportive of the Court, the relationships were not strong.[109] (However, diffuse support among white "opinion leaders" *was* affected by their policy views.) More significant in predicting diffuse support were "basic value orientations" (toward democracy and toward liberty as opposed to social order), educational level, Court attentiveness, and the "use of ideological schema." The implications of these new findings are uncertain. Clearly, their study taps into a new and different source of attitudes toward the Court, which are not, as is typically the case, powerfully affected by ideology and public policy views.

A final study by Caldeira provides both supporting and conflicting evidence regarding the primacy of political factors in explaining public support for the Court.[110] Caldeira sought to explain aggregate changes in public confidence in the Supreme Court from 1966 through 1984 (ranging from a high of 50 percent of the public expressing great confidence in the Court in 1966 to a low of 23 percent in 1971). After testing a variety of variables for their explanatory power, he concluded that

> during the period from 1966 through 1984, crime and economic conditions played relatively small roles as determinants of public confidence . . . [while] political events and judicial actions registered striking impacts on changes in the public's view of the justices. More specifically, in descending order, the Johnson administration, Watergate, judicial support for the accused, the salience of the Court, invalidations of federal laws, and presidential popularity brought about statistically signficant movements in public feelings toward the justices of the Supreme Court during this period.[111]

Of special relevance, increased judicial activism (expressed as an increasing number of Supreme Court invalidations of federal statutes) did in fact decrease public confidence in the Court, in contrast to an earlier study of a state supreme court.[112] In fact, "for each federal statute the Court has struck down in the past 17 years, public confidence in the justices has declined about 2.4%."[113] (Perhaps this explains why the Court overturns about ten times as many state laws as federal laws[114] and is more deferential to federal compared to state statutes.[115])

However, Caldeira's evidence also supports the scholarly consensus that citizens react to the substance of the Court's decisions and evaluate those decisions in terms of personal policy preferences. For example, the Court lost public confidence in direct relation to its greater solicitude for the rights of criminal defendants.[116] Clearly, "shifts in public confidence in the Court march to the beat of a markedly policy-oriented drummer. . . . In broad outlines, then, the dynamics of aggregate support for the Court bear a remarkable resemblance to those for Congress and the presidency."[117]

Reinforcing these conclusions regarding the importance of political factors in public evaluations of the Court is Caldeira and Smith's analysis of public opinion regarding the Clarence Thomas nomination. A number of factors influenced public attitudes toward Thomas, such as race, gender, and approval of President Bush. However, more powerful were political party and ideology: "opinion on Thomas, like evaluations of other political figures and issues, turned to a great extent on partisan commitment and ideological conviction."[118]

Public Support for the Court: A Summary

Support for the Supreme Court presents a puzzle. How is it that a nonelective institution without enforcement powers is able to command public support and compliance, even when it issues unpopular decisions? The conventional answer has been that the public views the Court in a unique way, as exalted and impartial, and that the Court benefits from the nation's reverence for the Constitution.

Public opinion research clearly and convincingly refutes the conventional wisdom. As Caldeira simply states the matter, "Citizens know surprisingly little about the Court and the workings of the judicial branch, manifest scant concern about its personnel and about most decisions, and offer support contingent upon agreement with specific public policies."[119] Additionally, ideology explains to a significant degree not only individual attitudes toward the Court, but changes in aggregate public support over time.[120]

One certainly cannot conclude that there exists *no* mythic attachment to or expectations regarding the Court among the general public.[121] However, the notion that the public possesses great reverence for the Court and its constitutional role is simply not supported. Also not receiving empirical verification is the conventional expectation that the Court's violation of norms regarding mechanical jurisprudence or impartiality greatly reduces public support. Support for the Court is lukewarm and does not greatly exceed support for other institutions. Perceptions of the Court's constitutional role or expectations of impartiality are not widely or strongly held. Support for and opposition to the Court are in fact best explained by political agreement or disagreement with the Court's policy decisions (and perhaps by broader "value-orientations").[122]

Revising and Reappraising the Puzzle

Perhaps one reason why the conventional explanation of reverence for the Court fails to solve the puzzle of the Court's power is that there is not much of a puzzle to solve. The mystery scholars attempt to unravel is public support for and compliance with the Court's unpopular decisions and countermajoritarian role. However, this assumes that, in fact, public support for the Court is high, that compliance is assured, that the Court's interventions are necessarily unpopular, and that the Court plays a countermajoritarian role.

Contrary to these assumptions, public opinion research does not indicate that the public supports the Court in a deep or profound way, except in the sense of not favoring its elimination.[123] Nor does the public in any case pay much attention to the Court. Furthermore, the Court does not always receive full or uncritical compliance, as numerous impact studies demonstrate; rather, compliance is often limited, incomplete, or uneven.[124]

Finally, the Court does not always issue unpopular decisions or play an unpopular role. This is not to say that the Court always acts in accordance with public opinion. Certainly its flag burning and school prayer decisions are proof of that.[125] However, as several studies have proven, the Court does not exclusively or persistently act in opposition to public opinion or the will of representative bodies. As Barnum's study of the relationship between public opinion and Supreme Court policies in the post–New Deal era indicates, the "countermajoritarian reputation" of the Court is greatly exaggerated.[126]

Except for the area of school prayer, the Court's decisions (e.g., regarding access to birth control, school desegregation, the role of women) occurred in the context of either increasing public support or even majority public support. The Court then often sided with national opinion against state law.[127] Additionally, where public opinion was divided or growing in opposition (e.g., affirmative action, busing, death penalty, legalization of homosexual activity), the Court was largely deferential or equivocal.

Mishler and Sheehan's examination of the "public mood" and the "liberalness" of the Court's decisions from 1956 to 1989 provided similar results. They found that "for most of the period since 1956, the Court has been highly responsive to majority opinion. Its decisions . . . have conformed closely to the aggregate policy opinions of the American public."[128] Marshall and Ignagni studied the Court's decisions in cases involving civil rights, civil liberties, and equality claims from 1953 to 1992 and similarly found that "the Court's record of supporting rights claims often follows public opinion. When public opinion opposed the claim, so typically did the Supreme Court, supporting less than half (40 percent) of these claims. When public opinion was either evenly divided or supported the claim, however, the Court supported 73 percent and 67 percent of these claims, respectively."[129] Similar conclusions were reached by Stimson, Mackuen, and Erikson. Their empirical evidence demonstrated that "court decisions do, in fact, vary in accord with current public preferences" although they do so less strongly and less quickly than for the president, House, and Senate.[130]

Marshall's study of public opinion and the Court is especially significant. He analyzed 146 instances in which national polls existed on an issue decided by the Supreme Court from 1935 through 1986. He found that "a clear majority [about 62 percent] of the 146 Supreme Court decisions were consistent with public opinion."[131] This is especially significant in light of the results of studies regarding the general relationship between public opinion and government policy. Monroe found that public opinion and public policy were consistent 64 percent of the time (in 222 instances between 1960 and 1974), and a study by Page and Shapiro revealed that policy change was congruent with public opinion change 66 percent of the time (in 231 instances between 1935 and 1979).[132] Thus, Marshall concludes, "The modern Court appears neither markedly more nor less consistent with the polls than are other policy makers."[133]

Marshall then tested a number of possible explanations for the Court's majoritarian decisionmaking behavior.[134] He found that the Court was especially likely to agree with public opinion during crisis times.[135] It was more deferential to Congress than to state or local governments, upholding 76 percent of federal laws compared to 49 percent of state and local laws.[136] (However, it is significant that state and local laws were less likely than congressional statutes to reflect nationwide public opinion.)[137] The Court was also more likely to uphold state or federal laws that were consistent with national opinion as compared to state or federal laws that were inconsistent with national opinion; nonetheless, the Court still upheld a clear majority (63 percent) of inconsistent federal laws.

Especially significant for our purposes here are Marshall's findings regarding the longevity of Supreme Court rulings.[138] A Court decision was more likely to "prevail" or persist through time if it was liberal and unanimously rendered, if it was made during a noncrisis time, *and* if it reflected popular opinion. Furthermore, "the Court's agreement with public opinion better explained a ruling's longevity than whether the decision was a full, written one; whether the decision involved fundamental freedoms or economic claims; or whether the ruling demonstrated judicial activism or judicial restraint."[139]

The evidence supports Marshall's conclusion that "overall, the modern Court has been an essentially majoritarian institution."[140] Additionally, about half of the time in which the Court practiced "judicial activism" in that it overturned a law, its decisions reflected rather than contradicted nationwide public opinion. Just as Barnum has argued, when the Court overturns a state law that lacks majority support nationally or a federal law that no longer commands majority support, the Court is in effect "making a direct contribution to the operation of majoritarian democracy in the United States."[141] Certainly the Court often rules against public opinion, as it did in one-third of its rulings in Marshall's survey.[142] However, the Court is not substantially or persistently a countermajoritarian institution.

We now return to the puzzle of how the Court maintains public support and respect in spite of it unpopular rulings. Clearly, there is not much of a puzzle to solve. The Court does not enjoy widespread support or complete and uncritical compliance with its decisions. Nor does the Court act primarily and consistently in opposition to majority opinion. Thus, attempting to explain the mysteriously high public support and compliance levels regarding the Court's persistently unpopular decisions is akin to studying the snake population of Ireland.

The question (and the answer) regarding the Court's legitimacy then may not be so unique. Public support for and obedience to the Court appears in the end to be little different from that concerning other political institutions. A variety of studies suggests that support for the Court and its decisions is contingent upon several political factors. To the degree that a number of political conditions prevail, the Court will receive public support or, more accurately, will not arouse or anger the public so that noncompliance or sanctions against the Court become a threat. Those conditions include: political agreement with the policy decisions of the Court among the public,[143] among strategically located political elites,[144] or among interest groups;[145] public support for and confidence in other institutions and the system as a whole;[146] divided public and elite opinion;[147] the existence of structural fragmentation in which "clipping the judicial wings" is made more difficult and is preventable even by a small core of Court supporters;[148] and restraint on the part of the Court in "goring too many oxen" at any one time.[149] Empirical research has, on the other hand, provided negligible support for the claim that judicial activism, careless legal reasoning, or failure to comply with myth-related expectations exact a significant price in terms of public support for the Court.[150]

Implications for Judicial Behavior

In *Dennis* v. *United States,* Justice Felix Frankfurter argued that "history teaches that the independence of the judiciary is jeopardized when courts become embroiled in the passions of the day and assume primary responsibility in choosing between competing political, economic, and social pressures."[151] Frankfurter's message is the conventional judicial restraint position that activism of a political sort exacts a great price in terms of loss of legitimacy and independence. The message or lesson learned from public opinion research, however, is quite different.

Of course, Frankfurter's advice that the Court not assume *primary* responsibility for resolving dominant political issues cannot be disputed on grounds of democratic theory or political prudence. However, his admonition that the Court refrain from entering the political fray as a general rule is nonsense and would likely prove to be costly. The Court is typically rather than atypically caught up in the controversial issues of the day. And it is brought into those controversies at the request of litigants, typically interest groups. The Court would be *more* rather than less likely to lose its relevance, and thus its power, should it consistently refuse to involve itself in such issues at the behest of groups dissatisfied with the results of their legislative or administrative resolution.

Furthermore, Frankfurter fails to recognize that the Court comes under political attack only when it is politically insensitive and politically "incorrect" in its handling of those issues. As always, the *Lochner* and anti–New Deal Courts loom large in judicial restraint advocacy. Presumably the Court "played with fire" by trying to dictate the nation's economic policies from the bench, and by additionally doing so armed only with a weak and unpersuasive interpretation of the due process clause, the Tenth Amendment, and Congress's commerce power. The Court did indeed come under severe political attack, including FDR's assault on the Court's independence via his Court-packing plan.

That attack, however, was a result of extreme political frustration with the Court's obstructionism. It was not the product of a clear and specific public attitude that the Court lacked the constitutional authority either to intervene at all or once it did, to decide as it did. Nor is it likely that the public was then considerably more knowledgeable regarding the specific content of the Court's opinions than is typically the case today. In fact, public opinion research shows that public support for or opposition to the Court at that time was principally a function of political party affiliation.[152] Quite simply, regardless of the textual or otherwise justifiable bases of the Court's opinions, both the public and political leaders disagreed quite fundamentally with the Court's general doctrine that government intervention in the economy was only rarely permissible. The Court unsuccessfully sought to advance a political viewpoint that had become quite unpopular, and the Court was made to retreat.

The lesson to be learned is not that the Court should stay away from controversial issues or even from economic issues. Nor is the lesson that the Court must stick closely to the text and the Framers' intent, since its subsequent doctrine—that the Constitution provides for *no* judicially enforced economic rights—is certainly less persuasive in those terms than was its pre-1937 doctrine. The lesson is simply that should the Court persistently issue decisions that are patently and substantially out of sync with dominant public opinion and the dominant political leadership, the Court can and will be brought to heel. Again, as the New Deal episode and public opinion research demonstrates, public support is determined by the *political* acceptability of its decisions rather than the presence of persuasive constitutional authority for the Court's intervention and its subsequent decisions.

There are a number of important lessons to be learned both from the Court's history and from public opinion research. First, given public inattention, divisions and ambiguities in public and elite opinion, and structural fragmentation, the Court enjoys considerable room in which to maneuver in its policymaking endeavors. Because of its protection from immediate electoral reprisal, the Court also enjoys relatively more room than other branches do. Thus, the Court does have some capacity to act in an unpopular fashion. However, the Court does not enjoy unlimited freedom to do so. Public and elite support is to a large extent conditioned on political agreement with the Court's policy decisions. Thus, the Court must exercise political caution and be sufficiently responsive or sensitive to public and elite opinion so as not to wake the sleeping lion.[153]

If it wishes to retain its relevance in American politics and its power to shape public policy, the Court needs mechanisms that enable it to make those critical political judgments. For example, it must be capable of deciding whether it can withstand political attacks if it rules against race discrimination or flag burning or the death penalty. That of course is a political judgment, a necessarily uncertain judgment regarding the strength and endurance of one's political allies and opponents.

The two previous chapters have outlined precisely those mechanisms which increase the likelihood that the Court's policies will prove acceptable and that the Court will accurately appraise its chances of surviving with its policy course and its legitimacy and power intact. For example, when the selection process is politically controlled and when ideology is the overriding selection criteria, we are more likely to end up with a Court whose members are representative in terms of their policy views. Furthermore, when the justices come from within the ranks of the political elite, the justices are more likely to possess the knowledge to anticipate and the contacts to discover the political reactions to its decisions.[154] To the degree that the justices care deeply about their policy goals, they will be attentive to and if need be respond to political opposition to its decisions, which is expressed in a variety of ways, from amicus and solicitor general briefs to Court-curbing bills in Congress to presidential speeches.[155]

The conventional wisdom that an active, political Court will inevitably violate widely held norms of apolitical, impartial decisionmaking and, thus, will lose its legitimacy and power is simply not true. In fact, it is when the Court persistently fails to involve itself in the political process or cares only about textual or legally defensible decisional criteria or excludes political calculations from its decisionmaking that it courts danger. In short, it is a political Court—a generally responsive, politically aware, and politically sensitive Court—that guarantees the ongoing public and elite support necessary to preserve its policymaking power.

Truth in Judging?

One might (although I do not) take this lesson regarding public support for the Court to its logical extreme. The Court's support is in large part a function of political agreement with its decisions. The Court's relative freedom to shape policy is also a function of public opinion often being divided, ambiguous, or weakly held, and a function as well of the ability of a small group of Court supporters to halt Court-curbing efforts.[156]

Why not then permit the Court to or even insist that it write its opinions in an honest and forthright manner? Why not require that the justices simply state that, in their view, a certain policy is beneficial to society (and is politically feasible), rather than arguing that their policy choice is dictated by legal text or precedent?

A number of scholars have in fact called for "truth in judging."[157] They ask the Court to defend its value and policy choices on the merits rather than in terms of consistency with legal text and precedent. The primary appeal of this decisionmaking model is its greater compatibility with democratic values: the people should be permitted to know what its leaders are deciding and why and should be permitted to judge for themselves whether those decisions constitute wise and desirable policy.

However, the evidence suggests that in fact the public *does* evaluate the Court's decisions in this way. Of course, one may decry the general lack of public attention and knowledge concerning the Court's decisions. But when the Court does engage the public, support or opposition ensues according to political agreement with the Court's policy decisions.

Additionally, I have not argued here nor does the evidence show that the public holds *no* myth-related expectations regarding the Court. For example, Casey's research findings show that "the strength of the myth's hold makes the suggestions . . . that the Supreme Court jettison its myth and function instead on the merits of its rulings alone appear risky."[158]

I have also not argued that the support of the academic and professional legal community, the standard bearers of the judicial myth, is of *no* consequence for the Court's legitimacy and support. As Martin Shapiro argues, the Court is stronger for the support of both the bar (as important opinion leaders) and the bench (lower court judges who must carry out the Court's rulings).[159] Accordingly, their demands for something more in a judicial opinion than statements of personal political preference—for example, principled decisions rooted in text and precedent—should be heeded. Thus, as a political strategy, the Court should be attentive to both public and professional expectations (e.g., of impartiality or consistency with text and precedent) and attempt to satisfy them where possible. Although satisfying myth-related expectations does not bear so directly or critically on the Court's legitimacy as the conventional wisdom tells us, not doing so may entail at least some risk. And, as has been previously discussed, the pursuit of a justice's policy preferences within the parameters of what is politically feasible does not necessarily act as a bar to writing an intelligent, coherent, and principled piece of legal reasoning.

As long as the political acceptability of the Court's policymaking performance is the overriding factor in influencing the Court's legitimacy, then the subsidiary goal of pleasing the bench and bar is not so problematic as the truth seekers assume. Judicial activism and decisionmaking based on personal political preference or calculations of political acceptability do not pose a great threat to the Court's power and independence. What does pose such a threat is extreme judicial restraint or, alternatively, judicial activism accompanied by political insensitivity and carelessness.

The Real Puzzle: Why the Legitimacy Crisis Argument Persists

Prescriptions that the Court avoid political entanglements and satisfy norms of legal certainty and judicial impartiality in order to preserve its legitimacy lack empirical grounding. The evidence consistently demonstrates the public's lack of knowledge of and affect toward the Supreme Court. It further reveals political factors to be more important than myth satisfaction in influencing public support for the Court. Why then do these prescriptions survive in spite of their dependence on erroneous empirical assertions? What might be the normative underpinnings and implications of the idea of popular reverence for the Court, which has enabled it to survive despite empirical evidence to the contrary?

Part of the answer may lie in the implications of the empirical evidence for the image of the Court and for its guardianship, traditionally performed by the academic and professional legal community. As Martin Shapiro notes, the interests of the lawyer and law professor and the interests of the political scientist with regard to the Court are quite different.

> The political scientist . . . does not yet worry much about the results of his teachings because he has seen so few. But the lawyer, and particularly the law teacher, knows that what he teaches concerning the nature of law and courts today will determine the attitudes and actions of the next generation at the bench and bar. He must worry about not only whether what he is saying is true, but how what he is saying affects the position of the courts and his profession. Furthermore, the political scientist feels no vested interest in the institution he studies; the student of the Interstate Commerce Commission does not care particularly whether it lives or dies. The lawyer, on the other hand, has a personal and professional loyalty to courts, a loyalty considerably reinforced by material considerations. Taken at its most cynical or most exalted level, the lawyer's interest in maintaining the health and prestige of the Supreme Court and other courts is a deep and abiding one.[160]

The legal community then has a personal stake in developing and preserving a special reverence for the Court.

There also exists a stake in preserving its mediating and guardianship role. If the public does and perhaps should evaluate the Court, like other institutions, in terms of the political acceptability of its decisions, then the appropriate mediators and guardians are political leaders rather than leaders in the law schools and organized bar.

Greg Caldeira has also questioned the curious survival of the idea that the Court's legitimacy is a function of mythical reverence for it. He suggests, accurately I believe, that the idea has "proved an invaluable fulcrum in the debate among lawyers, judges, and social scientists about the proper role of the Supreme Court in American political life ... [and] has been—and, I suspect, will continue to be—the deus ex machina of lawyers and social scientists of varying ideologies who wish to persuade readers or listeners to accept their own normative view of the Supreme Court."[161] In other words, the idea of the Court's legitimacy being closely tied to public reverence for its mythical attributes and function is a useful device in the conventional scholar's prescriptions. However, it is used in two distinct ways, even by those scholars previously grouped together under the "neutralist" label.[162]

For neutralist scholars like Herbert Wechsler and Alexander Bickel, reverence for the Court requires judicial restraint. These scholars desire a modest role for the Court, perhaps out of a fear of abuse of power by judges or a preference for the democratic process and legislative dominance. Emphasizing the precarious and myth-based character of the Court's legitimacy provides yet another piece of "evidence" supporting their call for restraint. Thus, neutralists advocating judicial modesty are able to use the public reverence notion to their advantage: "The Court has a reservoir of trust which it might lose if [it] became too 'active'; thus the Court should exercise 'restraint.' "[163] The idea that the Court is uniquely dependent on the public's reverence for it and its special function is rhetorically and ideologically useful for advocates of judicial restraint, even if it is not empirically correct.

The notion of public idealization of the Court may also prove useful to neutralist scholars advocating judicial activism, such as Michael Perry or Laurence Tribe. As Caldeira explains, "Similarly ... the notion can be used to justify ... activism—the Court has a reservoir of trust which it will retain regardless of specific decisions; thus the Court should assume a more 'active' role."[164] Reverence for the Court permits it to accomplish socially desirable ends, which legislatures are not free to pursue. For example, the Court can protect minority rights or advance "society's fundamental values," even if those decisions would prove unacceptable if rendered by elective bodies.

Underpinning this particular use of the public idealization thesis by non-interpretivists is not a fear of judicial abuse or a preference for the more democratic legislative process. Rather, it is a fear of or skepticism toward the democratic process, and legislative decisionmaking in particular. This leads the "neutralist-activist" scholar to emphasize the *freedom* for the Court that public reverence provides.

Quite simply, neutralist scholars advocating judicial activism do not trust the people or their elected representatives to "do the right thing." As Paul Brest notes, most conventional constitutional theorists "do not believe that 'majorities' and legislatures are willing or able to engage in serious, reflective moral discourse."[165] Michael Perry is without a doubt the most skeptical of the Skeptics. For example, he believes that, "as a matter of comparative institutional competence, the politically insulated federal judiciary is more likely, when the human rights issue is a deeply controversial one, to move us in the direction of a right answer . . . than is the political process left to its own devices, which tends to resolve such issues by reflexive, mechanical reference to established moral conventions."[166] When the legislature makes a policy decision, it does so based on "established moral conventions . . . [or] at least typically . . . does not challenge those conventions."[167] The Court on the other hand bases its decisions on a more open and thorough moral inquiry, thus leading to a "far more self-critical political morality than would otherwise appear, and therefore likely a more mature political morality as well . . . rather than a stagnant or even regressive morality."[168] Given this characterization of legislative and judicial decisionmaking, it is no wonder that Perry advocates judicial activism in human rights issues.[169]

Defending the quality of legislative decisionmaking is not the primary task here. Nonetheless, it is not difficult to challenge Perry's assumption that the legislature addresses issues of national importance in only a reflexive manner. Perhaps attending a legislative hearing or debate would alter Perry's view that legislators blindly reflect "stagnant moral conventions" or merely look to their morally impoverished constituents and interest group supporters. While not all issues receive the sort of thoughtful and comprehensive consideration we might desire, issues of great importance and salience (slavery, civil rights, environmental protection, welfare reform, even the wisdom of the Vietnam War or military aid to the contras) have received more than cursory treatment by the Congress.

One might argue (as I would) that the proper solution to a democracy or political process that is of poor quality, if indeed that is what we have, is to improve its quality. The "activist neutralist" solution to the moral impoverishment of the people and their elected representatives, however, is to bypass the democratic process and grant power to our moral superiors, Supreme Court justices. Fortunately, they are protected from political reprisal by the reverence the public holds for the Court.

As it was for neutralist scholars advocating judicial *restraint,* the notion that the Court possesses a reservoir of public trust based on reverence (although empirically incorrect) is of value to neutralists advocating *activism.* Skepticism toward politics generally and legislatures more particularly requires moral leadership from an institution that is best able to provide it and that is least likely to suffer politically as a result. Given its special qualities and attributes and the high esteem in which the public holds it, that institution is the Supreme Court.

Conclusion

The idea that public reverence for the Court is the key to its legitimacy plays an important role in conventional scholars' various prescriptions for the Court's constitutional role, as well as their opposition to a political Court. However, that particular pillar of conventional constitutional theory, like that of objectively constrained constitutional interpretation, is a faulty one.

The public does not hold the Court in particularly high regard and does not view it in exalted terms. When the public does pay attention to the Court's decisions, it evaluates them (and the Court) largely in political terms. Thus, the Court may risk its support by intervening in ongoing political controversies, but only if it persistently does so in callous disregard of the views of the public and other political leaders. Thus, it is not a political Court per se, which jeopardizes its legitimacy and its ability to play a role in the national policymaking process. In fact, continued legitimacy *demands* that the Court be policy motivated and, thus, politically sensitive and responsible in the exercise of its power.

CHAPTER 7

• •

Democratic Theory Revisited

CONVENTIONAL legal scholars regard constitutional decisionmaking motivated by the personal political preferences of the justices as illegitimate and as precisely the evil to be avoided. Those personal views after all have not been tested in elections and approved by voters. Nor do voters have the opportunity to reject those views, and the justices who hold them, via electoral retribution. And when the Court rests a decision on the Constitution rather than a statute, not even a majority in the electorate or in Congress is capable of reversing it. As these scholars point out, that is certainly not what one would expect in a democracy.

However, as this chapter seeks to prove, these conventional scholars, or "neutralists," rest their entire enterprise, their resolution of the legitimacy question, and their condemnation of value-voting on a view of American democracy that is fundamentally flawed. There are in fact two flaws to be examined here. The first is a serious one, the second is fatal.

As the first part of the chapter demonstrates, the neutralists overstate the degree to which the "political" branches are subject to majoritarian influences and understate the degree to which the Court is subject to democratic influences. Once acknowledged, the persuasiveness of the claim that the Court is *uniquely* deviant and antimajoritarian and, therefore, in need of some extraordinary form of legitimacy is greatly reduced.

The last half of the chapter then addresses the second and fatal flaw in the neutralists' arguments: their assertion that the central principles of American democracy are majority rule, electoral accountability, and legislative supremacy. While judicial review and value-voting would be correctly viewed as possessing dubious legitimacy in a majoritarian, legislative-centered system, the American political system is neither majoritarian nor legislative-centered. Rather, it is "pluralist" in structure and operation.

In a pluralist system, there are numerous and diverse political institutions that are nonhierarchically arranged. This increases the opportunities for groups to advance their interests effectively and contest policies with which they disagree. The legitimacy of each institution is determined not by its "democraticness" but by its instrumental value in providing access points for the expression of opposing views and interests. In this pluralist enterprise, judicial review and value-voting are not illegitimate but, rather, play a significant, integral, and legitimate part.

The Neutralist Theory of American Democracy

It is somewhat misleading to speak of a neutralist theory of American democracy as if there is a clearly elaborated and unanimously supported theory as such readily available in the literature. In fact, there is often scant attention given by these scholars to their assumptions regarding the nature of American democracy, an issue that is obviously critical to determining the Court's fit with or role in that system. Evidence of the neutralists' beliefs regarding the defining features of American democracy most often comes indirectly, in the context of their assertions regarding the Court. For example, the most common claim is that the Court is countermajoritarian, the logical inference being that the rest of the system is majoritarian. The majoritarian character of American democracy is a given, a take-off point for attending to the problematical nature of the Court, rather than itself a subject for explanation and defense.

Although this particular approach is most common, there are a few (but only a few) exceptions. For example, Alexander Bickel and Jesse Choper have taken greater care in explaining their use of the majoritarian label.[1] Even more unusual, Cass Sunstein has discussed the pluralist nature of the political process,[2] and Erwin Chemerinsky has confronted head on what he believes is a faulty yet dominant "majoritarian paradigm" in constitutional law scholarship.[3] Bruce Ackerman has also rejected what he terms a "monistic" version of American democracy, in which any interference with the decisions of the most recent electoral winners is presumptively antidemocratic.[4] However, as noted above, these are the exceptions. Most conventional scholars endorse, either explicitly or implicitly, the theory of American democracy that is outlined below.

The adjective most often used by the neutralists to describe American democracy is *majoritarian*. John Hart Ely states that "majoritarian democracy is . . . the core of our entire system."[5] Jesse Choper asserts that "whether one looks to such classical theorists as Aristotle, Locke, and Rousseau, to such mainstays of American political thinking as Madison, Jefferson, and Lincoln, or to this nation's constitutional development from its origin to the present time, majority rule has been considered the keystone of a democratic political system in both theory and practice."[6]

This central principle of majority rule is in turn used to conclude that the Court is undemocratic. For example, in a frequently cited passage Alexander Bickel asserts:

> The root difficulty is that judicial review is a countermajoritarian force in our system. . . . [W]hen the Supreme Court declares unconstitutional a legislative act or the action of an elected executive, it thwarts the will of representatives of the actual people of the here and now; it exercises control, not in behalf of the prevailing majority, but against it. That [is] the reason the charge can be made that judicial review is undemocratic.[7]

In asserting that judicial review is deviant and undemocratic, the neutralists additionally emphasize the Court's lack of electoral accountability, the absence of electoral recourse should the people disagree with the Court's decisions. However, this is regarded as problematic only with regard to constitutional rather than statutory review since Congress can reverse the Court's statutory interpretations by ordinary legislation. Thus, Ely argues that, unlike statutory review, judicial rulings of unconstitutionality are "not subject to 'correction' by the ordinary lawmaking process" leading to "the central problem . . . of judicial review: a body that is not elected or otherwise politically responsible in any significant way is telling the people's elected representatives that they cannot govern as they'd like."[8]

The neutralists, thus, appear to believe that the central component of American democracy is majority rule. The will of the majority is expressed through the electoral process and enforced through the norm of legislative supremacy. It is assumed that legislative decisions represent majority preferences since, at a minimum, they are subject to majority reversal through elections. Legislative decisions are therefore presumptively superior, perhaps inviolable. Accordingly, when the Supreme Court strikes down a statute as unconstitutional, it is thwarting the will of the majority and that majority has no recourse.

Given this version of the workings of American democracy and of judicial review, it is not surprising that the neutralists regard judicial review as "antithetical to democracy" and as "cut[ting] directly against the grain of traditional democratic philosophy."[9] Nor is it surprising that the traditional scholar must search for some extraordinary and exceptional justification for the Court's power. Typically, the legitimacy of judicial review rests on the availability of neutral grounds for the Court's decisions or on the special attributes, insights, or abilities of its members, for example as moral prophets (as in Perry's theory),[10] superior democratic theorists (as in Ely's),[11] or legal historians (as in Berger's).[12] Given their emphasis on electoral accountability, it is also not surprising that the neutralists oppose constitutional decisionmaking motivated by the personal values and political judgments of the justices. According to the neutralist perspective, those personal values and political judgments are an arbitrary and undemocratic decisionmaking source, given that they are untested and irreversible in the electoral marketplace.

This theory of American democracy as majoritarian, electorally driven, and legislative-centered is the source of and the engine driving the conventional approach to saving the Court's legitimacy. However, as a respected scholar of American politics and the Court, Martin Shapiro, pointed out over thirty years ago, that description of American democracy represents "the most starry-eyed political naivete" and seems to be based more on "the cliches of . . . high school civics books" rather than on an informed analysis of how American government actually works.[13] Simply put, "there can be no automatic and blanket equation of Congress or the Executive branch with the voice of the people."[14]

The Response of Political Science

It is stating the obvious to say that democracies are organized in different ways in order to achieve certain values over others. Majority rule is certainly one such option and has obvious advantages for the scholar in terms of intellectual simplicity. However, for a variety of reasons, it is not a concept or normative standard that can be accurately and profitably applied for purposes of understanding and evaluating American democracy. With regard to both electoral and decisionmaking processes, majorities simply have insufficient significance and force to warrant the conclusion that American democracy is majoritarian.

For a number of reasons, elections do not operate in the United States in such a way as to enable majority expression and control. As Robert Dahl explains, there are inherent limitations on the ability of elections to reveal the policy preferences of the majority.[15] It is unlikely that, but in any case is impossible to know whether, each member of the majority votes for a particular candidate for the same policy reasons, even assuming that the policy differences of each candidate are perceived and used as the basis of voting. As a result, "strictly speaking, all an election reveals is the first preference of some citizens among the candidates standing for office."[16] The policy meaning of the majority's vote is necessarily ambiguous.

Additionally, survey research consistently demonstrates that most Americans are not interested in, attentive to, or informed about politics.[17] They lack specific knowledge or firm opinions regarding most issues. Their views are not well organized, (i.e., they do not constitute a coherent ideology) and, at the individual level, they are quite unstable. Thus, public opinion in the United States regarding the major issues of the day is characterized by ambivalence, incoherence, instability, and diversity. This absence of clear and enduring policy-preference groupings necessarily makes majority formation and expression more difficult.

Of course, political parties, in order to attract broad popular support sufficient to win elections and gain control of the government, are supposed to aggregate and organize citizen preferences. However, political parties in the United States have historically been weak and highly decentralized.[18] In addition, their role and power in electoral and governing processes has declined considerably in the the last quarter century: voter attachment to political parties has declined; split-ticket voting has increased; and, with the rise of direct primaries, political consultants, and television's power to reach voters, parties have lost power in the election process itself.[19] Thus, American political parties possess only a limited capacity for organizing the morass of policy preferences into coherent and comprehensive policy packages (and for then enforcing adherence to that platform by all of the party's candidates). In other words, a policy-relevant majority does not exist in a natural state *or* as the result of citizens' identification with and votes for a political party.

At the same time that parties have declined, interest groups have proliferated.[20] This explosion in the number, variety, and independence of organized interests is yet another source of fragmentation in and splintering of the American electorate.[21]

Should a meaningful majority somehow arise, it would have to possess sufficient strength and unity to overcome the difficulties posed by the use of staggered and independent elections, devices created by the Framers specifically to inhibit majority rule. We do not simultaneously elect a national leadership corps in the United States. Instead, the president and the members of the House and Senate are elected independently of each other, by different constituencies, and for different terms of office. To transmit a policy message in an unequivocal manner would require that national majorities develop and sustain a meaningful policy unity in a sufficient number of congressional districts, states, and heavily populated geographical areas made relevant by the electoral college. That unity must additionally be maintained over a sufficient period of time, in order to gain control of the Senate (only one-third of which is elected every two years) and the presidency (elected every four years), while retaining control of the House (every member up for election every two years). And, of course, neither the Senate nor presidency is designed to represent a "national majority." In fact, as originally designed in the Constitution, neither was to be elected directly by the people. Additionally, distortions in popular representation occur in the Senate as small states receive more representation than their population size warrants. And the electoral college, particularly the winner-take-all rule, produces distortions in how the popular vote is translated into electoral votes; it may even award the presidency to a candidate who fails to win a majority, or even a plurality, of the popular votes.[22] To state it simply, elections in the United States are not well designed or well suited to ascertaining the will of the majority in a definitive manner.

Yet another blow to the claim that laws passed by Congress and signed by the President represent the majority will is the phenomenon of low, declining, and unrepresentative voter turnout.[23] Only half of all eligible voters have cast their ballots in recent presidential elections, and only 49 percent of eligible voters did so in 1996, the lowest level since 1924. Turnout in off-year congressional elections is even lower, dipping in recent years below the 40 percent mark. Those who vote are additionally unrepresentative of the population as a whole: they are older, better educated, and wealthier. Furthermore, the "class gap" in voter turnout is increasing.[24]

Finally, elections have, in any case, "become less decisive as mechanisms for resolving conflicts and constituting governments in the United States."[25] Emblematic of what Ginsberg and Shefter refer to as America's "postelectoral political order" are low voter turnout, a decline in the competitiveness of congressional races,[26] and an extraordinary level of interbranch conflict and stalemate. Replacing success in popular mobilization as the primary path to power is "institutional combat," characterized by legislative investigations, charges and countercharges played out in the media, and bitter battles over executive and judicial appointments. The result is "the decay of electoral democracy in the United States."[27]

Even if the majority was able to transmit its preferences through political parties and elections in a meaningful way, their effective translation into government policy confronts additional obstacles. For example, members of Congress increasingly devote themselves to activities that are electorally profitable (e.g., constituency service in the form of pork barrel and casework), but nonprogrammatic and, in a sense, nonlegislative.[28] In addition, the structure and decisionmaking processes of Congress greatly inhibit its capacity to act as a national policymaker on behalf of a national majority.[29] Congress is not only divided into two houses (which may be controlled by different parties), but is further divided into nearly three hundred committees and subcommittees. This is ostensibly for the sake of economy and the development of policy expertise. However, due to the workings of the norms of seniority and reciprocity, as well as the subcommittee bill of rights passed in the early 1970s, these committees have come to exercise considerable power over their policy domains, which they jealously guard. (Committee power remains substantial, despite the recent recentralization of power to the party leadership.) The power of subcommittees and individual members, it must be noted, is not a function of their insight into or ability and desire to represent "the majority will." Reinforcing the considerable decentralization within Congress is the tremendous growth in staff size and influence,[30] as well as the rising importance of informal caucuses. The filibuster and the "hold system" in the Senate represent additional ways in which majority-supported legislation may be impeded or halted.[31] Further complicating the picture are the growing role of political action committees in financing congressional elections[32] and the power of interest groups in shaping legislative outcomes. Congress, then, is increasingly devoted to nonlegislative constituency service and to interest group concerns, it is increasingly "fractured," and its members are increasingly individualistic.[33] It is simply not an institution that directly and automatically reflects (a fictional) majority will; nor can it easily or with certainty build a majority coalition within Congress that in turn represents majority preferences.

The president is elected by the nation as a whole, and the presidential election process has become more plebiscitary and more tied to national interests than the Framers intended; the strategy of "going public" to win popular and congressional approval of his initiatives and actions further strengthens presidential links with the electorate.[34] The President, thus, appears to have a much stronger claim to representing a national majority than the Congress. Additionally, presidential power has greatly increased in the last half century; "presidential government has become an established fact of American life."[35] It is thus surprising that the neutralists do not rest their claim for the majoritarian character of American politics more on the growing strength and democratization of the presidency; their emphasis on Congress and *legislative* supremacy as the path to majority rule is quite curious.

Nonetheless, there are limits to the claim that the president represents the majority will or that, as a consequence, American democracy is majoritarian. Although the presidential election process is indeed more plebiscitary, the electoral college remains a distorting factor in the translation of majority preferences (should they exist) into presidential victory. After all, President Clinton failed to receive a majority of the popular vote in both 1992 and 1996. However, even presidents who win a majority of the popular vote, including President Reagan in his "landslide" victories, cannot claim to have won a majority-supported mandate.[36] For example, in 1980, Reagan received slightly less than 51 percent of the popular vote, and the Democrats won a majority of seats in the House from 1980 through 1986 and a majority of Senate seats in 1986; furthermore, public opinion data collected throughout Reagan's two terms did not show a significant conservative shift despite his election victories.[37]

Additionally, scholars advance not only the notion of "presidential government," but also the theme of the "imperiled" presidency—a substantial and growing gap between presidential responsibilities and the power to fulfill them.[38] There are numerous and significant limitations on the ability of the president to enact the policies he (and perhaps a majority) desires[39]—a more fragmented and independent-minded (and therefore less easily led) Congress; an enormous (and enormously complex) bureaucracy dominated by the career civil servant, as well as agencies more responsive to congressional than presidential desires; a frighteningly fickle public, which reacts negatively to many domestic policy intiatives;[40] entrenched interests who can successfully fend off hostile policy proposals; and the double-edged sword of intense media scrutiny. The discretionary power of individual agencies throughout the executive branch and the growth in the size and power of the Executive Office of the President pose further difficulties for the simplistic majority-rule model.[41]

The most notable characteristic of the structure of American government is fragmentation. Power is dispersed among the separate branches and levels of government, between the House and Senate, within each house of Congress, between the president and Congress, and throughout the bureaucracy. It is an extraordinary task for a majority to build and maintain the requisite strength, unity, and endurance to control and direct the many separate and largely independent centers of decisionmaking power.

To summarize, the key assumption of the neutralists is that American democracy is majoritarian and the Court is, problematically, countermajoritarian. Political scientists have responded that, as an empirical matter, majorities simply have insufficient significance and force in American politics to justify using majority rule as a central explanatory concept. A majority of Americans do not often hold or express their opinions on the issues of the day. Policy preferences in the United States are weakly held and poorly organized and, consequently, resist simplistic majority-minority formulations. Additionally, our weak, decentralized political parties and independent, staggered elections are not structured in such a way as to ascertain or organize a policy-specific majority will. And, finally, the fractured nature of Congress, the numerous independent sites of power, and the fragmented structure of the political system as a whole do not, in any case, permit the swift and effective translation of such a majority will into government policy.

Clearly, the elective branches are not as majoritarian as the neutralists assume. Two implications follow. First, we cannot say with certainty that when the Court overturns a law, it is "thwarting the majority's will." Second, to the degree that the Court is countermajoritarian, it is not uniquely so.

In fact, not only are the "political" branches not as majoritarian or purely democratic as the neutralists would have us believe, neither is the Court so immune from popular and political influences. As previously discussed in chapters 4 and 5, there are a number of formal and informal checks on the Court's power that are democratic in character—most notably, the politically controlled selection process and the discretionary power of Congress and the executive to fund and enforce the Court's decisions. And as chapter 6 demonstrates, the Court's decisions correspond with national public opinion at roughly the same rate as the elective branches.[42]

This then is the response of political science to the claim that the Court is, problematically, a countermajoritarian institution in a majoritarian democracy. Choper has termed it "the sophisticated response" to reconciling judicial review with democratic values and has accurately explained it as follows: "Congress and the executive, the so-called political branches of our government, are by no means as democratic as standard belief would hold and . . . the Court is much more subject to the popular will than conventional wisdom would grant."[43]

The Neutralists' Counterresponse

Only a few of the neutralists have responded to this challenge. However, as will be seen, their theory of American democracy and their view of the Court as a deviant element in that system remain largely unchanged.

Alexander Bickel's approach is to weaken the definition of majority rule, while insisting that it retains its viability as a central explanatory concept. Bickel backs away from the strong assertion that legislative outcomes accurately and uniformly reflect majority preferences.

> Most assuredly, no democracy operates by taking continuous nose counts on the broad range of daily governmental activities. Representative democracies . . . function by electing certain men for certain periods of time, then passing judgment periodically on their conduct of public office. It is a matter of a laying on of hands, followed in time by a process of holding to account—all through the exercise of the franchise. . . . The whole operates under public criticism—but not at all times or in all parts. . . . Nevertheless, although democracy does not mean constant reconsideration of decisions once made, it does mean that a representative majority has the

power to accomplish a reversal. This power is of the essence, and no less so because it is often merely held in reserve.[44]

In this formulation, majority rule is made to mean generalized support by the majority for the cumulative or overall performance of their elected representatives. Emphasis is placed on the electoral threat posed by disgruntled majorities and the strong inducement thus provided legislators to satisfy the majority over time or, at a minimum, to avoid alienating voters to such a degree that electoral retribution is likely to occur. Thus, the norm of majority rule is satisfied, according to Bickel, to the degree that elected representatives are effectively limited to those decisions lying within the majority's "zone of acceptance" or "zone of indifference."[45] According to this interpretation, majority rule seems little more than a form of legitimacy—majority acceptance of specific legislative decisions deriving more from general approval of overall legislative performance than from specific approval of the policy content of individual decisions.

Jesse Choper, too, has responded to the charge that the Court is not so deviant or undemocratic when we recognize the mix of democratic and undemocratic features in the presumably majoritarian political branches. However, he believes that a careful analysis of those charges requires little in the way of revision or retreat. For example, with regard to such legislative features as bicameralism or the filibuster, Choper argues that they "actually [serve] democratic ends for forcing fuller and more open congressional consideration of great issues and by improving the flow of information to the electorate."[46] With regard to the power of committee chairs, party leaders, and conference committees, Choper argues that their power and success require that they operate within the constraints of the active and continuing support of the larger legislative body. Thus, they are subject to broader majoritarian pressures. Choper also takes note of a number of democratizing measures throughout the system: stripping the committee chairs of their dictatorial power, the increasing use of direct primaries rather than "smoke-filled rooms" in selecting presidential nominees, and campaign finance reforms such as disclosure requirements and contribution limits.

Choper also endorses Bickel's view that although interest groups may represent "an impurity or imperfection," they "often tend themselves to be majoritarian in composition and to be subject to broader majoritarian influences."[47] Furthermore, legislative success requires that groups join forces with other groups to form a majority, "and the price of what they sell or buy in the legislature is determined in the biennial or quadrennial electoral marketplace."[48] Thus, power flows only to those groups who "can command the votes of a majority of individuals in the legislature who can command the votes of a majority of individuals in the electorate."[49]

Choper further argues that the various antimajoritarian elements, in any case, "are negative ones, i.e., they work to *prevent* the translation of popular wishes into governing rules rather than to *produce* laws that are contrary to majority sentiment."[50] The legislation the Court reviews does in fact represent the majority's will since it has successfully survived the numerous opportunities for minority challenges. Thus, "the relatively few laws that finally overcome the Congressional obstacle course generally illustrate the national political branches operating at their majoritarian best while the process of judicial review depicts that element of the Court's work and that exertion of federal authority, with the most brittle democratic roots" (27–28). In concluding his reexamination of the political branches, Choper states that "it is clear that the national legislative process conducted by the political branches is not impeccable democracy in action. . . . Despite all the surface blemishes, however, closer examination reveals an underlying and unshrinking core of popular responsibility—not pure majority rule, but rule by government broadly accountable to the majority" (47–48).

Choper then turns to the Court and concludes (along with several other neutralist scholars) that the various political checks on the Court are unwieldy, rarely employed, and, in the end, ineffective (47–51).[51] Thus, the Court is not, as most political scientists claim, subject to significant political control by the people and their elected representatives. For example, Choper argues that "the sustained effort needed to reverse (or even halt) a course of constitutional interpretation through the appointing process is much greater than that required for virtually any legislative program"(50–51). Although he concedes that the Court's dependence on other government officials for enforcing and funding its decisions is a more effective check, it fails "to mak[e] judicial review compatible with majoritarian democracy as it is traditionally conceived or practiced," since few Supreme Court decisions "are capable of generating the intensity of opposition necessary to prevent enforcement," and, in any case, "impelling the Court to bend or draw up in developing doctrine falls far short of causing the Court to break or retreat" (57–58). Although "the antimajoritarian features of all three federal departments bear a certain similarity," there remains, in Choper's view, a critical distinction: "That a majority of the people may ultimately prevail vis-à-vis the Court by outright resistance or through methods of dubious legitimacy under a rule of law, even if a reality, is not the same as their ordained ability to change the composition of the political branches at regularly scheduled periodic elections" (58).

Choper concludes that "[t]he case may be an uneasy one, but given a realistic and balanced view of the operation of the political branches, and especially considering the predominantly negative quality of their antimajoritarianism, the Supreme Court is not as democratic as the Congress and President, and the institution of judicial review is not as majoritarian as the lawmaking process" (58).

This constitutes the three types of responses to the political science critique of the neutralists' theory of American democracy. The first is that, upon reexamination, the political branches are in fact roughly majoritarian in character and operation; in other words, political scientists have overstated their case. The second response is that the case made *for* the popular and elite influences on the Court is also exaggerated; those democratic checks are too weak and ineffective to allow us to regard the Court as a politically responsive and responsible institution. The final reply is that even if we accept that the political branches are imperfectly democratic or majoritarian, that does not change the fact that the Court remains less democratic and less majoritarian than the other branches.

Evaluating the Neutralist Response

In some respects, this reformulation of the neutralist theory of American democracy is correct. For example, elections do of course perform a critical function in insuring that leaders respond to voter desires, even if they fail to transmit a clear, specific, and comprehensive message regarding the policy preferences of the majority. It is also true that the different electoral bases of each institution operate to expand the size and variety of voters and groups that must be taken into account by leaders. Choper and Bickel are also correct that the committee chairs, agency heads, and interest group leaders exercise power over their individual policy domains only within the constraints imposed by the larger political leadership. In other words, their policy decisions are subject to the approval or at least the acquiescence of other political actors.

Where the neutralists err is in their *specific* use of the term *majority*. The notion that it is a majority to whom leaders are accountable is difficult to justify, at least to the degree that the majority versus minority distinction in electoral activity is to be given any great significance. The diverse and widely dispersed voters electing individual candidates to different institutions over time might constitute a numerical majority, but the ties among them are simply too tenuous to make any further claim. As Dahl notes,

> every aggregate of American citizens large enough to constitute a majority of voters is necessarily a rather heterogeneous collection of individuals and groups who may agree on some matters but are sure to disagree on others. No group of like-minded citizens can ever win a national election merely by mobilizing themselves and others who think exactly the way they do. In this sense, no single group can win national elections—only hetero-geneous combination[s] of groups can.[52]

Of course, no numerical majority simultaneously elects the national leadership. In response, Bickel and Choper both argue that the different constit-uencies of each institution "balance out" to constitute, in effect, true major-ity representation. However, there is nothing in those electoral processes to justify the specific use of the term *majority*. Instead, a more appropriate char-acterization is that "elections and political competition do not make for gov-ernment by majorities in any very significant way, but they vastly increase the size, number, and variety of minorities whose preferences must be taken into account by leaders in making policy choices."[53]

Another problem lies in the assertion that decisionmaking within Con-gress and between Congress and the president constitutes a form of majority building. The neutralists fail to note that policymaking does not always take place at the "aggregate" level. Instead, action with regard to individual poli-cies often occurs in what has been referred to as subgovernments or iron triangles.[54] Many policy decisions are a result of bargaining among a subset of congressional subcommittees, bureaucratic agencies, and interest groups most directly concerned with that policy area. These subgovernments usually operate, due to the norm of reciprocity, quite independently of one another and constitute relatively closed policymaking systems. Accordingly, specific policy choices are often shaped by intense, narrowly focused minorities, rather than by a broad majority coalition. Thus, Bickel's and Choper's argument that a minority must actively build a majority coalition before it can succeed in achieving the policy it desires is often incorrect. (They are, further, incorrect that the majority coalition in the legislature represents a majority in the electorate, given the structure of congressional elections and given what is known about public awareness and voter turnout.)

The question remains whether the term *majority* is the appropriate analytical focus and whether it is still deserving of the significance given it by the neutralists. Can we justify as "majoritarian" decisions that are the result of bargaining among a relatively small number of political actors and groups intensely and narrowly interested in that decision merely because they are subject to broad and passive validation by the rest of the political leadership and, even more indirectly, by the people they represent? There is the initial problem of raising this passive validation, although important and of consequence, to the level of a positive endorsement by the people and their representatives. In addition, there is the problem once again of justifying the claim that this general endorsement of or acquiescence in subgovernment policy decisions is specifically majoritarian in character. Given the vagaries of electoral and representational processes, the distribution of power, and institutional norms and habits, such a definitive conclusion is problematic.

Perhaps this makes too much of what is only a minor semantic difference. After all, the neutralists have taken note of the various imperfections and distortions that occur as majority preferences are translated into government policy. They have recast their definition of majority rule as "rule by government broadly accountable to the majority."[55] What is troubling, however, is their insistence that it is "the majority," a term connoting a relatively stable or identifiable group, to whom the political branches are accountable. Typically, the government acts to appease the demands of various groups (which may be large or small in size and number), subject to the validation but more often the passive acquiescence of other groups, the public, and political leaders. Shall we refer to this as "majority rule"? If we concede that it is, then the same standard should be, but in fact is not, applied to the Court to determine the degree to which it is "majoritarian."

The neutralists are much more forgiving of majoritarian imperfections with regard to the "democratic" branches than they are for the Court. For example, Choper has argued that the various formal checks on the Court's power, such as constitutional amendment, impeachment, and congressional power to regulate the Court's appellate jurisdiction, are unwieldy, rarely used, and, therefore, ineffective. However, he merely infers that those controls are ineffective because they are rarely used;[56] while a logical conclusion, it is not based on anything more, such as empirical evidence. As was argued in chapter 5, although it is true that these mechanisms of political control are not often used, this does not necessarily imply they are ineffective. If the Court takes care in its decisions to avoid tempting political leaders to invoke those sanctions, then the Court vitiates the need for their use. This would constitute a form of political responsiveness. In other words, the effectiveness of those mechanisms of political control need not be measured by how often they are successfully invoked, but rather by their *effect on the Court's behavior.*[57]

Choper acknowledges the "rule of anticipated reactions," but only with regard to Congress. For example, in his discussion of the nonmajoritarian-based power of committee chairs, conference committees, and party leaders, he argues that these actors are aware of and take into account the likely reactions of other leaders or the larger legislative body. Choper does not argue that those broader political influences are exerted through formal means, but that they are primarily felt and responded to by committee chairs and party leaders, in an informal, anticipatory manner. Yet, he is unwilling to concede that this same sort of influence might be at work with regard to the formal checks on the Court, though they too are typically held in reserve.

The criterion of majoritarianism that Choper applies is also altered when he turns to the Court. He argues that successfully changing the Court's policy course either through the appointment process or through popular and elite resistance to its rulings occurs only under extraordinary circumstances and requires an immense effort. Opposition to the Court's rulings must first be clear, strong, and unified. Translating that opposition into judicial change is then a lengthy and difficult process. With regard to the appointment process, it requires the focused attention and clairvoyance of successive, like-minded presidents and cooperative Senates. Or in the case of policy resistance, it requires the concerted efforts of citizens, groups, and leaders to communicate that message or threat effectively. Even then, he argues, change in the Court's policies is not certain, given the norm of *stare decisis* and the possibility of only a limited retreat by the Court.

Again, Professor Choper errs in assuming that the Court can be regarded as responsive only if we can observe repeated or continuously successful efforts to alter or defeat the Court's policies. He is correct that most decisions do not evoke the intense opposition necessary to exact vengeance on the Court. And he is no doubt correct as well that the cause is in part "inertia." However, he rules out two other possibilities. The first is the reality that the Court's decisions are neither consistently nor automatically implemented, as Rosenberg's work demonstrates; simply put, the Court does not always "prevail."[58] It is also possible that the Court is, over time, continuously responsive to popular and elite sentiment as a product of the appointment process and the justices' anticipation of the reactions of those who must obey, fund, and enforce the Court's rulings; in other words, there may not be significant opposition to the Court's decisions. Furthermore, when the Court does exceed the bounds of dominant public opinion, it can be (and has been) forced to retreat. One only need remember the events of the Court's New Deal crisis, in which public outcry, elite hostility, and the regular operation of turnover and the politically controlled appointment process produced a dramatic turnaround from the Court's unpopular anti-New Deal policies.

Choper's claims regarding the difficulties of changing or reversing the Court's policies apply as well to the policies of the other branches. Breaking the hold that iron triangles possess over their policy domain (they are called *iron* triangles for a reason) also requires extraordinary effort. There must be intense, focused policy opposition, which must then be reflected in successive elections in separate institutions. There must then be concerted action by a sufficient number of political actors in each institution. It may additionally require further time and effort in order to effect real change in the career bureaucracy and independent boards and commissions that also possess discretionary policymaking power. However, this standard of political responsibility, used for the Court, is not applied by Choper. He asks of the political branches, "What are the variety of ways in which popular or majority preferences are expressed and reflected in their policymaking activities?" For the Court, the standard is, "What are the difficulties involved in defeating or reversing the Court's policy decisions?" Such a comparison is inconsistent and unfair. There are a variety of ways in which popular preferences are expressed and enforced in each institution, and there are great difficulties as well in overturning their established policies.

Choper does in fact concede this point. He admits that "the leeway afforded the political branches by the people and the tenacity of popular feeling needed for radical change through election revolt are not absolutely different from the independence granted the judiciary by the Constitution and the assiduous efforts required to affect the Court and its decisions through the restraints ultimately retained by the citizenry and their elected representatives."[59] However, Choper concludes that they are different to a "substantial degree," since majority pressure on the Court to retreat from or reverse its policy course, even if successful, is "not the same as their ordained ability to change the composition of the political branches at regularly scheduled periodic elections."[60] Thus, even though there are means by which the people and their elected representatives can influence the Court (or "prevail"), those procedures are insufficient for us to regard the Court as democratic because they are not formal, regularized, and electorally based. Bickel echoes this theme:

> There are other means than the electoral process, though subordinate and subsidiary ones, of making institutions of government responsive to the needs and wishes of the governed. Hence we may infer that judicial review, although not responsible, may have ways of being responsive. But nothing can finally depreciate the central function that is assigned in democratic theory and practice to the electoral process, nor can it be denied that the policy-making power of representative institutions, born of the electoral process, is the distinguishing characteristic of the system. Judicial review works counter to this characteristic.[61]

This conclusion seems to me quite curious given the analysis that precedes it. Both Choper and Bickel accept the weaknesses of elections in transmitting and enforcing popular preferences in a meaningful way. They both acknowledge that there are a number of alternative, nonelectoral means for expressing and enforcing those preferences, which are in fact significant and effective. Yet those important observations are ignored when they turn to the Court. Choper and Bickel resort to a formalism, an argument that even if the Court might be responsive to popular desires, that is inconsequential if those desires are not enforced through formal, regularized elections. That conclusion is unjustified and inconsistent with their analysis of other institutions and actors. (After all, the policymaking power of committee chairs, agency heads, independent regulatory commissions, career bureaucrats, or even lame-duck presidents is not electorally based in the sense that a national majority can easily vote out those officeholders or easily alter their policies.)

The variety of more indirect means of accomplishing policy change and the more diffuse "majority" support or acquiescence necessary for continued policy success in the political branches are regarded by the neutralists as sufficient to overcome the weaknesses (or absence) of a direct, immediate, and meaningful electoral sanction. Yet that same forgiving attitude is not granted the Court. Instead, the neutralists resort to more abstract, theoretical arguments, for example, regarding the "central role of formal elections in a democracy" and the theoretical distinction between the Court's role of constitutional versus statutory review.[62] This seems to be a "cop-out," a way of ignoring the implications of the neutralists' own qualifications to their majority-rule, electorally driven, legislative-centered version of American democracy. Yet that subterfuge is necessary to reach the desired subject matter—justifying the deviant, undemocratic power of judicial review and condemning constitutional decisionmaking motivated by personal political preference.

The obvious weaknesses in their theory of American democracy forces the neutralists to engage in a number of contradictions and sleights of hand. They must significantly weaken their majority rule and electoral accountability criteria, while insisting they retain their viability as central explanatory and normative concepts of American democracy that sharply distinguish the Court from the other branches. Various countermajoritarian features are acknowledged as operating throughout the system, yet the Court's countermajoritarian aspects or functions are regarded as somehow different and in need of extraordinary justification. Bickel and Choper also acknowledge that the Court is subject to popular and elite influences and can be regarded in some sense as responsive. Yet that is regarded as inconsequential, presumably because of the "central importance of elections in a democracy." This is additionally in spite of the recognition that elections typically exert only a diffuse and indirect force in terms of producing specific policies and are supplemented by a variety of other means of expressing and enforcing popular desires.

The neutralists seem to recognize these weaknesses and inconsistencies in their arguments. Their inability to maintain a sharp distinction between the democratic properties of the political branches as compared to those of the Court lead them in the end to abandon that strategy. Thus, Choper's final response is that, in any case, the Court is less democratic and less majoritarian than the other branches. Similarly, Bickel argues that "impurities and imperfections, if such they be, in one part of the system are no argument for total departure from the desired norm in another part."[63] Professor Ely goes even further. He argues that the various antimajoritarian elements are themselves problematic. To the degree that limits exist on the majority's ability to direct and reverse legislative decisions, "such failures of accountability are properly regarded as constitutional defects in their own right and thus number among the things courts should be actively engaged in correcting."[64]

According to this line of reasoning, the neutralist theory would need to be revised in one of two ways. First, it would have to be argued that American democracy *should* be majoritarian and that any deviation from that norm requires reform. However, it is then no longer possible to argue that the Court is unique in its "undemocraticness" and in need of extraordinary justification because it is antimajoritarian. A second possibility, in line with Bickel's response, is to argue that the political branches are a little antimajoritarian and the Court is greatly antimajoritarian. Again, the argument that the Court is undemocratic and the rest of the system is democratic is accordingly more tenuous. However, the logical implications of this type of response are not acknowledged, and the neutralists' theory is not altered accordingly.

This fallback position represents an admission of failure. The neutralists cannot maintain the sharp distinction between the Court and the political branches that is necessary to regard the Court as uniquely deviant and, therefore, subject to special, extraordinary legitimacy requirements. The neutralists' own analysis is, thus, quite capable of supporting Professor Shapiro's conclusion:

> [S]o long as the Supreme Court functions within a governmental matrix of mixed democratic and nondemocratic elements, whether or not to assign certain tasks to the Justices is no more and no less a question of democracy than whether or not to assign those tasks to any other government agency. Certainly nothing can be solved by calling down a plague on both their houses because neither is selected by annual elections.[65]

Shapiro's response, while correct and buttressed by an abundance of empirical evidence regarding the actual workings of the American political system, is inadequate or, more accurately, incomplete. First, it fails to address directly the neutralists' irrefutable assertion that indeed the Court *is* different and it *is* less democratic than the other branches, at least according to traditional democratic criteria. Might not such differences, regardless of how one characterizes them (i.e., insignificant versus minimal versus substantial), dictate a specialized judicial role such as that which the neutralists advance? This claim must be addressed more directly.

Additionally, the message of Shapiro's response is that since all U.S. political institutions are a mixed bag of democratic and undemocratic elements, let's stop worrying about "the Court's legitimacy" and simply proceed to studying how each operates and interacts. While sound advice in the main, Shapiro's implicit message devalues the normative inquiry. There remains a normative vacuum, which is filled almost entirely by neutralist scholars.

In all fairness to Professor Shapiro, he does go on to say that rather than being consumed by the nonissue of justifying the Court's unique deviance in our democracy, "it seems preferable to determine in each separate policy area whether judicial policy-making contributes to well rounded representation of interests or to popular control more or less than policy-making by some rival agency."[66] While this also appears to be sound and defensible on democratic grounds and worthy of exploration, there must be a stronger, more affirmative response. This is particularly so given the long-standing dominance of the neutralist approach and the limited development of any alternative normative perspective. As the next and concluding section will argue, pluralist theory provides a more powerful rebuttal to the neutralist theory of American democracy and a more sound and productive theoretical foundation for advancing our normative inquiry.

The Pluralist Theory of American Democracy

The many electoral and structural oddities and complexities in the American political system are described by the neutralists as "impurities and imperfections" in an essentially majoritarian, electorally driven, and legislative-centered system. What the neutralists fail to understand is that those imperfections are themselves critical elements constituting an alternate form of government—a pluralist system. Pluralist theory provides an alternative explanation and defense of American politics.[67] It goes beyond merely chiding the neutralists for failing to acknowledge that the political branches do not truly reflect the majority will or that the Court is, in a significant way, a politically responsive institution. Pluralist theory makes comprehensible and rational what the neutralists see as irrational and exceptional features of a majoritarian democracy, *including* the discretionary power of a nonelective institution such as the Court.

In the neutralist perspective, there are three principles of American democracy: the legitimacy and sanctity of majority preferences; the critical role of regularized elections in holding leaders accountable to majority preferences; and the vindication of majority preferences through the norm of legislative supremacy. The Court, even though perhaps responsive through nonelectoral means, violates these principles.

It is not enough to note that in the actual workings of American government, there are a number of deviations from a pure majority rule, electorally controlled, legislative-centered model. The more appropriate response is that American democracy is not in *any* way intended or designed to vindicate those principles of majority rule and electoral and legislative supremacy. The majority possesses no special empirical force or normative significance in American politics. Instead, a premium is placed on the rights of groups to challenge, in any forum they choose, governmental action they find inimical to their interests. Elections are not to be regarded as the exclusive or superior means of insuring the responsiveness of governmental leaders; instead, diversity in the forms of responsiveness is deemed desirable and paramount. And finally, rather than legislative and electoral supremacy, there is no hierarchical order, in theory or practice, among these various forms of responsiveness or among the various branches of government.

These alternative principles—minorities or groups rule, diversity in political representation, and a nonhierarchical arrangement among alternative and competing institutions—make little sense in the context of a majority rule model. They are, however, quite rationally related to the fundamental normative premise of a pluralist system regarding the virtues, particularly in a large polity, of reliability and stability in ascertaining the more enduring bases of political consent.

The American political system specifically and deliberately rejects majority rule as a normatively desirable end. Rather than representing either isolated and inconsequential imperfections (Bickel, Choper) or some sort of systemic failure (Ely), the various structural features that impede the ability of the majority to effect its will through governmental means are quite deliberate and rational and form a coherent whole. It was precisely the Framers' fear of majorities that motivated their many choices regarding the system's structure and design.

That fear is most clearly expressed by Madison in *Federalist No. 10*.[68] Madison believed that the greatest threat to the stability and survival of any political system was the existence of "factions" and their tendency to seek to control the coercive powers of government in order to impose their will on others and further their selfish interests, even if minorities or the national good are harmed.[69] This not only amounts to tyranny, an intolerable condition, but also serves as a source of discontent and instability.[70] Disgruntled minority losers are forced to obey laws with which they disagree and are thus denied their liberty. Further, they are likely to regard the system as illegitimate, thus representing a threat to political stability.

A primary objective of the Framers then was to construct a system that would limit the ability of groups both to perceive and act on their common interests and to gain full control of the governmental apparatus. Because minority tyranny could be prevented by the majority outvoting them, the greater concern was with guarding against majority tyranny.[71]

Protection against majority tyranny was provided for in numerous ways. For example, a republic or indirect democracy was preferred to a direct democracy, which is nothing less than a prescription for majority tyranny, according to the Framers.[72] Elected representatives could refine and moderate the majority's selfish and emotional demands.[73] Further limiting the majority's control of government, only the House was to be directly elected by the people. Senators were selected by state legislators, presidents by the electoral college, and members of the judiciary by the president and Senate. Additionally, the Framers sought to "extend the sphere"—that is, to rely on a large republic and large electoral districts in which size and diversity would weaken majority strength and unity.[74] The electoral college, indirect election of senators, and staggered, independent elections among the House, Senate, and presidency are all devices that prevent a majority from directly and simultaneously electing the entire government leadership. Structural fragmentation, through the creation of separate branches of government, further limits the majority's ability to use the government for its tyrannous ends. Thanks to a system of checks and balances, no single branch would possess unilateral power to enact the majority's will should a majority gain momentary control of one branch. Further fragmentation is provided by a federal structure. Restrictions on the majority using the national government for its purposes are insured by limiting and enumerating the powers of the national government. Specific written limitations on the powers of the national government, including a statement of individual rights and liberties in the Bill of Rights, provide a final safeguard should a majority manage to overcome those various obstacles and gain control of the whole apparatus of government.[75]

The thrust of this system is negative in the sense of impairing the ability of groups, particularly majorities, to effect their will through government. However, there is a positive aspect as well. Granting groups the legitimacy and power to intervene effectively in the political process when their interests are threatened, even by a majority, is a way of insuring that before the coercive powers of the government can be used, political consent of a broad, certain, and enduring nature must be won.

This goal of insuring that government policy reflect a more stable and enduring consensus, rather than a momentary majority passion, is operationalized by expanding the opportunities for groups to advance and protect their interests. That expansion occurs through the use of redundancy and diversity in political representation. Structurally, this means a system of numerous and diverse (i.e., differently representative) institutions, which are additionally deliberately arranged in a nonhierarchical manner.

Having many institutions rather than a single institution possessing policymaking authority and employing a number of separate elections rather than a single national election are both examples of redundancy. In general, systems that are redundant use duplication of effort and overlap of function in order to achieve greater reliability and stability. Failure by one unit is not fatal to the achievement of the system's goal.[76] In the United States, the determination of a political consensus is not left to a single election or single institution. This, of course, would increase the possibility of error, of incorrectly reading the popular will and increasing the risks of popular dissatisfaction and political instability. This is particularly so in a large polity where preferences are diverse, complex, and poorly organized. By employing multiple channels and multiple arenas for the expression of citizen and group preferences, reliability and certainty in discovering the bases of political consensus are increased.

In addition to increasing the number of arenas in which groups can advance their interests and contest policies with which they disagree, there is *planned* diversity among those arenas. Each branch of government is organized differently and subject to different forms of popular and elite influence. For example, the president, members of the House, and members of the Senate are elected separately, by different electorates, and for different terms of office. Executive branch agencies and the judiciary offer not only additional sites for effective group intervention, but additional diversity in the types of group resources and claims to which they must respond. This diversity is then multiplied by virtue of its replication at the state and local levels. Decentralized political parties offer additional opportunities for political access and influence.

Diversity among and within the various branches and levels of government operates to expand the opportunities for groups to influence government decisions. As Dahl explains,

> Groups weighty in a presidential election may be much weaker in House and Senate elections. . . . A group may be strong in one executive agency, weak in another; strong in a particular House or Senate committee, weak elsewhere. A group may have individual spokesmen and opponents located at various places in the executive agencies, the regulatory commissions, the House, the Senate, the standing committees, a conference committee. . . . A minority may be defeated at the presidential nominating convention, yet retain its strength in state and local party organizations; it cannot be pushed aside. . . . Again and again in the history of the Supreme Court, a minority coalition that could not win the Presidency or majorities in Congress has preserved a majority within the Supreme Court to fight a rear-guard delaying action. . . . Even if they rarely win their wars in the Congress, minorities well represented on the Court can win some impressive battles.[77]

The numerous and diverse political institutions with policymaking power dispersed throughout our system are intended to and, in fact, do "offer organized minorities innumerable sites in which to fight, perhaps to defeat, at any rate to damage an opposing coalition."[78]

There is not only diversity among political institutions, but the absence of any clear hierarchy among them.

> Neither the Constitution, constitutional doctrine, nor American ideology have ever treated all these institutions, national and federal, as components of an ordered hierarchy in which some constitutional units are

invariably subordinate to others. Constitutionally speaking, the President does not dominate Congress, nor, on the other hand, is the President a mere agent of Congress; the Senate is not constitutionally superior to the House, nor Congress and President to the Judiciary, nor the governors and state legislatures to the President and Congress.... If in constitutional theory there is no hierarchy of legitimate authorities, then fact . . . conforms with theory.[79]

The absence of a hierarchical ordering among our political institutions is assured through a system of checks and balances or sharing of powers among institutions. Thus, no institution has complete or unilateral power over another. The House may enact a legislative program, but only with the agreement of a Senate majority, the acquiescence of a Senate minority unwilling to use the filibuster, and the approval of the president as well. The president may enact treaties and appoint federal judges and executive department heads, but only with the advice and consent of the Senate. The judiciary may interpret the Constitution and statutes in the course of resolving individual disputes and, as a result, is able to exercise significant policymaking power; however, the president and Senate select the judiciary's membership, and the executive and Congress are responsible for the enforcement and funding of the Court's policies. The system is replete with such examples of the ability of one institution to block or damage the policy initiatives of another.

Not only does one institution not possess hierarchical authority over another but, accordingly, no single form of representation or responsiveness is deemed superior to another. There is diversity among the House, Senate, and the presidency in how voters and interests are represented, and no single form of representation among them is granted greater significance or legitimacy, in theory or in practice. The House is not "more democratic" and, therefore, "more legitimate" than the Senate. Nor is the president regarded as "more democratic" than the Congress. Similarly, although the insight of the House of Representatives into current public opinion may be greater than that of the Senate, a lame-duck president, or the Court, that does not imply that policy initiatives issuing from the House are more legitimate or worthy of greater deference. Each form of representation, each institutional site for group access and influence, is regarded in a pluralist system as *instrumentally* valuable in terms of providing the building blocks for a more complete and stable political consensus rather than as intrinsically valuable and superior to another.

This failure to order competing institutions in a clear, hierarchical manner has as its consequence an increase in the effectiveness of these various channels of group participation. To the degree that a group can win in one of those arenas, it can effectively alter or halt policies it deems harmful. Thus, its interests must be taken into account.

Redundancy, diversity, and a lack of hierarchy are the tools to achieve what Professor Dahl regards as the "single principle of legitimate decision-making" in American politics: "Unanimity, though unattainable, is best; institutions must therefore be so contrived that they will compel a constant search for the highest attainable degree of consent."[80] The existence of many institutions increases the number of arenas in which groups can articulate their interests and contest policies with which they disagree. Organizing each institution differently, making each subject to a different form of popular influence, operates to increase the likelihood that a group will succeed in one of those arenas. And ordering those numerous and diverse institutions in a nonhierarchical manner (via a system of checks and balances) can help to insure that a victory in one arena is of real consequence for policymaking outcomes. Thus, the likelihood of the perennial minority loser whose interests are overlooked, whose liberty is denied, and who represents a threat to political stability is reduced. Or stated more affirmatively, policy that is the product of agreement among the many and diverse representative institutions in a pluralist system should reflect a more encompassing and, thus, a more enduring and stable consensus.

As both a normative and empirical matter, government decisions in the American pluralist system are not deemed superior by virtue of the particular institution that produced them nor by the size of the group which supports them. Rather, any group of any size may legitimately contest a decision in any institution. For example, although President Reagan won office handily, particularly in 1984, he did not receive a clear, specific, and comprehensive policy mandate.[81] That is even more true for President Clinton, who failed to receive a majority of the popular vote in both of his elections. Thus, Clinton's policy proposals, for example regarding gays in the military and health care reform, required continued "testing"—in Congress, in the bureaucracy, in the states, and in the courts. And groups opposed to Clinton, whether antiabortion and antigay groups or health insurers, were not cast aside by virtue of his election. Rather, they retained the legitimacy to contest his policies in any arena of their choosing.[82]

The appropriate standard in a pluralist system for determining an institution's legitimacy and value is *not* whether it is majoritarian or subject to elections. Rather, that standard is the degree to which it adds to the number and diversity of arenas in which groups can regularly and effectively advance their interests, thereby contributing to the reliability and stability of the political process as a whole in ascertaining the enduring bases of political consent.

Pluralist Critiques

The pluralist defense of American democracy is not without its critics, including Robert Dahl himself.[83] It should be acknowledged that pluralist theory, in fact, encompasses much more than what has been presented here. It includes a variety of assumptions and assertions regarding a significant number of issues—the definition of power, empirical methods appropriate to its study, the distribution of political power, interest group formation and influence, the representativeness of policy that results from interest group struggles, and the nature (or existence) of "the public interest." There has been considerable criticism and debate on each issue, primarily from the "ruling elite" school, which regards policy in American democracy as too interest-group driven and power as much more concentrated and much less accessible than the pluralists assert.[84]

My use of pluralist theory is obviously more limited. Emphasis here is placed on the heavy reliance in the United States on redundancy, diversity, and nonhierarchy in political institutions and the resulting expansion in group access and veto points. My only point is that this pluralist perspective is more appropriate for understanding the operation of American politics, and thus the Court's role in it, than is the neutralists' emphasis on majority rule and legislative supremacy. That point is easily proven. And it is a limited point, one that does not reach such issues as whether pluralist democracy is the best form of democracy or whether it is better than a parliamentary form. Such questions need not be entertained here; they do not bear on the *empirical* question of whether majority rule or pluralist governance better captures the reality of American politics.

That limited point also does not extend further to the clearly false assertion that pluralist democracy in the United States in fact achieves equality of access and equality in political influence. It does not. Political participation and political power is strongly related to income and education, with voting rates, interest group membership, and political influence increasing with class status. Schattschneider correctly points out that "the flaw in the pluralist heaven is that the heavenly chorus sings with a strong upper-class accent."[85] It remains true, however, that the chance that a group will find a receptive ear somewhere in government is greater in a pluralist scheme as compared to a majority rule, legislative-centered system lacking such redundancy and diversity.

Conclusion

The neutralists' claims that judicial review is deviant and that value-voting is objectionable rest upon a foundation that is not only weak but fundamentally and fatally flawed. The neutralists argue that the Court is a deviant and undemocratic institution in need of extraordinary justification and that value-voting represents an arbitrary and illegitimate expression of a politically unaccountable justice.

One simply cannot accept those conclusions, at least not for the reasons the neutralists have traditionally supplied—that in American democracy, the majority possesses unique legitimacy and empirical significance; that elections are exclusive or superior means of inducing political responsiveness; that Congress and the executive possess a unique claim to representing the majority will, and thus possess hierarchical authority over other political institutions; and that, for all of these reasons, their decisions are and should be accorded greater legitimacy and are presumptively superior. On all of these counts, the neutralist theory of American democracy is incorrect, and the standards thus supplied for evaluating the Court are inappropriate.

Well armed with an impressive array of empirical and conceptual work, political scientists have provided an effective challenge to the neutralists' theory. They have criticized the neutralists' abstract and naive model of American democracy, pointing out the many ways in which the political branches fail to satisfy the principle of majority rule and the many ways (albeit nonelectoral) in which the Court is made to be politically responsive.

Although few neutralist scholars have responded directly, some concessions have been made. The neutralists are reduced, in the end, to making the more tenuous assertion that while all three branches are imperfectly democratic, the Court is the *most* imperfectly democratic (i.e., the least democratic) branch.

The result it seems is a stalemate, a difference in interpretation. The problem is transformed into a decision over how much is to be made of the difference between the Court and the other political institutions. Are those differences sufficiently significant to regard the Court as unique or deviant and, accordingly, as needing a different sort of justification for its policymaking power? Or is Shapiro correct that those differences are minimal, consequently leaving only the issue of which institution is better or more democratic in particular policy areas? That question of interpretation and its implications, I have argued, misses the point entirely.

The neutralists have retreated to the position that it is of no consequence that the political branches are imperfectly democratic since the Court is, in any case, the least democratic. This is so, they argue, because the ways in which the Court can be made to be politically responsive are less direct, more difficult to employ, and of uncertain effectiveness as compared to the formal, regularized electoral process to which the other branches are subject. While such a distinction can be and typically is exaggerated, there is a more important point to be made. Assigning the democratic label, exclusive legitimacy, and a preeminent policymaking role to the most majoritarian or most directly electorally accountable institution is not a universal democratic criterion. More importantly, it is not one upon which American democracy in particular rests.

The neutralists' primary error is not in incorrectly interpreting the degree of difference between the Court and the political branches in their "democraticness." There is a more fundamental error—the failure to understand that the pluralist system of American government makes such differences *inconsequential* in determining an institution's legitimacy, value, or power in the governing process.

The central teaching of pluralist theory is that there are a variety of forms of political representation and responsiveness, none of which needs be regarded as superior to or more democratic than another. Rather, each has instrumental or systemic value. By employing redundant and diverse forms of political representation and arranging them nonhierarchically, two objectives can be achieved. First, the opportunities for groups to gain access to and an effective voice in government policymaking are greatly expanded. Second, the political system as a consequence will possess a greater capacity to discover, with more certainty and reliability, the stable and enduring bases of political consensus.

Accordingly, the appropriate response to the neutralists' claim that the Court is less majoritarian, not electorally controlled, and least democratic is: "So what?" In a pluralist system, it is of *no* consequence that the Court is representative or responsive in a different—that is, nonelectoral—way. Redundancy and diversity in the expression of citizen and group desires is intended and valued. And no particular form of representation and no particular institution is intrinsically better or more democratic; none is granted greater legitimacy or greater policymaking power.

Pluralist theory provides an alternative and superior explanation of American politics. It, therefore, also serves as an alternative and superior vehicle for reappraising the Court's fit with and role in that system. Rather than being viewed as anachronistic and deviant, the Court in a pluralist system can be seen as quite "normal"—a rational, integral, indeed *critical* component of the governing process. It can serve as an alternative arena in which dissatisfaction with legislative or administrative decisions can be aired. For example, groups such as the NAACP and Jehovah's Witnesses have turned to the courts after failing to win their political battles in legislative or executive forums.[86] The effort necessary to bring an issue to the attention of the Court indicates that some group feels sufficiently threatened by a particular policy to expend its resources to seek judicial redress.[87] If the intense dissatisfaction of some group is to be considered of legitimate concern to political leaders, then the Court's "interference" with legislative or administrative judgments at the behest of such a group need not be considered undemocratic. (And that is equally the case for white males taking their complaints regarding affirmative action policies to the Rehnquist Court.) In fact, having the Court serve as an institutional recourse for legislative or administrative losers, in a pluralist system, is regarded as a desirable redundancy in the process of developing policies that command widespread agreement.

That the Court serves as an additional arena for interest group activity is well documented by empirical research. Pluralism, in the form of broad and intensive interest group involvement, exists not only in the so-called political branches, but in the Court as well. The frequency of interest group participation in Supreme Court cases, whether through direct sponsorship or the filing of amicus curiae briefs, is quite high[88] and consistently high across a variety of issues.[89] Furthermore, participation is not limited to certain types of groups, such as the disadvantaged.[90] As Epstein has noted, "nearly 75 percent of all organizations have litigated at least once"[91] and "between 1952 and 1986, almost 2,400 organizations, falling into twenty substantive categories . . . appeared before the Court."[92] Caldeira and Wright found considerable diversity in amicus curiae participation during the 1982 term; for example, they found that "more than 40% of the amicus briefs filed during the 1982 term were filed by citizen or advocacy groups; business, trade, or professional associations; unions; and peak organizations."[93] Additionally, Caldeira and Wright found considerable competition among groups at the plenary stage, with opposing briefs filed in a majority of the cases (803). The pluralist notion of a variety of groups competing for power and policymaking influence is appropriate not only for Congress and the executive, but for the Court as well.

Although the evidence is limited, existing research also suggests that there is considerable overlap between the interest group environment of the Court and that of the other branches; to this degree, the Court is indeed one of many redundant arenas for interest group access and pressure. For example, Caldeira and Wright found that the variety of amici participating in the Court was "quite representative of the general mix of organizations represented in Washington" (803). Most frequent participants included state governments; business, trade, and professional associations; and citizen groups (794).

Nonetheless, it is important to note that business and governmental interests participated at much higher rates in the certiorari stage than did citizen groups, giving the former much more influence in the agenda-setting stage (794–95). Additionally, the participation of states and corporations was more focused and intense (i.e., fewer briefs and fewer cases), while business, trade, and professional associations participated in a larger number of cases and filed a larger number of briefs, thus making the latter "much more prominent players" than the overall numbers indicate (795). Epstein similarly found that governmental and commercial interests were well represented among amici curiae, accounting for almost 50 percent of all briefs filed in 1987.[94] With regard to direct sponsorship of litigation, "commercial interests (such as a chamber of commerce, Delta Airlines) dominated pressure group activity in the Court. Indeed, if we exclude governmental concerns . . . , commercial interests sponsored more litigation than all others combined."[95] Not surprisingly, the upper-class and business bias of the interest group community carries over to Supreme Court litigation, showing the relevance of pluralist theory and pluralist critiques to the Court as well as to the other branches.

Although the research again does not speak directly to this point, it does appear that the interest group environment of the Court, while similar, is not identical to that of the other branches. In the view of Caldeira and Wright, the Court "is remarkably accessible to a wide array of organized interests. . . . Participation is not restricted to prestigious individuals, public or private law firms, corporations, or units of federal and state government" (802–3). Despite the Court's lack of an electoral motive, the evidence "testifies to the surprising openness of the Court to the articulation of interests from a broad array of membership organizations" (797). Several empirical studies also suggest that the Court is quite receptive (and not merely "accessible") to the claims of "underdogs," such as the poor, minorities, and criminal defendants; they are quite successful in Supreme Court litigation, even when pitted against litigants with more resources and experience such as the government,[96] and in contrast to the advantages enjoyed by "upperdogs" in state supreme courts[97] and U.S. Courts of Appeals.[98] Numerous case studies provide further evidence that lower-status groups which found access or influence limited in the legislature succeeded in the Supreme Court—Jehovah's Witnesses,[99] the NAACP regarding race discrimination in housing and school segregation,[100] the Legal Defense Fund regarding the death penalty,[101] and the Legal Services Program regarding the rights of the poor.[102] In terms of interest group access, the Court has at times been more receptive than the other branches.

Of course, it is not only the Court's availability as an alternative forum that gives it value in a pluralist system, but additionally the fact that it is subject to quite different forms of popular and elite influence. It is the diversity among institutions, not only their number, that is valued in a pluralist system. If each institution was composed in precisely the same manner, a reasonable expectation would be that the same groups would win and the same groups would lose in each arena. This form of redundancy or fragmentation would then serve no purpose, or at least would not contribute to the goal of broadening the range of interests to be taken into account in policymaking. Institutions that are instead organized differently may be responsive to different groups and may weigh the normative arguments and political resources of groups (e.g., size, unity, wealth, expertise) in different ways. In other words, the prospects of any group's success will vary from one arena to another, thereby laying the groundwork for a more inclusive and stable consensus.

It is quite easy to take note of periods in the Court's history in which it has in fact been responsive to groups and values different from those well represented in other institutions. In the early-twentieth century through the mid-1930s, the Court protected and advanced the values of free-market capitalism and the interests of business, even though such groups and values were losing their dominance in many state legislatures and, in the 1930s, in Congress and the executive branch. The Warren Court was notable for advancing the cause of equality and the interests of particular groups who had not fared well in the legislature—for example, racial minorities, the poor, and criminal defendants.

An important study by Stimson, Mackuen, and Erikson provides additional verification. Their evidence reveals that although all government institutions reflect or represent public opinion, the Court does so distinctively. For example, while each of the elective institutions "represents . . . the previous year's public opinion . . . almost all of the Court's reflection of public opinion is driven by the events of the past seven years."[103] Overall, compared to the House, Senate, and president, the Court was found to respond more modestly and more slowly to changes in public preferences.

As noted earlier, however, redundancy and diversity in political representation serve only to lay the groundwork for a more inclusive and more stable political consensus. Intended to effectuate that result is the nonhierarchical arrangement among these numerous and diverse representative institutions. Each institution has some degree of independent power, although not complete power, to force the inclusion of "their" interests or constituency into the policy process. Thus, it is only through the exercise of its power, through judicial activism, that the Court can give effect to its alternative representation and thereby add to or improve on the efforts of other institutions to achieve a meaningful consensus.

This in fact is little different from the added contribution that the president makes to the initial consensus as represented by legislative proposals. His independent power to advance policies and force concessions from Congress, if need be, on behalf of his allies or constituency is a function of the strength of his popular and group following, a following to some degree independent of that of Congress. The same is true for members of Congress in relation to the president. Since neither possesses complete power over the other, policies that are the result of bargaining between the two should, at least over time, be satisfactory to the constituencies of both. Consensus is thereby broadened. To the extent that little bargaining is needed, that only implies that a consensus has to some degree already been achieved, via party or electoral activities or perhaps the strength and durability of a recently forged alliance.

The Court's contribution is similar. To the degree that the Court responds to groups or values even slightly different from those of the president or Congress and, because it too possesses some measure of independent power, it can insure that policies respond to those groups and values as well. Thus, the Court too is capable of contributing to the goal of widespread consent.

Justices are appointed on the basis of their loyalty to certain policy views and group interests. Their tenure on the Court can be used by the justices to act on those loyalties and to protect those group interests and values that a recently elected president and Senate have chosen to promote and that have consequently received political approval. Similarly to administrative agencies or career bureaucrats, a justice or group of justices may serve to protect and preserve a recently reached consensus, at least until those bargains are decisively and consensually voided. The Court's behavior during the *Lochner* era can in this way be viewed as legitimate. A majority of justices acted according to the policy premises upon which they were appointed; they were merely protecting past political winners (business interests and laissez-faire values) from being expelled or cast aside by newly elected representatives with new and significantly different group loyalties. Rather than acting "arbitrarily," the *Lochner* Court was merely protecting those interests which they were put into office to protect. Political stability is thereby enhanced; groups cannot be transformed from winners into losers by virtue of one or two elections.[104]

Of course, the independence of the Court in indefinitely protecting those interests is limited, and rightly so. The strength of the New Deal coalition and the loss in political favor of business interests did not permit the Court to continue in its devotion to laissez-faire principles and business groups. The survival and strength of the New Deal consensus, in any case, insured that the Court, as a product of membership turnover, would itself become protectors of and partners in that new coalition. Thus, the "independent" power to protect past political winners in the making of new policy is popularly and politically checked.

The Court can also *expand* the bases of consensus, by bringing in new groups into the bargaining process. Yet again, this activity is subject to political validation by other powerful groups and leaders. The race discrimination cases are the prime example of this capability. The Court's promotion of the interests of racial minorities insured that policy embraced those interests, but only as much and as far as other political leaders and groups were willing to permit. The Court was not acting arbitrarily or against the popular will. Rather, it was capable of advancing the goal of racial equality only as a result of the growing strength and respectability of civil rights groups and the sympathetic view of an increasing number of groups and leaders toward that goal. Of course, even then, the Court could not achieve its goal as fully or as quickly as it wished. Similarly, to the extent that the Court cultivates and reflects popular and elite expectations that its role is one of protecting the fairness of the criminal justice system, free speech, or other diffuse values, it retains some degree of independence to protect criminal defendants and political dissidents and to force their inclusion into the building of consensual policies.

This power to protect past political winners or to bring in new winners should be of obvious relevance to pluralist goals. The Court assists in expanding and preserving the consensual basis of government policies, thereby preserving liberty and political stability and increasing the opportunities for groups to express and advance their interests.

However, quite importantly, that power is politically and popularly checked. The Court cannot protect groups or values when overwhelmingly opposed by a strong political alliance.[105] This, of course, is as it should be. If, in a democracy, policy is to be derived from and reflect the expressed interests and desires of various groups in society, the Court should not be permitted to create or protect a "group" that is unable to command any significant political resources or win any political battles.

An important aspect of the Court's role is, thus, the maintenance and expansion of the bases of political consensus. Of course, the Court is typically part of any enduring and cohesive political alliance. However, it does possess sufficient independence to promote new and sustain old bases of consensus, thereby serving the ends of stable political change. It is only by recognizing the pluralist intent and structure of our political system that the value and legitimacy of judicial intervention can be perceived.

The following chapter will further explore such implications of recognizing that the Court operates in and is an integral part of a pluralist system. It is sufficient to note at this point that the objections raised by conventional scholars regarding the deviance and undemocraticness of judicial review generally and policy-motivated decisionmaking more particularly rest upon a theory of American democracy that is quite simply wrong.

CHAPTER 8

• •

Whither the Court and Constitution?

A LIKELY response to the view of the Court as "just another political agency" is, why then should we bother with a Court or Constitution at all? Of what value is the Court or Constitution if constitutional decisionmaking is nothing more than the personal, idiosyncratic views of nine unelected, life-tenured judges? However, as previous chapters have shown, decisionmaking by policy-motivated, politically sensitive judges who are constrained by democratic forces is hardly the sort of idiosyncratic, democratically indefensible decisionmaking that we have been told to expect. Accordingly, the response of "Whither the Court and Constitution?" must be recast and the questions reformulated.

While policy-motivated decisionmaking may be defensible on democratic grounds, there remains the difficult task of ascertaining its limits as well as its particular value in the policymaking process as a whole. What is the appropriate role of value-voting judges in American pluralist democracy? What are the boundaries and appropriate uses of judicial activism motivated by personal political preference? For example, might not repeated judicial protection of legislative and administrative losers become too great a strain on the process of reaching some degree of closure in policymaking, thus inhibiting the system from responding at all to public interests and needs? How then can we evaluate when judicial intervention is appropriate, and how can we judge the substantive content of those interventions?

Before addressing those questions, it will first be helpful to review the primary conclusions reached thus far. I have not attempted to present a comprehensive theory of constitutional interpretation or of the Court's role in American democracy. Rather, I have only thus far examined and subjected to critical analysis the dominant themes and assumptions regarding those two issues we presently find in constitutional law scholarship. For example, in place of the dominant premise of legal autonomy, I have argued for the inevitability of constitutional indeterminacy and judicial subjectivity. Rather than assuming that policy motivation and political sensitivity should play no role in constitutional decisionmaking, I have demonstrated their many benefits. Rather than assuming we need the Court to save us from our politics, I argue that we must confront the necessity and value of our politics (and if need be change them). And rather than regarding the Court as a deviant element in a majoritarian and legislative-centered democracy, we should see the Court as a quite normal and integral part of a pluralist system of governance. After reviewing these thematic shifts in constitutional theory, we can then examine their implications.

Legal Autonomy versus Constitutional Indeterminacy

Conventional constitutional law scholars see their central task as "saving the Court's legitimacy." They must discover a justification for the apparently undemocratic power of judicial review. Their solution proceeds along two complementary tracks. First, they attempt to present constitutional interpretation as an objectively determined or at least an objectively constrained process of decisionmaking. Thus, constitutional answers exist and can be discovered apart from the personal political views of the justices. Second, and apparently a fallback position, they seek to persuade us that the judicial process and judges themselves possess special qualities or attributes, which in turn justifies delegating certain matters not appropriately handled in the political sphere. Such qualities include legal training and methods of reasoning, capacities for dealing with matters of principle and, in particular, insulation from political pressure. Thus, the Court's legitimacy in a democracy is saved by "keeping the judicial function distinct from the legislative and thus capable of being justified."[1]

As chapter 2 explained, the conventional scholars' hope for objectively constrained constitutional interpretation carried out by wise moral philosophers (or in Ely's view, by wise democratic theorists)[2] has thus far proven illusory. As conventional scholars' criticism of each others' theories and the work of Critical Legal Studies scholars demonstrate, it is a quite simple task to demonstrate that every theory of judicial review offered is capable of rendering different, and even contradictory, constitutional answers. Accordingly, constitutional decisions cannot be defended in any objective way.

Rather, they can only be explained and defended according to the interpreter's personal, subjective, and ultimately biased views. Thus, the neutralists' endeavor is futile, because the Constitution is significantly indeterminate and judicial subjectivity is inevitable.

Political Motivation: Virtue or Vice?

Recognition of constitutional indeterminacy and judicial subjectivity means recognition of the inevitable role of personal political preference in constitutional decisionmaking. However, this is for many a difficult pill to swallow, given the horror with which politically motivated judicial decisionmaking is typically regarded. For the conventional scholar, subjective and politically motivated decisionmaking permits unelected justices to impose their personal, unprincipled, and idiosyncratic views against the people's will. For the Critical Legal Studies scholar, such a justice necessarily imposes his own elitist views or is the servant of liberal-capitalist oppression.

However, these scholars mischaracterize politically motivated decisionmaking, relying on little more than a stereotype of the biased, self-interested judge choosing winners and losers in an ad hoc and arbitrary fashion. That mischaracterization includes erroneously regarding intellectual rigor and legal craftsmanship in opinion writing as inherently incompatible with political motivation in constitutional decisionmaking.

The traditional scholar also overlooks the many benefits that derive from politically motivated decisionmaking. For example, policy motivation and value-voting constitute a form of political representation. By voting her values, the policy-motivated justice is carrying out the value premises of her appointment, premises actively and deliberately selected by elected officials—the president and Senate.

Policy motivation also activates the various political controls on the Court and renders them effective. Only a policy-motivated justice would care about the success of his policy goals and would, therefore, be attentive to the existence of political support and opposition. He would further attempt to persuade opponents with more rigorous legal and policy arguments, build political support for those policy goals and, if need be, accommodate the views and interests of the opposition. This is a form of consensus building, a political activity of tremendous value in a diverse society such as ours and in a fragmented political system such as ours.

American Democracy: Majoritarian or Pluralist?

Some scholars, such as Jesse Choper[3] and Alexander Bickel,[4] are willing to concede these points. They do acknowledge that there are a variety of ways of making the Court responsive. However, they regard this as insufficient to reconcile judicial review with democratic values or to sanction policy-motivated decisionmaking as legitimate. This is due to their misguided view of American democracy as majoritarian, electorally controlled, and legislative centered.

Both Choper and Bickel acknowledge that there are many countermajoritarian features throughout the system and that there are a variety of mechanisms of political responsiveness supplementing electoral ones. However, they fail to take those observations seriously. Their theory of American democracy, as an essentially majority-rule system in which the legislature is supreme, is so riddled with exceptions that the exception becomes the rule. This should but does not lead the neutralists to adopt the view that American democracy as a whole is exceptional and deviant, at least when evaluated in the context of traditional democratic notions like majority rule or the centrality of elections.

Another way of expressing the complex and exceptional nature of American democracy is the term *pluralist.* Our political system is not directed to the goal of majority rule; it is in virtually all aspects an antimajoritarian system, including its rejection of legislative supremacy. Rather, our system provides numerous and diverse political institutions, none of which is hierarchically superior to another, whether in theory or practice. The underlying purpose is to provide groups, especially minorities, with a variety of arenas in which to advance their interests and contest policies with which they disagree. As a result, it is less likely that government will pursue a policy course that is opposed by any group.

Accordingly, denigrating the Court for interfering with the definitive and presumptively superior electoral and legislative determinations of political winners, at least in the context of pluralist politics, makes little sense. This standard of evaluation is simply inappropriate. The appropriate standard in a pluralist system for determining an institution's legitimacy is *not* simply whether it is majoritarian or subject to formal, regularized elections. Rather, its value or legitimacy is a function of the degree to which it adds constructively to the number and diversity of arenas in which groups can regularly and effectively advance their interests, thus contributing to the reliability and stability of the political process as a whole in ascertaining the more enduring bases of political consent. In this *pluralist* system, judicial review is neither deviant nor illegitimate. Rather, it is a quite normal expression of the pluralist principles of redundancy and diversity in political representation.

Shall the Court Protect Us from or become Part of Our Politics?

The reason why conventional scholars cannot be dissuaded from the untenable position that American democracy is majoritarian and legislative-centered is that they so desperately want to arrive at that conclusion. They *want* the Court to play a special undemocratic role in our system and, accordingly, must defend their curious theory of American democracy that permits them to arrive at that prescriptive conclusion.

At least for those neutralists advocating judicial activism, such as Perry[5] and Tribe,[6] the desire for an undemocratic though legitimate Court simply reflects a lack of faith in democracy generally and in legislatures more particularly. Registering and weighing the competing preferences of individuals and gratifying some rather than others is the stuff of politics and the function of legislatures. In that crass, utilitarian sort of process, there is little room, they imagine, for moral reflection about rights, principles, and the social good. That special function of principled, moral discourse is thus relegated exclusively to the Court. And justifying that desirable though undemocratic role—the Court as moral guardian—requires distinguishing the Court from the rest of the political system. Portraying the other branches as majoritarian and electorally driven serves that need.

Similarly, dire warnings about the loss of legitimacy and power which will ensue if the Court is "political" do not, as chapter 6 demonstrated, receive empirical support. This too is simply a way of trying to justify the empty hope for Platonic Guardians to "save us from our politics."

Contemporary constitutional theory, thus, expresses a profound and unjustified skepticism about politics generally and American politics more particularly. This lack of faith in politics produces a solution little different from that of the Progressives. They both seek to "take the politics out of politics." The Progressives sought to do so by, for example, substituting independent and impartial decisionmaking bodies for political or partisan ones. The neutralists do so by substituting morally superior judges for morally impoverished politicians.[7] However, the solution to an imperfect democratic process, if that is indeed what we have, is not less democracy but better democracy. Of course, that inquiry is not even pursued because of the negative and skeptical attitude of most conventional scholars toward politics and democracy generally. Conventional constitutional theory is at every turn a product of this fear of politics. It is a fear and skepticism regarding politics that masquerades as a debate over constitutional indeterminacy or as a debate over how to characterize American democracy.

However, embracing politics—its inevitability, desirability, virtues, and vices—does not have the negative consequences the neutralists fear. Recognizing the role of political motivation in constitutional decisionmaking and perceiving the Court as an integral part of a pluralist political system does not require that we denigrate the Court, its function, or its members. In fact, the political leadership role envisioned here for the Court is, I believe, a quite noble one in itself. There is no need to apologize for it or to invent an alternative, such as moral prophet or guardian of our democratic ideals.

It is now time to examine more closely the implications for the Court and the Constitution of the thematic shifts suggested here: constitutional indeterminacy and judicial subjectivity; the value of policy and political motivation in constitutional decisionmaking; pluralist principles of governance; and embracing rather than fleeing from our politics.

Whither the Court?

The first question implied by these thematic shifts is, of course, what role does and should the Court play in American politics? If its members do little more than decide in accordance with their personal views as to wise policy, in light of what they can get away with politically, of what value is the Court?

At least part of the answer is supplied by pluralist theory. To reiterate, our system of government consists of numerous and diverse political institutions arranged nonhierarchically. The purpose of this type of system is to expand the number and diversity of opportunities for groups to advance their interests and contest policies that they believe will harm their interests. The end result is intended to be government policy that is disagreeable to the fewest interests possible. A pluralist system should thus result in a higher degree of "nonarbitrariness," liberty, and political stability as compared to a system without such redundancy and diversity. What then does this imply for the Court's role?

The Court quite simply serves as another step in the policy process. The Court provides yet another, and a still different, forum in which interest groups may challenge the policy initiatives of other branches and levels of government. Accordingly, the chance that government policy will in the end prove more satisfactory to the diverse interests in our nation is increased, as is the stability of the system as a whole.

This is the normative value of the Court, *in theory*. Whether the Court in fact contributes over time to a more broadly based consensus, rather than merely substituting its favored groups as winners for those chosen by the legislature, is an important empirical question. One example of the type of research that is relevant to this inquiry is Ulmer's empirical examination of the success of government litigants in the Supreme Court in cases in which it was pitted against an "underdog" litigant.[8] Despite its tremendous resources and an impressive success record in the Court overall, the government's success against underdog litigants declined quite dramatically from 1903 to 1968. Sheehan's subsequent research revealed that government success when opposing underdogs has in fact varied, with the federal government winning only 37 percent of such cases from 1953 to 1970, but 74 percent from 1981 to 1988, a rather dramatic reflection of the Court's conservative shift.[9] It is precisely this sort of research, conducted over time, that may support, modify, or disprove the hypothesis that the Court's value lies in its capacity to give another chance to legislative losers and thereby to promote a broader consensus and system stability.

While the Court *may*, in the process of reviewing and revising existing policies, protect minorities or individual rights or "diffuse values" (some of the roles suggested by other scholars), there is absolutely no *guarantee* that the Court will in fact do so.[10] This is so because it is elected officials who select Supreme Court justices and, of course, they quite legitimately do so on the basis of ideology. Accordingly, the Court inevitably changes, and in a democracy should change, in accordance with the political views of the people and their elected representatives.

Every Court, to the degree that it is politically feasible, pursues its own political vision or agenda. Additionally, every Court does so *not* on account of some imperative from the constitutional text, the Framers' intentions, moral philosophy, or democratic theory. For example, the conservative

Lochner Court sought to protect economic liberty from what it perceived as arbitrary or ill-conceived restrictions imposed by popular and legislative majorities. The Warren Court perceived its role as promoting equality and protecting economic and political underdogs. While the Burger and Rehnquist Courts were no less eager to exercise their power, they were certainly less committed to the egalitarian ethic, particularly to its pursuit by judges. (If forced to do so, I would select "tradition" or traditional morality as a value that has served as a significant guide in the Rehnquist Court's decision-making.)[11]

None of these Courts was "wrong" in its choices. There are simply no absolute imperatives about the particular values or group interests that the Court must advance and protect.[12] However, because the Court is another site for reconsideration of policy decisions and because it is a differently organized and differently responsive forum, the chances that the Court will advance some group or value different from what has been advanced in other institutions is increased. (While the Court chose to do so for flag burners and free speech in *Texas* v. *Johnson*,[13] it did not for members of the Native American Church and the free exercise of religion in *Employment Division* v. *Smith*.[14]) The pluralist goal is thus met: the opportunity for a group to amend, damage, or halt policies perceived as inimical to its interests is enhanced (though not guaranteed), as is the likelihood that government policy as a whole will be more responsive to the diverse interests in society.

The values and group interests that the Court chooses to advance and is capable of advancing are not timeless or universal or derived from some external source, such as the Framers' intentions or moral philosophy. Rather, they are dictated by the personal values and experiences of the justices as constrained by the political environment in which the Court seeks to advance them. Thus, with regard to the question of the proper limits of judicial activism, there simply are none, at least not with regard to the types of issues or values with which the Court must consistently concern itself. Rather, the limits are set continuously according to the personal prudential judgments of the Court as to when judicial intervention is desirable and politically feasible.

Accordingly, the value and "special" role of the Court is not significantly different from the value of other redundant institutions in American politics. This will no doubt be perceived as a significant devaluation and "deflation" of the Court's role.[15] It does, of course, seem to lack the flair and eloquence of other prescriptions, for example "the Court as moral prophet." However, it is a role that is sensible in light of the pluralist character of American politics and a role that is quite valuable in a system such as ours in which achieving any sort of meaningful political consensus is quite difficult.

The Court as a Redundant, "Transformative" Institution

As was discussed in the previous chapter, consensus is never completely realized privately, which is why we create political institutions. That is particularly true in a large and diverse country such as ours. Nor is a consensus completely or meaningfully realized in the United States through the mobilization activities of our elections and political parties. In other words, the end result of our electoral and party activities is not a clear, specific, or comprehensive policy consensus.

As a consequence, the task of building and sustaining a consensus for specific government policies rests upon our governing institutions. They must develop "transformative" powers or capacities—the ability to transform the diverse, competing, and ambiguous interests and demands of a large population into *specific* government programs and policies.[16] Thus, the policy choices of our leaders cannot be objectively checked for their "democraticness" against some a priori, identifiable consensus since that so rarely exists, whether in some natural state or as the product of national elections.

Given such conditions, how do leaders make decisions and why do we sanction those choices as democratic? With regard to elected officials, the answer at first glance seems clear and simple. "Politicians subject to elections must operate within the limits set . . . by their expectations about what policies they can adopt and still be reelected."[17] Leaders are induced to discover, anticipate, and shape the reactions of voters and groups and, on that basis, choose policies that command enough support to insure policy success and continuance in office. And those decisions are regarded as democratic because their performance is subject to political validation, although perhaps of a crude sort given the difficulties of transmitting and interpreting policy approval, whether through parties, elections, or perhaps public opinion polls.

The task for political leaders in the United States is the more difficult and inexact one of anticipating and mobilizing a popular consensus for government policies amid considerable uncertainty as to where that actual or potential consensus lies. The difficulty of this task is directly and inversely related to the aggregative and integrative capacities of existing ideologies and alliances as well as of parties and electoral mechanisms. The accountability relationship to which U.S. political leaders are consequently subject induces behavior that tends more toward maintaining legitimacy via specific policy choices. This is in contrast to the "responsible party leader" who merely votes the party position that has been clearly, directly, and specifically endorsed by a majority of voters.[18]

The weaknesses in the policy guidance provided by elections and parties requires that our political leaders and institutions develop transformative capacities. Political leaders in the United States must be capable of transforming an ambiguous and complex array of popular policy preferences into specific decisions that sufficiently respond to popular desires to insure that they remain in office and retain their legitimacy and power to act. This general requirement exists for the Court no less than for other political institutions.

Neither party identification nor elections dictate congressional decisions. Instead, members who wish to be reelected must try to discern and organize a consensus behind their policy proposals or at least make specific policy choices they believe will command popular support sufficient for continuance in office. Nor do congressional mandates dictate bureaucratic decisions. Bureaucrats must devise specific rules and regulations that will not alienate the interest group, congressional, presidential, and judicial support they need to retain or expand their power.

Given that the Court also requires some degree of popular and elite support to maintain its power and legitimacy and to pursue its policy goals, it is faced with the same problem. The Constitution does not dictate judicial choice, and such choices might not in any case command the requisite political support. Nor does some prior consensus exist that would clearly indicate acceptable or unacceptable constitutional decisions. The Court no less than Congress, the president, and bureaucratic officials must choose specific decisions that insure the popular and elite support necessary for policy success and the continued power and legitimacy to act. Although the Court is not induced to do so specifically because of an electoral sanction, its need for popular and elite backing is very real nonetheless and carries with it similar sorts of consequences for the Court's decisionmaking behavior.

The Supreme Court, like other political institutions, bears the responsibility for placing before the people policy initiatives they hope and have predicted will command a sufficient level of support. This is, in the United States, a most difficult and valuable function, one that requires political leadership skills. Our leaders must do more than merely reflect public wishes. They must, through their policy choices, anticipate public wishes and provoke a public reaction, and if need be revise the initial policy decision.

The "echo chamber" analogy developed by V. O. Key is useful here.[19] In *The Responsible Electorate,* Key argued that "the voice of the people is but an echo chamber. The output of an echo chamber bears an inevitable and invariable relation to the input. As candidates and parties clamor for attention and vie for popular support, the people's verdict can be no more than a selective reflection from among the alternatives and outlooks presented to them."[20] In a large and diverse country such as exists in the United States, there are inherent limitations on the ability of the people to communicate a meaningful and coherent set of policy instructions to the government. For example in elections, the vocabulary of the people is largely restricted to two words—*yes* and *no.* They may vote for one candidate and his or her set of policies or for another. A high premium is, thus, placed on the quality of the choices given to voters. To the degree that the people are given a clear and meaningful choice regarding competing policies, their simple yes or no response has meaning. This is what permits them to have a meaningful measure of control over government policy.

In short, "the people" are largely restricted to *reacting* and must be given something meaningful to which to react. This responsibility for putting before the people meaningful policy initiatives is shared by many political leaders, including Supreme Court justices. The Court is a partner and competitor in this process of developing policy initiatives that, it is hoped, will succeed in commanding a consensus and then revising those initiatives in accordance with popular and elite feedback. The Court, by being a differently representative and responsive institution, can add to the volume and diversity of information regarding which policies are capable of receiving broad and enduring support.

This then is at least part of the value in having the Court serve as yet another set of political representatives seeking to "make good policy" as they see it. That value is the additional opportunity provided for groups to contest the actions (or inactions) of other officials, thereby contributing, like other redundant institutions, to a governing process that promotes consensus and stability.

Yet this cannot be the end of the inquiry regarding the value and proper scope of policy-motivated judicial activism in a pluralist system. It must be acknowledged that, at some point, the Court might be forcing reconsideration of existing policies that produces little added value in terms of consensus building but significantly greater costs in terms of policy clarity and coherence. It is doubtful that each and every delaying "bite at the policy apple" by the Court is equally valuable in terms of consensus building or equally insignificant in terms of the costs to policy coherence and closure. (This is particularly so given the numerous "bites" no doubt already taken by others.) Thus, the question that must be examined more closely is of what *particular* value is the Court's additional intervention and what might that imply for any limits on its intervention?

The Unique Contribution of the Court as a Redundant Institution

The question at hand is, "What of value does the Court add to the policy process?" This is a question of comparative institutional performance. For example, we would want to know whether the Court is only needlessly adding to the noise and confusion of the endless reconsideration of existing policies or merely substituting its preferred winners for those of the legislature.

Our political system is replete with institutional redundancies, a multiplicity of arenas available for reconsideration of existing policies. Achieving some sort of closure or agreement on policy is accordingly quite difficult. When the Court accepts the invitation to review and revise an existing policy, there may be some value in terms of expanded group representation or more cautious consideration of policy consequences. However, it may come at a cost to the development of clarity, coherence, and finality in policymaking. The question then is whether the Court serves as a *particularly valuable* redundancy.

Of course, this is a question for all redundant institutions and not only the Court. The value in having diverse, redundant policymaking bodies is the different insight each has into the question of the desirability and political acceptability of various policy alternatives. What then might be the nature of the Court's "insight"?

Although it can be and typically is exaggerated, one difference for the Court is the more indirect and diffuse form of popular and elite influence to which it is subject. This relative freedom from direct and immediate political reprisals may be used to defend groups or values that do not receive adequate representation in the other branches (apart from whether they have a special place in the Constitution).[21] Certainly this is the case with regard to *Brown* and the then politically dangerous course of combating race discrimination. It is also true with regard to protecting street demonstrations, picketing, and even flag burning as forms of political expression protected by the First Amendment.

As discussed previously, although that opportunity exists, there is nothing that demands or that can guarantee that the Court will protect unpopular ideas and groups consistently. And to insist that the Court do so aggressively and exclusively is a dangerous prescription in terms of preserving the Court's power and legitimacy. Yet the Court can choose to use its freedom in that way if it does so carefully and prudently.[22]

Certainly in a society as large and diverse as ours, there is value in having an institution that can guard against the development of a class of permanent political losers who may then threaten the stability of the system. In this way, the Court's intervention on behalf of African Americans may have resulted in a less painful and violent movement toward racial equality and justice than would have occurred if a single legislative institution provided the only available avenue of change. In this instance, the Court's contribution as a redundant institution proved more valuable than the redundancies offered by the Senate in relation to the House or the president in relation to the Congress. This may be seen as a systemic safety valve function.

However, the Court may choose to protect political losers even though they cannot threaten the system. Certainly that is the case with regard to criminal suspects, aliens, and "far-out" religious and political dissidents. This may promote the values of tolerance and fair play, thereby also contributing to systemic legitimacy and stability.

The Court can also serve as an often-needed counterweight to the dominance of wealthy and well-organized groups in legislative and administrative decisionmaking. The Framers were particularly concerned about "factional tyranny." They feared the ability of a single group, especially a majority, to dominate government and impose policies on the nation that benefited themselves at the expense of others and the general good. They hoped that in a large republic, there would be a diversity of interests, none of which would be able, with staggered elections and a fragmented government structure, to control simultaneously all the various "pieces" of governmental power and use them selfishly and tyrannously.

However, legislative and administrative policymaking typically rewards groups that are well organized, well financed, and unified around narrow (typically economic) interests. Accordingly, certain interests are inherently advantaged. For example, dairy farmers are intensely interested in the issue of dairy price supports. The economic stakes for them are quite high, and they are a small group with inherent organizational advantages. The economic stake for consumers, while substantial, is spread thinly among a large, diffuse population that has greater difficulty organizing to protect their common interest in low prices. The same dynamics are at work for doctors and hospitals as compared to patients, producers in relation to consumers, and polluters compared to environmentalists.

When well-organized groups with narrow economic interests are able to dominate the legislative and administrative process, we have precisely the sort of factional tyranny the Framers feared.[23] The Court, however, is not so dependent as legislators or executive branch agencies on those groups for ongoing political support. It possesses relatively greater capacity to protect underrepresented, diffuse interests. Thus, they can require legislatures and bureaucratic agencies to justify granting policy benefits exclusively and arbitrarily to such traditionally dominant groups.

Certainly, the Court's relaxation of standing requirements for challenging agency decisions represents an increase in its capacity to serve precisely that role. Throughout the 1960s and 1970s, the Court abandoned its traditional requirement that only those with a substantial economic stake in agency decisions possessed the requisite standing to challenge those decisions in court.[24] This change in access thus enabled diffuse and weakly organized interests like consumers and environmentalists to serve as a counterweight to narrow, well-organized economic interests.

Similarly, the Court's reapportionment decisions can be characterized as an effort to protect the majority (i.e., urban interests, especially the poor and minorities) from laws favoring overrepresented minorities (i.e., rural conservatives). Recent antiaffirmative action decisions[25] are no doubt a reflection of the increased conservatism of the Rehnquist Court. However, they might also be seen as an attempt to check the power of minorities to win advantages for themselves at the expense of the majority, or at least minority power to do so absent some compelling justification.

The Court then is capable of fulfilling the Framers' expectations that redundant institutions serve as a check against factional dominance. This is another example of the *unique* contribution that the Court, as a redundant institution, can provide.

In addition to possessing relatively greater freedom to protect unpopular or inadequately represented groups and values, the Court approaches and resolves policy disputes differently, which may serve as a valuable redundancy. For example, policy questions for the Court are more likely to arise in the context of vivid, individualized stories that may reveal the unexpected and adverse consequences of the policy generalizations rendered by legislatures. Thus, greater precision in the design and execution of policies may result from the Court's intervention in the face of unacceptable consequences in the individual and perhaps marginal case.[26]

Appraising the Court's added contribution to the policy process is an empirical question, requiring empirical research. A collection of studies presented in Robert Mnookin's *In the Interest of Children* provides precisely this sort of analysis.[27] The typical pattern revealed by these case studies is a legislative-judicial dialogue, initiated by the Court's sensitivity to deviant cases and unanticipated legislative consequences.

One such case study examined *Smith* v. *Offer*,[28] a class-action suit challenging the power of New York State officials to remove a child from a foster home without providing a hearing for the foster parents.[29] The authors legitimately conclude that the judges involved in this case did not demonstrate a *superior* sensitivity to the needs of foster children than the New York State legislature and its Temporary Commission on Child Welfare. However, the Court did prove to be "a valuable, if limited, forum for nudging government toward more humane treatment of children and families."[30]

Most significantly, the Court's decision requiring a hearing for transfers of foster children limited the potential for arbitrary agency actions. The new rules enabled more and better information to be gathered and thus potentially provided better protection for children. They also were cited as "one of several factors contributing to a higher degree of trust between foster parents and the agency because the foster parents knew they were entitled to a review of decisions to remove by an impartial examiner."[31] Judicial intervention, thus, at least partially succeeded in increasing administrative caution and sensitivity and in decreasing the likelihood of arbitrary removals.

Legal battles in the 1970s over the issue of coercing single mothers receiving welfare to pursue child support from the fathers of their children also provide evidence of the special value of judges in the policymaking process.[32] As a result of *Roe* v. *Norton,* the legislature was forced to deal with the minority of cases in which providing information about the absent father could produce retaliation against the mother or her children. Although it came after years of litigation and deadlock, the Court did encourage a fuller and more careful exploration of the costs of a general coerced maternal cooperation rule in the marginal though not insignificant case.

Bellotti v. *Baird*[33] presents a less clearly successful case of judicial intervention.[34] *Bellotti* involved a challenge to a Massachusetts law requiring parental consent for pregnant minors to obtain an abortion. The class representative in the litigation, Mary Moe, claimed that her father would kick her out of the house and kill her boyfriend if she were forced to seek his consent for an abortion. Judges thus evaluated the law in the context of an individual and possibly deviant case in which a minor would not benefit and might be harmed by the parental consent requirement.

Judicial intervention could have alerted legislators to consider the consequences of their parental consent policy more thoroughly and carefully, providing protection to the marginal case like Mary Moe's. Judicial intervention could have also demanded that the legislature do more than simply reward prolife groups intent on restricting *Roe* and promoting prolife and family values (which is what the Massachusetts legislature seemed to be doing). It could have required the legislature to engage in a more thorough examination of the moral and policy issues at stake. However, the Court in the end did little more than impose its own policy on the legislature, a policy that largely fudged the underlying moral and policy issues.

The Court decided that while a pregnant minor's rights were not coextensive with those of a pregnant adult, a parental veto of a mature minor's decision to abort was unconstitutional. In order to protect the minor's rights and the state's concern for the minor's welfare, the Court encouraged judicial authorization as an alternative to parental consent. Massachusetts followed Justice Powell's "advice" in *Bellotti* to the letter. The result, however, was a judicial "rubber-stamp" operation,[35] which most people involved in the process (abortion counselors, lawyers, and judges) found quite unsatisfactory.

The Court, thus, did not seem to perform much better than the legislature, merely replacing legislative winners, prolife groups, with the judicially favored prochoice groups. While the judges involved were concerned, and legitimately so, with the deviant case of Mary Moe, they were not attentive to the more ordinary case in which a pregnant minor would benefit from parental involvement (and which, in the typical case, produces parental consent).

The Court could have heightened legislative awareness of the harmful consequences of the parental consent rule in the marginal case and consequently initiated a more productive legislative-judicial dialogue. Instead, it substituted its preference for prochoice values and chose judicial consent over parental consent.

It is precisely this type of research that is capable of revealing the *variable* value of judicial intervention. As a general rule, the Court's role as a redundant institution has value in terms of providing groups and values receiving insufficient attention elsewhere to have at least a chance at being included and represented in the policymaking process. This, in and of itself, should contribute over time to a broader consensus, increased systemic legitimacy, and greater political stability.

However, we would also want that intervention to improve the policy product and to provide something of value that offsets the costs which judicial reconsideration adds to policy clarity, coherence, and finality. This discussion suggests two distinctive contributions that the Court can make in the endless consideration and reconsideration of existing policies.

First, the Court possesses the ability (if not always the will) to protect unpopular or underrepresented groups and values. This can be of tremendous value in a diverse society such as exists in the United States and in a system in which the legislative and executive branches are often overly responsive to moralistic majorities or to well-organized groups with narrow economic interests. Of great value to the system's legitimacy and stability, the Court can intervene on behalf of the perennial legislative loser, as in the case of the Court's battle against state-sanctioned and state-encouraged racial discrimination and in its protection of criminal suspects, aliens, and religious and political dissidents.

The Court also considers the wisdom of legislative and administrative policies in the context of individual cases, often marginal and deviant cases. Thus, the Court is likely to be more sensitive than legislatures to the adverse effects of policy generalizations at the margins. Judges are likely to see, in often dramatic fashion, the problems of policy over- and underinclusiveness. The special contribution of the Court then is more precision in fashioning public policy—policymaking with a scalpel rather than a hatchet.

A political Court pursuing its policy goals in light of what is politically feasible is not then simply one of many redundant institutions possessing equal value. While we may grant value to all redundancies for providing more forums for disgruntled groups seeking to advance their interests, we must be aware of the costs of excessive redundancy to policy clarity, policy coherence, and timeliness. However, the Court's distinctive contribution to the process of policy agreement is of greater value than the added contribution of, for example, redundant subcommittees in Congress or the shared jurisdiction of half a dozen executive branch agencies. Thus, the Court possesses the capacity for serving as a particularly profitable redundancy in the policymaking process, by invoking interests and values overlooked in other branches and by being sensitive to unintended or harmful policy consequences in individual cases.

Evaluating the Court

While the previous discussion is suggestive regarding how we then should evaluate the Court and its particular decisions, a more direct inquiry is called for. How do we evaluate the Court as a redundant institution in a pluralist system? How does such an evaluation differ from conventional approaches?

Conventional scholars attempt to provide us with a clear and objective way for the Court to interpret the Constitution without relying on personal preference or some other subjective source. In the process, scholars are provided with a clear and objective way to evaluate the Court. We can determine when the Court is exceeding its legitimate role or exercising its power arbitrarily or inappropriately. However, as chapter 2 explained, these scholars fail to deliver on that promise. If constitutional decisionmaking is inherently subjective and legitimately premised on the justices' personal values, how are we to evaluate the Court?

Although the Critical Legal Studies scholars are persuasive in their critique of conventional approaches and in their view that constitutional decisionmaking is inherently subjective and "political," their final conclusion is inadequate. These Critics despair and throw up their hands, denigrating all exercises of judicial power as arbitrary and illegitimate due to our inability to stop judges from making subjective and personally biased judgments when interpeting the Constitution. However, the lack of objective constraints on judicial power is not, I have argued, such a troublesome matter in a democracy.

If there are no objectively correct constitutional answers, and if there are only politically defensible or subjectively defensible constitutional decisions, *and* if we truly care about democracy, then there is a very simple answer to the question of when the Court is exceeding its legitimate authority. That simple answer is, "Let the people (and their interest group and political leaders) decide."

In other words, it is not a scholarly judgment, but a political judgment when the Court is exceeding its legitimate role or deciding inappropriately. That judgment is one that properly belongs in the public sphere; it is a proper subject for public debate and political action. The task of scholars is only to examine the variety of ways in which the people can express their satisfaction or dissatisfaction with the Court, to suggest how they might do so more effectively, and, further, to evaluate particular decisions or doctrines in terms of the consequences for public policy and the quality of the democratic process.

What then does this mean for how we might evaluate the Court? At least in part that evaluation should consist of an assessment of the processes by which there is a meaningful political dialogue over the Court's policy decisions and direction. There are four distinct elements here which insure that the Court is better equipped to pursue policies likely to command a consensus, which additionally insure that the people can respond in a meaningful way, and which further insure that the Court will pay attention and respond to such information. We can be assured that the Court is not exceeding its legitimate role to the degree that:

1. the selection process works properly, as a device for examining, debating, and sanctioning the political preferences of the justices;

2. the Court is clear and honest in its policymaking, in order to enable a meaningful response to its policy initiatives by the public and other political leaders;

3. there are effective opportunities for the people and other political leaders to respond; and

4. the justices possess the desire and ability to listen and respond to such information, a product of policy motivation, political sensitivity, and political experience and skill.

The Selection Process

The selection process should serve as an opportunity for political dialogue and deliberation on the values the Court should be pursuing. This is precisely what occurred with President Reagan's nomination of Judge Bork to the Supreme Court. While media and Senate scrutiny is not typically so vigorous (unfortunately, I believe), the stakes were quite high, given that Bork would be replacing Justice Powell and, thus, be placing in jeopardy a number of significant Court policies, such as those concerning abortion and affirmative action. There was significant public and media attention, substantial interest group involvement, and intense Senate scrutiny and debate. This is just as it should be.[36] We should be quite conscious of the policy consequences of placing a new justice on the Court. This then is a critical way in which the people and their elected representatives can influence the Court and its future policy direction; "we the people" are deciding the proper bounds of judicial policymaking.

The Quality of the Policy Message

The Court should be clear and honest about the fundamental value choices involved in its decisions.[37] To the degree that the Court resorts to legalisms or vague constitutional reasoning, it is ignoring and fleeing from the value conflicts inevitably underlying its decisions. This does a great disservice to the political process and to the people who deserve the opportunity to understand and respond to the Court's discretionary political choices. By dealing with those value conflicts clearly and honestly, the Court can bring a focus and energy to public debate and can thereby facilitate a dialogue and political response on the issues of the day.

Even the Court's failures, its occasional failures to predict accurately the degree of political support for its policies, constitute democratic successes, at least when the Court is clear and forthright in its policy objectives. For example, the conservative anti–New Deal justices, consistent with the value premises of their appointments, protected the values of economic liberty and laissez-faire from legislative interference. They did so until such strict allegiance to those values was clearly and overwhelmingly repudiated by the people and their elected representatives. Thus, the Court provided a final and definitive check on the breadth and depth of that new political consensus.

Similarly, the Warren Court pursued the goal of economic and political equality on a variety of fronts. In doing so, the justices put to a clear test the commitment of the American people and their political leaders to equality as an *overriding* value in public policy. The resulting political backlash, along with the new conservative Nixon and Reagan justices it produced, resulted in a more moderate egalitarian course, one more consistent with the popular and elite consensus.

The point here is not the "correctness" of the policy decisions of either the anti–New Deal Court or the egalitarian Warren Court. Rather, the clarity and consistency of the policy pursuits of each gave the American people and their leaders something to which to react, a clear choice that provided valuable information regarding a political consensus on those issues. Without leaders engaging us in such a clear, value-focused debate, policy consensus cannot emerge, due to, as previously discussed, the ambiguity and complexity of policy preferences in the society and weaknesses of our party and electoral mechanisms in mobilizing them.

The clarity of the Court's policy message and thus the clarity of the political response to that message can also be hampered by the Court "overextending" itself. If the Court has no clear or simple policy agenda and instead nibbles away willy-nilly at too many different and discrete policies, a political response is necessarily inhibited. Similarly, the ideological divisons within the Burger Court, the lack of leadership within that Court, and its tendency to favor "balancing approaches" over establishing general value and policy principles also inhibited our ability to "label" that Court and, thus, be capable of responding to its general policy course.

Of course, wise politics on the Court, as in other institutions, may require fudging the value conflicts a bit in the service of other goals, such as consensus building within the Court. However, particularly when the Court pursues a new policy, it should not and probably cannot expect to build substantial and long-term support for that policy by hiding behind unclear, unpersuasive, or false grounds, as the Court did in *Roe* v. *Wade.*

Opportunities for a Political Response

To facilitate a political dialogue on the Court's policy decisions, there must then be effective opportunities for the people and their interest group and governmental representatives to respond to the Court's policy initiatives. There are, as previously discussed, a variety of such opportunities. Supreme Court decisions often become election campaign issues, with candidates pledging to pursue certain selection or policy implementation strategies. Senate confirmation hearings are often a vehicle for sanctioning or criticizing the Court's policy course. Interest group litigation is another option, as is pressuring congressional or executive officials to pursue policy change or retaliatory action against the Court.

The adequacy of those mechanisms for responding to the Court must be an important and ongoing area of inquiry for political scientists. For example, Mark Silverstein and Benjamin Ginsberg have argued that because of its liberalized justiciability rules and its ability to attract supportive interest groups who benefited from judicial activism, the Court has substantially increased its power and its independence from executive control.[38] They believe that "the opportunity for the president to transform the Court and the federal judiciary through the appointment power has narrowed considerably."[39] Although recent appointments (especially by Reagan) suggest otherwise, such claims require our attention and our concern that the Court not become too independent from political checks on its policymaking power.

Policy Motivation on the Part of Supreme Court Justices

The mechanisms that enable a political response to and check on the Court are directed to insuring responsiveness in the Court's policymaking and to providing adequate feedback to the justices regarding their policy choices. However, these mechanisms will matter little if the justices do not care about the ultimate success of their policy initiatives. Thus, policy motivation, combined with a keen sense of the political limitations regarding what the Court can in fact accomplish, are valuable judicial traits.

Congress on occasion considers whether a certain amount of judicial experience might be a worthwhile statutory requirement for Supreme Court justices. They may as well have done so, as recent presidents have overwhelmingly chosen to elevate judges to the High Bench, rather than transferring prominent politicians there. However, we would be much better served by a requirement for legislative experience (and perhaps administrative experience, given the growth in judicial oversight of administrative decisionmaking). It is legislative experience that would better enable justices to anticipate popular and elite reaction to its decisions and which would give them the requisite political acuity and sensitivity in making those difficult judgments. These sorts of qualities should be an important part of the Senate's inquiry into the fitness of a nominee for the Court. Thus, the Senate was quite legitimately troubled by what appeared to be a lack of political sensitivity and awareness on the part of Judge Bork as to the consequences of his purportedly intellectually rigorous and coherent theory of constitutional interpretation.[40]

A substantial part of our evaluation of the Court and its policymaking activities should, thus, be process oriented. In other words, the Court's policy pursuits are legitimate as long as the processes by which the values expressed in Supreme Court opinions are a product of the politically controlled selection process and, further, are debated and responded to by the public and their political leaders. However, there is a supplemental evaluation that can be made.

Substantive Evaluation of the Court's Policies

The general process-based evaluation can be supplemented by an evaluation of specific policies or doctrines. The purpose of such an evaluation is not whether the Court was correct in some objective sense. Rather, the question is whether the Court exercised sound political judgment—that is, whether its judgments are sound and valid regarding which policies prove, in the long term, both beneficial to society and capable of commanding and sustaining a consensus.[41] This is, after all, how we evaluate other political leaders as well, not according to whether their policies accurately reflect some momentary "public mood." And as previously noted, even if the Court's judgments ultimately prove wrong, there may be value in terms of the quality of the policy-consensus information thereby generated.

For example, the anti–New Deal Court of the early 1930s sorely miscalculated the degree of political opposition to its decisions; in other words, it misread (or dangerously ignored) the consensus that had emerged. Of course, by forthrightly pursuing that policy course, the Court did enable "the people" to have their say and to repudiate clearly and definitively the old consensus as to the legitimacy and desirability of government intervention in the economy.[42]

With regard to *Brown*, the Court exercised political judgment and political vision and concluded that the time was right for such a decision. The Court was acutely aware of the political risks involved and certainly took them into account. However, it was also aware of the consequences of continuing to put off the resolution of the race issue. The justices took notice of the group support and opposition, considered the possible political reactions, and developed strategies to increase the likelihood of ultimate success. To the degree that *Brown* was successful, it was not because the justices were brilliant legal theoreticians, but because they were wise and experienced politicians.

With regard to *Roe*, the story is still being told. Certainly the Court's initial policy decision, granting full freedom of choice during the first trimester (and, in effect, through the second), was not widely supported, but then neither was the type of restrictive Texas law struck down in *Roe*. We can, of course, fault the Court (and Justice Blackmun in particular) for the failure to talk honestly and persuasively about what it was doing and why. Instead, the Court resorted to an evaluation of the medical information, sanctified the doctor-patient relationship, and relied on some rather unpersuasive constitutional hocus-pocus. That has likely hurt its ability to build and maintain political support for its initial policy goal.

Additionally, the Court at least initially permitted virtually no restriction on access to abortions in the first trimester. This position has never been supported by even a substantial minority of the people. This is not necessarily a sign that the Court was wrong. However, it failed to persuade us *why* overriding public opinion on this issue was necessary or desirable. The Court also failed to acknowledge *any* legitimate governmental interest in regulating abortion in the first trimester. For a considerable length of time, it preempted the field of abortion policy and foreclosed the possibility of compromise or abortion policy reform in legislatures.

A judicial veto of restrictive abortion statutes can perhaps be justified in light of changes in medical conditions and the difficulties poor and working-class women had in organizing effectively to challenge those statutes, many of which were in fact passed before women could vote. However, the quality of the Court's intervention can be criticized as dishonest and as a foreclosure on rather than an invitation to abortion policy reform.

The abortion decisions of the West German Constitutional Court were in this sense superior to *Roe* and its progeny.[43] The West German Court ruled against a relatively lenient abortion law, liberalized by the Bundestag in 1974.

However, it did so on the basis that the law did not sufficiently protect human life. The Court, however, granted considerable discretion to the legislature to revise its abortion regulations, provided that "abortion is not to be completely decriminalized . . . and [provided] that the total effect of the laws in the area is to support and protect the value of human life."[44] The result was that the Bundestag was permitted to and did in fact develop a workable compromise on the issue.

The U.S. Supreme Court, on the other hand, "virtually closed down the state legislative process with respect to abortions prior to viability."[45] The Supreme Court elevated the woman's individual right of privacy over all other rights. The right of privacy was made supreme over the rights of the fetus, which of course the Court refused to acknowledge. And at least in the first trimester, a woman's right of privacy was made weightier than the right of the legislature to affirm the value of human life or to communicate a messsage regarding the seriousness and moral concern that should accompany the decision to abort human life. Although the Rehnquist Court has given legislatures more freedom to restrict access to and use of abortion,[46] the Court for over twenty years foreclosed the sort of compromise and abortion reform that occurred in Western Europe. As compared to the West German Court, the Supreme Court's approach represents a far less politically sensitive "resolution" of the issue and one that has proven far more divisive.

This certainly does not exhaust all of the possible implications of viewing the Court as a redundant, differently representative policymaking institution in a pluralist system. However, the primary purpose of this effort has been to dismantle the old theoretical foundation and develop and defend an alternative one. Such questions briefly explored here simply do not emerge from contemporary constitutional debate. For example, while we may wish to evaluate the internal logic and consistency of a decision, that is only a very small part of the issue of how responsibly the Court exercises its power and whether we are better off for the Court's intervention. Recognizing the discretionary, subjective nature of judicial decisionmaking, dispensing with negative and stereotyped views regarding political motivation and its consequences, and acknowledging the redundancy value and democratic legitimacy of judicial review in our pluralist system enables us to expand our inquiry. The Court exercises discretionary political power, and our evaluation must consist of how responsibly and profitably the Court exercises that power.

Whither the Constitution?

In *The Tempting of America*, Bork provides an anecdote (which he hopes is not authentic) about a new state supreme court chief justice "who, upon first meeting a United States Supreme Court Justice, said, 'I'm delighted to meet you in person because I have just taken an oath to support and defend whatever comes into your head.' "[47] The notion that the Constitution is not "law" but the arbitrary preferences of those individuals lucky enough to reach the Court is terribly troubling to Bork. Such a notion challenges the very existence of rights and liberties that individuals possess, it belittles the oath of all government officials to obey the Constitution, and it calls into question the legitimacy of all of the statutes, treaties, and judicial decisions made throughout American history. As a result, the notion that the Constitution is not law profoundly changes the nature of political obligation; if there are no laws or no ground rules as to how to identify "legitimate" commands of the government, why should anyone obey? The decision as to "what is law" becomes individualized, "incoherent and chaotic."[48]

If, as I have argued, the Court is merely one of many redundant, transformative institutions, adding its own views and insights to the consensus building process, then of what significance is the Constitution itself? If the Constitution is significantly indeterminate and capable of manipulation by politically motivated (and unelected) judges, then why bother with a written Constitution at all? Are the consequences indeed as terrifying as Bork and others suggest?[49]

It is important to point out first that these predicted consequences flow from an exaggerated and distorted view of politically motivated constitutional decisionmaking. No one is suggesting that a justice does or should arbitrarily make the Constitution mean "whatever comes into her head" at the moment. Constitutional meaning can only be given by at least five justices, who have been approved by elected officials, and only when the public and political leaders have accepted that meaning as well. Additionally, precedent conditions (though it does not control) that process, thus also limiting the likelihood of a radical breakdown in the shared understandings of what the Constitution means.

A dose of realism regarding the source of the Court's decisions or the indeterminacy of the Constitution is highly unlikely in any case to produce the conditions Bork describes. It will not produce noncompliance on a mass scale or a "lawless" society, in the sense that all citizens decide individually and arbitrarily whether every law is truly a law or merely the personal preference of a few black-robed politicians. There certainly is a middle ground between the extremes of "no political obligation to obey" and "no political obligation (or need) to question."

There are benefits to accepting that we have an unwritten Constitution, or at least one continually rewritten by unelected judges who decide in accordance with their personal political preferences in light of their political acceptability. The idea that we can avoid confronting and resolving difficult moral and political choices by easy resort to a hallowed document interpreted by Platonic Guardians undermines democracy. Weakening if not dispensing with notions of certainty and objectivity in constitutional interpretation may strengthen the will and ability of the people and their representatives to evaluate the Court and its policies more closely. When constitutional interpretation is regarded and practiced as a broadly shared democratic exercise, even if Court led, the values to which the Constitution variously speaks should in the end be more rather than less broadly and meaningfully felt.[50]

If the only function of the Constitution is its utility in helping the justices to mislead us into accepting their discretionary and personal preference–driven decisions as "constitutional truths" deserving of obedience, then perhaps the Constitution is a threat rather than a boon to democracy. What functions then, aside from that of myth and power protector, might the Constitution serve?

One obvious and profitable function the Constitution serves is that it establishes a basic structural framework. It sets down, in a formal way, the "rules of the game," which are not continually open for debate and change. Thus, the Constitution cordons off some political issues for purposes of simplicity, manageability, and stability.

The Constitution can also serve to channel and limit political debate. Although there are substantial limits to the ability of the text to dictate constitutional outcomes, when combined with legal norms of *stare decisis,* constitutional doctrines can narrow and focus political debate. Every political issue in every forum, for practical reasons, cannot provoke a far-ranging and comprehensive philosophical inquiry or cost-benefit analysis. Even evolving constitutional doctrine shapes the arguments and evidence that are to be regarded as legitimate matters of inquiry. Thus, agreement on the parameters of debate, as set in text-based doctrine, can serve as an anchor, an agreed-upon starting point for argumentation and even for deciding what constitutes a legal or constitutional issue.

Such text-based rules and limits are constructive for debate within the Court and for lower court judges as well. Compromise and agreement within the Court is more difficult in the absence of any textual or doctrinal guidance. Polarization within the Court is less likely when constitutional change proceeds along a narrower doctrinal path bounded to a degree by text and precedent. For lower courts as well, precedents serve as guideposts that limit permissible arguments and decisions. Thus, each and every case does not become yet another opportunity to make policy anew on a blank slate. Incremental change rather than unguided wholesale policy change is encouraged.

Where conventional scholars err is in assuming that the *content* of that textual or doctrinal anchor can be regarded as objectively correct in some sense, for example as dictated by the Framers' intent, moral philosophy, or democratic theory. The content of Court doctrine, while relatively stable, is not driven by the words of the Constitution nor by the existence of some coherent theory of moral principles. It is instead significantly driven by the personal values and policy preferences of the justices, as well as by the consensus reached and affirmed in the recent past. However, what is distinctive is that each justice does not possess full freedom to rewrite constitutional doctrines in toto from those personal views. Those doctrines evolve—from what has gone before, from what results from compromise within the Court, and from what is politically permissible.

Thus, the Constitution, far from establishing given moral principles that philosopher kings interpret for us, merely establishes a structural framework and, when combined with *stare decisis,* channels political debate. Compromise, incremental change, and, thus, political stability are thereby promoted.

Owen Fiss,[51] like Bork, is fearful of the consequences of what he refers to as the "nihilistic view" that the Constitution has no clear or definitive meaning and that the Court "simply beats the text into a shape which will serve [its] own purpose."[52] Interestingly, the consequences that Fiss fears would occur if the nihilistic view were to take root in the public mind are similar to what I have just described with regard to the Constitution's role.

> The great public text of modern America, the Constitution, would be drained of meaning. It would be debased. It would no longer be seen as embodying a public morality to be understood and expressed through rational processes like adjudication; it would be reduced to a mere instrument of political organization—distributing political power and establishing the modes by which that power will be exercised. Public values would be defined only as those held by the current winners in the processes prescribed by the Constitution; beyond that, there would be only individual morality, or even worse, only individual interests.[53]

Like many conventional legal scholars, Fiss expresses a fear of placing too much faith in the political process as the forum for debate over our public values. In contrast, I am concerned that traditional constitutional scholarship has placed too much faith in the Constitution as an exclusive and objective source of our public values and too much faith as well in the justices as sole and superior arbiters of their meaning. The Constitution is better conceived as providing, in the interest of consensus and stability, a complex system of alternative political arenas for an ongoing debate about public values—their meaning and their application; the Court is better conceived as one of those arenas.[54]

Neither the Constitution nor the Court need to be granted a role more profound and exalted than this. The justices are and should be regarded as politicians who share in the difficult but noble task of political leadership, in generating consensual solutions to the often vexing and contentious issues of the day. However, political responsibility must attend the Court's fulfillment of that task. Insuring that political responsibility is a Court composed of justices, chosen by elected officials on the basis of ideology, who wish to advance a clear and coherent policy agenda and who possess political experience and sensitivity. Enforcing that responsibility is both the will and the capacity of the people and their representatives to respond clearly and effectively to the Court's policy choices. Contrary to the conventional wisdom, these "political" factors do not permit or promote judicial tyranny, but instead go far to prevent it.

NOTES

•••

INTRODUCTION

1. Charles Evans Hughes, *Addresses of Charles Evans Hughes* 185–86 (New York: Putnam's, 1916).

2. To be more accurate, most political scientists readily accept Hughes's assertion as truth, while most conventional constitutional law scholars vehemently reject it (at least as an inevitable truth).

3. However, I do not advocate judicial *supremacy*—the view that the Court has the exclusive or final say as to the Constitution's meaning.

4. Mark Tushnet, *Red, White, and Blue: A Critical Analysis of Constitutional Law*, 1–4 (Cambridge: Harvard University Press, 1988).

5. The term *legal autonomy* and its definition are provided by Phillip Johnson in "Do You Sincerely Want to Be Radical?" 36 *Stanford Law Review* 247, 252 (1984).

CHAPTER 1

1. Bernard H. Siegan, *The Supreme Court's Constitution: An Inquiry into Judicial Review and Its Impact on Society* (New Brunswick, N.J.: Transaction Books, 1987).

2. Only one Supreme Court justice, Samuel Chase, was impeached by the House of Representatives. However, the Senate failed to convict Chase by the required two-thirds vote, and he served out his term.

3. *Chisholm* v. *Georgia*, 2 U.S. 419 (1793), overruled by the Eleventh Amendment; *Dred Scott* v. *Sandford*, 60 U.S. 393 (1857), reversed by the Civil War Amendments (Thirteenth, Fourteenth, and Fifteenth); *Pollock* v. *Farmers' Loan & Trust Co.*, 157 U.S. 429 (1895), overruled by the Sixteenth Amendment; and *Oregon* v. *Mitchell*, 400 U.S. 112 (1970), overruled by the Twenty-sixth Amendment.

4. This is referred to as the Madisonian dilemma. See Bork's characterization in Robert H. Bork, *The Tempting of America: The Political Seduction of the Law* 139–41 (New York: Free Press, 1990).

5. *Lochner* v. *New York*, 198 U.S. 45 (1905).

6. The modern day example of such judicial arrogance and overreaching, for many scholars, is the Court's *Roe* v. *Wade* abortion ruling. 410 U.S. 113 (1973).

7. For an interesting and detailed account of the *Lochner* case and the social, economic, and political conditions prevailing at the time, see Paul Kens, *Judicial Power and Reform Politics* (Lawrence: University Press of Kansas, 1992).

8. The need for a theory of constitutional interpretation that objectively constrains judicial discretion was also a function of the need to rebut the Legal Realists. The Legal Realists, like their present day counterparts in the Critical Legal Studies movement, argued that judicial decisionmaking is subjective and arbitrary and that notions of mechanical jurisprudence and legal autonomy were devoid of meaning or relevance for judicial decisionmaking and failed as a restraint on "raw judicial power." See G. Edward White, "The Evolution of Reasoned Elaboration: Jurisprudential Criticism and Social Change," 59 *Virginia Law Review* 279 (1973).

9. Alexander M. Bickel, *The Least Dangerous Branch* 55 (Indianapolis: Bobbs-Merrill, 1962).

10. Thomas Grey originated the interpretivist-noninterpretivist distinction. "Do We Have an Unwritten Constitution?" 27 *Stanford Law Review* 703 (1975).

11. John Hart Ely, *Democracy and Distrust: A Theory of Judicial Review* (Cambridge: Harvard University Press, 1980).

12. A significant oversight, for example, is the group of "republican revivalists" or "civic republicans." For example, see Frank I. Michelman, "Bringing the Law to Life: A Plea for Disenchantment," 74 *Cornell Law Review* 256 (1989); Frank I. Michelman, "Law's Republic," 97 *Yale Law Journal* 1493 (1988); Suzanna Sherry, "Civic Culture and the Feminine Voice in Constitutional Adjudication," 72 *University*

of Virginia Law Review 543 (1986); Cass R. Sunstein, "Beyond the Republican Revival," 97 *Yale Law Journal* 1539 (1988); Cass R. Sunstein, *The Partial Constitution* (Cambridge: Harvard University, 1993).

Short shrift is, unfortunately, also given to Bruce Ackerman's interesting (but flawed) account of American democracy as "dualist." *We the People: Foundations* (Cambridge: Harvard University Press, 1991 and *We the People: Transformations* (Cambridge: Harvard University Press, 1998). According to Ackerman, during that rare occasion he labels a "constitutional moment," an unusually aroused and politically active public enacts higher lawmaking principles, which the Court is to preserve from ordinary politicians during more ordinary political times. If required to place him, I would put Ackerman in the interpretivist category, although he is quite different from the typical interpretivist. The Court's role, in his view, is to protect the people's deep and fundamental beliefs and desires. These may be expressed formally and textually in the Constitution and its amendments or, alternatively, informally through a "structural" amendment, in which We the People, after full and vigorous debate and definitive electoral victories, approve momentous constitutional change such as occurred in the New Deal period. In this sense, the Court merely interprets the formal and "informal" text.

13. Philip Bobbitt, *Constitutional Fate: Theory of the Constitution* 43 (New York: Oxford University Press, 1982).

14. Herbert Wechsler, "Toward Neutral Principles of Constitutional Law," 73 *Harvard Law Review* 1 (1959); Henry M. Hart, Jr., "Foreword: The Time Chart of the Justices," 73 *Harvard Law Review* 84 (1959).

15. Bickel especially emphasizes the Court's enhanced capacity for principled deliberation and decisionmaking. *The Least Dangerous Branch*, 25–26. See also Harry H. Wellington, *Interpreting the Constitution: The Supreme Court and the Process of Adjudication* (New Haven: Yale University Press, 1990).

16. Owen Fiss, "Foreword: The Forms of Justice," 93 *Harvard Law Review* 1 (1979).

17. Ibid. at 51. See also John Hart Ely, "Another Such Victory: Constitutional Theory and Practice in a World Where Courts Are No Different from Legislatures," 77 *Virginia Law Review* 833 (1991).

18. E.g., Wechsler, "Toward Neutral Principles."

19. E.g., Fiss, "The Forms of Justice"; Bickel, *The Least Dangerous Branch.*

20. Martin M. Shapiro, "The Supreme Court and Constitutional Adjudication: Of Politics and Neutral Principles," 31 *George Washington Law Review* 587 (1963); Arthur S. Miller and Ronald F. Howell, "The Myth of Neutrality in Constitutional Adjudication," 27 *University of Chicago Law Review* 661 (1960); Arthur S. Miller and Alan W. Scheflin, "The Power of the Supreme Court in the Age of the Positive State: A Preliminary Excursus, Part One: On Candor and the Court, or, Why Bamboozle the Natives?" 1967 *Duke Law Journal* 273 (1967). For a more glowing review, see Kent Greenawalt, "The Enduring Significance of Neutral Principles," 78 *Columbia Law Review* 982 (1978).

21. Ely, *Democracy and Distrust*, 1.

22. Ibid. at 1.

23. Ibid. at 12.

24. Bork, *The Tempting of America.* Other interpretivists include Raoul Berger, *Government by Judiciary: The Transformation of the Fourteenth Amendment* (Cambridge: Harvard University Press, 1977); J. Clifford Wallace, "The Jurisprudence of Judicial Restraint: A Return to the Moorings," 50 *George Washington Law Review* 1 (1981); Christopher Wolfe, *How to Read the Constitution* (Lanham, Md.: Rowman and Littlefield Publishers, 1996); Christopher Wolfe, *Judicial Activism*, 2d ed. (Lanham, Md.: Rowman and Littlefield, 1997); Lino Graglia, *Disaster by Decree: The Supreme Court Decisions on Race and the Schools* (Ithaca: Cornell University Press, 1976); Joseph Grano, "Judicial Review and a Written Constitution in a Democratic Society," 28 *Wayne Law Review* 1 (1981); William Van Alstyne, "A Graphic Review of the Free Speech Clause," 70 *California Law Review* 107 (1982); Richard A. Epstein, "Substantive Due Process by Any Other Name: The Abortion Cases," 1973 *Supreme Court Review* 159 (1973); Richard E. Morgan, *Disabling America: The "Rights Industry" in Our Time* (New York: Basic Books, 1984). See also Edwin Meese III, "The Supreme Court of the United States: Bulwark of a Limited Constitution," 27 *South Texas*

Law Journal 455 (1986). Gerber claims to be an originalist but, with his emphasis on the Court's protection of natural rights and the Declaration of Independence as a source of those rights, I would place him in the noninterpretivist category. Scott Douglas Gerber, *To Secure These Rights* (New York: New York University Press, 1995). An originalist who generally reaches liberal results is Akhil Reed Amar. See *The Bill of Rights* (New Haven: Yale University Press, 1998).

25. Bork, *The Tempting of America*, 153.
26. Ibid. at 176.
27. Ibid. at 144.
28. Bobbitt, *Constitutional Fate*.
29. Charles L. Black, Jr., *Structure and Relationship in Constitutional Law* (Baton Rouge: Louisiana State University Press, 1969).
30. Cass R. Sunstein, *Legal Reasoning and Political Conflict* 173 (New York: Oxford University Press, 1996).
31. Berger, *Government by Judiciary*.
32. *McCulloch* v. *Maryland*, 17 U.S. (4 Wheat) 316, 414 (1819).
33. Sunstein, *Legal Reasoning and Political Conflict*, 173.
34. E.g., see Leslie Friedman Goldstein, *In Defense of the Text* (Lanham, Md.: Rowman & Littlefield Publishers, 1991).
35. It may seem odd to label Bork a "moderate interpretivist." However, he does in fact provide a more supple theory of judicial review than generally acknowledged and is more moderate than Raoul Berger. Of course, the appropriate response is, "Who isn't?"
36. Bork, *The Tempting of America*, 163.
37. Ibid. at 163.
38. Ibid. at 169.
39. Ely, *Democracy and Distrust*, 2.
40. Wallace, "The Jurisprudence of Judicial Restraint," 71. Similarly, Bork asserts that "the attempt to adhere to the principles actually laid down in the historic Constitution will mean that entire ranges of problems and issues are placed off-limits for judges." *The Tempting of America*, 163.
41. According to Hoffman, this is not an infrequent problem. Daniel N. Hoffman, *Our Elusive Constitution* (Albany: State University of New York Press, 1997).
42. Bork, *The Tempting of America*, 257–59.
43. Ibid. at 242.

44. Ibid. at 167, 51.
45. Berger, *Government by Judiciary*, 364, quoting letter to Wilson Cary Nicholas, September 7, 1803.
46. Raoul Berger, "The Imperial Court," *New York Times Magazine* 40, 55 (October 8, 1977).
47. Ibid. at 56.
48. Wallace, "The Jurisprudence of Judicial Restraint," 83.
49. William H. Rehnquist, "The Notion of a Living Constitution," 54 *Texas Law Review* 693 (1976).
50. James Bradley Thayer, *John Marshall* 106–7 (Boston: Houghton Mifflin, 1901). See also Robert F. Nagel, *Constitutional Cultures: The Mentality and Consequences of Judicial Review* (Berkeley: University of California Press, 1989); Gary C. Leedes, "The Supreme Court Mess," 57 *Texas Law Review* 1361 (1979).
51. Ely, *Democracy and Distrust*, 8. However, Ely regards this argument as "largely a fake."
52. Grey, "Do We Have an Unwritten Constitution?" 705.
53. See, e.g., Hadley Arkes, *Beyond the Constitution* (Princeton: Princeton University Press, 1990).
54. Richard B. Saphire, "The Search for Legitimacy in Constitutional Theory: What Price Purity?" 42 *Ohio State Law Journal* 335, 344 (1981).
55. Ibid. at 348.
56. Kenneth Karst, "Foreword: Equal Citizenship under the Fourteenth Amendment," 91 *Harvard Law Review* 1 (1977); Kenneth L. Karst and Harold W. Horowitz, "The *Bakke* Opinions and Equal Protection Doctrine," 14 *Harvard Civil Rights–Civil Liberties Law Review* 7 (1979).
57. Laurence H. Tribe, *American Constitutional Law*, 1st ed., 52 (Mineola, N.Y.: Foundation Press, 1978). Similarly, the "ultimate test of the Justices' work must be goodness." J. Skelly Wright, "Professor Bickel, the Scholarly Tradition, and the Supreme Court," 84 *Harvard Law Review* 769 (1971). This certainly was the dominant approach employed by Chief Justice Earl Warren.
58. Harry H. Wellington, "Common Law Rules and Constitutional Double Standards: Some Notes on Adjudication," 83 *Yale Law Journal* 221 (1973); Michael Perry, "Abortion,

The Public Morals, and the Police Power: The Ethical Function of Substantive Due Process," 23 *UCLA Law Review* 689 (1976); Michael Perry, "Substantive Due Process Revisited: Reflections on (and beyond) Recent Cases," 71 *Northwestern University Law Review* 417 (1977).

59. Laurence H. Tribe, *American Constitutional Law*, 2d ed. (Mineola, N.Y.: Foundation Press, 1988).

60. David A. J. Richards, "Unnatural Acts and the Constitutional Right to Privacy: A Moral Theory," 45 *Fordham Law Review* 1281 (1977); David A. J. Richards, "Sexual Autonomy and the Constitutional Right to Privacy: A Case Study in Human Rights and the Unwritten Constitution," 30 *Hastings Law Journal* 957 (1979); David A. J. Richards, *Conscience and the Constitution* (Princeton: Princeton University Press, 1993). For a similar approach, see J. Harvey Wilkinson and G. Edward White, "Constitutional Protection for Personal Lifestyles," 62 *Cornell Law Review* 563 (1977).

61. Rogers M. Smith, *Liberalism and American Constitutional Law* 200 (Cambridge: Harvard University Press, 1985); Sotirios A. Barber, *On What the Constitution Means* (Baltimore: Johns Hopkins University Press, 1984).

62. Arthur S. Miller, *Toward Increased Judicial Activism: The Political Role of the Supreme Court* 230 (Westport, Conn.: Greenwood Press, 1982). In Miller's view, the Court's other substantive concerns should be: equality, the shortcomings of our pluralistic politics, minimum economic well-being, and reassessment of the meaning of *constitutionalism.*

63. William J. Brennan, Jr., "The Constitution of the United States: Contemporary Ratification," 27 *South Texas Law Journal* 433 (1986).

64. Ronald M. Dworkin, *Taking Rights Seriously* (London: Duckworth, 1977). See also David A. J. Richards, *The Moral Criticism of Law* (Encino, Calif.: Dickenson Publishing, 1977).

65. Kenneth L. Karst, *Belonging to America* 3 (New Haven: Yale University Press, 1989). An argument could be made, I think, for placing Karst in the interpretivist category, as his theory is more textually based than other noninterpretivist approaches. After all, the Constitution's Fourteenth Amendment does contain an equal protection clause.

66. Thomas Gerety, "Doing without Pri-

vacy," 42 *Ohio State Law Journal* 143 (1981).

67. Stephen Macedo, *The New Right v. the Constitution* (Washington, D.C.: Cato Institute, 1987).

68. Also advocating a return to judicial concern with economic rights are Bernard Siegan, *Economic Liberties and the Constitution* (Chicago: University of Chicago Press, 1981); Richard Epstein, *Takings: Private Property and the Power of Eminent Domain* (Cambridge: Harvard University Press, 1985); Gary Jacobsohn, *The Supreme Court and the Decline of Constitutional Aspiration* (Totowa, N.J.: Rowman and Littlefield, 1986); Richard Epstein, "Toward a Revitalization of the Contract Clause," 51 *University of Chicago Law Review* 703 (1984); Clint Bolick, *Unfinished Business: A Civil Rights Strategy for America's Third Century* (San Francisco: Pacific Research Institute for Public Policy, 1990). For an excellent account of the Framers' views on property, see Jennifer Nedelsky, *Private Property and the Limits of American Constitutionalism: The Madisonian Framework and Its Legacy* (Chicago: University of Chicago Press, 1990).

69. Macedo, *The New Right v. the Constitution*, 60.

70. A notable exception is Michael Perry, *The Constitution, the Courts, and Human Rights: An Inquiry into the Legitimacy of Constitutional Policymaking by the Judiciary* (New Haven: Yale University Press, 1982). Perry argues that the Court's noninterpretive decisions, because their legitimacy is suspect, should be subject to congressional approval via its power to restrict the Court's appellate jurisdiction. Thus, Perry claims to have reconciled noninterpretive review with democratic values. (In chapter 3, I argue that he has not in fact succeeded.)

71. Bork, *The Tempting of America*, 199, 201.

72. Laurence H. Tribe and Michael C. Dorf, *On Reading the Constitution* 14 (Cambridge: Harvard University Press, 1991).

73. Ibid. at 14–15.

74. *Democracy and Distrust.* In *Carolene Products*, the Court announced a new agenda: economic regulations would be presumed constitutional, but not laws affecting the Bill of Rights, the political process, or religious or racial minorities, *U.S.* v. *Carolene Products Co.*, 304 U.S. 144, 152 n. 4 (1938).

75. Louis Lusky, *By What Right? A Commentary on the Supreme Court's Power to Revise the Constitution* (Charlottesville, Va.: Michie Co.,

1975); Charles L. Black, Jr., "The Unfinished Business of the Warren Court," 46 *Washington Law Review* 3 (1970); Milner S. Ball, "Judicial Protection of Powerless Minorities," 59 *Iowa Law Review* 1059 (1974), although Ball has mildly objected to being placed in the process-perfecting category. "Don't Die, Don Quixote: A Response and Alternative to Tushnet, Bobbitt, and the Revised Texas Version of Constitutional Law," 59 *Texas Law Review* 789, 794–96 (1981); and more recently, Guido Calabresi, "Foreword: Antidiscrimination and Constitutional Accountability (What the Bork-Brennan Debate Ignores)," 105 *Harvard Law Review* 80 (1991), although Ely would certainly object to Calabresi's use of fundamental rights language. Jesse Choper similarly argues that the Court should use its limited political capital to serve those who cannot protect themselves politically. However, for Choper this means that, the Constitution notwithstanding, the Court need not bother with separation of powers issues involving Congress and the executive branch, since each is well equipped to do battle with the other. Nor should the Court intervene to protect states' rights from invasion by the federal government, since the states are well represented there, most explicitly in the U.S. Senate. Instead, the Court need only protect (1) the national government from state encroachments, (2) the federal judiciary from encroachments by the other two branches, and (3) individual rights that the Constitution has placed beyond the reach of majorities. Jesse H. Choper, *Judicial Review and the National Political Process: A Functional Reconsideration of the Role of the Supreme Court* (Chicago: University of Chicago Press, 1980).

76. Ely, *Democracy and Distrust*, 11–41. Subsequent page references appear parenthetically in text.

77. For a similar view regarding the Constitution's emphasis on structure and process, see Martin H. Redish, *The Constitution as Political Structure* (New York: Oxford University Press, 1995).

78. *Democracy and Distrust*, 103. Subsequent page references appear parenthetically in text.

79. Laurence H. Tribe, "The Puzzling Persistence of Process-Based Constitutional Theories," 89 *Yale Law Journal* 1063 (1980).

80. Mark Tushnet, "Darkness on the Edge

of Town: The Contributions of John Hart Ely to Constitutional Theory," 89 *Yale Law Journal* 1037 (1980).

81. Bork, *The Tempting of America*, 16–132. Subsequent page references appear parenthetically in text.

82. *Reynolds* v. *Sims*, 377 U.S. 533 (1964).

83. *Harper* v. *Virginia State Board of Elections*, 383 U.S. 663 (1966).

84. *Katzenbach* v. *Morgan*, 384 U.S. 641 (1966).

85. *Griswold* v. *Connecticut*, 381 U.S. 479 (1965).

86. Bork disagrees with the "conservative" label. He argues that the Court remains "more liberal than the American people and is only moderately and occasionally less radical than the Warren Court." *The Tempting of America*, 102, 126.

87. Ibid. at 101–10. Bork is especially critical of *Griggs* v. *Duke Power Co.*, 401 U.S. 424 (1971); *United Steelworkers of America* v. *Weber*, 443 U.S. 193 (1979); and *Johnson* v. *Transportation Agency of Santa Clara County*, 480 U.S. 616 (1987); but he approves of the "moderate adjustments" made by the Court in *Richmond* v. *J. A. Croson Co.*, 488 U.S. 469 (1989) and *Wards Cove Packing Co.* v. *Atonio*, 490 U.S. 642 (1989).

88. *Roe* v. *Wade*, 410 U.S. 113 (1973).

89. *Bowers* v. *Hardwick*, 478 U.S. 186 (1986).

90. *Texas* v. *Johnson*, 491 U.S. 397 (1989).

91. Berger, *Government by Judiciary*, 134–56; Raoul Berger, "Incorporation of the Bill of Rights in the Fourteenth Amendment: A Nine-Lived Cat," 42 *Ohio State Law Journal* 435 (1981).

92. Bork, *The Tempting of America*, 93–95.

93. A limited sampling of this voluminous literature includes: John Noonan, "The Root and Branch of *Roe* v. *Wade*," 63 *Nebraska Law Review* 668 (1984); John Hart Ely, "The Wages of Crying Wolf: A Comment on *Roe* v. *Wade*," 82 *Yale Law Journal* 920 (1973); Joseph Grano, "Judicial Review and a Written Constitution in a Democratic Society," 28 *Wayne Law Review* 1 (1981); Sylvia Law, "Rethinking Sex and the Constitution," 132 *University of Pennsylvania Law Review* 955 (1984); Perry, "Substantive Due Process Revisited"; Louis Henkin, "Privacy and Autonomy," 74 *Columbia Law Review* 1410 (1974); Archibald Cox, *The Role of the Supreme Court in American Government* 113–14 (New York: Oxford University Press, 1976); Catha-

rine MacKinnon, "*Roe* v. *Wade*: A Study in Male Ideology," in Jay L. Garfield and Patricia Hennessey, eds., *Abortion: Moral and Legal Perspectives* 45 (Amherst: University of Massachusetts Press, 1984); Robert W. Bennett, "Abortion and Judicial Review: Of Burdens and Benefits, Hard Cases and Some Bad Law," 75 *Northwestern University Law Review* 978 (1981); Epstein, "Substantive Due Process by Any Other Name"; Andrea Asaro, "The Judicial Portrayal of the Physician in Abortion and Sterilization Decisions," 6 *Harvard Women's Law Journal* 51 (1983).

94. Tushnet, *Red, White, and Blue*, 54.

95. R. Smith, *Liberalism and American Constitutional Law*.

96. Ibid. at 226. Similarly, Karst's principle of equal citizenship is asserted to be "an informing principle" rather than a "limiting principle" and is "inescapably open-ended"; it is "a perspective" and "a way of not seeing." "Equal Citizenship," 40, 67.

97. R. Smith, *Liberalism and American Constitutional Law*, 237. Hereafter, page references appear parenthetically in text.

98. *Miranda* v. *Arizona*, 384 U.S. 436 (1966); *Gideon* v. *Wainwright*, 372 U.S. 335 (1963); *Mapp* v. *Ohio*, 367 U.S. 643 (1961); *Griffin* v. *Illinois*, 351 U.S. 12 (1956).

99. In *Williamson* v. *Lee Optical Company*, the Court upheld against a due process challenge a state law prohibiting opticians from replacing lenses in frames without a prescription from an optometrist or ophthalmologist. 348 U.S. 483 (1955).

100. *San Antonio Independent School District* v. *Rodriguez*, 411 U.S. 1 (1973).

101. Paul Brest, "The Fundamental Rights Controversy: The Essential Contradictions of Normative Constitutional Scholarship," 90 *Yale Law Journal* 1063, 1089 (1981).

102. Wellington, "Common Law Rules," 305–11.

103. Perry, "Abortion," 733; "Substantive Due Process," 447–48.

104. Ely believes that the Warren Court was primarily concerned in its decisions with participational or process rights rather than substantive values. For a similar revisionist account of the Warren Court, see Ronald Kahn, *The Supreme Court and Constitutional Theory, 1953–1993* (Lawrence: University Press of Kansas, 1994).

105. Ely, *Democracy and Distrust*, 148–61. Subsequent page references appear parenthetically in text.

106. John Hart Ely, "The Constitutionality of Reverse Racial Discrimination," 41 *University of Chicago Law Review* 723 (1974).

107. Despite Ely's assertion that homosexuals should be treated as a suspect class, since they have long been victims of prejudice and stereotyping, he curiously would permit laws criminalizing homosexual condut to be upheld if based on the legislature's sincere moral belief that such conduct was immoral. Ibid. at 255–56, n. 92. The problems with this distinction are discussed in chapter 2.

108. Ely did, however, advocate strict judicial scrutiny for gender classifications in an earlier article. See "The Wages of Crying Wolf," 933.

109. In fact, Ely regards the *Roe* decision as lacking *any* legitimate constitutional basis. He believes *Roe* is not simply "bad constitutional law," it is "*not* constitutional law and gives almost no sense of an obligation to try to be." "The Wages of Crying Wolf," 947, fn. excluded.

110. Bickel, *The Least Dangerous Branch*, 40.

CHAPTER 2

1. I continue to find the need to defend this idea quite curious (if not bizarre). It seems to me that it is the contrary notion—that judges are capable of resolving constitutional issues *without* recourse to their personal views—which is counterintuitive and in need of defense. Nonetheless, insofar as conventional neutralist approaches persist and continue to be introduced anew, the curious and counterintuitive idea that constitutional outcomes can be generated in a neutral or objective manner must be addressed.

2. See chapter 4 for a review of the judicial behavior literature that verifies empirically the existence of value voting.

3. Frederick Schauer, "Easy Cases," 58 *Southern California Law Review* 399 (1985).

4. Ibid. at 439.

5. Phillip Johnson, "Do You Sincerely Want to Be Radical?" 36 *Stanford Law Review* 247, 252 (1984).

6. Jerome Frank, *Law and the Modern Mind* (New York: Coward McCann, 1930); Karl Lle-

wellyn, "Some Realism about Realism—Responding to Dean Pound," 44 *Harvard Law Review* 1222 (1931); Karl Llewellyn, "A Realistic Jurisprudence—The Next Step," 30 *Columbia Law Review* 431 (1930).

7. For a sampling of this extensive literature, see Mark Tushnet, *Red, White, and Blue: A Critical Analysis of Constitutional Law* (Cambridge: Harvard University Press, 1988); Roberto Mangabeira Unger, *The Critical Legal Studies Movement* (Cambridge: Harvard University Press, 1986); Duncan Kennedy and Karl E. Klane, "A Bibliography of Critical Legal Studies," 94 *Yale Law Journal* 461 (1984); "Symposium on Critical Legal Studies," 6 *Cardozo Law Review* 691 (1985); "Critical Legal Studies Symposium" 36 *Stanford Law Review* 1 (1984); " 'Round and 'Round the Bramble Bush: From Legal Realism to Critical Legal Scholarship," 95 *Harvard Law Review* 1669 (1982); Sanford Levinson, "Law as Literature," 60 *Texas Law Review* 373 (1982); "Interpretation Symposium," 58 nos. 1 and 2, *Southern California Law Review* 1 (1985); Robert Post, ed., *Law and the Order of Culture* (Berkeley: University of California Press, 1991); Allan C. Hutchinson, ed., *Critical Legal Studies* (Lanham, Md.: Rowman and Littlefield Publishers, 1989); David Kairys, *The Politics of Law: A Progressive Critique*, 3d ed. (Boulder, Colo.: Basic Books, 1998).

8. Paul Brest, "The Fundamental Rights Controversy: The Essential Contradictions of Normative Constitutional Scholarship," 90 *Yale Law Journal* 1063 (1981).

9. Leslie Friedman Goldstein, "Indeterminacy and Constitutional Theory: A Critique of CLS and Its Fellow-Travelers" (paper delivered at the Western Political Science Association meeting, San Francisco, 1988).

10. Mark Tushnet, "Legal Realism, Structural Review, and Prophecy," 8 *University of Dayton Law Review* 809, 828 (1983).

11. Mark Tushnet, "Darkness on the Edge of Town: The Contributions of John Hart Ely to Constitutional Theory," 89 *Yale Law Journal* 1037, 1038 (1980). Rogers Smith also acknowledges weaknesses and tensions in the philosophical foundations of liberalism. However, he is far more optimistic that they can be minimized and that liberalism can remain a useful and coherent source of constitutional principle. *Liberalism and American Constitutional Law* (Cambridge: Harvard University Press, 1985).

12. Goldstein, "Indeterminacy and Constitutional Theory," 15–16. Scholars in this group include Levinson, "Law as Literature"; Sanford Levinson, " 'The Constitution' in American Civil Religion," 1979 *Supreme Court Review* 123 (1979); Lief Carter, *Contemporary Constitutional Lawmaking: The Supreme Court and the Art of Politics* (New York: Pergamon Press, 1985); Lief H. Carter, *Reason in Law*, 5th ed. (New York: Longman, 1998); Robert Gordon, "New Developments in Legal Theory," in David Kairys, ed., *The Politics of Law: A Progressive Critique*, 281–93 (New York: Pantheon Books, 1982).

13. Tushnet, "Legal Realism," 810.

14. Raoul Berger, *Government by Judiciary* (Cambridge: Harvard University Press, 1977).

15. See Mark Tushnet's critique of Berger's "supplementary evidentiary rules." *Red, White, and Blue*, 36–37.

16. Ibid. at 46.

17. Ibid. at 35–36, fn. excluded. For similar critiques regarding the problematical nature of discovering the Framers' intent, see Ronald Dworkin, *Law's Empire* 359–63 (Cambridge: Harvard University Press, Belknap Press, 1986); Leonard W. Levy, *Original Intent and the Framers' Constitution* (New York: Macmillan, 1988); Stephen Macedo, *The New Right v. the Constitution* 11–16 (Washington, D.C.: Cato Institute, 1987); Jack N. Rakove, *Original Meanings* (New York: Knopf, 1995).

This criticism that considerable judicial discretion remains with interprevist approaches applies as well to Ackerman's version of originalism. Bruce Ackerman, *We the People* (Cambridge: Harvard University Press, 1991). According to Ackerman, the Court is to ascertain the meaning of and to protect the higher lawmaking principles established by the people, whether formally in the text or informally through "structural" amendments. However, perceiving and interpreting constitutional moments and their results, especially structural amendments, is not a simple, straightforward task; uncertainty and manipulability remain. For example, McConnell provides a different reading of constitutional moments in American history using Ackerman's own criteria. Michael W. McConnell, "The Forgotten Constitutional Moment," 11 *Constitutional Commentary* 115 (1994). For additional critiques of Ackerman's theory, see Terrance Sandalow, "Abstract Democracy: A Review of Ackerman's *We the People*," 9 *Constitutional Commentary* 309 (1992); Frederick Schauer, "Deliberating about Deliberation," 90 *Michigan Law Review* 1187 (1992); Christy Scott, "Constitutional Moments and Crackpot Revolutions," 25 *Connecticut Law Review* 967 (1993); Suzanna Sherry, "The Ghost of Liberalism Past," 105 *Harvard Law Review* 918 (1992). For a critique of the second volume in Ackerman's *We the People* trilogy (*We the People: Transformations* [Cambridge: Harvard University Press, 1998]), see Richard A. Posner, "This Magic Moment," *New Republic* 32 (April 6, 1998).

18. Paul Brest, "The Misconceived Quest for the Original Understanding," 60 *Boston University Law Review* 204, 215–17, 220 (1980); Ronald Dworkin, "The Forum of Principle," 56 *New York University Law Review* 469, 493–97 (1981); Levy, *Original Intent and the Framers' Constitution*; Rakove, *Original Meanings*.

19. H. Jefferson Powell, "The Original Understanding of Original Intent," 98 *Harvard Law Review* 886 (1985).

20. Macedo, *The New Right v. the Constitution*, 17–19.

21. Brest, "The Misconceived Quest," 222–23.

22. Ibid. at 223.

23. Robert Bork, "Neutral Principles and Some First Amendment Problems," 47 *Indiana Law Journal* 1, 15 (1971).

24. Brest, "The Fundamental Rights Controversy," 1091.

25. Mark Tushnet, "Following the Rules Laid Down: A Critique of Interpretivism and Neutral Principles," 96 *Harvard Law Review* 781, 802 (1983). See also Ronald Dworkin, *Taking Rights Seriously* 134–36 (London: Duckworth, 1977); Erwin Chemerinsky, "Foreword: The Vanishing Constitution," 103 *Harvard Law Review* 44, 94–95 (1989).

26. Owen Fiss, "Objectivity and Interpretation," 34 *Stanford Law Review* 739, 745 (1982).

27. Stanley Fish, "Fish v. Fiss," 36 *Stanford Law Review* 1325, 1326 (1984).

28. Paul Brest, "Interpretation and Interest," 34 *Stanford Law Review* 765, 771–72 (1982).

29. Ackerman, *We the People: Foundations*; Ackerman, *We the People: Transformations*.

30. Commentary regarding interpretivist approaches, mostly negative, is quite voluminous. Regarding originalist approaches, see Stephen R. Munzer and James W. Nickel, "Does the Constitution Mean What It Always Meant?" 77 *Columbia Law Review* 1029 (1977); Larry G. Simon, "The Authority of the Framers of the Constitution: Can Originalist Interpretation Be Justified?" 73 *California Law Review* 1482 (1985); Michael Perry, "The Authority of Text, Tradition, and Reason: A Theory of Constitutional 'Interpretation,'" 58 *Southern California Law Review* 551 (1985); Richard S. Kay, "Adherence to the Original Intentions in Constitutional Adjudication: Three Objections and Responses," 82 *Northwestern University Law Review* 226 (1988); Earl Maltz, "Some New Thoughts on an Old Problem—The Role of the Intent of the Framers in Constitutional Theory," 63 *Boston University Law Review* 811 (1983); Walter F. Murphy, "Constitutional Interpretation: The Art of the Historian, Magician, or Statesman?" 87 *Yale Law Journal* 1752 (1978); Erwin Chemerinsky, "The Constitution Is Not 'Hard Law': The Bork Rejection and the Future of Constitutional Jurisprudence" 6 *Constitutional Commentary* 29 (1989). Regarding textualist arguments, see Tushnet, *Red, White, and Blue*, 60–69, especially his response to Douglas Laycock, "Taking Constitutions Seriously: A Theory of Judicial Power," 59 *Texas Law Review* 343 (1981); "Interpretation Symposium"; "Law and Literature" (symposium), 60 *Texas Law Review* (1982); Sanford Levinson and Steven Mailloux, eds., *Interpreting Law and Literature: A Hermeneutic Reader* (Evanston, Ill.: Northwestern University Press, 1988); Thomas Grey, "The Constitution as Scripture," 37 *Stanford Law Review* 1 (1984). Regarding the ongoing debate between originalism and nonoriginalism, see pt. 2 of Kenneth L. Grasso and Cicelia Rodriguez Castillo, eds., *Liberty under Law: American Constitutionalism, Yesterday, Today, and Tomorrow*, 2d ed. (Lanham, Md.: Rowman and Littlefield Publishers, 1997).

31. John Hart Ely, *Democracy and Distrust* 14 (Cambridge: Harvard University Press, 1980).

32. Tushnet, *Red, White, and Blue*, 109–10.

33. Ely, *Democracy and Distrust*, 58.

34. Ibid. at 50–52, 54.

35. Tushnet, *Red, White, and Blue*, 114–19.

36. Ibid. at 134.

37. Ely, *Democracy and Distrust*, 60. See also Tushnet, *Red, White, and Blue*, 140–41.

38. *Michael H. v. Gerald D.*, 491 U.S. 110 (1989).

39. For critical analysis of Scalia's suggested approach in fn. 6 of *Michael H.*, see Laurence H. Tribe and Michael C. Dorf, *On Reading the Constitution* 73–74, 97–109 (Cambridge: Harvard Univiersity Press, 1991); J. M. Balkin, "Tradition, Betrayal, and the Politics of Deconstruction," 11 *Cardozo Law Review* 1613 (1990); and more generally, David A. Schultz and Christopher E. Smith, *The Jurisprudential Vision of Justice Antonin Scalia* (Lanham, Md.: Rowman & Littlefield Publishers, 1996).

40. *Bowers v. Hardwick*, 478 U.S. 186 (1986).

41. Tushnet, *Red, White, and Blue*, 120. I thoroughly defend this claim in chapter 4.

42. Ibid. at 121. Michael Perry strongly disagrees. Perry's justification of noninterpretivist judicial review as a form of moral prophecy rests critically on his belief that "in the modern period . . . noninterpretivist review has functioned, *on balance*, as an instrument of deepening moral insight and of moral growth." *The Constitution, the Courts, and Human Rights: An Inquiry into the Legitimacy of Constitutional Policymaking by the Judiciary* (New Haven: Yale University Press, 1982).

43. Ibid. at 136–37.

44. Ely, *Democracy and Distrust*, 59, fnn excluded. Robert Bork echoes Ely's complaint that the values which judges and scholars typically single out as "fundamental" are rooted in "intellectual class attitudes," resulting in the "gentrification of the Constitution." Bork, *The Tempting of America: The Political Seduction of the Law* 242 (New York: Free Press, 1990).

45. Lawrence G. Sager, "Rights Skepticism and Process-Based Responses," 56 *New York University Law Review* 417 (1981).

46. Brest, "The Fundamental Rights Controversy," 1093.

47. Laurence H. Tribe, "The Puzzling Persistence of Process-Based Constitutional Theories," 89 *Yale Law Journal* 1063, 1064 (1980). See also Guido Calabresi, "Foreword: Antidiscrimination and Constitutional Accountability (What the Bork-Brennan Debate Ignores)," 105 *Harvard Law Review* 80, 84, n. 9 (1991); R. M. Smith, *Liberalism and American Constitutional Law*, 172–74.

48. Tushnet, "Darkness on the Edge of Town," 1045.

49. Ely, *Democracy and Distrust*, 75 n.

50. Ibid. at 75.

51. Tribe, "The Puzzling Persistence," 1065. See also Joseph D. Grano, "Ely's Theory of Judicial Review: Preserving the Significance of the Political Process," 42 *Ohio State Law Journal* 167, 174–77 (1981).

52. Samuel Estreicher, "Platonic Guardians of Democracy: John Hart Ely's Role for the Supreme Court in the Constitution's Open Texture," 56 *New York University Law Review* 547, 580 (1981).

53. 430 U.S. 144 (1977). However, the case involved a statutory rather than a constitutional challenge.

54. Richard B. Saphire, "The Search for Legitimacy in Constitutional Theory: What Price Purity?" 42 *Ohio State Law Journal* 335, 363 (1981).

55. Tushnet, *Red, White, and Blue*, 87.

56. See also Harry H. Wellington, "The Importance of Being Elegant," 42 *Ohio State Law Journal* 427, 432–34 (1981).

57. Tribe, "The Puzzling Persistence," 1072.

58. Ely, *Democracy and Distrust*, 148–61.

59. Ibid. at 164–69.

60. Bruce Ackerman, "Beyond *Carolene Products*," 98 *Harvard Law Review* 713, 745 (1985).

61. Paul Brest, "The Substance of Process," 42 *Ohio State Law Journal* 131, 137 (1981).

62. Ibid. at 131.

63. Ely, *Democracy and Distrust*, 256, n. 92.

64. Brest, "The Fundamental Rights Controversy," 1095.

65. Brest, "The Substance of Process," 136.

66. Raoul Berger, "Ely's 'Theory of Judicial Review,'" 42 *Ohio State Law Journal* 87 (1981); Berger, "Government by Judiciary: John Hart Ely's 'Invitation,'" 54 *Indiana Law Journal* 277 (1979); Tribe, "The Puzzling Persistence." Former Supreme Court Justice Lewis Powell makes the same point regarding *Carolene Products*, the primary source of Ely's theory. Justice Lewis Powell, "*Carolene Products* Revisited," 82 *Columbia Law Review* 1087 (1982).

67. Richard Davies Parker, "The Past of Constitutional Theory—And Its Future," 42 *Ohio State Law Journal* 223, 239 (1981).

68. Tushnet, *Red, White, and Blue*, 94, 103–6;

Parker, "The Past of Constitutional Theory," 239–46.

69. For interpretivists, the range of issues Ely finds appropriate for judicial resolution is arbitrarily broad, particularly in including reapportionment. E.g., see Berger, "Government by Judiciary: John Hart Ely's 'Invitation.'" For most noninterpretivists, that range is arbitrarily narrow, particularly in excluding privacy. Thomas Gerety, "Doing without Privacy," 42 *Ohio State Law Journal* 143 (1981); Saphire, "What Price Purity?" 364. David Richards, a noninterpretivist, argues that Ely is unwilling or, more likely, unable to comprehend moral philosophy and properly appraise its value in constitutional law. For Richards, it is this inexcusable failing on Ely's part that leads him arbitrarily to limit judicial intervention to neutral "process" values. David A. J. Richards, "Moral Philosophy and the Search for Fundamental Values in Constitutional Law," 42 *Ohio State Law Journal* 319, 328 (1981).

70. Tribe, "The Puzzling Persistence," 1067.

71. Estreicher, "Platonic Guardians of Democracy," 578, fn. excluded.

72. The phrase in the subheading, "The Critics against Themselves," belongs to Paul Brest. "The Fundamental Rights Controversy," 1089. Alan Freeman, "Truth and Mystification in Legal Scholarship," 90 *Yale Law Journal* 1229 (1981); Mark Kelman, "Interpretive Construction in the Substantive Criminal Law," 33 *Stanford Law Review* 591 (1981).

73. Brest, "The Fundamental Rights Controversy," 1096.

74. Ibid. at 1063.

75. For example, Mark Tushnet sees his role as "intellectual historian" and "cultural critic"—examining "the structure of arguments to expose their sometimes unarticulated presuppositions about the nature of American society" and "the way in which constitutional doctrine constitutes—shapes and defends—important social institutions." *Red, White, and Blue*, viii, ix.

76. Robert G. McCloskey, "Economic Due Process and the Supreme Court: An Exhumation and Reburial," 1962 *Supreme Court Review* 34 (1962); Martin M. Shapiro, "The Constitution and Economic Rights," in M. Judd Harmon, ed., *Essays on the Constitution of the United States* 74 (Port Washington, N.Y.: Kennikat

Press, 1978); Macedo, *The New Right v. the Constitution.*

77. Shapiro, "The Constitution and Economic Rights," 85.

78. Johnson, "Do You Sincerely Want to be Radical?" 281.

79. Duncan Kennedy, "Cost-Reduction Theory as Legitimation," 90 *Yale Law Journal* 1275, 1283 (1981). Kennedy also dreams of a "shared vision of a social harmony so complete as to obviate the need for any rules at all." "Form and Substance in Private Law Adjudication," 95 *Harvard Law Review* 1685, 1746 (1976).

80. Roberto Mangabeira Unger, *Law in Modern Society: Toward a Criticism of Social Theory* 261 (New York: Free Press, 1976).

81. Peter Gabel, review of *Taking Rights Seriously*, by Ronald Dworkin, 91 *Harvard Law Review* 302, 315 (1977).

82. Brest, "The Fundamental Rights Controversy," 1109, fn. excluded.

83. Parker, "The Past of Constitutional Theory," 258 n. 146.

84. Tushnet, *Red, White, and Blue*, 187.

85. Johnson, "Do You Sincerely Want to Be Radical?" 283.

86. Ibid. at 262. For Robert Bork, the Critics' belief that there is "no defensible theory of judicial supremacy" must necessarily be followed by the conclusion that "the institution is illegitimate and should be dropped." *The Tempting of America*, 208. However, as the Critics would respond, dispensing with judicial review in order to prevent *judicial* tyranny reintroduces unchecked *legislative* tyranny. Thus, the dilemma for constitutional theory created by liberalism remains.

87. John Agresto, *The Supreme Court and Constitutional Democracy* 38 (Ithaca: Cornell University Press, 1984).

88. *Dred Scott* v. *Sandford*, 60 U.S. 393 (1857).

89. Adolf Berle, *The Three Faces of Power* 51 (New York: Harcourt, Brace and World, 1967).

CHAPTER 3

1. Primary proponents of some form of provisional review are John Agresto, *The Supreme Court and Constitutional Democracy* (Ithaca: Cornell University Press, 1984); Robert A. Burt, *The Constitution in Conflict* (Cambridge: Har-

vard University Press, 1992); Robert Lowry Clinton, Marbury v. Madison *and Judicial Review* (Lawrence: University of Kansas Press, 1989); Paul R. Dimond, *The Supreme Court and Judicial Choice: The Role of Provisional Review in a Democracy* (Ann Arbor: University of Michigan Press, 1989); Michael J. Perry, *The Constitution, the Courts, and Human Rights: An Inquiry into the Legitimacy of Constitutional Policymaking by the Judiciary* (New Haven: Yale University Press, 1982); Harry H. Wellington, "Common Law Rules and Constitutional Double Standards: Some Notes on Adjudication," 83 *Yale Law Journal* 221 (1973); Harry H. Wellington, "The Nature of Judicial Review," 91 *Yale Law Journal* 486 (1982); Harry H. Wellington, *Interpreting the Constitution: The Supreme Court and the Process of Adjudication* (New Haven: Yale University Press, 1991). See also Terrance Sandalow, "Constitutional Interpretation," 79 *Michigan Law Review* 1033 (1981); Charles L. Black, Jr., *Decision according to Law* (New York: Norton, 1981); Gary L. McDowell, "Judicial Activism: Toward a Constitutional Solution," in Gary L. McDowell, ed., *Taking the Constitution Seriously* (Dubuque, Iowa: Kendall/Hunt Publishing, 1981); Daniel Conkle, "Nonoriginalist Constitutional Rights and the Problem of Judicial Finality," 13 *Hastings Constitutional Law Quarterly* 9 (1985). This is similar (but not identical) to what Mark Tushnet calls "structural review." *Red, White, and Blue* 196–213 (Cambridge: Harvard University Press, 1988); and what Calabresi calls "Type III review: judicial enforcement of constitutional accountability." Guido Calabresi, "Foreword: Antidiscrimination and Constitutional Accountability (What the Bork-Brennan Debate Ignores)," 105 *Harvard Law Review* 80, 103–8, 134–37 (1991).

2. Robert Dahl, "Decision-Making in a Democracy: The Supreme Court as a National Policy-Maker," 6 *Journal of Public Law* 279, 293, 291 (1957). For further discussion and debate regarding this model, see David W. Adamany, "Legitimacy, Realigning Elections, and the Supreme Court," 1973 *Wisconsin Law Review* 790 (1973); Jonathan D. Casper, "The Supreme Court and National Policy Making," 70 *American Political Science Review* 50 (1976); Richard Funston, "The Supreme Court and Critical Elections," 69 *American Political Science Review* 795 (1975); John B. Gates, *The Supreme Court*

and Partisan Realignment: A Macro- and Microlevel Perspective (Boulder, Colo.: Westview Press, 1992); Mark Silverstein and Benjamin Ginsberg, "The Supreme Court and the New Politics of Judicial Power," 102 *Political Science Quarterly* 371 (1987).

3. For an excellent empirical study of the limited capacity of courts to achieve social change, see Gerald N. Rosenberg, *The Hollow Hope: Can Courts Bring about Social Change?* (Chicago: University of Chicago Press, 1991). There is a voluminous literature on judicial impact and implementation. See Charles A. Johnson and Bradley C. Canon, *Judicial Policies: Implementation and Impact* (Washington, D.C.: Congressional Quarterly Press, 1984); Theodore L. Becker and Malcolm Feeley, eds., *The Impact of Supreme Court Decisions*, 2d ed. (New York: Oxford University Press, 1973); Bradley C. Canon, "Courts and Policy: Compliance, Implementation, and Impact," in John B. Gates and Charles A. Johnson, eds., *The American Courts: A Critical Assessment* 435 (Washington, D.C.: Congressional Quarterly Press, 1991); Kenneth M. Dolbeare and Phillip E. Hammond, *The School Prayer Decisions: From Court Policy to Local Practice* (Chicago: University of Chicago Press, 1971); Micheal Giles and Douglas Gatlin, "Mass Level Compliance with Public Policy: The Case of School Desegregation," 42 *Journal of Politics* 722 (1980); Susan B. Hansen, "State Implementation of Supreme Court Decisions: Abortion Rates since *Roe* v. *Wade*," 42 *Journal of Politics* 372 (1980); Roger Hanson and Robert Crew, "The Policy Impact of Reapportionment," 8 *Law and Society Review* 69 (1973); Richard M. Johnson, *The Dynamics of Compliance: Supreme Court Decisionmaking from a New Perspective* (Evanston, Ill.: Northwestern University Press, 1967); Matthew D. McCubbins and Thomas Schwartz, "Congress, the Courts, and Public Policy: Consequences of the One Man, One Vote Rule," 32 *American Journal of Political Science* 388 (1988); William K. Muir, Jr., *Prayer in the Public Schools: Law and Attitude Change* (Chicago: University of Chicago Press, 1967); Myron W. Orfield, Jr., "The Exclusionary Rule and Deterrence: An Empirical Study of Chicago Narcotics Officers," 54 *University of Chicago Law Review* 1016 (1987); Gordon Patric, "The Impact of a Court Decision: Aftermath of the *McCollum* Case," 6 *Journal of Public Law* 455 (1957); Traciel V. Reid,

"Judicial Policy-Making and Implementation: An Empirical Examination," 41 *Western Political Quarterly* 509 (1988); Harrell R. Rodgers, Jr., and Charles S. Bullock III, *Law and Social Change: Civil Rights Laws and Their Consequences* (New York: McGraw-Hill, 1972); Frank J. Sorauf, "*Zorach v. Clauson*: The Impact of a Supreme Court Decision," 53 *American Political Science Review* 777 (1959); Stephen Wasby, *The Impact of the United States Supreme Court: Some Perspectives* (Homewood, Ill.: Dorsey Press, 1970); Christopher E. Smith, *The Rehnquist Court and Criminal Punishment* (Hamden, Conn.: Garland Publishing, 1997).

4. This point is fully defended in chapters 4 and 5. Primary sources include Walter F. Murphy, *Congress and the Court* (Chicago: University of Chicago Press, 1962); Stuart S. Nagel, "Court-Curbing Periods in American History," 18 *Vanderbilt Law Review* 925 (1965); Roger Handberg and Harold F. Hill, Jr., "Court Curbing, Court Reversals, and Judicial Review: The Supreme Court versus Congress," 14 *Law and Society Review* 309 (1980); John R. Schmidhauser and Larry L. Berg, *The Supreme Court and Congress* (New York: Free Press, 1972); and more generally, Louis Fisher, *Constitutional Dialogues: Interpretation as Political Process* (Princeton: Princeton University Press, 1988); Jeffrey A. Segal, "Courts, Executives, and Legislatures," in John B. Gates and Charles A. Johnson, eds., *The American Courts: A Critical Assessment* 373 (Washington, D.C.: Congressional Quarterly Press, 1991). Regarding the success of presidents in packing the Courts, see my discussion in chapter 4, as well as Henry J. Abraham, *Justices and Presidents: A Political History of Appointments to the Supreme Court*, 3d ed. (New York: Oxford University Press, 1992); John B. Gates and Jeffrey E. Cohen, "Presidents, Justices, and Racial Equality Cases, 1954–1984," 10 *Political Behavior* 22 (1988); Robert Scigliano, *The Supreme Court and the Presidency* (New York: Free Press, 1971); and Laurence H. Tribe, *God Save This Honorable Court* (New York: Random House, 1985). Of course, the most notable example of a judicial retreat in the face of political attack is the Court's dramatic shift in 1937 from barring to permitting governmental regulation of the economy. See Robert H. Jackson, *The Struggle for Judicial Supremacy: A Study of a Crisis in American Power Pol-*

itics (New York: A. A. Knopf, 1941); Joseph Alsop and Turner Catledge, *The 168 Days* (Garden City, N.Y.: Doubleday, Doran and Co., 1938); William E. Leuchtenberg, *The Supreme Court Reborn* (New York: Oxford University Press, 1995).

5. Louis Fisher, *Constitutional Dialogues: Interpretation as Political Process* (Princeton: Princeton University Press, 1988); Louis Fisher and Neal Devins, *Political Dynamics of Constitutional Law* (St. Paul, Minn.: West Publishing Co., 1992); Susan R. Burgess, *Contest for Constitutional Authority: The Abortion and War Powers Debates* (Lawrence: University Press of Kansas, 1992). For an interesting account of state constitutional law as an ongoing interbranch political dialogue, see Janet S. Lindgren, "Beyond Cases: Reconsidering Judicial Review," 1983 *Wisconsin Law Review* 583 (1983).

6. Wellington, "The Nature of Judicial Review," 501–2.

7. Perry, *The Constitution, The Courts, and Human Rights*, 3.

8. Ibid. at 24.

9. Perry has since abandoned this distinction, for reasons that will be made clear by the chapter's end. Michael J. Perry, "The Authority of Text, Tradition, and Reason: A Theory of Constitutional 'Interpretation,'" 58 *Southern California Law Review* 551, 580 n. 89 (1985).

10. Perry, *The Constitution, The Courts, and Human Rights*, 10. Subsequent page references appear parenthetically in text.

11. Dimond, *The Supreme Court and Judicial Choice*, 18. Subsequent page references appear parenthetically in text.

12. Dimond finds interpretivist theories especially lacking in this regard (9).

13. Dimond notes, however, that the Court's enforcement of constitutional restrictions on congressional power is still subject to a subsequent political dialogue and revision, though in a different and more demanding form—"new appointments to the Court, case-by-case adjudication, and constitutional amendment that [have] by now become familiar" (80).

14. The Court would use such tools as the clear statement rule, suspensive veto, or rational relationship review "with teeth." Ibid. at 93–94 n. 30.

15. In an earlier article introducing his the-

ory of provisional review, Dimond expressed his hope that acceptance of his approach as a legitimate alternative would "encourage the Court, commentators, Congress, and the people to expend their energies discussing the merits of policy choices rather than further debating the legitimacy of judicial review." Paul R. Dimond, "Provisional Review: An Exploratory Essay on an Alternative Form of Judicial Review," 12 *Hastings Constitutional Law Quarterly* 201, 203 (1985). In this respect, he differs from Perry. Perry is much more in the mainstream of conventional constitutional theory. Perry "flatly rejects" the claims of Critical Legal Studies scholars that the legitimacy question at the heart of constitutional theory is "incoherent and unresolvable," and instead hopes that his book "demonstrates that the controversy is both coherent and resolvable (although, to be sure, the eventual resolution may be other than I imagine it to be)." *The Constitution, The Courts and Human Rights*, xi.

16. John Hart Ely, *Democracy and Distrust* (Cambridge: Harvard University Press, 1980).

17. Dimond, *The Supreme Court and Judicial Choice*, 24 n. 36. Brest similarly notes that Perry's solution of allowing one party in the conversation to silence the other makes little sense. "Participants in 'dialogue' usually talk rather than choke each other." Paul Brest, "Congress as Constitutional Decisionmaker and Its Power to Counter Judicial Doctrine," 21 *Georgia Law Review* 57, 103 n. 148 (1987).

18. Agresto, *The Supreme Court and Constitutional Democracy*, 10.

19. Ibid. at 11–12. See also Raoul Berger, *Government by Judiciary: The Transformation of the Fourteenth Amendment* (Cambridge: Harvard University Press, 1977); Lino Graglia, *Disaster by Decree* (Ithaca: Cornell University Press, 1976); Nathan Glazer, "Towards an Imperial Judiciary?" 41 *Public Interest* 104 (1975).

20. Agresto, *The Supreme Court and Constitutional Democracy*, 12–14. Subsequent page references appear parenthetically in text.

21. Agresto endorses the notion that the "primary purpose of the [Fourteenth] Amendment was to augment the power of Congress, not the judiciary." The unlikely source of Agresto's quote is Justice William Brennan, hardly a practitioner of judicial restraint. Ibid. at 131.

22. Quoting Alexander M. Bickel, *The Least Dangerous Branch: The Supreme Court at the Bar of Politics* 240 (Indianapolis, Ind.: Bobbs-Merrill, 1962).

23. Mark Tushnet, "Legal Realism, Structural Review, and Prophecy," 8 *University of Dayton Law Review* 809, 828 (1983).

24. This particular criticism is found in virtually all of the reviews of Perry's theory, of which there are many. See, e.g., "Judicial Review and the Constitution—The Text and Beyond," 8 *University of Dayton Law Review* (symposium) 443 (1983); "Constitutional Adjudication and Democratic Theory," (symposium) 56 *New York University Law Review* 259 (1981); Telford Taylor, review of *The Constitution, the Courts, and Human Rights: An Inquiry into the Legitimacy of Constitutional Policymaking by the Judiciary*, by Michael J. Perry, 5 *Cardozo Law Review* 223 (1983).

25. Perry, *The Constitution, The Court, and Human Rights*, 130.

26. Taylor, review of Perry, *The Constitution, the Courts, and Human Rights*, 230.

27. Larry A. Alexander, "Painting without the Numbers: Noninterpretive Judicial Review," 8 *University of Dayton Law Review* 447, 454–455 (1983).

28. Laurence H. Tribe, "The Puzzling Persistence of Process-Based Constitutional Theories," 89 *Yale Law Journal* 1063 (1980); Paul Brest, "The Fundamental Rights Controversy: The Essential Contradictions of Normative Constitutional Scholarship," 90 *Yale Law Journal* 1063 (1981); Mark Tushnet, "Darkness on the Edge of Town: The Contributions of John Hart Ely to Constitutional Theory," 89 *Yale Law Journal* 1037 (1980).

29. Alexander, "Painting without the Numbers," 453. Critics of Perry disagree as to the practical consequences of his theory of provisional review. For example, Wellington believes Perry gives Congress too much control; after all, "what kind of dialogue is it in which one participant can silence the other by cutting out his tongue when offended by his words?" "History and Morals in Constitutional Adjudication," 97 *Harvard Law Review* 326, 333 (1983). Earl Maltz, on the other hand, believes that jurisdictional control is and will remain an ineffective congressional check. The Court's *constitutional* decisions tend to discourage and

inhibit any dialogue, and Congress will continue to have serious and quite reasonable doubts as to the legitimacy and wisdom of using its jurisdiction-restricting powers. "Murder in the Cathedral: The Supreme Court as Moral Prophet," 8 *University of Dayton Law Review* 623 (1983).

30. Michael J. Perry, "The Authority of Text, Tradition, and Reason: A Theory of Constitutional 'Interpretation,'" 58 *Southern California Law Review* 551, 580 n. 89 (1985).

31. Dimond, *The Supreme Court and Judicial Choice,* 79.

32. Ibid. at 80 ("the substantive restrictions that the Bill of Rights places on Congress can be interpreted by the Court as relatively narrow"); at 87 (the Court has erroneously "chosen to read the due process clauses of the fifth and fourteenth amendments as open-ended invitation to articulate substantive rights"); at 88 ("the Court must refuse to interpret the ninth amendment as an invitation to declare open-ended rights . . . as against the national government").

33. Calabresi's provisional review approach suffers from precisely the same difficulties. See "Antidiscrimination and Constitutional Accountability," 134–37. According to the Critics, we are thus back to the original problem—"the incoherence of liberal theory. . . . We [do] not end up with a system devoid of tyranny, but with one in which the forms of tyranny [legislative v. judicial] continually replace each other." Tushnet, "Legal Realism," 811.

34. Agresto, *The Supreme Court and Constitutional Democracy,* 165.

35. Wellington, "History and Morals," 335.

36. Wellington, "The Nature of Judicial Review," 509.

37. Perry, *The Constitution, the Courts, and Human Rights,* 100–101.

38. Agresto, *The Supreme Court and Constitutional Democracy,* 144.

39. Ibid. at 156.

40. Telford Taylor similarly regards this idea as "bizarre." Review of Perry, *The Constitution, the Courts, and Human Rights,* 235–38.

41. Agresto, *The Supreme Court and Constitutional Democracy,* 157.

42. Perry, *The Constitution, the Courts, and Human Rights,* 118.

43. Agresto, *The Supreme Court and Constitutional Democracy,* 157.

44. Taylor, review of Perry, *The Constitution, the Courts, and Human Rights,* 236.

45. Ibid. at 236–37.

46. See Sanford Levinson, "The Turn toward Functionalism in Constitutional Theory," 8 *University of Dayton Law Review* 567, 570–71 (1983).

47. See also Gary C. Leedes, "A Critique of Illegitimate Noninterpretivism," 8 *University of Dayton Law Review* 533 (1983).

48. Berger, *Government by Judiciary.*

49. Hand's often-cited objection to judicial activism was that "for myself, it would be most irksome to be ruled by a bevy of Platonic Guardians, even if I knew how to choose them, which I assuredly do not. If they were in charge, I should miss the stimulus of living in a society where I have, at least theoretically, some part in the direction of public affairs." Learned Hand, *The Bill of Rights* 73–74 (Cambridge: Harvard University Press, 1958).

50. Similarly, Grey argues that we abandon the "judge as prophet" analogy and recognize that Supreme Court justices are "comfortably middle-of-the-road senatorially confirmable lawyer-politicians . . . not so different from those on the Senate Judiciary Committee or your state utilities commission." Thomas C. Grey, "The Constitution as Scripture," 37 *Stanford Law Review* 1, 24 (1984).

51. Agresto, *The Supreme Court and Constitutional Democracy,* 114.

52. See Owen Fiss, "Foreword: The Forms of Justice," 93 *Harvard Law Review* 1, 10 (1979) ("Legislatures are entirely of a different order. They are not ideologically committed or institutionally suited to search for the meaning of constitutional values."); Perry, *The Constitution, the Courts, and Human Rights,* 111 (Supreme Court justices, in contrast to legislators, "deal with moral problems, not passively, by bowing to established moral conventions, but actively, creatively, by subjecting those conventions to critical reevaluation." The Court's "morality is 'open,' not 'closed.'"); Bickel, *The Least Dangerous Branch,* 25–26 ("courts have certain capacities for dealing with matters of principle that legislatures and executives do not possess. Judges have, or should have, the leisure, the training, and the insulation to follow the ways of the scholar in pursuing the ends of government."); Paul Brest, "Congress as Constitutional Decisionmaker and Its Power to

Counter Judicial Doctrine," 21 *Georgia Law Review* 57, 103 (1987) ("Congress' traditions and practices of considering constitutional questions are so weak and untrustworthy that it is not ready to enter into a dialogue. It needs a tutorial first. For all of the criticisms of the federal judiciary or of particular Supreme Court decisions, Congress is not playing in the same league.") For a quite different view, see Louis Fisher, "Constitutional Interpretation by Members of Congress," 63 *North Carolina Law Review* 707, 717–31 (1985) (Congress possesses significant resources which are appropriately geared to informed constitutional decisionmaking.); Louis Fisher, "Congress and the Fourth Amendment," 21 *Georgia Law Review* 107 (1986) (With regard to constitutional issues, "wisdom is concentrated in neither branch.") See also Mark C. Miller, "Congress and the Constitution: A Tale of Two Committees," 3 *Constitutional Law Journal* 317 (1993), and Mark C. Miller, "Courts, Agencies, and Congressional Committees: A Neo-Institutional Perspective," 55 *Review of Politics* 471 (1993), arguing that congressional committees vary considerably in how carefully and responsibly they deal with constitutional issues.

nificant share of national policymaking power, the appropriate focus is insuring its effectiveness and responsibility. In other words, if the Court lacks certain capacities to be an effective policymaker (e.g., in data gathering or oversight), the solution is to *enhance* those capacities. Most of the critiques like that of Horowitz, in any case, suffer from overstatement. They tend to exaggerate the Court's limitations, typically by: resting analysis of judicial capacities on an abstract, idealized model of the judicial process, rather than on empirical evidence; ignoring judicial adaptations to new policymaking demands, such as the use of special masters in complex, multiparty litigation; and evaluating the capacities of courts in isolation, rather than in comparison to the legislative and executive branches. See Ralph Cavanagh and Austin Sarat, "Thinking about Courts: Toward and beyond a Jurisprudence of Judicial Competence," 14 *Law and Society Review* 371 (1980); Judicially Managed Institutional Reform (symposium) 32 *Alabama Law Review* 267 (1981); Elizabeth Warren, *The Legacy of Judicial Policy-Making—"Gautreaux v. Chicago Housing Authority": The Decision and Its Impact* (Lanham, Md.: University Press of America, 1988).

INTRODUCTION TO PART II

1. Harry H. Wellington, "The Nature of Judicial Review," 91 *Yale Law Journal* 486 (1982); Michael J. Perry, *The Constitution, the Courts, and Human Rights: An Inquiry into the Legitimacy of Constitutional Policymaking by the Judiciary* 125 (New Haven: Yale University Press, 1982).

2. Martin M. Shapiro, "The Supreme Court and Constitutional Adjudication: Of Politics and Neutral Principles," 31 *George Washington Law Review* 587, 590 (1963).

3. Yet another complaint is that courts lack the institutional capacity to carry out an active, policymaking role effectively and, thus, inevitably perform it poorly. See, e.g., Donald L. Horowitz, *The Courts and Social Policy* (Washington, D.C.: Brookings Institution Press, 1977); and Jeremy Rabkin, *Judicial Compulsions: How Public Law Distorts Public Policy* (New York: Basic Books, 1989). This last charge will not be addressed, largely due to limitations of space and time and the consequent choice of focusing on the normative issues. However, it seems to me that if the Court inevitably exercises a sig-

CHAPTER 4

1. Martin M. Shapiro, "The Supreme Court and Constitutional Adjudication: Of Politics and Neutral Principles," 31 *George Washington Law Review* 587 (1963).

2. Archibald Cox, *The Role of the Supreme Court in American Government* 107 (New York: Oxford University Press, 1976).

3. John Hart Ely, "Foreword: On Discovering Fundamental Values," 92 *Harvard Law Review* 5 (1978), fn. excluded.

4. John Hart Ely, *Democracy and Distrust: A Theory of Judicial Review* 44 (Cambridge: Harvard University Press, 1980). See also John Hart Ely, "Another Such Victory: Constitutional Theory and Practice in a World Where Courts Are No Different from Legislatures," 77 *Virginia Law Review* 833, 835 (1991).

5. Cox, *The Role of the Supreme Court*, 106, 109.

6. Phillip B. Kurland, *Politics, the Constitution, and the Warren Court* xxiv (Chicago: University of Chicago Press, 1970).

7. Ibid. at xxv.

8. Cox, *The Role of the Supreme Court*, 108–9 (emphasis added). See also Alexander Bickel, *The Least Dangerous Branch: The Supreme Court at the Bar of Politics* 40 (Indianapolis, Ind.: Bobbs-Merrill, 1962). (The key to the Court's legitimacy is "keeping the judicial function distinct from the legislative and thus capable of being justified.")

9. See Henry M. Hart, Jr., "Foreword: The Time Chart of the Justices," 73 *Harvard Law Review* 84 (1959); Archibald Cox, *The Warren Court: Constitutional Decision as an Instrument of Reform* (Cambridge: Harvard University Press, 1968); Kurland, *Politics, the Constitution, and the Warren Court*; Alexander M. Bickel, *Politics and the Warren Court* (New York: Harper and Rowe, 1965). See also Clifford M. Lytle, *The Warren Court and Its Critics* (Tucson: University of Arizona Press, 1968). And for a more recent critique of the Warren Court in the area of criminal procedure, see Joseph D. Grano, *Confessions, Truth, and the Law* (Ann Arbor: University of Michigan Press, 1993).

10. Shapiro, "The Supreme Court and Constitutional Adjudication," 591.

11. Ibid. at 591–92.

12. That, of course, is one of the tasks of teaching law, including constitutional law: teaching students to make reasonable, persuasive arguments supporting either party or any number of different outcomes.

13. Mark Tushnet makes a similar point in "Following the Rules Laid Down: A Critique of Interpretivism and Neutral Principles," 96 *Harvard Law Review* 781, 819–21 (1983).

14. Robert H. Bork, *The Tempting of America: The Political Seduction of the Law* 6 (New York: Free Press, 1990).

15. John R. Schmidhauser, *The Supreme Court: Its Politics, Personalities, and Procedures* 56–57 (New York: Holt, Rinehart and Winston, 1960). The unwritten requirement of significant political experience, unfortunately I believe, seems to have changed if recent appointments are any indication. Anonymity—the *absence* of any high-profile political experience or public record that might make a nominee more controversial and less confirmable—seems to make a potential nominee more appealing to the president. This may be a result of divided party control between the president and Senate, as well as the growth in public visibility of and interest group involvement in the Senate confirmation process. See Terri Jennings Peretti, "Restoring the Balance of Power: The Struggle for Control of the Supreme Court" 20 *Hastings Constitutional Law Quarterly* 69 (1992); Mark Silverstein, "The People, the Senate, and the Court: The Democratization of the Judicial Confirmation System," 9 *Constitutional Commentary* 41 (1992).

16. *Nomination of Robert H. Bork to be Associate Justice of the Supreme Court of the United States: Hearings before the Senate Committee on the Judiciary*, 100th Congress, 1st session, 511 (1987).

17. J. Braxton Craven, "Paean to Pragmatism," 50 *North Carolina Law Review* 977, 979 (1972).

18. Ibid. at 980.

19. Sheldon Goldman, "Federal Judicial Recruitment," in John B. Gates and Charles A. Johnson, eds., *The American Courts: A Critical Assessmet* 189–90 (Washington, D.C.: Congressional Quarterly Press, 1991).

20. For example, Flemming and Wood note: "To the extent the choices of presidents and voting decisions of senators reflect the public mood when new justices are nominated and confirmed, the elected branches adjust the Court's ideological makeup to bring it in line with the public's views. In this way, prevailing popular sentiment is filtered through the electoral process to shape the Supreme Court's policy direction. *Empirical substantiation for this link is very strong* as both our analysis and the literature indicate, *and is no longer a matter of controversy.*" Roy B. Flemming and B. Dan Wood, "The Public and the Supreme Court: Individual Justice Responsiveness to American Policy Moods," 41 *American Journal of Political Science* 468, 492 (1997) (emphasis added).

21. Goldman, "Federal Judicial Recruitment," 189.

22. Henry J. Abraham, *Justices and Presidents*, 3d ed., 6 (New York: Oxford University Press, 1992).

23. William E. Hulbary and Thomas G. Walker, "The Supreme Court Selection Process: Presidential Motivations and Judicial Performance," 33 *Western Political Quarterly* 185, 189 (1980). See also John Massaro, *Supremely Political: The Role of Ideology and Presidential Management in Unsuccessful Supreme Court Nominations* (Albany: State University of New York Press, 1990).

24. Goldman, "Federal Judicial Recruitment," 193–94.

25. See the background paper by David M. O'Brien in *Judicial Roulette: Report of the Twentieth Century Fund Task Force on Judicial Selection* 35 (New York: Priority Press Publications, 1988).

26. Ibid. at 194; Lawrence Baum, *The Supreme Court*, 3d ed., 43 (Washington, D.C.: Congressional Quarterly Press, 1989). For Presidents Roosevelt and Reagan, 97 percent of their judicial appointees belonged to the president's political party. O'Brien, *Judicial Roulette*, 37.

27. Thomas G. Walker and Lee Epstein, *The Supreme Court of the United States* 36 (New York: St. Martin's Press, 1993).

28. Thomas Marshall, "Symbolic versus Policy Representation on the U.S. Supreme Court," 55 *Journal of Politics* 140 (1993).

29. Sheldon Goldman, "Judicial Appointments and the Presidential Agenda," in Paul Brace, Christine B. Harrington, and Gary King, eds., *The Presidency in American Politics* 19, 41 (New York: New York University Press, 1989).

30. Elliot Slotnick, "Federal Judicial Recruitment and Selection Research: A Review Essay," 71 *Judicature* 317 (1988).

31. Rayman Solomon, "The Politics of Appointment and the Federal Courts' Role in Regulating America: U.S. Courts of Appeals Judgeships from T.R. to F.D.R.," 2 *American Bar Foundation Research Journal* 285 (1984).

32. V. O. Key, "A Theory of Critical Elections," 17 *Journal of Politics* 4 (1955); Thomas P. Jahnige, "Critical Elections and Social Change: Toward a Dynamic Explanation of National Party Competition in the United States," 3 *Polity* 465 (1971); Walter Dean Burnham, *Critical Elections and the Mainsprings of American Politics* (New York: Norton, 1980); James L. Sundquist, *Dynamics of the Party System: Alignment and Realignment of Political Parties in the United States*, rev. ed. (Washington, D.C.: Brookings Institution, 1983).

33. Goldman, "Judicial Appointments and the Presidential Agenda," 22–41, 42–43.

34. Walter F. Murphy, "Reagan's Judicial Strategy," in Larry Berman, ed., *Looking Back on the Reagan Presidency* 207, 218 (Baltimore: Johns Hopkins University Press, 1990) (quoting Everett Dirksen).

35. Ibid. at 207–10.

36. Ibid. at 218.

37. Charles M. Cameron, Albert D. Cover, and Jeffrey A. Segal, "Supreme Court Nominations and the Rational Presidency" (paper presented at the annual meeting of the American Political Science Association, 1990).

38. See Sheldon Goldman, *Picking Federal Judges: Lower Court Selection from Roosevelt through Reagan* (New Haven: Yale University Press, 1997).

39. Henry J. Abraham, *Justices and Presidents: A Political History of Appointments to the Supreme Court*, 237–38, 2d ed. (New York: Oxford University Press, 1985). Goldman's examination of the Justice Department files of appellate court appointees revealed that only 17 percent of the Truman appointees' files contained references to policy views. In contrast, 75 percent of the files on FDR's appointees made some reference to ideology or policy views. Sheldon Goldman, "Judicial Appointments and the Presidential Agenda," 30–31, citing his earlier study, "Judicial Appointments to the United States Courts of Appeals," 1967 *Wisconsin Law Review* 186 (1967).

40. David M. O'Brien, "The Politics of Professionalism: President Gerald R. Ford's Appointment of John Paul Stevens," 21 *Presidential Studies Quarterly* 103 (1991).

41. David M. O'Brien, "The Reagan Judges: His Most Enduring Legacy?" in Charles O. Jones, ed., *The Reagan Legacy: Promise and Performance* 62 (Chatham, N.J.: Chatham House Publishers, 1988).

42. Ibid. The fact that Ford's appointment of Republicans "only" 81 percent of the time is regarded as unusual should serve to reinforce the importance of partisanship in the judicial selection process.

43. Christopher Madison, "A Class Apart," *National Journal* 564 (March 9, 1991).

44. O'Brien, "The Reagan Judges," 65.

45. Ibid. at 62.

46. Jon Gottschall, "Carter's Judicial Appointments: The Influence of Affirmative Action and Merit Selection on Voting on the U.S. Courts of Appeals," 67 *Judicature* 164, 173 (1983); see also Sheldon Goldman, "Carter's Judicial Appointments: A Lasting Legacy," 64 *Judicature* 344 (1981).

47. Goldman, "Judicial Appointments and the Presidential Agenda," 29–31, 33–35, 39–41.

48. Goldman, "Federal Judicial Recruitment," 194. See also O'Brien, "The Reagan Judges," 60–71; Murphy, "Reagan's Judicial Legacy," 210–21; Goldman, "Judicial Appointments and the Presidential Agenda," 36–41; Sheldon Goldman, "Reaganizing the Judiciary: The First Term Appointments," 68 *Judicature* 313 (1985); Sheldon Goldman, "Reagan's Second Term Judicial Appointments: The Battle at Midway," 70 *Judicature* 324 (1987). The Reagan administration record on judicial appointments was unusual with respect to, first, the clarity and intensity of its desire to achieve legal policy change and, second, the institutional mechanism developed to select nominees committed to such change. Under Reagan, the locus of power moved from the Deputy Attorney General's Office to the Office of Legal Policy. To insure White House influence, the President's Committee on Federal Judicial Selection was created, permitting close presidential aides such as Ed Meese, James Baker, and Fred Fielding to play a dominant role. The committee met frequently and was active in generating lists of potential candidates and in evaluating them. Furthermore, candidates were subjected to intensive screening and interviewing, including questions regarding their views on abortion, affirmative action, and criminal justice.

49. Sheldon Goldman, "The Bush Imprint on the Judiciary: Carrying on a Tradition," 74 *Judicature* 294 (1991); Sheldon Goldman, "Bush's Judicial Legacy: The Final Imprint," 76 *Judicature* 282 (1993). As further evidence that Bush "carried on the Reagan tradition," Goldman points out that nine of the ten judges elevated to the U.S. Courts of Appeals by Bush in his first two years were initially appointed to the bench by Reagan. "The Bush Imprint on the Judiciary," 306.

50. Sheldon Goldman, "Judicial Selection under Clinton: A Midterm Examination," 78 *Judicature* 276 (1995); Sheldon Goldman and Elliot Slotnick, "Clinton's First Term Judiciary: Many Bridges to Cross," 80 *Judicature* 254 (1997); David W. Neubauer, *Judicial Process: Law, Courts, and Politics in the United States*, 2d ed., 165 (New York: Harcourt Brace, 1997).

51. Goldman and Slotnick, "Clinton's First Term Judiciary," 256.

52. Ibid. at 265, 270. For example, only 2.4 percent of Clinton's first-term, district

court appointees were opposition party, compared to 4.5 percent for Carter, 4.8 percent for Reagan, and 5.4 percent for Bush. Ibid. at 261.

53. Sheldon Goldman and Matthew D. Saronson, "Clinton's Nontraditional Judges: Creating a More Representative Bench," 78 *Judicature* 68 (1994); Goldman and Slotnick, "Clinton's First Term Judiciary"; Neubauer, *Judicial Process*, 2d ed., 165.

54. In addition to those previously cited, see George L. Watson and John A. Stookey, *Shaping America: The Politics of Supreme Court Appointments* 57–66 (New York: HarperCollins, 1995); Slotnick, "Federal Judicial Recruitment and Selection Research"; W. Gary Fowler, "A Comparison of Initial Recommendation Procedures: Judicial Selection under Reagan and Carter," 1 *Yale Law and Policy Review* 299 (1983); Neil D. McFeeley, *Appointment of Judges* (Austin: University of Texas Press, 1987); Laurence H. Tribe, *God Save This Honorable Court* (New York: Random House, 1985); Daniel S. McHargue, "Factors Influencing the Selection and Appointment of Members of the United States Supreme Court, 1789–1932" (Ph.D. diss. University of California, Los Angeles, 1949); Robert Scigliano, *The Supreme Court and the Presidency* (New York: Free Press, 1971); David J. Danelski, *A Supreme Court Justice Is Appointed* (New York: Random House, 1964); John P. Frank, "The Appointment of Supreme Court Justices: Prestige, Principles, and Politics," 1941 *Wisconsin Law Review* 343 (1941).

55. Abraham, *Justices and Presidents*, 3d ed., 39. For similar lists, see Joel B. Grossman and Stephen L. Wasby, "The Senate and Supreme Court Nominations: Some Reflections," 1972 *Duke Law Journal* 557, 567–68 (1972); Wayne Sulfridge, "Ideology as a Factor in Senate Consideration of Supreme Court Nominations," 42 *Journal of Politics* 560, 562 (1980).

56. Jeffrey Segal, "Senate Confirmation of Supreme Court Justices: Partisan and Institutional Politics," 49 *Journal of Politics* 998, 1007 (1987); Jeffrey A. Segal and Harold J. Spaeth, *The Supreme Court and the Attitudinal Model* 144–45 (New York: Cambridge University Press, 1993). See also Goldman and Slotnick, "Clinton's First Term Judiciary," 255 (regarding the reduced rate of confirmation success for Clinton's judicial nominations following the Re-

publicans regaining control of the Senate in the 104th Congress).

57. P. S. Ruckman, Jr., "The Supreme Court, Critical Nominations, and the Senate Confirmation Process," 55 *Journal of Politics* 793, 797 (1993).

58. Ibid. at 798. Christopher Smith's use of the term "critical judicial nominations" is quite different from Ruckman's. Christopher E. Smith, *Critical Judicial Nominations and Political Change: The Impact of Clarence Thomas* (Westport, Conn.: Praeger Publishers, 1993). For Smith, "Critical judicial nominations are nominations that serve as catalytic events for important changes in politics and public policy that were not anticipated by the political actors who initiated the nominations." For example, Clarence Thomas's nomination was "critical" in that President Bush did not intend or anticipate its effects—a mobilization of women candidates and voters and a new concern of existing officials with issues of particular concern to women. Ruckman's more sensible definition turns on whether a critical change in the partisan balance on the Court is attempted.

59. John D. Felice and Herbert F. Weisberg, "The Changing Importance of Ideology, Party, and Region in Confirmation of Supreme Court Nominees, 1953–1988," 77 *Kentucky Law Journal* 509, 518, 521 (1989). The nine nominations studied were those of Harlan, Stewart, Marshall, Fortas (for chief justice), Haynsworth, Carswell, Rehnquist (for both associate and chief justice), and Bork.

60. Segal and Spaeth, *The Supreme Court and the Attitudinal Model*, 139, 142.

61. This relationship is, in some cases, confounded by the conservatism of southern Democrats. For example, only 77 percent of Democratic senators supported the nomination of Thurgood Marshall, compared to 97 percent of Republicans. Ibid. at 521.

62. Scigliano, *The Supreme Court and the Presidency*, 97–98; Jan Palmer, "Senate Confirmation of Appointments to the U.S. Supreme Court," 41 *Review of Social Economy* 152 (1983); Charles M. Cameron, Albert D. Cover, and Jeffrey A. Segal, "Senate Voting on Supreme Court Nominees: A Neoinstitutional Model," 84 *American Political Science Review* 525, 531 (1990); Jeffrey A. Segal, Albert D. Cover, and Charles M. Cameron, "The Role of Ideology in

Senate Confirmation of Supreme Court Justices," 77 *Kentucky Law Journal* 485 (1988–89); McHargue, "Factors Influencing the Selection and Appointment of Members of the United States Supreme Court, 1789–1932."

63. Segal, "Senate Confirmation," 1008.

64. Stephen Wasby, *The Supreme Court in the Federal Judicial System*, 3d ed., 128 (Chicago: Nelson-Hall Publishers, 1988); Palmer, "Senate Confirmation"; Cameron, Cover, and Segal, "Senate Voting on Supreme Court Nominees"; Segal, Cover, and Cameron, "The Role of Ideology"; Thomas Halper, "Senate Rejection of Supreme Court Nominees," 22 *Drake Law Review* 102 (1972).

65. Halper found support for his "jackal theory" of Senate confirmation: when presidents are politically vulnerable (i.e., if they are lame-duck or unpopular, or they have reached office via presidential death), the Senate is more likely to reject their nominees to the Court. "Senate Rejection of Supreme Court Nominees," 108–10. However, Segal found no effect on confirmation success for elected as compared to succession presidents. For example, the Senate rejected a record five of six nominees put forward by President Tyler; however, all occurred during the fourth year of his presidency. Segal also found that popular support for the president, measured as the percentage of the electoral college vote received, did not influence confirmation probabilities. "Senate Confirmation of Supreme Court Justices," 1009.

66. Palmer, "Senate Confirmation of Appointments," 160. See also Jeffrey Segal and Harold Spaeth, "If a Supreme Court Vacancy Occurs, Will the Senate Confirm a Reagan Nominee?" 69 *Judicature* 187 (1986); John Stookey and George Watson, "The Bork Hearings: Rocks and Roles," 71 *Judicature* 194 (1988). Segal did not find, as Scigliano and Palmer have both suggested, that "the combination of a fourth-year nomination to an opposition Senate creates more trouble than the simple effects of the two variables combined." Segal, "Senate Confirmation of Supreme Court Justices," 1011.

67. Segal and Spaeth, *The Supreme Court and the Attitudinal Model*, 144. See also Ruckman, "The Supreme Court, Critical Nominations, and the Senate Confirmation Process," 800–801: "Nominees who are not members of the

president's cabinet are almost nine times more likely to be confirmed by the Senate."

68. Sulfridge, "Ideology as a Factor," 560. See also Baum, *The Supreme Court*, 3d ed., 49: "Where nominees in this century have received ten or more negative votes, the most important reason for opposition nearly always has been disagreement about policy."

69. Cameron, Cover, and Segal, "Senate Voting on Supreme Court Nominees," 530; Segal, Cover, and Cameron, "The Role of Ideology." Regarding the significant impact of senators' party affiliation and ideology on the Clarence Thomas confirmation vote, see L. Marvin Overby, Beth M. Henschen, Michael H. Walsh, and Julie Strauss, "Courting Constituents: An Analysis of the Senate Confirmation Vote on Justice Clarence Thomas," 86 *American Political Science Review* 997, 999 (1992).

70. Segal and Spaeth, *The Supreme Court and the Attitudinal Model*, 135–37, 138–42. "Liberalism" was determined by senators' scores compiled by Americans for Democratic Action (ADA).

71. David Rohde and Harold Spaeth, *Supreme Court Decision Making* 79 (San Francisco: W. H. Freeman, 1976).

72. Donald R. Songer, "The Relevance of Policy Values for the Confirmation of Supreme Court Nominees," 13 *Law and Society Review* 927, 946 (1979).

73. Felice and Weisberg, "The Changing Importance of Ideology," 525.

74. Ibid. at 530. In contrast, Segal, Cameron, and Cover ("The Role of Ideology") argue that ideological distance does not *directly* affect Senate confirmation voting, but is conditioned by other political factors, such as whether the president is a lame duck or whether the president's party controls the Senate.

75. Most notably, see Bruce Fein, "A Circumscribed Senate Confirmation Role," 102 *Harvard Law Review* 672 (1989); Richard D. Friedman, "Balance Favoring Restraint," 9 *Cardozo Law Review* 15 (1987); Richard D. Friedman, "Tribal Myths: Ideology and the Confirmation of Supreme Court Nominations," 95 *Yale Law Journal* 1283 (1986); Robert H. Bork, *The Tempting of America: The Political Seduction of the Law* (New York: Free Press, 1990); and, more generally with regard to all presidential appointments, Stephen L. Carter,

The Confirmation Mess (New York: Basic Books, 1995).

76. Halper, "Senate Rejection of Supreme Court Nominees," 104. See also Songer "The Relevance of Policy Values," 927–29.

77. Halper, "Senate Rejection of Supreme Court Nominees," 104, 112.

78. Ibid. at 107. Additionally, Segal found that a nominee's professional experience had a very limited impact on the likelihood of Senate confirmation. More specifically, judicial and executive branch experience had virtually no effect, while legislative experience helped the nominee only marginally. However, in Segal's view, this is more likely due to institutional loyalty rather than senators' high regard for "professional experience." "Senate Confirmation of Supreme Court Justices," 1010.

79. Cameron, Cover, and Segal, "Senate Voting on Supreme Court Nominees," 531. See also Segal, Cover, and Cameron, "The Role of Ideology"; Segal and Spaeth, *The Supreme Court and the Attitudinal Model*, 150–52.

80. Cameron, Cover, and Segal, "Senate Voting on Supreme Court Nominees," 531.

81. See also Watson and Stookey, *Shaping America*, 177–89, 199–204. For two brief historical accounts, emphasizing the role of partisanship and politics in Senate confirmation, see William F. Swindler, "The Politics of 'Advice and Consent,'" 56 *American Bar Association Journal* 533 (1970); Tribe, *God Save This Honorable Court*, 93–111. See also Massaro, *Supremely Political.*

82. Gregory A. Caldeira, "Commentary on Senate Confirmation of Supreme Court Justices: The Roles of Organized and Unorganized Interests," 77 *Kentucky Law Journal* 531 (1988–89).

83. Abraham, *Justices and Presidents*, 3d ed.; Richard Watson, "The Defeat of Judge Parker: A Study in Pressure Groups and Politics," 50 *Mississippi Valley Historical Review* 213 (1963–64); Peter G. Fish, "*Red Jacket* Revisited: The Case That Unraveled John J. Parker's Supreme Court Appointment," 5 *Law and History Review* 1 (1987); Peter G. Fish, "Spite Nominations to the United States Supreme Court: Herbert Hoover, Owen J. Roberts, and the Politics of Presidential Vengeance in Retrospect," 77 *Kentucky Law Journal* 545 (1989); O'Brien, *Judicial*

Roulette, 100–101; Baum, *The Supreme Court*, 3d ed., 33–34; Michael Pertschuk and Wendy Schaetzel, *The People Rising: The Campaign against the Bork Nomination* (New York: Thunder's Mouth Press, 1989).

84. One exception is Palmer, who asserts that the satisfaction of interest group allies is the "one consistent element" in the president's nomination decision and, further, that conflict between the president and Senate over a nomination is a function of whether each branch is responding to the same or different interests. "Senate Confirmation of Supreme Court Appointments," 152, 154. However, his subsequent empirical analysis fails to follow up on those assumptions. The same is true for Cameron, Cover, and Segal (in "Senate Voting on Supreme Court Nominees"), whose stated objective is to use "the electoral connection" as an explanatory variable for confirmation roll call votes.

85. Caldeira, "Commentary on Senate Confirmation of Supreme Court Justices," 536–37.

86. Ibid. See also John Anthony Maltese, *The Selling of Supreme Court Nominees* (Baltimore: Johns Hopkins University Press, 1995); Gregory A. Caldeira and Charles E. Smith, Jr., "Campaigning for the Supreme Court: The Dynamics of Public Opinion on the Thomas Nomination," 58 *Journal of Politics* 655 (1996); Mark Silverstein, *Judicious Choices: The New Politics of Supreme Court Confirmations* (New York: W. W. Norton Co., 1994); Silverstein, "The People, the Senate, and the Court."

87. Caldeira and Smith, "Campaigning for the Supreme Court," 656.

88. Caldeira, "Commentary on Senate Confirmation of Supreme Court Justices," 537.

89. Ibid. at 538. See also Martin Shapiro, "Interest Groups and Supreme Court Appointments," 84 *Northwestern University Law Review* 935 (1990); Watson and Stookey, *Shaping America*, 97–108.

90. Segal and Spaeth, *The Supreme Court and the Attitudinal Model*, 153–54, 157–78.

91. Jeffrey A. Segal, Charles M. Cameron, and Albert D. Cover, "A Spatial Model of Roll Call Voting: Senators, Constituents, Presidents, and Interest Groups in Supreme Court Confirmations," 36 *American Journal of Political Science* 96 (1992). See also Watson and Stookey, *Shaping America*, 118–22, 195–98.

92. Segal and Spaeth, *The Supreme Court and the Attitudinal Model*, 151.

93. Overby et al., "Courting Constituents."

94. Ibid. at 1002.

95. Similarly, Caldeira and Smith argue that "the activation of public opinion during these dramatic 'campaigns' for and against confirmation, along with concomitant attention to public attitudes by those formally charged with the disposition of a nomination, raises the prospect of a genuine contribution by ordinary citizens to the makeup of the Supreme Court." "Campaigning for the Supreme Court," 656. See also Silverstein's argument that the confirmation process is much more democratic than before, in *Judicious Choices* and "The People, the Senate, and the Court."

96. For a summary of the evolution of the ABA's role and methods in evaluating judicial nominees, see O'Brien, *Judicial Roulette*, 81–94; Abraham, *Justices and Presidents*, 2d ed., 32–39; Watson and Stookey, *Shaping America*, 83–85, 108–12.

97. Joel B. Grossman, *Lawyers and Judges* 250–51 (New York: Wiley, 1965). See also John R. Schmidhauser, *Judges and Justices: The Federal Appellate Judiciary* 23–26 (Boston: Little, Brown, 1979).

98. Elliot E. Slotnick, "The ABA Standing Committee on Federal Judiciary: A Contemporary Assessment," 66 *Judicature* 349, 393 (1983).

99. Ibid. As a result, Slotnick expresses strong reservations about the ABA's "most favored status" and its "monopoly as an institutionalized, nongovernmental voice in the federal judicial selection process."

100. O'Brien, *Judicial Roulette*, 81–82; Bork, *The Tempting of America*, 292–93.

101. Songer, "The Relevance of Policy Values"; Sulfridge, "Ideology as a Factor"; Segal, Cover, and Cameron, "The Role of Ideology"; Nina Totenberg, "The Confirmation Process and the Public: To Know or Not to Know," 101 *Harvard Law Review* 1213 (1988); O'Brien, *Judicial Roulette*.

102. See Peretti, "Restoring the Balance of Power."

103. Tribe, *God Save This Honorable Court*, 78.

104. Ibid. at 92. For a similar view, see Albert Melone, "The Senate's Confirmation Role in Supreme Court Nominations and the

Politics of Ideology versus Impartiality," 75 *Judicature* 68, 72–75 (1991).

105. Walker and Epstein note that "the Senate has rejected only twelve cabinet appointments during the nation's entire history—and fully half of those occurred during the turbulent administration of John Tyler in the 1840s." *The Supreme Court of the United States*, 46. In contrast, the Senate rejected, refused to act, indefinitely postponed, or forced the withdrawal of twenty-seven Supreme Court nominees. (This figure does not include the nomination of William Patterson, withdrawn by George Washington to allow Patterson to resign from the Senate; he was renominated and approved five days later. It also does not include the nomination of Homer Thornberry by President Lyndon Johnson. The Senate did not act on the nomination because the withdrawal of Abe Fortas's nomination for the chief justiceship eliminated the vacancy Thornberry was to fill.) For a list of all Supreme Court nominations and the resulting Senate action, see Lee Epstein, Jeffrey A. Segal, Harold J. Spaeth, and Thomas G. Walker, *The Supreme Court Compendium: Data, Decisions, and Developments* 284–90 (Washington, D.C.: Congressional Quarterly Press, 1994).

106. The Senate rejected President Hoover's nomination of Judge John Parker in 1930, Nixon's nominations of Clement Haynsworth in 1969 and G. Harrold Carswell in 1970, and Reagan's nomination of Robert Bork in 1987. President Johnson's nomination of Justice Abe Fortas to fill the chief justice seat was withdrawn in 1968 after the Senate failed to approve a motion to end floor debate and bring the nomination to a vote. (Not included are Homer Thornberry, withdrawn after the Fortas nomination failed, and Douglas Ginsburg, who withdrew him name from consideration due to media reports of marijuana use.)

107. Mark Silverstein and William Haltom, "Can There Be a Theory of Supreme Court Confirmations?" (paper presented at the Western Political Science Association meeting, 1990), 5. It is Clarence Thomas's confirmation vote that increases their stated "5 of 25 nominations" to 6.

108. Abraham, *Justices and Presidents*, 2d ed., 39; Gary J. Simson, "Taking the Court Seriously: A Proposed Approach to Senate Confirmation of Supreme Court Nominees," 7 *Constitutional Commentary* 283, 324 (1990).

109. Simson, "Taking the Court Seriously," 323.

110. Sulfridge, "Ideology as a Factor," 562–63.

111. Richard D. Friedman, "The Transformation in Senate Response to Supreme Court Nominations: From Reconstruction to the Taft Administration," 5 *Cardozo Law Review* 1 (1983).

112. Ibid. at 4.

113. Ibid.

114. Ibid. at 5. The decline in the importance of sectional concerns in the selection of Supreme Court justices was verified empirically by Segal, "Senate Confirmation of Supreme Court Justices," 1010.

115. The "White House script" in the Reagan-Bush years, according to Strauss and Sunstein, was to assert that "the nominee is open-minded, has 'no agenda,' enthusiastically accepts both *Brown* v. *Board of Education* and *Griswold* v. *Connecticut*, is humbled by the difficulty of being a Justice, and admires Justice Harlan." David A. Strauss and Cass R. Sunstein, "The Senate, the Constitution, and the Confirmation Process," 101 *Yale Law Journal* 1491, 1492 (1992). Watson and Stookey also discuss the president's role in initiating "the nomination discourse" and the constraints on that role, in *Shaping America*, 85–96.

116. Calvin R. Massey, "The Duty of Keeping Political Power Separated," 20 *Hastings Constitutional Law Quarterly* 1, 2 (1992), summarizing my argument in "Restoring the Balance of Power."

117. Segal, "Senate Confirmation of Supreme Court Justices," 1009–10.

118. Ibid. at 1008.

119. Ibid. at 1010. Scigliano, *The Supreme Court and the Presidency*.

120. Baum, *The Supreme Court*, 3d ed., 49.

121. David W. Neubauer, *Judicial Process: Law, Courts, and Politics in the United States*, 1st ed., 400 (Pacific Grove, Calif.: Brooks/Cole Publishing Co., 1991).

122. Ibid.

123. Baum, *The Supreme Court*, 3d ed., 47.

124. Ibid. See also Silverstein, "The People, the Senate and the Court." Senate scrutiny and "contentiousness," measured in terms of

confirmation success and confirmation delay, has increased for federal judicial nominees generally. See Roger E. Hartley and Lisa M. Holmes, "Increasing Senate Scrutiny of Lower Federal Court Nominees," 80 *Judicature* 274 (1997); Garland Allison, "Delay in Senate Confirmation of Federal Judicial Nominees," 80 *Judicature* 8 (1996).

125. Watson and Stookey, *Shaping America,* 64.

126. Cameron, Cover, and Segal, "Supreme Court Nominations and the Rational Presidency," 1, 12–16.

127. Goldman and Slotnick, "Clinton's First Term Judiciary," 255–56.

128. Abraham, *Justices and Presidents,* 2d ed., 126.

129. According to Abraham, "Twenty-four hours before Hoover had indicated he would announce his candidate publicly, he called for Borah. In an often-told, dramatic confrontation between two proud men, the President, after discussing the vacancy generally, suddenly handed Borah a list on which he had ranked those individuals he was considering for the nomination in descending order of preference. The name at the bottom was that of Benjamin N. Cardozo. Borah glanced at it and replied: 'Your list is all right, but you handed it to me upside down.' " Ibid. at 202–3.

130. See O'Brien, "The Reagan Judges," 73–74.

131. Ibid. at 74. Similarly, "confirmation delay" by the Senate in reviewing Reagan's lower court nominees increased dramatically in 1987, when Biden took over the Judiciary Committee. Hartley and Holmes, "Increasing Senate Scrutiny of Lower Federal Court Nominees," 274, 276.

132. Thomas was hurt by Hill's charges of sexual harassment, although there is some question of how much. "Both sides estimate that Thomas lost about 10 votes that he might have had before the Hill allegations emerged—narrowing an outcome that still would have been one of the closest in history. But only three senators publicly shifted positions." Joan Biskupic, "Thomas' Victory Puts Icing on the Reagan-Bush Court," 49 *Congressional Quarterly* 3026, 3030 (October 19, 1991).

133. According to Ethan Bronner, the White House campaign on behalf of Bork was an exception. *Battle for Justice: How the Bork Nomination Shook America* 348 (New York: Norton, 1989). Bruce Fein would agree. ("A Circumscribed Senate Confirmation Role," 102 *Harvard Law Review* 672, 685–87 (1989).

134. The same follows for a Democratic president, such as Clinton, facing a Republican-controlled Senate. During his first term, Clinton deliberately chose a less confrontational path, nominating noncontroversial federal judges to fill Supreme Court vacancies and, further, for his judicial appointments generally, employing a process of consultation, compromise, and accommodation with key Republicans in the Senate. Goldman and Slotnick, "Clinton's First Term Judiciary," 255–56.

135. Robert Bork correctly predicted this to be one of the undesirable results of his defeat in the Senate. See Bork, *The Tempting of America,* 347–48; Robert H. Bork, "The Full Court Press: The Drive for Control of the Courts," *American Enterprise* 58 (1990).

136. For example, Souter and Kennedy provided the fourth and fifth votes in upholding the Reagan administration's "gag rule" forbidding abortion counseling and referral in federally funded family planning clinics. *Rust* v. *Sullivan,* 500 U.S. 173 (1991). Congress's attempt to reverse the *Rust* decision met with a Bush veto, which it failed to override. Justice Kennedy provided the critical fifth vote in several employment discrimination decisions in 1989 that met with congressional disapproval. See especially *Wards Cove Packing Co.* v. *Atonio,* 490 U.S. 642 (1989) (holding that employees challenging employment practices having racially discriminatory impact bear the burden of proving that such practices are motivated by discriminatory intent rather than business necessity, thus overruling *Griggs* v. *Duke Power Co.,* 401 U.S. 424 [1971]); *Patterson* v. *McClean Credit Union,* 491 U.S. 164 (1989) (holding that sec. 1981 of the 1866 Civil Rights Act forbids racial discrimination in hiring but not in on-the-job racial harassment); and *Martin* v. *Wilks,* 490 U.S. 755 (1989) (allowing white employees to challenge court-approved consent decrees embodying affirmative action plans). Congress subsequently passed the 1990 Civil Rights Act, which would have reversed these decisions. President Bush, however, vetoed the act, and the Senate failed to override by one vote. The Civil Rights Act of 1991, signed by

Bush, overturned twelve Supreme Court rulings, including *Wards Cove, Patterson,* and *Martin* v. *Wilks.* See David M. O'Brien, *Supreme Court Watch—1992* 26–27 (New York: Norton, 1992). In the *Casey* decision upholding most of Pennsylvania's abortion regulations, Clarence Thomas joined both the Rehnquist and Scalia opinions, which provided scathing attacks of *Roe* and argued for its reversal. *Planned Parenthood of Southeastern Pennsylvania* v. *Casey,* 505 U.S. 833 (1992). Thomas's impact on the Court was less notable than that of Kennedy and Souter, as he was so often a member of an already existent conservative majority on the Court; in contrast, Souter cast the deciding vote in twelve of the thirteen five-to-four decisions during the Court's 1991 term. See Christopher E. Smith and Scott Patrick Johnson, "The First-Term Performance of Justice Clarence Thomas," 76 *Judicature* 172, 175 (1993).

137. In the nineteenth century, Congress altered the size of the Court to secure a particular membership and ideological bent several times. In the Judiciary Act of 1801, the "lame-duck" Federalist Congress reduced the number of justices from six to five (effective with the next vacancy) and created new judgeships, which were promptly filled with loyal Federalists. The new Congress repealed the act and postponed the Court's next term to insure that it could not hear a legal challenge to the repealing legislation. The number of justices was increased from six to eight in the final days of Andrew Jackson's administration. The size of the Court was increased to ten to benefit President Lincoln, after a close five-to-four decision upholding the blockade of the Confederacy. *The Prize Cases,* 67 U.S. (2 Black) 635 (1862). To prevent President Andrew Johnson from appointing justices who might fail to uphold its Reconstruction program, the powerful Republican Congress reduced the Court's size, as each vacancy occurred, from ten to seven justices. The embattled Johnson was never permitted an appointment to the Court, and the existing majority of Lincoln appointees remained secure. After Ulysses Grant's election, Congress again expanded the size of the Court, this time to nine, where it remains to this day. President Grant promptly used the new vacancies to engineer a reversal of the *Hepburn* decision, which had denied Congress

the power to authorize the use of paper currency. *The Legal Tender Cases,* 12 Wallace 457 (1871). Franklin Roosevelt's failure to win support from an overwhelmingly friendly and Democratic Congress for his court-packing plan (to increase the size of the Court by, in effect, six members to insure that his New Deal programs would be upheld) was clear evidence that times had changed. Court-curbing and Court-influencing attempts by Congress in the twentieth century are quite rare. See my fuller discussion in "Restoring the Balance of Power," 79–82.

138. However, this is an advantage that Clinton has largely not chosen to use.

139. In addition to his poor civil rights record, Carswell was widely regarded, in Henry Abraham's words, as a "patently inferior [candidate], simply on the basis of fundamental juridical and legal qualifications." *Justices and Presidents,* 2d ed., 16. Louis Pollak, then dean of the Yale Law School, asserted that Carswell possessed "more slender credentials than any Supreme Court nominee put forth in this century." Ibid. Even the floor manager of the nomination in the Senate, Roman Hruska of Nebraska, had a difficult time defending Carswell; he argued to his Senate colleagues that "even if he is mediocre, there are a lot of mediocre judges and people and lawyers. They are entitled to a little representation, aren't they, and a little chance? We can't have all Brandeises, Cardozos and Frankfurters, and stuff like that there." Ibid. at 16–17. In addition, Carswell held the dubious record of having been reversed by appellate courts more than any of the other then-sitting federal jurists except seven. Ibid. at 17.

140. While some have challenged the validity of this claim, Bork was certainly widely *perceived* as a judicial radical. See Fein, "A Circumscribed Senate Confirmation Role," 685–86, discussing the Justice Department's statistical study of Bork's judicial record, provided in "A Response to the Critics of Judge Robert H. Bork," 9 *Cardozo Law Review* 373 (1987) (reprint from the U.S. Department of Justice, Office of Public Affairs).

141. Cameron, Cover, and Segal regard such nominations by the president as puzzling and the resulting rejection by senators as "sensible, predictable, and readily understandable." Presidents invite rejection when they

"nominate a less well qualified, ideologically extreme candiate, especially when the president is in a weak position." Yet such irrational presidential behavior occasionally occurs. "Senate Voting on Supreme Court Nominees," 532.

142. The phrase belongs to Laurence Tribe, *God Save This Honorable Court*, 76.

143. In fact, it may be the Senate's failure to challenge the Reagan-Bush nominations more vigorously that produced the interesting trend discovered by Mishler and Sheehan: the "liberalness" of the Court's decisions corresponded with the "public mood" from 1956 to 1981, but deviated from it after 1981. William Mishler and Reginald S. Sheehan, "The Supreme Court as a Countermajoritarian Institution? The Impact of Public Opinion on Supreme Court Decisions," 87 *American Political Science Review* 87 (1993).

Presidential dominance in selecting the Court's membership and shaping its ideological character is problematic in two other respects. In addition to weakening the Court's representative character, it undermines the principle of separation of powers. In contrast to executive branch appointments requiring Senate confirmation, the federal judiciary is intended to be a coequal and not a presidentially subordinate branch of government. Presidents should not control two branches of government, nor should they be permitted to select the mediator of disputes in which they are a direct party. See Strauss and Sunstein, "The Senate, the Constitution, and the Confirmation Process," 1491. Second, presidential dominance in judicial selection threatens to create a dangerous "two-against-one" situation in the lawmaking and statutory construction process. See Biskupic, "Thomas' Victory Puts Icing on Reagan-Bush Court." Especially in the late 1980s and early 1990s, the Court often provided a conservative interpretation of a congressional statute or deferred to a conservative statutory interpretation by the executive branch. Congress would then reverse that interpretation by rewriting the statute, only to face a presidential veto, which it narrowly failed to override. Two examples include Congress's efforts to override the Court's *Rust* v. *Sullivan* decision, 500 U.S. 173 (1991) and several of its employment discrimination decisions (most notably *Wards Cove*

Packing v. *Atonio*, 490 U.S. 642 (1989). In the latter case at least, Congress was ultimately successful when a politically weakened President Bush decided to sign the Civil Rights Act of 1991.

144. This discussion is not meant to imply that the propriety of aggressive and ideologically based Senate review of Supreme Court nominees is a settled issue. Rather, the focus here has been on examining, as an empirical matter, the degree to which the Senate in fact injects its political preferences in a consistent and aggressive manner, thereby leading to fuller, more effective political representation on the Court. For a discussion of the normative issue of whether the Senate should play such a role, see Peretti, "Restoring the Balance of Power"; "Essays on the Supreme Court Appointment Process," (symposium) 101 *Harvard Law Review* 1146 (1988); "Confirmation Controversy: The Selection of a Supreme Court Justice" (symposium), 84 *Northwestern University Law Review* 832 (1990); Fein, "A Circumscribed Senate Confirmation Role"; Strauss and Sunstein, "The Senate, the Constitution, and the Confirmation Process"; Simson, "Taking the Court Seriously"; "What's the Alternative? A Roundtable on the Confirmation Process," 78 *American Bar Association Journal* 41 (1992); Tribe, *God Save This Honorable Court*; Richard D. Friedman, "Tribal Myths: Ideology and the Confirmation of Supreme Court Nominations," 95 *Yale Law Journal* 1283 (1986); Friedman, "The Transformation in Senate Response to Supreme Court Nominations"; Bork, *The Tempting of America*; Watson and Stookey, *Shaping America*, 212–23; James E. Gauch, "The Intended Role of the Senate in Supreme Court Appointments," 56 *University of Chicago Law Review* 337 (1989); Charles L. Black, Jr., "A Note on Senatorial Considerations of Supreme Court Nominees," 79 *Yale Law Journal* 657 (1970); Henry J. Abraham, Griffin B. Bell, Charles E. Grassley, Eugene W. Hickok, Jr., Judge John W. Kern III, Stephen J. Markman, and William Bradford Reynolds, *Judicial Selection: Merit, Ideology, and Politics* (Washington, D.C.: National Legal Center for the Public Interest, 1990); "Gender, Race, and the Politics of Supreme Court Appointments," (symposium) 65 *Southern California Law Review* 1279 (1992); Donald Lively, "The Supreme Court Appointment Process: In Search of Con-

stitutional Roles and Responsibilities," 59 *Southern California Law Review* 563 (1986); Joseph Larisa, "Popular Mythology: The Framers' Intent, the Constitution, and Ideological Review of Supreme Court Nominees," 69 *Boston College Law Review* (1989); David Danelski, "Ideology as a Ground for the Rejection of the Bork Nomination," 84 *Northwestern University Law Review* (1990); Melone, "The Senate's Confirmation Role in Supreme Court Nominations and the Politics of Ideology versus Impartiality"; Michael Comiskey, "Can the Senate Examine the Constitutional Philosophies of Supreme Court Nominees?" 26 *PS: Political Science and Politics* 495 (1993); William Bradford Reynolds, "The Confirmation Process: Too Much Advice and Too Little Consent," 75 *Judicature* 80 (1991); A. Mitchell McConnell, Jr., "Haynsworth and Carswell: A New Senate Standard of Excellence," 59 *Kentucky Law Journal* 7 (1970).

145. The solution, I have argued, is to strengthen the political checks on the president's power to influence the Court, by revitalizing the Senate's critical role in the confirmation process and removing normative constraints on the power of Congress to alter the Court's size. Peretti, "Restoring the Balance of Power," 95–103.

146. Murphy, "Reagan's Judicial Strategy," 210.

147. John Hart Ely, "Another Such Victory: Constitutional Theory and Practice in a World Where Courts Are No Different from Legislatures," 77 *Virginia Law Review* 833, 877 (1991). See also Robert Dahl, "Decision-Making in a Democracy: The Supreme Court as a National Policy-Maker," 6 *Journal of Public Law* 279 (1957). Certainly as President Carter discovered, this average rate can mask periods of greater stability in the Court's membership. However, only four presidents did not have the opportunity to appoint a member to the Court. Of the four, both William Harrison and Zachary Taylor died soon after reaching office. The Senate failed to confirm Andrew Johnson's only Supreme Court nominee, and Congress reduced the size of the Court each time a vacancy occurred during Johnson's term in office. The fourth, Jimmy Carter, was simply unlucky (in this and other matters); he is the only president to serve a full term without a single Court vacancy occurring. Ten presi-

dents appointed but one Supreme Court justice, and eleven presidents appointed four or more, with Washington and FDR appointing ten and nine justices, respectively.

For evidence that justices time their retirements strategically, for political (and particularly policy) reasons, see Timothy M. Hagle, "Strategic Retirements: A Political Model of Turnover on the United States Supreme Court," 15 *Political Behavior* 25 (1993); Peverill Squire, "Politics and Personal Factors in Retirement from the United States Supreme Court," 10 *Political Behavior* 180 (1988); Deborah J. Barrow, Gary Zuk, and Gerard S. Gryski, *The Federal Judiciary and Institutional Change* (Ann Arbor: University of Michigan Press, 1996).

148. Of course, that is Robert Dahl's argument in "Decision-Making in a Democracy." For critical commentary, see David W. Adamany, "Legitimacy, Realigning Elections, and the Supreme Court," 1973 *Wisconsin Law Review* 790 (1973); Jonathan Casper, "The Supreme Court and National Policy Making," 70 *American Political Science Review* 50 (1976); Richard Funston, "The Supreme Court and Critical Elections," 69 *American Political Science Review* 795 (1975); John B. Gates, *The Supreme Court and Partisan Realignment: A Macro- and Microlevel Perspective* (Boulder, Colo.: Westview Press, 1992). Regarding the relevance of partisanship in the executive and legislative branches for the federal judiciary, see Barrow, Zuk, and Gryski, *The Federal Judiciary and Institutional Change.*

149. There are obvious methodological problems in testing the correspondence between the political views of Supreme Court justices, other national political elites, and the general population. For now, I propose only to examine whether the policy views of the justices have dominated their recruitment and selection and whether those views in turn exert a great influence on their subsequent decisions. Chapter 6 will more directly examine the relationship between public opinion and the Court's decisions.

150. Mishler and Sheehan, "The Supreme Court as a Countermajoritarian Institution?"

151. After 1981, the Court became more conservative, in line with presidential desires but in opposition to the ideological composition of Congress and the increasingly liberal

public mood. Mishler and Sheehan ("The Supreme Court as a Countermajoritarian Institution?") and Helmut Norpoth and Jeffrey Segal ("Popular Influence on Supreme Court Decisions: Comment," 88 *American Political Science Review* 711 [1994]) hypothesize that the Court's conservatism was likely due to the character of presidential elections during this period. To the degree that the president is elected for reasons other than his domestic policy views (e.g., personality or foreign policy), the Court is less likely to reflect the public's policy preferences. In contrast, I would attribute this to the failure of the Senate to challenge or reject Reagan-Bush nominees whose conservative views were not in line with the Senate Democratic majority. See Peretti, "Restoring the Balance of Power."

152. Norpoth and Segal, "Popular Influence on Supreme Court Decisions"; William Mishler and Reginald S. Sheehan, "Popular Influence on Supreme Court Decisions: A Response to Helmut Norpoth and Jeffrey A. Segal," 88 *American Political Science Review* 716 (1994); James A. Stimson, Michael B. MacKuen, and Robert S. Erikson, "Dynamic Representation," 89 *American Political Science Review* 543 (1995). See also Michael W. Link, "Tracking Public Mood in the Supreme Court: Cross-Time Analysis of Criminal Procedure and Civil Rights Cases," 48 *Political Research Quarterly* 61 (1995), finding that the relationship held for cases involving civil rights but not criminal procedure.

153. Segal and Spaeth, *The Supreme Court and the Attitudinal Model*, 69 (although I would dispute the lack of *political* accountability).

154. David Adamany, "The Supreme Court," in John B. Gates and Charles A. Johnson, eds., *The American Courts: A Critical Assessment* 12 (Washington, D.C.: Congressional Quarterly Press 1991).

155. Sheldon Goldman and Austin Sarat, eds., *American Court Systems*, 2d ed., 383 (New York: Longman, 1989).

156. Thomas G. Walker, Lee Epstein, and William J. Dixon, "On the Mysterious Demise of Consensual Norms in the United States Supreme Court," 50 *Journal of Politics* 361, 362 (1988). See also Stacia L. Haynie, "Leadership and Consensus on the U.S. Supreme Court," 54 *Journal of Politics* 1158 (1992). Further evidence of growing dissensus on the Court is the

number of five-to-four decisions. The Court averaged only one five-to-four decision during the nineteenth century, but sixteen during the Warren Court (1956–69), and thirty from 1982 through 1990. David G. Barnum, *The Supreme Court and American Democracy* 81 (New York: St. Martin's Press, 1993). For the finding that (and an exploration of why) lower court judges become "less consensual" when they become Supreme Court justices, see Scott D. Gerber and Keeok Park, "The Quixotic Search for Consensus on the U.S. Supreme Court: A Cross-Judicial Empirical Analysis of the Rehnquist Court Justices," 91 *American Political Science Review* 390 (1997).

157. Walker, Epstein, and Dixon, "On the Mysterious Demise of Consensual Norms," 362–63.

158. C. Herman Pritchett, *The Roosevelt Court: A Study in Judicial Politics and Values, 1937–47* (New York: Macmillan, 1948).

159. Glendon Schubert, *Quantitative Analysis of Judicial Behavior* (Glencoe, Ill.: Free Press, 1959); Glendon Schubert, *The Judicial Mind* (Evanston, Ill.: Northwestern University Press, 1965). See also Glendon Schubert, *The Judicial Mind Revisited* (New York: Oxford, 1974).

160. Schubert, *The Judicial Mind*, 38.

161. Glendon Schubert, "The 1960–1961 Term of the Supreme Court: A Psychological Analysis," 56 *American Political Science Review* 90 (1962); S. Sidney Ulmer, "The Analysis of Behavior Patterns on the United States Supreme Court," 22 *Journal of Politics* 629 (1960); S. Sidney Ulmer, "Supreme Court Behavior and Civil Rights," 13 *Western Political Quarterly* 288 (1960); S. Sidney Ulmer, "Scaling Judicial Cases: A Methodological Note," 4 *American Behavioral Scientist* 31 (1961); S. Sidney Ulmer, "Toward a Theory of Sub-Group Formation in the United States Supreme Court," 27 *Journal of Politics* 133 (1965); Harold J. Spaeth, "An Approach to the Study of Attitudinal Differences as an Aspect of Judicial Behavior," 5 *Midwest Journal of Political Science* 165 (1961); Harold J. Spaeth, "An Analysis of Judicial Attitudes in the Labor Relations Decisions of the Warren Court," 25 *Journal of Politics* 290 (1963); Harold J. Spaeth, "Warren Court Attitudes toward Business: The 'B' Scale," in Glendon Schubert, ed., *Judicial Decision-Making* 79 (New York: Free Press, 1963); Joseph Tanenhaus, "Supreme

Court Attitudes toward Federal Administrative Agencies, 1947–1956—An Application of Social Science Methods to the Study of the Judicial Process," 14 *Vanderbilt Law Review* 482 (1961); Joseph Tanenhaus, "The Cumulative Scaling of Judicial Decisions," 79 *Harvard Law Review* 1583 (1966).

162. Rohde and Spaeth, *Supreme Court Decision Making.*

163. Epstein, et. al., *The Supreme Court Compendium,* 427–29.

164. Ibid.

165. In their study of the Warren and Burger Courts, Segal and Spaeth found that support for the liberal position in nonunanimous civil liberties cases ranged from a high of 96.1 percent for Justice Douglas (while on the Warren Court) to a low of 5.6 percent for Justice Rehnquist (while on the Burger Court). Jeffrey A. Segal and Harold J. Spaeth, "Decisional Trends on the Warren and Burger Courts: Results from the Supreme Court Data Base Project," 73 *Judicature* 103, 106 (1989). For additional data and analysis regarding the apparently ideology-based voting patterns of justices on the Warren, Burger, and Rehnquist Courts, see Segal and Spaeth, *The Supreme Court and the Attitudinal Model,* 245–55; Goldman and Sarat, *American Court Systems,* 2d ed., 385, table 2; Baum, *The Supreme Court,* 3d ed., 137–42; Lawrence Baum, "Explaining the Burger Court's Support for Civil Liberties," 20 *Political Science Quarterly* 21 (1987); Epstein et al., *The Supreme Court Compendium,* 423–55.

166. Walker and Epstein, *The Supreme Court of the United States,* 125–26.

167. Segal and Spaeth, "Decisional Trends," 107. They also note that Justice Goldberg never dissented from a liberal civil liberties decision and dissented from only one of twenty-three liberal economic decisions, while Justice Clark never dissented from a conservative civil liberties decision.

Dissent behavior is not a function of a justice's social background, as some studies have suggested. John R. Schmidhauser, "*Stare Decisis,* Dissent, and the Background of the Justices of the Supreme Court of the United States," 14 *University of Toronto Law Journal* 194 (1962); S. Sidney Ulmer, "Dissent Behavior and the Social Background of Supreme Court Justices," 32 *Journal of Politics* 580 (1970). Rather, dissent behavior is consistent with an attitudinal

model. Segal and Spaeth, "Decisional Trends" 107.

168. Epstein et al., *The Supreme Court Compendium,* 425.

169. Ibid; Neubauer, *Judicial Process,* 409–10. See also Barnum, *The Supreme Court and American Democracy,* 229–31; Baum, *The Supreme Court,* 3d ed., 142–43; Epstein et al., *The Supreme Court Compendium,* 456–508.

170. "The Supreme Court, 1994 Term," 109 *Harvard Law Review* 340 (1995).

171. Segal and Spaeth, *The Supreme Court and the Attitudinal Model,* 280.

172. Ibid. at 279–90. See also Harold J. Spaeth and Michael F. Altfeld, "Influence Relationships within the Supreme Court: A Comparison of the Warren and Burger Courts," 38 *Western Political Quarterly* 70 (1985).

173. Segal and Spaeth, "Decisional Trends," 104.

174. Computed from data supplied by Segal and Spaeth. Ibid. at 104.

175. Lawrence Baum, "Membership Change and Collective Voting Change in the United States Supreme Court," 54 *Journal of Politics* 3 (1992); Lawrence Baum, "Measuring Policy Change in the U.S. Supreme Court," 82 *American Political Science Review* 905 (1988); Baum, *The Supreme Court,* 3d ed., 145–47; Charles A. Johnson, "Personnel Change and Policy Change in the U.S. Supreme Court," 62 *Social Science Quarterly* 751 (1981). Regarding the impact of the Nixon appointees in producing a considerable ideological realignment on the Court, see Norpoth and Segal, "Popular Influence on Supreme Court Decisions," 714. Significant but more limited support was found by Thomas Hensley and Christopher E. Smith in "Membership Change and Voting Change: An Analysis of the Rehnquist Court's 1986–1991 Terms," 48 *Political Research Quarterly* 837 (1995).

Membership change, however, is not the only factor causing decisionmaking change on the Court; two other factors are issue change and change in the voting patterns of "continuing" justices. See especially Hensley and Smith, "Membership Change and Voting Change."

For an interesting attempt to develop a more complex model of "legal" change, but one that does include and verify the influence of "judicial policy views," see Paul J. Wahlbeck,

"The Life of the Law: Judicial Politics and Legal Change," 59 *Journal of Politics* 778 (1997).

176. Reginald S. Sheehan, William Mishler, and Donald R. Songer, "Ideology, Status, and the Differential Success of Direct Parties before the Supreme Court," 86 *American Political Science Review* 464 (1992).

177. For two strong reviews of judicial behavior research, see James L. Gibson, "From Simplicity to Complexity: The Development of Theory in the Study of Judicial Behavior," 5 *Political Behavior* 7 (1983); and James L. Gibson, "Decision Making in Appellate Courts," in John B. Gates and Charles A. Johnson, eds., *The American Courts* 255 (Washington, D.C.: Congressional Quarterly Press, 1991). See also Spaeth, *Supreme Court Policy Making*; John D. Sprague, *Voting Patterns of the United States Supreme Court* (Indianapolis, Ind.: Bobbs-Merrill, 1968); Baum, *The Supreme Court*, 3d ed., 136–49; Robert L. Dudley and Craig R. Ducat, "The Burger Court and Economic Liberalism," 39 *Western Political Quarterly* 236 (1986); Craig R. Ducat and Robert L. Dudley, "Dimensions Underlying Economic Policy Making in the Early and Later Burger Courts," 49 *Journal of Politics* 521 (1987); Lee Epstein, Thomas G. Walker, and William J. Dixon, "The Supreme Court and Criminal Justice Disputes: A Neo-Institutional Perspective," 33 *American Journal of Political Science* 825 (1989); Timothy M. Hagle and Harold J. Spaeth, "The Business Decisions of the Burger Court: The Emergence of a New Ideology," 54 *Journal of Politics* 120 (1992); Timothy M. Hagle and Harold J. Spaeth, "Ideological Patterns in the Justices' Voting in the Burger Court's Business Cases," 55 *Journal of Politics* 492 (1993); Joseph A. Ignagni, "U.S. Supreme Court Decision-Making and the Free Exercise Clause," 55 *Review of Politics* 511 (1993). Additional studies finding ideology-based differences in decisionmaking for judges on lower federal courts and state supreme courts include: Sheldon Goldman, "Conflict on the U.S. Courts of Appeals, 1965–1971: A Quantitative Analysis," 42 *University of Cincinnati Law Review* 635 (1973); Charles Lamb, "Warren Burger and the Insanity Defense: Judicial Philosophy and Voting Behavior on a U.S. Court of Appeals," 24 *American University Law Review* 91 (1974); Daryl Fair, "An Experimental Application of Scalogram Analysis to State Supreme Court Decisions,"

1967 *Wisconsin Law Review* 449 (1967); Robert Bradley and S. Sidney Ulmer, "An Examination of Voting Behavior in the Supreme Court of Illinois, 1971–1975," *Southern Illinois University Law Journal* 245 (1980); G. Alan Tarr and Mary Cornelia Porter, *State Supreme Courts in State and Nation* (New Haven: Yale University Press, 1988). However, see Melinda Hall, "An Examination of Voting Behavior in the Louisiana Supreme Court," 71 *Judicature* 40 (1987). For several excellent review articles on decision-making at all levels of the judiciary, federal and state, see John B. Gates and Charles A. Johnson, *The American Courts* (Washington, D.C.: Congressional Quarterly Press, 1991).

178. Gibson, "From Simplicity to Complexity," 10.

179. For example, in Pritchett's study of the Roosevelt Court, only 30 percent of the Court's decisions were nonunanimous. *The Roosevelt Court.*

180. Segal and Spaeth, "Decisional Trends," 105–6; Donald Songer, "Consensual and Nonconsensual Decisions in Unanimous Opinions of the United States Courts of Appeals," 26 *American Journal of Political Science* 225 (1982); Harold J. Spaeth, "Consensus in the Unanimous Decisions of the U.S. Supreme Court," 72 *Judicature* 274 (1989); Epstein et al., *The Supreme Court Compendium*, 427–29.

181. Segal and Spaeth, "Decisional Trends," 105.

182. David J. Danelski, "Values as Variables in Judicial Decision-Making: Notes toward a Theory," 19 *Vanderbilt Law Review* 721 (1966).

183. Jeffrey A. Segal and Albert D. Cover, "Ideological Values and the Votes of U.S. Supreme Court Justices," 83 *American Political Science Review* 557 (1989).

184. The four newspapers were the *New York Times, Washington Post, Chicago Tribune,* and *Los Angeles Times.*

185. Segal and Cover, "Ideological Values," 561.

186. Segal and Spaeth, *The Supreme Court and the Attitudinal Model*, 226–29.

187. Mishler and Sheehan, "The Supreme Court as a Countermajoritarian Institution?" 90–91.

188. Jeffrey A. Segal, Lee Epstein, Charles M. Cameron, and Harold J. Spaeth, "Ideological Values and the Votes of U.S. Supreme

Court Justices Revisited," 57 *Journal of Politics* 812 (1995).

189. See also Spaeth, *Supreme Court Policy Making.*

190. Segal and Spaeth, *The Supreme Court and the Attitudinal Model,* 222–24.

191. See Segal's earlier analysis of the role of facts in justices' decisions regarding search and seizure: Jeffrey A. Segal, "Predicting Supreme Court Cases Probabilistically: The Search and Seizure Cases, 1962–1981," 78 *American Political Science Review* 891 (1984); and Jeffrey A. Segal, "Supreme Court Justices as Human Decision Makers: An Individual-Level Analysis of the Search and Seizure Cases," 48 *Journal of Politics* 938 (1986). See also Fred Kort, "Content Analysis of Judicial Opinions and Rules of Law," in Glendon Schubert, ed., *Judicial Decision-Making* 133–97 (New York: Free Press, 1963); Fred Kort, "Quantitative Analysis of Fact-Patterns in Cases and Their Impact on Judicial Decisions," 79 *Harvard Law Review* 1595 (1966); Jilda Aliotta, "Combining Judges' Attributes and Case Characteristics: An Alternative Approach to Explaining Supreme Court Decisionmaking," 71 *Judicature* 277 (1988).

192. Segal and Spaeth, *The Supreme Court and the Attitudinal Model,* 229–31. See also Saul Brenner and Theodore S. Arrington, "Unanimous Decision Making on the U.S. Supreme Court: Case Stimuli and Judicial Attitudes," 9 *Political Behavior* 75 (1987); Tracey E. George and Lee Epstein, "On the Nature of Supreme Court Decision Making," 86 *American Political Science Review* 323 (1992), arguing that the addition of legally relevant facts to the "extralegal" (primarily attitudinal) decisionmaking model significantly improves prediction of outcomes in death penalty cases from 1971 to 1988. The "judicial ideology of the appointing president" variable used by Segal and Spaeth was developed by C. Neal Tate and Roger Handberg, "Time Binding and Theory Building in Personal Attribute Models of Supreme Court Voting Behavior, 1916–1988," 35 *American Journal of Political Science* 460, 465–67 (1991). This will be discussed shortly in the section covering social background studies.

193. Segal and Spaeth, *The Supreme Court and the Attitudinal Model,* 229.

194. John R. Schmidhauser, "Judicial Behavior and the Sectional Crisis of 1837–1860," 23 *Journal of Politics* 615 (1961).

195. Due to methodological obstacles, most studies have focused on state and lower federal courts. Stuart S. Nagel, "Political Party Affiliation and Judges' Decisions," 55 *American Political Science Review* 92 (1961); Stuart S. Nagel, "Ethnic Affiliations and Judicial Propensities," 24 *Journal of Politics* 92 (1962); Stuart S. Nagel, "Multiple Correlation of Judicial Backgrounds and Decisions," 2 *Florida State University Law Review* 258 (1974); Kenneth N. Vines, "Federal District Judges and Race Relations Cases in the South," 26 *Journal of Politics* 338 (1964); Sheldon Goldman, "Voting Behavior in the United States Courts of Appeals, 1961–1964," 60 *American Political Science Review* 374 (1966); Sheldon Goldman, "Voting Behavior on the U.S. Courts of Appeals Revisited," 69 *American Political Science Review* 491 (1975); Donald Songer and Sue Davis, "The Impact of Party and Region on Voting Decisions in the United States Courts of Appeals, 1955–1986," 43 *Western Political Quarterly* 317 (1990); David W. Adamany, "The Party Variable in Judges' Voting: Conceptual Notes and a Case Study," 63 *American Political Science Review* 59 (1969); S. Sidney Ulmer, "The Political Party Variable in the Michigan Supreme Court," 11 *Journal of Public Law* 352 (1962); Malcolm Feeley, "Another Look at the 'Party Variable' in Judicial Decision-Making: An Analysis of the Michigan Supreme Court," 4 *Polity* 91 (1971); S. Sidney Ulmer, "Dissent Behavior and the Social Background of Supreme Court Justices, 32 *Journal of Politics* 580 (1970); S. Sidney Ulmer, "Social Background as an Indicator to the Votes of Supreme Court Justices in Criminal Cases," 17 *Midwest Journal of Political Science* 622 (1973); Richard E. Johnston, "Supreme Court Voting Behavior: A Comparison of the Warren and Burger Courts," in Robert L. Peabody, ed., *Cases in American Politics* 71 (New York: Praeger, 1976); Robert A. Carp and C. K. Rowland, *Policymaking and Politics in the Federal District Courts* chap. 2 (Knoxville: University of Tennessee Press, 1983); C. K. Rowland and Robert A. Carp, *Politics and Judgment in Federal District Courts* chap. 2 (Lawrence: University of Kansas Press, 1996); Gerard Gryski and Eleanor Main, "Social Backgrounds as Predictors of Votes on State Courts of Last Resort: The Case of Sex Discrimination," 39 *Western*

Political Quarterly 528 (1986); Robert A. Carp and Ronald Stidham, *Judicial Process in America* 264–70 (Washington, D.C.: Congressional Quarterly Press, 1990); Philip Dubois, "The Illusion of Judicial Consensus Revisited: Partisan Conflict on an Intermediate State Court of Appeals," 32 *American Journal of Political Science* 946 (1988). Regarding the possible influence of race and gender in judicial decisionmaking, see Jennifer A. Segal, "The Decision Making of Clinton's Nontraditional Judicial Appointees," 80 *Judicature* 279 (1997).

196. C. Neal Tate, "Personal Attribute Models of the Voting Behavior of U.S. Supreme Court Justices' Liberalism in Civil Liberties and Economics Decisions, 1946–1978," 75 *American Political Science Review* 355 (1981); Tate and Handberg, "Time Binding and Theory Building."

197. Segal and Spaeth dispute the significance of Tate's study due to the large number of variables employed. *The Supreme Court and the Attitudinal Model*, 232.

198. Tate and Handberg categorized presidents according to how ideologically conscious their appointments were and the ideological direction of those intentions. Seven presidents were classified as ideologically conscious, with Taft, Harding, Nixon, and Reagan possessing conservative intentions, and Wilson, Franklin Roosevelt, and Johnson possessing liberal intentions. "Time Binding and Theory Building," 465–67.

199. Segal and Spaeth, *The Supreme Court and the Attitudinal Model*, 232.

200. Additional studies that demonstrate the explanatory power of the appointing president variable will be discussed in the next section, entitled "Presidential Expectations and Judicial Performance."

201. The role of interest groups and the solicitor general in Supreme Court decisionmaking, particularly at the agenda-setting stage, is discussed in the next chapter.

202. Joseph Tanenhaus, Marvin Schick, Matthew Muraskin, and Daniel Rosen, "The Supreme Court's Certiorari Jurisdiction: Cue Theory," in Glendon Schubert, ed., *Judicial Decision Making* (New York: Free Press, 1963); Virginia Armstrong and Charles A. Johnson, "Certiorari Decisionmaking by the Warren and Burger Courts: Is Cue Theory Time Bound?" 15 *Polity* 141 (1982); Baum, *The Su-*

preme Court, 3d ed., 101–2; Gregory A. Caldeira and John R. Wright, "Organized Interests and Agenda Setting in the U.S. Supreme Court," 82 *American Political Science Review* 1109 (1988); H. W. Perry, Jr., "Agenda Setting and Case Selection," in John B. Gates and Charles A. Johnson, eds., *The American Courts: A Critical Assessment* 238 (Washington, D.C.: Congressional Quarterly Press, 1991); Doris Marie Provine, *Case Selection in the United States Supreme Court* 87 (Chicago: University of Chicago Press, 1980); Stuart H. Teger and Douglas Kosinski, "The Cue Theory of Supreme Court Certiorari Jurisdiction: A Reconsideration," 42 *Journal of Politics* 834 (1980); S. Sidney Ulmer, "The Decision to Grant Certiorari as an Indicator to Decision 'On the Merits,' " 4 *Polity* 429 (1972); S. Sidney Ulmer, William Hintze, and Louise Kirklosky, "The Decision to Grant or Deny Certiorari: Further Consideration of Cue Theory," 6 *Law and Society Review* 637 (1972).

203. Tanenhaus et al., "The Supreme Court's Certiorari Jurisdiction"; Armstrong and Johnson, "Certiorari Decisionmaking"; Caldeira and Wright, "Organized Interests and Agenda Setting"; H. W. Perry, Jr., *Deciding to Decide: Agenda Setting in the United States Supreme Court* (Cambridge: Harvard University Press, 1991); S. Sidney Ulmer, "Conflict with Supreme Court Precedent and the Granting of Plenary Review," 45 *Journal of Politics* 474 (1983); S. Sidney Ulmer, "The Supreme Court's Certiorari Decisions: Conflict as a Predictive Variable," 78 *American Political Science Review* 901 (1984).

204. Caldeira and Wright, "Organized Interests and Agenda Setting in the U.S. Supreme Court."

205. Provine and Perry have each studied the case selection process exhaustively and are more equivocal than other scholars regarding the role of ideology in case selection and the validity of the decisionmaking models and theoretical assumptions underlying much of the literature. Clearly, both political and legal considerations influence the Court's decision to accept cases for review. However, Perry is more likely to emphasize legal over political factors. See Perry, "Agenda Setting and Case Selection"; Perry, *Deciding to Decide*; Lawrence Baum, "Case Selection and Decisionmaking in the U.S. Supreme Court," 27 *Law and Society Review* 443 (1993); Doris Marie Provine, "De-

ciding What to Decide: How the Supreme Court Sets Its Agenda," 64 *Judicature* 320 (1981); Provine, *Case Selection in the United States Supreme Court.* See Segal and Spaeth's response to Provine in *The Supreme Court and the Attitudinal Model,* 191–92.

206. Lawrence Baum, "Policy Goals in Judicial Gatekeeping: A Proximity Model of Discretionary Jurisdiction," 21 *American Journal of Political Science* 13 (1977); Lawrence Baum, "Judicial Demand—Screening and Decisions on the Merits: A Second Look," 7 *American Politics Quarterly* 109 (1979); Glendon Schubert, "The Certiorari Game," in Glendon Schubert, ed., *Judicial Behavior: A Reader in Theory and Research* (Chicago: Rand McNally, 1964); Jan Palmer, "An Econometric Analysis of the U.S. Supreme Court's Certiorari Decisions," 39 *Public Choice* 387 (1982); Perry, *Deciding to Decide*; Ulmer, "The Decision to Grant Certiorari."

207. Saul Brenner and John F. Krol, "Strategies in Certiorari Voting on the United States Supreme Court," 51 *Journal of Politics* 828 (1989); John F. Krol and Saul Brenner, "Strategies in Certiorari Voting on the United States Supreme Court: A Reevaluation," 43 *Western Political Quarterly* 335 (1990); Provine, *Case Selection*; Ulmer, "The Decision to Grant Certiorari."

208. "The Supreme Court, 1986 Term," 101 *Harvard Law Review* 366 (1987), cited in Baum, *The Supreme Court*, 3d ed., 99.

209. Neubauer, *Judicial Process*, 385. Additionally, Segal and Spaeth find that the Rehnquist Court has been even more likely than previous Courts to affirm lower court decisions. Segal and Spaeth, *The Supreme Court and the Attitudinal Model,* 194–95, 199–202.

210. "The Supreme Court, 1994 Term," 109 *Harvard Law Review* 340 (1995).

211. Armstrong and Johnson, "Certiorari Decision Making by the Warren and Burger Courts"; Baum, "Policy Goals in Judicial Gatekeeping"; Baum, "Judicial Demand"; Caldeira and Wright, "Organized Interests and Agenda Setting"; Palmer, "An Econometric Analysis"; Perry, *Deciding to Decide*; Provine, *Case Selection*; Donald R. Songer, "Concern for Policy Outputs as a Cue for Supreme Court Decisions of Certiorari," 41 *Journal of Politics* 1185 (1979); S. Sidney Ulmer, "Supreme Court Justices as Strict and Not-So-Strict Constructionists: Some Implications," 8 *Law and Society Review*

13 (1973); S. Sidney Ulmer, "Selecting Cases for Supreme Court Review: An Underdog Model," 72 *American Political Science Review* 902 (1978); Ulmer, "The Supreme Court's Certiorari Decisions."

212. Baum, *The Supreme Court*, 3d ed., 100.

213. Virginia C. Armstrong and Charles A. Johnson, "Certiorari Decisions by the Warren and Burger Courts: Is Cue Theory Time Bound?" in Sheldon Goldman and Austin Sarat, eds., *American Court Systems*, 2d ed., 166, 168–69 (New York: Longman, 1989). First published in 15 *Polity* 141 (1982).

214. Caldeira and Wright, "Organized Interests and Agenda Setting."

215. Baum, *The Supreme Court*, 3d ed., 100–101.

216. Richard L. Pacelle, Jr., *The Transformation of the Supreme Court's Agenda: From the New Deal to the Reagan Administration* (Boulder, Colo.: Westview Press, 1991).

217. Saul Brenner, "The New Certiorari Game," 41 *Journal of Politics* 649 (1979); Brenner and Krol, "Strategies in Certiorari Voting"; Krol and Brenner, "Strategies in Certiorari Voting: A Reevaluation"; Robert Boucher and Jeffrey Segal, "Supreme Court Justices as Strategic Decision Makers: Aggressive Grants and Defensive Denials on the Vinson Court," 57 *Journal of Politics* 824 (1995); Palmer, "An Econometric Analysis"; Perry, *Deciding to Decide*; Schubert, "The Certiorari Game"; Glendon Schubert, "Policy without Law: An Extension of the Certiorari Game," 14 *Stanford Law Review* 224 (1962); Nina Totenberg, "Behind the Marble, Beneath the Robes," 60 *New York Times Magazine* (March 16, 1975); Ulmer, "Selecting Cases for Supreme Court Review."

218. Gregory J. Rathjen and Harold J. Spaeth, "Access to the Federal Courts: An Analysis of Burger Court Policy Making," 23 *American Journal of Political Science* 360 (1979); Gregory J. Rathjen and Harold J. Spaeth, "Denial of Access and Ideological Preferences: An Analysis of the Voting Behavior of the Burger Court Justices, 1969–1976," 36 *Western Political Quarterly* 71 (1983).

219. Segal and Spaeth, *The Supreme Court and the Attitudinal Model,* 165.

220. If the Chief Justice does not vote with the majority, the power to assign the opinion falls to the senior justice voting with the majority.

221. Segal and Spaeth, *The Attitudinal Model*, 263.

222. Ibid. at 265–68. See also Elliot Slotnick, "Who Speaks for the Court? Majority Opinion Assignment from Taft to Burger," 23 *American Journal of Political Science* 60 (1979); Harold J. Spaeth, "Distributive Justice: Majority Opinion Assignments in the Burger Court," 67 *Judicature* 299 (1984); David M. O'Brien, *Storm Center: The Supreme Court in American Politics*, 4th ed., 298–99 (New York: W. W. Norton, 1996); Sue Davis, "Power on the Court: Chief Justice Rehnquist's Opinion Assignments" 74 *Judicature* 66 (1990).

223. Segal and Spaeth, *The Supreme Court and the Attitudinal Model*, 271–72; Elliot E. Slotnick, "The Chief Justice and Self-Assignment of Majority Opinions," 31 *Western Political Quarterly* 219 (1978); Slotnick, "Who Speaks for the Court?"; Spaeth, "Distributive Justice"; Saul Brenner, "The Chief Justice's Self-Assignment of Majority Opinions in Salient Cases," 30 *Social Science Journal* 143 (1993); O'Brien, *Storm Center*, 297; Davis, "Power on the Court."

224. Segal and Spaeth, *The Supreme Court and the Attitudinal Model*, 268–71, 273. See also David W. Rohde, "Policy Goals, Strategic Choice, and Majority Opinion Assignments in the U.S. Supreme Court," 16 *American Journal of Political Science* 652 (1972); Slotnick, "Who Speaks for the Court?"; Spaeth, "Distributive Justice"; Rohde and Spaeth, *Supreme Court Decision Making*; S. Sidney Ulmer, "The Use of Power on the Supreme Court: The Opinion Assignments of Earl Warren, 1953–1960," 30 *Journal of Public Law* 49 (1970); Davis, "Power on the Court." However, for the view that Rehnquist emphasizes organizational needs rather than ideological preferences in opinion assignments, see Forrest Maltzman and Paul J. Wahlbeck, "May It Please the Chief? Opinion Assignments in the Rehnquist Court," 40 *American Journal of Political Science* 421 (1996).

225. Saul Brenner and Harold J. Spaeth, "Issue Specialization in Majority Opinion Assignment on the Burger Court," 39 *Western Political Quarterly* 520 (1986).

226. Segal and Spaeth, *The Supreme Court and the Attitudinal Model*, 272–73. See also Saul Brenner, "Issue Specialization as a Variable in Opinion Assignment on the U.S. Supreme Court," 46 *Journal of Politics* 1217 (1984).

227. David J. Danelski, "The Influence of the Chief Justice in the Decisional Process of the Supreme Court," in Sheldon Goldman and Austin Sarat, eds., *American Court Systems: Readings in Judicial Process and Behavior* 486 (San Francisco: W. H. Freeman and Co., 1978); Rohde and Spaeth, *Supreme Court Decision Making*, chap. 8; Rohde, "Policy Goals, Strategic Choice, and Majority Opinion Assignments." However, evidence shows that assigning opinions to the marginal justice does not increase the probability that the majority coalition will hold together, nor does it increase the size of the majority. Saul Brenner and Harold J. Spaeth, "Majority Opinion Assignments and the Maintenance of the Original Coalition on the Warren Court," 32 *American Journal of Political Science* 72 (1988); Saul Brenner, Timothy M. Hagle, and Harold J. Spaeth, "Increasing the Size of the Minimum Winning Coalitions on the Warren Court," 23 *Polity* 309 (1990); Segal and Spaeth, *The Supreme Court and the Attitudinal Model*, 274–75.

228. J. Woodford Howard, "On the Fluidity of Judicial Choice," 52 *American Political Science Review* 43 (1968). Voting fluidity is distinct from "issue fluidity," in which the issues presented by the parties are different from the issues ultimately resolved by the Court in its decision. Unlike voting fluidity, issue fluidity does not challenge the validity of the attitudinal model and is likely to be compatible with it. See Kevin McGuire and Barbara Palmer, "Issue Fluidity on the U.S. Supreme Court" 89 *American Political Science Review* 691 (1995).

229. Saul Brenner, "Fluidity on the United States Supreme Court: A Re-examination," 24 *American Journal of Political Science* 526 (1980). Similar results were found for the 1956 to 1967 period of the Warren Court, in Saul Brenner, "Fluidity on the Supreme Court, 1956–1967," 26 *American Journal of Political Science* 388 (1982). See also O'Brien, *Storm Center*, 301.

230. Saul Brenner, "Ideological Voting on the Vinson Court: A Comparison of the Original Vote on the Merits with the Final Vote," 21 *Polity* 102 (1989); Brenner and Spaeth, "Majority Opinion Assignments and the Maintenance of the Original Coalition on the Warren Court"; Saul Brenner, Timothy M. Hagle, and Harold J. Spaeth, "The Defection of the Marginal Justice on the Warren Court," 42 *Western Political Quarterly* 409 (1989); Timothy M. Hagle and Harold J. Spaeth, "Voting Fluidity

and the Attitudinal Model of Supreme Court Decision Making," 44 *Western Political Quarterly* 119 (1991); Forrest Maltzman and Paul J. Wahlbeck, "Strategic Policy Considerations and Voting Fluidity on the Burger Court," 90 *American Political Science Review* 581 (1996); Segal and Spaeth, *The Supreme Court and the Attitudinal Model*, 213–14.

231. Baum, *The Supreme Court*, 3d ed., 150.

232. Segal and Spaeth, *The Supreme Court and the Attitudinal Model*, 211–12, citing William H. Rehnquist, *The Supreme Court: How It Was, How It Is* 290–91 (New York: Morrow, 1987), and William H. Rehnquist, "Ruing Fixed Opinions," *New York Times* (February 22, 1988), 20, reprinted in Harold J. Spaeth and Saul Brenner, eds., *Studies in U.S. Supreme Court Behavior* 256–57 (New York: Garland, 1990).

233. Segal and Spaeth, *The Supreme Court and the Attitudinal Model*, 235–37; Baum, *The Supreme Court*, 3d ed., 147–49. Methodological difficulties in testing this question do remain, however, and the issue is not yet closed. There is *some* evidence that role orientations may matter for judges other than Supreme Court justices, although the impact on voting behavior is indirect. James Gibson, "Judges' Role Orientations, Attitudes, and Decisions: An Interactive Model," 72 *American Political Science Review* 911 (1978); J. Woodford Howard, "Role Perceptions and Behavior on Three U.S. Courts of Appeals," 39 *Journal of Politics* 916 (1977); J. Woodford Howard, *Courts of Appeals in the Federal Judicial System: A Study of the Second, Fifth, and District of Columbia Circuits* (Princeton: Princeton University Press, 1981); John Wold, "Political Orientations, Social Backgrounds, and Role Perceptions of State Supreme Court Judges," 27 *Western Political Quarterly* 239 (1974); John M. Scheb II and Thomas D. Ungs, "Competing Orientations to the Judicial Role: The Case of Tennessee Judges," 54 *Tennessee Law Review* 391 (1987); John M. Scheb II, Terry Bowen, and Gary Anderson, "Ideology, Role Orientations, and Behavior in the State Courts of Last Resort," 19 *American Politics Quarterly* 324 (1991). However, see Melinda Hall, "An Examination of Voting Behavior in the Louisiana Supreme Court," 71 *Judicature* 40 (1987).

234. Segal and Spaeth, *The Supreme Court and the Attitudinal Model*, chap. 8; regarding Frankfurter, see 316–18. See also Harold J.

Spaeth, "The Judicial Restraint of Mr. Justice Frankfurter—Myth or Reality?" 8 *American Journal of Political Science* 22 (1964); Epstein et al., *The Supreme Court Compendium*, 425, 509–13.

235. Segal and Spaeth, *The Supreme Court and the Attitudinal Model*, 326; see also Epstein et al., *The Supreme Court Compendium*, 425, 509–13. The tests used by Segal and Spaeth are superior to the one used by Gibson, in which he found considerable variation in "restraint-tism" among the justices (1953–88), based on the degree to which their values as reported by Segal and Cover ("Ideological Values") corresponded to their decisions. James L. Gibson, "Decision Making in Appellate Courts," in Gates and Johnson, *American Courts*, 255, 264. Anecdotal evidence that "judicial restraint" is used selectively and politically includes Justice Blackmun's insistence in his dissent in *Furman* v. *Georgia* that his personal opposition to the death penalty should be set aside out of respect for and deference to the democratic process, yet his willingness in *Roe* v. *Wade* to overturn existing abortion policy in most states and rewrite it in a thoroughly detailed manner, with little in the way of textual and doctrinal justification. Segal and Spaeth, *The Supreme Court and the Attitudinal Model*, 235. Similarly, Justice Marshall, late in his career, criticized the Court for giving insufficient respect to precedent; this was of course a politically transparent strategy to protect the liberal Warren Court precedents which he helped to create. Walker and Epstein, *The Supreme Court of the United States*, 129–30. See also Baum, *The Supreme Court*, 3d ed., 147–49; Harold J. Spaeth and Stuart H. Teger, "Activism and Restraint: A Cloak for the Justices' Policy Preferences," in Stephen C. Halpern and Charles M. Lamb, eds., *Supreme Court Activism and Restraint* (Lexington, Mass.: D. C. Heath, 1982); Walker and Epstein, *The Supreme Court of the United States*, 156–58.

236. Saul Brenner and Harold J. Spaeth, *Stare Indecisis: The Alteration of Precedent on the Supreme Court, 1946–1992* (Cambridge: Cambridge University Press, 1995).

237. Jeffrey A. Segal and Harold J. Spaeth, "The Influence of *Stare Decisis* on the Votes of United States Supreme Court Justices," 40 *American Journal of Political Science* 971 (1996).

238. Saul Brenner and Marc Stier, "Retesting Segal and Spaeth's *Stare Decisis* Model," 40 *American Journal of Political Science* 1036 (1996); Jack Knight and Lee Epstein, "The Norm of *Stare Decisis*," 40 *American Journal of Political Science* 1018 (1996); Donald R. Songer and Stefanie A. Lindquist, "Not the Whole Story: The Impact of Justices' Values on Supreme Court Decision Making," 40 *American Journal of Political Science* 1049 (1996); Richard A. Brisbin, Jr., "Slaying the Dragon: Segal, Spaeth and the Function of Law in Supreme Court Decision Making," 40 *American Journal of Political Science* 1004 (1996). For a response to the critics, see Jeffrey A. Segal and Harold J. Spaeth, "Norms, Dragons, and *Stare Decisis*: A Response," 40 *American Journal of Political Science* 1064 (1996).

239. Lee Epstein and Joseph Kobylka, *The Supreme Court and Legal Change* (Chapel Hill: University of North Carolina Press, 1993); John Brigham, *Constitutional Language: An Interpretation of Judicial Decision* (Westport, Conn.: Greenwood Press, 1978); Wahlbeck, "The Life of the Law."

240. Lawrence Baum, "What Judges Want: Judges' Goals and Judicial Behavior," 47 *Political Research Quarterly* 749 (1994); Lawrence Baum, *The Puzzle of Judicial Behavior* (Ann Arbor: University of Michigan Press, 1997).

241. Songer and Lindquist, "Not the Whole Story," 1049.

242. Tribe, *God Save This Honorable Court*, chap. 4.

243. Charles Warren, *The Supreme Court in United States History* 2:22 (Boston: Little, Brown, 1937). Quoted in Abraham, *Justices and Presidents*, 2d ed., 69.

244. *Time* (May 23, 1969), 24. Quoted in Abraham, *Justices and Presidents*, 2d ed., 70.

245. John Hart Ely, *Democracy and Distrust: A Theory of Judicial Review* 47 (Cambridge: Harvard University Press, 1980). See also Philip B. Kurland, "The Appointment and Disappointment of Supreme Court Justices," 1972 *Law and Social Order* 183 (1972); Ronald Kahn, *The Supreme Court and Constitutional Theory, 1953–1993* 57 (Lawrence: University Press of Kansas, 1994) ("presidents cannot reliably predict the juicial policy directions of their appointees"); Christopher E. Smith and Kimberly A. Beuger, "Clouds in the Crystal Ball: Presidential Expectations and the Unpredictable Behavior of Supreme Court Appointees," 27 *Akron Law Review* 115, 116 (1993) ("many presidents are ultimately disappointed by the decisions which their nominees produce").

Ely has since suggested that several factors have enhanced the predictability of a justice's future decisions—more intensive ideological screening of nominees, recruitment nearly exclusively from the U.S. Courts of Appeals, and the declining importance of legal process decisionmaking norms. Ely, "Another Such Victory," 869–70.

246. Lecture at Columbia University, April 28, 1959. Quoted in Abraham, *Justices and Presidents*, 2d ed., 70.

247. Quoted in Spaeth, *Supreme Court Policy Making*, 103.

248. Quoted in Tribe, *God Save This Honorable Court*, 51.

249. Quoted in Abraham, *Justices and Presidents*, 2d ed., 70.

250. Comment to Anthony Lewis, "A Talk with Warren on Crime, the Court, the Country," *New York Times Magazine* (October 19, 1969), 128–29. Quoted in Abraham, *Justices and Presidents*, 2d ed., 70.

251. Lecture at University of Minnesota, October 19, 1984. William H. Rehnquist, "Presidential Appointments to the Supreme Court," 2 *Constitutional Commentary* 319 (1985).

252. Watson and Stookey, *Shaping America*, 67–68. See also Smith and Beuger "Clouds in the Crystal Ball."

253. Baum, "Membership Change and Collective Voting Change"; Hensley and Smith, "Membership Change and Voting Change." For Hensley and Smith, voting change by continuing members and issue change were found to be more significant in causing decisionmaking change on the Rehnquist Court from 1986 to 1992. For Baum, membership change was the primary cause of decisionmaking change for the Vinson, Warren, and Burger Courts.

254. Sources include Abraham, *Justices and Presidents*, 3d ed.; Leon Friedman and Fred L. Israel, eds., *The Justices of the United States Supreme Court, 1789–1969: Their Lives and Major Opinions*, 4 vols. (New York: Chelsea House, 1969); R. Friedman, "Tribal Myths"; Scigliano, *The Supreme Court and the Presidency*; Tribe, *God Save This Honorable Court*. To sum-

marize their conclusions requires in some cases (e.g., Friedman and Israel, Abraham) inferring the numbers of presidential successes and failures; in others (Scligliano, Tribe, Friedman), such a conclusion is supplied directly. Providing a summary rather than another exhaustive historical review here is justified in light of the substantial agreement among these scholars (with the exception of Richard Friedman) in support of the proposition in question.

255. Scigliano, *The Supreme Court and the Presidency*, 148.

256. Ibid. at 146.

257. Tribe, *God Save This Honorable Court*, 50.

258. Ibid. at 76. This conclusion is echoed by Lawrence Baum in *American Courts*, 4th ed., 292–294 (Boston: Houghton Mifflin Company, 1998).

259. Friedman, "Tribal Myths," 1292.

260. Friedman's list of presidential surprises includes Justices Story (appointed by Madison), McLean, Baldwin, and Taney (all appointed by Jackson), Swayne, Miller, Davis, Field, and Chase (all appointed by Lincoln), Holmes and Day (T. Roosevelt), McReynolds (Wilson), Stone (Coolidge), Hughes (Hoover), Reed and Frankfurter (FDR), Burton, Vinson, and Clark (Truman), Warren (Eisenhower), White (Kennedy), and Blackmun (Nixon). Ibid. at 1291–1302. It is not clear, however, that this is Friedman's complete list. He may have felt that these instances were sufficient to refute Tribe's analysis.

261. The list of presidents who clearly succeeded in their appointments, in that their ideological and policy expectations were fulfilled by their Supreme Court appointees, includes: Presidents Washington, Adams, Jackson (for Taney, Barbour, and Catron), Van Buren, Lincoln (excepting Chase), Grant, Cleveland, Harrison, McKinley, Theodore Roosevelt (for Justice Moody only), Taft, Wilson (excepting McReynolds), Harding, Franklin Roosevelt, Truman (excepting Clark), Lyndon Johnson, Nixon (excepting Blackmun), Reagan, Bush (for Thomas only), and Clinton (with the long-term verdict still out). The twenty justices who clearly failed to live up to presidential expectations or desires include the appointees of Presidents Jefferson, Madison, Monroe, John Quincy Adams, Jack-

son (with Justice McLean and, to a lesser degree, Baldwin and Wayne), Theodore Roosevelt (Day), Wilson (McReynolds), Coolidge (Stone), Hoover (Cardozo, Hughes, and Roberts), Eisenhower (Warren and Brennan), Nixon (Blackmun), and Ford (Stevens). The decisionmaking performance of the remaining justices provides either unclear or mixed results regarding their fulfillment of presidential expectations.

262. The most glaring differences are the inclusion, in my list of presidential failures, of the seven appointees from Justice Johnson (the first of three appointments by Jefferson) to Trimble (the only appointment of John Quincy Adams), and my exclusion from that list of four of Lincoln's five appointees, two of FDR's (Frankfurter and Reed), and all four of Truman's appointees.

263. Rohde and Spaeth, *Supreme Court Decisionmaking*, 107–10, 114–15.

264. Edward V. Heck and Steven A. Shull, "Policy Preferences of Justices and Presidents: The Case of Civil Rights," 4 *Law and Policy Quarterly* 327 (1982).

265. Ibid. at 333.

266. Ibid. at 330–31. Another problem with the Heck and Shull study is their classification scheme. Justices are categorized as liberal or conservative not by their individual civil rights support score, but in relation to the score of the Court on which they served. Thus, Stewart is categorized as a conservative who failed to fulfill Eisenhower's liberal civil rights intentions because his 64.2 percent support score is lower than the liberal Warren Court support score of 74.8 percent. In contrast, they regard Ford's conservative civil rights views as inconsistent with the performance of Stevens, who is considered a liberal with a support score of 65.1 percent, which is very close to Stewart's but higher than the increasingly conservative Burger Court. Meanwhile, Blackmun, who supported civil rights claims 63.1 percent of the time, is labeled a conservative who accurately reflected Nixon's conservative civil rights views. (Of course, Blackmun is widely regarded as a presidential failure.)

267. Ibid. at 335. This is quite similar to Tribe's conclusion that "for the most part, and especially in areas of particular and known concern to a President, Justices have been loyal to the ideals and perspectives of the men

who have nominated them." Tribe, *God Save This Honorable Court*, 50.

268. John B. Gates and Jeffrey E. Cohen, "Presidents, Justices, and Racial Equality Cases: 1954–1984," 10 *Political Behavior* 22 (1988).

269. Ibid. at 33, 31.

270. Jeffrey A. Segal, "Judicial-Executive Interactions: The Effect of Presidential Ideology" (manuscript, State University of New York at Stony Brook, 1989).

271. Sue Davis, "The Supreme Court: Rehnquist's or Reagan's?" 44 *Western Political Quarterly* 87 (1991). See also David W. Rohde and Harold J. Spaeth, "Ideology, Strategy and Supreme Court Decisions: William Rehnquist as Chief Justice," 72 *Judicature* 247 (1989). For a bit of the conventional wisdom regarding the Court's conservative shift, see David G. Savage, *Turning Right: The Making of the Rehnquist Supreme Court* (New York: John Wiley and Sons, 1992); Christopher Smith, "The Supreme Court's Emerging Majority: Restraining the High Court or Transforming Its Role?" 24 *Akron Law Review* 393 (1990); Murphy, "Reagan's Judicial Strategy." For the contrary view that the Rehnquist Court is not as conservative as either its reputation or, in some years, the Burger Court, see Christopher E. Smith and Thomas R. Hensley, "Assessing the Conservatism of the Rehnquist Court," 76 *Judicature* 83 (1993); Hensley and Smith, "Membership Change and Voting Change."

272. Tate, "Personal Attribute Models."

273. Tate and Handberg, "Time Binding and Theory Building."

274. Thomas R. Marshall and Joseph Ignagni, "Supreme Court and Public Support for Rights Claims," 78 *Judicature* 146 (1994). The study examined cases involving civil rights, civil liberties, and equality claims from the 1953 to 1991 terms.

275. C. K. Rowland, Robert A. Carp, and Donald Songer, "Presidential Effects on Criminal Justice Policy in the Lower Federal Courts: The Reagan Judges," 22 *Law and Society Review* 191 (1988).

276. Ronald Stidham and Robert A. Carp, "Support for Labor and Economic Regulation among Reagan and Carter Appointees to the Federal Courts," 26 *Social Science Journal* 433 (1989).

277. Steve Alumbaugh and C. K. Rowland,

"The Links between Platform-Based Appointment Criteria and Trial Judges' Abortion Judgments," 74 *Judicature* 153 (1990).

278. Ronald Stidham and Robert A. Carp, "Judges, Presidents, and Policy Choices: Exploring the Linkages," 68 *Social Science Quarterly* 395 (1987).

279. C. K. Rowland and Bridget Jeffery Todd, "Where You Stand Depends on Who Sits: Platform Promises and Judicial Gatekeeping in the Federal District Courts," 53 *Journal of Politics* 175 (1991).

280. C. K. Rowland and Robert A. Carp, *Political Appointments and Political Jurisprudence in the Federal District Courts* (Lawrence: University Press of Kansas, 1992).

281. Stidham and Carp, "Support for Labor and Economic Regulation."

282. Carp and Rowland, *Policymaking and Politics in the Federal District Courts.*

283. Robert A. Carp and Ronald Stidham, *Judicial Process in America* 235–38 (Washington, D.C.: Congressional Quarterly Press, 1990); Robert A. Carp, Donald Songer, C. K. Rowland, Ronald Stidham, and Lisa Richey-Tracy, "The Voting Behavior of Judges Appointed by President Bush," 76 *Judicature* 298, 299 (1993).

284. Jon Gottschall, "Reagan's Appointments to the U.S. Courts of Appeals: The Continuation of a Judicial Revolution," 70 *Judicature* 48, 52 (1986). The differences persisted but decreased when unanimous decisions were included.

285. Smaller differences were found in the area of personal injury, with Kennedy/Johnson and Carter appointees voting the liberal position 53 and 65 percent of the time respectively, and Nixon/Ford and Reagan appointees voting the liberal outcome 31 and 55 percent of the time respectively. Ibid. at 52.

286. In addition, see Craig R. Ducat and Robert L. Dudley, "Federal District Judges and Presidential Power during the Postwar Era," 51 *Journal of Politics* 98 (1989); C. K. Rowland and Robert A. Carp, "The Relative Effects of Maturation, Time Period, and Appointing President on District Judges' Policy Choices: A Cohort Analysis," 5 *Political Behavior* 109 (1983); C. K. Rowland, Robert A. Carp, and Ronald Stidham, "Judges' Policy Choices and the Value Basis of Judicial Appointments: A Comparison of Support for Criminal Defendants among Nixon, Johnson and Kennedy Appoin-

tees to the Federal District Courts," 46 *Journal of Politics* 886 (1984); Ronald Stidham, Robert A. Carp, and C. K. Rowland, "Patterns of Presidential Influence on the Federal District Courts: An Analysis of the Appointment Process," 14 *Presidential Studies Quarterly* 548 (1984); Sue Davis, "President Carter's Selection Reforms and Judicial Policymaking," 14 *American Politics Quarterly* 328 (1986); Gottschall, "Carter's Judicial Appointments"; Donald R. Songer, "The Policy Consequences of Senate Involvement in the Selection of Judges in the United States Courts of Appeal," 35 *Western Political Quarterly* 107 (1982); Timothy B. Tomasi and Jess A. Velona, "All the President's Men? A Study of Ronald Reagan's Appointments to the U.S. Courts of Appeals," 87 *Columbia Law Review* 766 (1987); Rowland and Carp, *Politics and Judgment in Federal District Courts*, chaps. 2 and 5; Carp et al. "The Voting Behavior of Judges Appointed by President Bush"; Ronald Stidham, Robert A. Carp, and Donald R. Songer, "The Voting Behavior of President Clinton's Judicial Appointees," 80 *Judicature* 16 (1996); Songer and Davis, "The Impact of Party and Region"; William E. Kovacic, "Reagan's Judicial Appointees and Antitrust in the 1990s," 60 *Fordham Law Review* 49 (1991); William E. Kovacic, "The Reagan Judiciary and Environmental Policy: The Impact of Appointments to the Federal Courts of Appeals," 18 *Boston College Environmental Affairs Law Review* 669 (1991); Ronald Stidham, Robert Carp, Donald Songer, and Donean Surratt, "The Impact of Major Structural Reform on Judicial Decisionmaking: A Case Study of the U.S. Fifth Circuit," 45 *Western Political Quarterly* 143 (1992); Lettie Wenner and Cynthia Ostberg, "Restraint in Environmental Cases by Reagan-Bush Judicial Appointees," 77 *Judicature* 217 (1994).

287. Tribe, *God Save This Honorable Court*, 51.

288. Carp and Rowland, *Politics and Policymaking in the Federal District Courts*. See also Stidham, Carp, and Rowland, "Patterns of Presidential Influence on the Federal District Courts."

289. This echoes the findings previously discussed of Heck and Shull ("Policy Preferences of Justices and Presidents") and Gates and Cohen ("Presidents, Supreme Court Justices, and Racial Equality Cases").

290. Carp et al., "The Voting Behavior of Judges Appointed by President Bush"; Stidham, Carp, and Songer, "The Voting Behavior of President Clinton's Judicial Appointees."

291. Those factors which Carp and Rowland identify as contributing to increased presidential influence on the ideological propensities of judicial appointees are also echoed explicitly by Tribe and Scigliano and implicitly by Abraham.

292. The following discussion comes from a variety of sources, including Abraham, *Justices and Presidents*, 2d ed.; Sheldon Goldman, *Constitutional Law: Cases and Essays*, 2d ed., chaps. 2, 3, and 4 (New York: HarperCollins Publishers, 1991); Tribe, *God Save This Honorable Court*. Regarding the policy impact of recent appointees, see Baum, *The Supreme Court*, 3d ed., 145–47; Baum, "Membership Change and Collective Voting Change"; Johnson, "Personnel Change and Policy Change"; Segal and Spaeth, "Decisional Trends."

293. Two prominent exceptions were the Burger Court's sex discrimination and abortion decisions.

294. The phrase is from Nixon's speech, reported in *New York Times* (October 22, 1971), 24.

295. In Blackmun's early years on the Court, he agreed with Chief Justice Burger so frequently that he and Burger, his childhood friend from Minnesota, were labeled the "Minnesota Twins." He then moved to the Court's center and then farther to the liberal wing of the Court. During the 1973 term, Blackmun joined Burger's opinions 84 percent of the time, but Brennan's opinions only 49 percent of the time. However, by 1985, the opposite pattern prevailed. During the 1985 term, Burger's last term on the Court, Blackmun agreed with Brennan in 80 percent of the cases and Burger only half the time. Baum, *The Supreme Court*, 3d ed., 144–45; David G. Barnum, *The Supreme Court and American Democracy* 232–33 (New York: St. Martin's Press, 1993); Epstein et al., *The Supreme Court Compendium*, 432–33; Stephen L. Wasby, "Justice Harry A. Blackmun: Transformation from Minnesota Twin to Independent Voice," in Charles M. Lamb and Stephen C. Halphern, eds., *The Burger Court: Political and Judicial Profiles* (Urbana, Ill.: University of Illinois Press, 1991).

296. Segal and Spaeth, "Decisional Trends,"

106. According to Segal and Spaeth, during his tenure on the Burger Court, Blackmun voted the liberal position in criminal procedure cases only 32.6 percent of the time. More generally, 40.9 percent of his votes in nonunanimous civil liberties decision were liberal, compared to 29.7 percent for Burger, 37.7 percent for Powell, and 19.6 percent for Rehnquist.

297. Smith and Hensley offer a different view: "Although individual decisions and doctrinal changes produced by the Rehnquist Court moved constitutional law and judicial policymaking in the conservative direction sought by Reagan and Bush, systematic analysis of the Court's decisions indicates that the Court did not shift as far right as the Presidents had hoped and intended." "Unfulfilled Aspirations," 1124.

298. Clinton also appears to have been successful in appointing justices who vote, as he intended, in a moderately liberal manner. However, it is too early at this point to provide a definitive conclusion. See Christopher E. Smith, Joyce Ann Baugh, Thomas R. Hensley, and Scott Patrick Johnson, "The First-Term Performance of Justice Ruth Bader Ginsburg," 78 *Judicature* 74 (1994); Christopher E. Smith, Joyce A. Baugh, and Thomas R. Hensley, "The First-Term Performance of Justice Stephen Breyer," 79 *Judicature* 74 (1995).

299. Abraham, *Justices and Presidents*, 2d ed., 69.

300. There was much evidence supporting the president's expectations that his nominee was and would continue to be a moderate Republican. However, there was also evidence of Warren's independence and progressivism and his ties with Democrats, leading some senators to attack Warren as "ultraliberal." Additionally, Eisenhower chose Warren at least in part for his leadership and administrative abilities and also as payment of a political debt owed Warren, who was responsible for swinging the California delegation behind Eisenhower at a critical point during the 1952 Republican nominating convention. Complicating the picture further were the lobbying efforts of California Republican Party leaders (including Vice President Nixon) to be rid of Warren, considered to be too independent-minded, too progressive, and too popular with Democrats and independent voters. To the degree that Eisenhower ignored evidence of Warren's latent liberalism and relied on criteria other than purely ideological ones, such as payment of a political debt, then the president's claim of surprise and disappointment is at least somewhat more tenuous. Justice Blackmun certainly fits the model of the unpredictable judicial metamorphosis that legal scholars emphasize, executing a clear conservative to liberal shift while on the Court. However, at least one commentator suggested at the time that Blackmun was in fact not the conservative Warren Burger clone that both Nixon and Burger expected him to be. Thus, his early conservatism on the Court may have been the product of an indecisive, freshman justice following the lead of his friend and mentor Warren Burger. See Fred Graham, "Blackmun May Prove a Surprise to Nixon," *New York Times* (April 19, 1970), 10.

301. In one such attempt, Donald Songer found a positive correlation between the ideological views (i.e., votes) of home state senators of the president's party and the subsequent votes of appellate court appointees. "The Policy Consequences of Senate Involvement."

302. Walter F. Murphy, *Elements of Judicial Strategy* (Chicago: University of Chicago Press, 1964).

303. Conventional legal scholars demand from the Court clarity, coherence, *and* consensus, a typically incompatible combination.

304. See Murphy, *Elements of Judicial Strategy*, chap. 3; S. Sidney Ulmer, *Courts as Small and Not So Small Groups* (New York: General Learning Press, 1971); S. Sidney Ulmer, "Earl Warren and the *Brown* Decision," 33 *Journal of Politics* 689 (1971); Danelski, "The Influence of the Chief Justice in the Decisional Process of the Supreme Court"; Haynie, "Leadership and Consensus on the U.S. Supreme Court." Baum argues that changes in the ideological balance on the Court may also produce a shift in a justice's views. For example, he regards Potter Stewart's moderate leftward shift as a response to the addition of new conservative members to the Court. Baum, *The Supreme Court*, 3d ed., 144.

305. Tribe, *God Save This Honorable Court*, 56.

306. Abraham, *Justices and Presidents*, 2d ed., 92.

307. Murphy, *Elements of Judicial Strategy*, 53–54.

308. "The movement of such Justices as Kennedy, O'Connor, and Souter away from their usual conservative allies on key issues may . . . reflect an effort to disassociate themselves from the judicial style and behavior of Justices Scalia and Thomas. Justice Scalia consistently employs sarcasm, strident condemnations, and other undiplomatic language in castigating both liberal and conservative colleagues when they disagree with him. Such irritating attacks on colleagues may have driven Kennedy and O'Connor, in particular, away from Scalia in key cases." Smith and Hensley, "Unfulfilled Aspirations," 1129 (fnn. excluded).

309. Smith and Beuger, "Clouds in the Crystal Ball," 126.

310. For example, Roberts wrote the opinion in *Nebbia*, upholding New York's regulation of milk prices. *Nebbia* v. *New York*, 291 U.S. 502 (1934). Also the vote in another critical case, *West Coast Hotel*, upholding a state minimum wage law, had in fact already been made prior to FDR's announced plan. *West Cast Hotel Co.* v. *Parrish* 300 U.S. 379 (1937). See Alpheus T. Mason, *The Supreme Court: Vehicle of Revealed Truth or Power Group?* (Boston: Boston University Press, 1953); Robert H. Jackson, *The Struggle for Judicial Supremacy: A Study of a Crisis in American Power Politics* (New York: A. A. Knopf, 1941); Joseph Alsop and Turner Catledge, *The 168 Days* (Garden City, N.Y.: Doubleday, Doran and Co., 1938); Robert L. Stern, "The Commerce Clause and the National Economy, 1933–1946," 59 *Harvard Law Review* 645 (1946).

311. This, I believe, should be regarded as a call for more careful and aggressive ideological evaluation by presidents, rather than for less value-voting by the justices.

312. This will be more fully explained in chapter 7, "Democratic Theory Revisited."

CHAPTER 5

1. Walter F. Murphy, *Elements of Judicial Strategy* (Chicago: University of Chicago Press, 1964). For a similar account of justices as strategic actors, see Lee Epstein and Jack Knight, *The Choices Justices Make* (Washington, D.C.: Congressional Quarterly Press, 1998).

2. Murphy, *Elements of Judicial Strategy*, 3–4. Unlike many scholars, Murphy does not bring to his analysis any assumptions regarding the legitimacy of policy motivation. He describes his book as "neither an effort to debunk or belittle, nor an effort to praise or defend. It is an attempt to understand" (vii). In this respect, Murphy's effort is different from the journalistic enterprise of *The Brethren*, which seemed an attempt to tarnish the Court's image (or at least the image of the authors' least favorite justices) with their reporting of the political motivations and behind-the-scenes maneuverings of the justices. Nonetheless, the book failed in that endeavor, coming up with little in the way of serious ethical failings. Bob Woodward and Scott Armstrong, *The Brethren* (New York: Avon Books, 1979).

3. Murphy draws most heavily from the papers and activities of former president and chief justice Taft, no doubt one of the most political of all the Court's members.

4. As the previous chapter proves, the justices' views are not, in any case, idiosyncratic. They are largely predictable, coherent, and traceable to elected officials.

5. Murphy, *Elements of Judicial Strategy*, 12. Subsequent page references will appear parenthetically in the text.

6. The primary sources used include David G. Barnum, *The Supreme Court and American Democracy* chap. 12 (New York: St. Martin's Press, 1993); Lawrence Baum, *The Supreme Court*, 3d ed. (Washington, D.C.: Congressional Quarterly Press, 1989); Louis Fisher and Neal Devins, *Political Dynamics of Constitutional Law* (St. Paul, Minn.: West Publishing Co., 1992); Edward Keynes, *The Court versus Congress: Prayer, Busing, and Abortion* (Durham, N.C.: Duke University Press, 1989); Murphy, *Elements of Judicial Strategy*; Walter F. Murphy, *Congress and the Court* (Chicago: University of Chicago Press, 1962). See also Adam Carlyle Breckenridge, *Congress against the Court* (Lincoln: University of Nebraska Press, 1970); C. Herman Pritchett, *Congress versus the Supreme Court, 1857–1960* (Minneapolis: University of Minnesota Press, 1962); Robert Scigliano, *The Supreme Court and the Presidency* (New York: Free Press, 1971); John R. Schmidhauser and Larry L. Berg, *The Supreme Court and Congress* (New York: Free Press, 1972).

7. The Jeffersonian Republicans led the impeachment against Chase, who was the most

outspoken and partisan Federalist on the Court (and therefore its easiest target). Among other things, Chase was accused of making seditious statements against the Jefferson administration and of misconduct in the trial of Republicans under the Sedition Act.

8. The following discussion is from my article "Restoring the Balance of Power: The Struggle for Control of the Supreme Court," 20 *Hastings Constitutional Law Quarterly* 69, 79–80 (1992).

9. *The Prize Cases,* 67 U.S. (2 Black) 635 (1862).

10. Due to the new appointees, *Hepburn* v. *Griswold* (8 Wallace 603 [1870]) was overruled in *The Legal Tender Cases* (12 Wallace 457 [1871]).

11. This is largely due to significant changes by the end of the nineteenth century in the perceived propriety of such congressional interference with the judiciary. See Peretti, "Restoring the Balance of Power." See also Richard Friedman, "The Transformation in Senate Response to Supreme Court Nominations: From Reconstruction to the Taft Administration and Beyond," 5 *Cardozo Law Review* 1 (1983).

12. Roosevelt did not directly propose expanding the Court by six members. Rather, his transparently political proposal was to improve the Court's capacity to handle its workload by creating a new position for every justice over the age of seventy years. Thus, for each of the then six sitting justices over that age refusing to resign, Roosevelt would get an appointment.

13. See Joseph Alsop and Turner Catledge, *The 168 Days* (Garden City, N.Y.: Doubleday, Doran and Co., 1938); Robert H. Jackson, *The Struggle for Judicial Supremacy: A Study of a Crisis in American Power Politics* (New York: A. A. Knopf, 1941).

14. 7 Wallace 506 (1869).

15. See Friedman, "The Transformation in Senate Response."

16. See Jeffrey A. Segal, "Courts, Executives, and Legislatures," in John B. Gates and Charles A. Johnson, eds., *The American Courts: A Critical Assessment* 385–86 (Washington, D.C.: Congressional Quarterly Press, 1991); Murphy, *Congress and the Court,* 245–46.

17. 350 U.S. 497 (1956).

18. 354 U.S. 178 (1957).
19. 354 U.S. 298 (1957).
20. 360 U.S. 109 (1959).
21. 360 U.S. 72 (1959).
22. Murphy, *Congress and the Court,* 246.
23. Segal, "Courts, Executives, and Legislatures," 386.
24. Stuart S. Nagel, "Court-Curbing Periods in American History," 18 *Vanderbilt Law Review* 925 (1965). See also Schmidhauser and Berg, *The Supreme Court and Congress*; Roger Handberg and Harold F. Hill, Jr., "Court Curbing, Court Reversals, and Judicial Review: The Supreme Court versus Congress," 14 *Law and Society Review* 309 (1980).
25. Fisher and Devins, *Political Dynamics of Constitutional Law,* 40–41.
26. From 1972 to 1985, 128 Court-curbing bills were introduced in Congress. Segal, "Courts, Executives, and Legislatures," 387.
27. Ibid. at 388.
28. Under article V, amendments may also be proposed by a national convention upon the petition of two-thirds of the states and ratified by special state conventions. All existing amendments, however, have been proposed by Congress, and all but one have been ratified by state legislatures. (The Twenty-first Amendment, which repealed Prohibition, was ratified by state conventions.)
29. 2 U.S. 419 (1793).
30. 60 U.S. 393 (1857).
31. 157 U.S. 429 (1895).
32. 400 U.S. 112 (1970).
33. Barnum, *The Supreme Court and American Democracy,* 145.
34. Ibid. at 145–46.
35. Fisher and Devins, *Political Dynamics of Constitutional Law,* 213.
36. 491 U.S. 397 (1989).
37. 496 U.S. 310 (1990).
38. Barnum, *The Supreme Court and American Democracy,* 213.
39. 463 U.S. 783 (1983).
40. 465 U.S. 668 (1984).
41. Baum, *The Supreme Court,* 3d ed., 134.
42. For a good review of such efforts, see William N. Eskridge, Jr., "Overriding Supreme Court Statutory Interpretation Decisions," 101 *Yale Law Journal* 331 (1991). See also Harry Stumpf, "Congressional Response to Supreme Court Rulings: The Interaction of Law and Politics," 14 *Journal of Public Law* 377 (1965);

Harry Stumpf, "The Political Efficacy of Judicial Symbolism," 19 *Western Political Quarterly* 293 (1966); Richard A. Pascal, "The Continuing Colloquy: Congress and the Finality of the Supreme Court," 8 *Journal of Law and Politics* 143 (1991); Beth M. Henschen, "Congressional Response to the Statutory Interpretations of the Supreme Court," 11 *American Political Quarterly* 441 (1983); Keynes and Miller, *The Court vs. Congress*; Michael E. Solimine and James L. Walker, "The Next Word: Congressional Response to Supreme Court Statutory Decisions," 65 *Temple Law Quarterly* 425 (1992); Joseph Ignagni and James Meernik, "Explaining Congressional Attempts to Reverse Supreme Court Decisions," 47 *Political Research Quarterly* 353 (1994); James Meernik and Joseph Ignagni, "Congressional Attacks on Supreme Court Rulings Involving Unconstitutional State Laws" 48 *Political Research Quarterly* 43 (1995); James Meernik and Joseph Ignagni, "Judicial Review and Coordinate Construction of the Constitution," 41 *American Journal of Political Science* 447 (1997); Abner J. Mikva and Jeff Bleich, "When Congress Overrules the Court," 79 *California Law Review* 729 (1991).

43. Most notably, the Civil Rights Act of 1991 reversed *Wards Cove Packing Co.* v. *Atonio*, 490 U.S. 642 (1989) (holding that employees challenging employment practices having a racially discriminatory impact bear the burden of proving such practices are motivated by discriminatory intent rather than business needs); *Patterson* v. *McClean Credit Union*, 491 U.S. 164 (1989) (holding that sec. 1981 of the 1866 Civil Rights Act forbids racial discrimination in hiring but not on-the-job racial harassment); and *Martin* v. *Wilks*, 490 U.S. 755 (1989) (allowing white employees to challenge court-approved consent decrees embodying affirmative action plans).

44. *Zurcher* v. *Stanford Daily*, 436 U.S. 547 (1978).

45. *United States* v. *Eichman*, 496 U.S. 310 (1990).

46. Fisher and Devins, *Political Dynamics of Constitutional Law*, 212. There was also widespread response in the states as well. That was particularly the case after the *Webster* decision, in which the Court weakened *Roe* and permitted greater state regulation of abortion. See ibid. at 232–44.

47. Barnum, *The Supreme Court in American Democracy*, 210.

48. Stephen L. Wasby, *The Supreme Court in the Federal Judicial System*, 4th ed., 318 (Chicago: Nelson-Hall Publishers, 1993). Henschen reports very similar numbers (Beth M. Henschen, "Statutory Interpretations of the Supreme Court: Congressional Response," 11 *American Politics Quarterly* 441 [1983], while Ignagni and Meernik find a much higher rate of success ("Explaining Congressional Attempts to Reverse Supreme Court Decisions"). Baum reports that "over the past three decades, on average, more than ten statutory decisions have been overturned in each two-year Congress." Lawrence Baum, *The Supreme Court*, 6th ed., 246 (Washington, D.C.: Congressional Quarterly Press, 1998).

49. Additional factors found to increase the likelihood of a congressional response include: executive branch opposition; a Court invitation to Congress to review its decision; the relative newness of the law; and the type of law (i.e., state rather than federal law). Ignagni and Meernik, "Explaining Congressional Attempts to Reverse Supreme Court Decisions"; Meernik and Ignagni, "Congressional Attacks on Supreme Court Rulings Involving Unconstitutional State Laws"; Meernik and Ignagni "Judicial Review and Coordinate Construction of the Constitution"; Solimine and Walker, "The Next Word."

50. Eugenia Froedge Toma, "Congressional Influence and the Supreme Court: The Budget as a Signaling Device," 20 *Journal of Legal Studies* 131, 134 (1991).

51. See Fisher and Devins, *Political Dynamics of Constitutional Law*, 87–89, 96–97; David M. O'Brien, *Constitutional Law and Politics* 172 (New York: W. W. Norton and Co., 1991). For other congressional efforts to affect the partisan makeup of the federal judiciary by manipulating incentives to retire, see Deborah J. Barrow, Gary Zuk, and Gerard S. Gryski, *The Federal Judiciary and Institutional Change* (Ann Arbor: University of Michigan Press, 1996).

52. Toma, "Congressional Influence and the Supreme Court," 146.

53. Toma does find changes in the ideological distance between the Court's decisions and congressional votes following Congress's budgetary signals. However, there are significant difficulties in determining Congress's

ideological ranking and especially in attributing causation.

54. Toma, "Congressional Influence and the Supreme Court," 145.

55. *Miranda* v. *Arizona*, 384 U.S. 436 (1966). Also targeted were *Mallory* v. *United States*, 354 U.S. 449 (1957), and *United States* v. *Wade*, 388 U.S. 218 (1967).

56. Fisher and Devins, *Political Dynamics of Constitutional Law*, 213.

57. See, e.g., Jesse H. Choper, *Judicial Review and the National Political Process* chap. 1 (Chicago: University of Chicago Press, 1980); Ely, *Democracy and Distrust*, 44–48; John Agresto, *The Supreme Court and Constitutional Democracy* (Ithaca: Cornell University Press, 1984).

58. This is similar (but not identical) to the "rational anticipation" model in James A. Stimson, Michael B. Mackuen, and Robert S. Erikson, "Dynamic Representation," 89 *American Political Science Review* 543 (1995).

59. Conventional scholars tend to paint the picture differently: the Court finally and fortuitously discovered the correct and true interpretation of the Constitution, i.e., that it should never interfere in economic policy. See Martin Shapiro's discussion of this "folk history" in M. Judd Harmon, ed., *Essays on the Constitution of the United States* (Port Washington, N.Y.: Kennikat Press, 1978). See also Bruce Ackerman, *We the People: Foundations* (Cambridge: Harvard University Press, 1991).

60. Shapiro would argue that the Court continues to involve itself in economic policymaking; it simply does so on behalf of members of the New Deal coalition—workers, the poor, and racial and ethnic minorities. Shapiro, "The Constitution and Economic Rights."

61. The law of averages simply did not work to FDR's advantage. He was not afforded an opportunity to appoint a single Supreme Court justice until his second term. Meanwhile, the nation had undergone a major realignment, with an extraordinary takeover of the presidency and Congress by the Democratic Party.

62. Baum, *The Supreme Court*, 3d ed., 133.

63. R. Friedman, "The Transformation in Senate Response."

64. Gerald N. Rosenberg, "Judicial Inde-

pendence and the Reality of Political Power," 54 *Review of Politics* 369, 371 (1992).

65. Ibid. at 394.

66. Ibid. at 397.

67. Richard C. Cortner, *The Supreme Court and Civil Liberties Policy* vi (Palo Alto, Calif.: Mayfield, 1975).

68. Nathan Hakman, "Lobbying the Supreme Court: An Appraisal of Political Science 'Folklore,' " 35 *Fordham Law Review* 15 (1966); Nathan Hakman, "The Supreme Court's Political Environment: The Processing of Non-Commercial Litigation," in Joel B. Grossman and Joseph Tanenhaus, eds., *Frontiers of Judicial Research* (New York: Wiley, 1969). The primary target of Hakman's challenge was Clement E. Vose, "Litigation as a Form of Pressure Group Activity," 319 *Annals of the American Academy of Political and Social Science* 20 (1958). See also Lucius Barker, "Third Parties in Litigation: A Systematic View of the Judicial Function," 29 *Journal of Politics* 41 (1967); Robert H. Birkby and Walter F. Murphy, "Interest Group Conflict in the Judicial Arena: The First Amendment and Group Access to the Courts," 42 *Texas Law Review* 1018 (1964); Samuel Krislov, "The Amicus Curiae Brief: From Friendship to Advocacy," 72 *Yale Law Journal* 694 (1963); Clement E. Vose, "National Consumers' League and the Brandeis Brief," 1 *Midwest Journal of Political Science* 178 (1957).

69. Lee Epstein, "Courts and Interest Groups," in John B. Gates and Charles A. Johnson, *The American Courts: A Critical Assessment* 335, 353 (Washington, D.C.: Congressional Quarterly Press, 1991). See also Baum, *The Supreme Court*, 3d ed., 79–88; Gregory A. Caldeira and John R. Wright, "Amici Curiae before the Supreme Court: Who Participates, When, and How Much?" 52 *Journal of Politics* 782 (1990); Robert Bradley and Paul Gardner, "Underdogs, Upperdogs and the Use of the Amicus Brief: Trends and Explanations," 10 *Justice System Journal* 78 (1985); Karen O'Connor and Lee Epstein, "An Appraisal of Hakman's 'Folklore,' " 16 *Law and Society Review* 701 (1982); Karen O'Connor and Lee Epstein, *Public Interest Law Groups* (Westport, Conn.: Greenwood Press, 1989). For case studies of interest group participation in Supreme Court litigation, see Richard Kluger, *Simple Justice* (New York: Knopf, 1976); Joseph F. Kobylka, *The Politics of Obscenity: Group Litigation in a*

Time of Legal Change (Westport, Conn.: Greenwood Press, 1991); Susan E. Lawrence, *The Poor in Court* (Princeton: Princeton University Press, 1990); David R. Manwaring, *Render unto Caesar: The Flag Salute Controversy* (Chicago: University of Chicago Press, 1962); Michael Meltsner, *Cruel and Unusual: The Supreme Court and Capital Punishment* (New York: Random House, 1973); Karen O'Connor, *Women's Organizations' Use of the Court* (Lexington, Mass.: Lexington Books, 1980); Susan M. Olson, *Clients and Lawyers—Serving the Rights of Disabled People* (Westport, Conn.: Greenwood Press, 1984); Leo Pfeffer, "Amici in Church-State Litigation," 44 *Law and Contemporary Problems* 83 (1981); Mark Tushnet, *The NAACP's Legal Strategy against Segregated Education, 1925–1950* (Chapel Hill: University of North Carolina Press, 1987); Clement E. Vose, *Caucasians Only: The Supreme Court, the NAACP, and the Restrictive Convenant Cases* (Berkeley: University of California Press, 1959); Vose, "National Consumers' League and the Brandeis Brief"; Lettie M. Wenner, *The Environmental Decade in Court* (Bloomington: Indiana University Press, 1982).

70. Epstein, "Courts and Interest Groups," 350.

71. Susan Behuniak-Long, "Friendly Fire: Amici Curiae and *Webster* v. *Reproductive Health Services*," 74 *Judicature* 261 (1991).

72. Richard C. Cortner, "Strategies and Tactics of Litigants in Constitutional Cases," 17 *Journal of Public Law* 287 (1968).

73. Caldeira and Wright, "Amici Curiae before the Supreme Court"; Lee Epstein, *Conservatives in Court* (Knoxville: University of Tennessee Press, 1985); Epstein, "Courts and Interest Groups," 354–57; Karen O'Connor and Lee Epstein, "The Rise of Conservative Interest Group Litigation," 45 *Journal of Politics* 479 (1983). See also Susan M. Olson, "Interest-Group Litigation in Federal District Court: Beyond the Political Disadvantage Theory," 52 *Journal of Politics* 854 (1990).

74. Gregory A. Caldeira and John R. Wright, "Organized Interests and Agenda Setting in the Supreme Court of the United States," 82 *American Political Science Review* 1109 (1988); Kevin T. McGuire and Gregory A. Caldeira, "Lawyers, Organized Interests, and the Law of Obscenity: Agenda Setting in the Su-

preme Court," 87 *American Political Science Review* 717 (1993). See also Meltsner, *Cruel and Unusual*; O'Connor, *Women's Organizations' Use of the Court*; Vose, *Caucasians Only*.

75. Baum, *The Supreme Court*, 3d ed., 87–88.

76. Kobylka, *The Politics of Obscenity*.

77. Karen O'Connor and Lee Epstein, "Court Rules and Workload: A Case Study of Rules Governing Amicus Curiae Participation," 8 *Justice System Journal* 35 (1983). Caldeira and Wright similarly conclude that "the Court is clearly receptive to a large number of [amicus] briefs." "Amici Curiae before the Supreme Court," 800.

78. "When a case involves real conflict or when the federal government is a petitioner, the addition of just one amicus curiae brief in support of certiorari increases the likelihood of plenary review by 40%–50%." Caldeira and Wright, "Organized Interests and Agenda Setting," 1122. See also Kevin T. McGuire and Gregory A. Caldeira, "Lawyers, Organized Interests, and the Law of Obscenity: Agenda Setting in the Supreme Court," 87 *American Political Science Review* 717 (1993).

79. O'Connor and Epstein, "Court Rules and Workload"; Epstein, "Courts and Interest Groups," 361; Lee Epstein, Jeffrey A. Segal, Harold J. Spaeth, and Thomas G. Walker, *The Supreme Court Compendium: Data, Decisions, and Developments* 582 (Washington, D.C.: Congressional Quarterly Press, 1994). See also Bruce L. Ennis, "Effective Amicus Briefs," 33 *Catholic University Law Review* 603 (1984); Pfeffer, "Amici in Church-State Litigation."

80. Greg Ivers and Karen O'Connor, "Friends as Foes: The Amicus Curiae Participation and Effectiveness of the American Civil Liberties Union and Americans for Effective Law Enforcement in Criminal Cases, 1969–1982," 9 *Law and Policy* 161 (1987); Lawrence, *The Poor in Court*; Meltsner, *Cruel and Unusual*; Steven Puro, "The Role of Amicus Curiae in the United States Supreme Court, 1920–1966" (Ph.D. diss., State University of New York at Buffalo, 1971); Vose, *Caucasians Only*.

81. Lee Epstein and C. K. Rowland, "Interest Groups in the Courts: Do Groups Fare Better?" in Allan J. Cigler and Burdett A. Loomis, eds., *Interest Group Politics*, 2d ed. (Washington, D.C.: Congressional Quarterly Press, 1986).

82. Epstein, "Courts and Interest Groups," 361.

83. Kevin T. McGuire, "Obscenity, Libertarian Values, and Decision Making in the Supreme Court," 18 *American Politics Quarterly* 47 (1990).

84. Donald R. Songer and Reginald S. Sheehan, "Interest Group Success in the Courts: Amicus Participation in the Supreme Court," 46 *Political Research Quarterly* 339 (1993).

85. Epstein and Rowland, "Interest Groups in the Courts."

86. Lee Epstein and C. K. Rowland, "Debunking the Myth of Interest Group Invincibility in the Courts," 85 *American Political Science Review* 205 (1991).

87. Reginald S. Sheehan, William Mishler, and Donald R. Songer, "Ideology, Status, and the Differential Success of Direct Parties before the Supreme Court," 86 *American Political Science Review* 464 (1992); McGuire and Caldeira, "Lawyers, Organized Interests, and the Law of Obscenity"; Reginald S. Sheehan, "Governmental Litigants, Underdogs, and Civil Liberties: A Reassessment of a Trend in Supreme Court Decisionmaking," 45 *Western Political Quarterly* 27 (1992).

88. The primary source for the following discussion is Segal, "Courts, Executives, and Legislatures," 376–82. See also Virginia Armstrong and Charles A. Johnson, "Certiorari Decisionmaking by the Warren and Burger Courts: Is Cue Theory Time Bound?" 15 *Polity* 141 (1982); Caldeira and Wright, "Organized Interests and Agenda Setting"; Lincoln Caplan, *The Tenth Justice* (New York: Knopf, 1987); Karen O'Connor, "The Amicus Curiae Role of the U.S. Solicitor General in Supreme Court Litigation," 66 *Judicature* 256 (1983); H. W. Perry, Jr., "Agenda Setting and Case Selection," in John B. Gates and Charles A. Johnson, eds., *The American Courts: A Critical Assessment* 235 (Washington, D.C.: Congressional Quarterly Press, 1991); Doris Marie Provine, *Case Selection in the United States Supreme Court* (Chicago: University of Chicago Press, 1980); Steven Puro, "The United States as Amicus Curiae," in S. Sidney Ulmer, ed., *Courts, Law, and Judicial Processes* (New York: Free Press, 1981); Robert Scigliano, *The Supreme Court and the Presidency* (New York: Free Press, 1971); Jeffrey A. Segal, "Amicus Curiae Briefs by the So-

licitor General during the Warren and Burger Courts," 41 *Western Political Quarterly* 135 (1988); Jeffrey A. Segal, "Supreme Court Support for the Solicitor General: The Effect of Presidential Appointments," 43 *Western Political Quarterly* 137 (1990); Rebecca Mae Salokar, *The Solicitor General: The Politics of Law* (Philadelphia, Penn.: Temple University Press, 1992); Joseph Tanenhaus, Marvin Schick, Matthew Muraskin, and Daniel Rosen, "The Supreme Court's Certiorari Jurisdiction: Cue Theory," in Glendon Schubert, ed., *Judicial Decision Making* (New York: Free Press, 1963); Stuart H. Teger and Douglas Kosinski, "The Cue Theory of Supreme Court Certiorari Jurisdiction: A Reconsideration," 42 *Journal of Politics* 834 (1980); S. Sidney Ulmer, William Hintze, and Louise Kirklosky, "The Decision to Grant or Deny Certiorari: Further Consideration of Cue Theory," 6 *Law and Society Review* 637 (1972).

89. Segal, "Courts, Executives, and Legislatures," 377.

90. Handberg and Hill, "Court Curbing, Court Reversals, and Judicial Review"; Epstein et al., *The Supreme Court Compendium*, 569–570.

91. Epstein et al., *The Supreme Court Compendium*, 571–572.

92. Puro, "The United States as Amicus Curiae." For the period 1952–90, solicitor general success as amicus curiae varied from 65.1 percent for Carter to 87.5 percent for Kennedy. Epstein et al., *The Supreme Court Compendium*, 571.

93. Jeffrey A. Segal, "Predicting Supreme Court Cases Probabilistically: The Search and Seizure Cases, 1962–1981," 78 *American Political Science Review* 891 (1984); Jeffrey A. Segal and Cheryl D. Reedy, "The Supreme Court and Sex Discrimination: The Role of the Solicitor General," 41 *Western Political Quarterly* 553 (1988).

94. Caldeira and Wright, "Organized Interests and Agenda Setting."

95. Segal, "Courts, Executives, and Legislatures," 378–79.

96. Ibid. at 378; Segal, "Amicus Curiae Briefs by the Solicitor General."

97. Segal, "Supreme Court Support for the Solicitor General."

98. Ibid. at 149.

99. Baum, *The Supreme Court*, 3d ed., 88–90;

Caplan, *The Tenth Justice*; Segal, "Courts, Executives, and Legislature," 380–82.

100. Gerald N. Rosenberg, *The Hollow Hope: Can Courts Bring about Social Change?* (Chicago: University of Chicago Press, 1991). Subsequent page references to this work will be given parenthetically in the text.

101. Krislov regards this as a straw-man argument. I agree that we should not be surprised by the "No" answer to the question of whether the Court can singlehandedly (and quickly) achieve momentous, nationwide social change. However, in Rosenberg's defense, the belief in judicial independence and court efficacy is quite strong, at least in most law schools and among many interest groups as well. It is a still-current assumption that deserves to be challenged and carefully repudiated. Samuel Krislov, Review of *The Hollow Hope*, by Gerald Rosenberg, 9 *Constitutional Commentary* 367 (1992).

102. There is a sizable literature regarding the impact of judicial decisions. Lawrence Baum, "Implementation of Judicial Decisions: An Organizational Analysis," 4 *American Politics Quarterly* 86 (1976); Theodore L. Becker and Malcolm Feeley, eds., *The Impact of Supreme Court Decisions*, 2d ed. (New York: Oxford University Press, 1973); Jon Bond and Charles A. Johnson, "Implementing a Permissive Policy: Hospital Abortion Services after *Roe v. Wade*," 26 *American Journal of Political Science* 1 (1982); Charles S. Bullock III and Charles M. Lamb, "Toward a Theory of Civil Rights Implementation," 2 *Policy Perspectives* 376 (1982); Bradley C. Canon, "Courts and Policy: Compliance, Implementation, and Impact," in John B. Gates and Charles A. Johnson, eds., *American Courts: A Critical Assessment* 435–66 (Washington D.C.: Congressional Quarterly Press 1991); Bradley C. Canon, "Testing the Effectiveness of Civil Liberties Policies at the State and Federal Levels: The Case of the Exclusionary Rule," 5 *American Politics Quarterly* 57 (1977); Jesse H. Choper, "Consequences of Supreme Court Decisions Upholding Individual Constitutional Rights," 83 *Michigan Law Review* 1 (1984); Kenneth M. Dolbeare and Phillip E. Hammond, *The School Prayer Decisions: From Court Policy to Local Practice* (Chicago: University of Chicago Press, 1971); Douglas G. Feig, "Expenditures in the American States: The Impact of Court-Ordered Reapportion-

ment," 6 *American Politics Quarterly* 309 (1978); Michael Giles and Douglas Gatlin, "Mass Level Compliance with Public Policy: The Case of School Desegregation," 42 *Journal of Politics* 711 (1980); Susan B. Hansen, "State Implementation of Supreme Court Decisions: Abortion Rates since *Roe v. Wade*," 42 *Journal of Politics* 372 (1980); Charles A. Johnson and Bradley C. Canon, *Judicial Policies: Implementation and Impact* (Washington, D.C.: Congressional Quarterly Press, 1984); Richard M. Johnson, *The Dynamics of Compliance: Supreme Court Decision-Making from a New Perspective* (Evanston, Ill.: Northwestern University Press, 1967); Matthew D. McCubbins and Thomas Schwartz, "Congress, the Courts, and Public Policy: Consequences of the One Man, One Vote Rule," 32 *American Journal of Political Science* 388 (1988); William K. Muir, Jr., *Prayer in the Public Schools: Law and Attitude Change* (Chicago: University of Chicago Press, 1967); Walter Murphy, "Lower Court Checks on Supreme Court Power," 53 *American Political Science Review* 1017 (1959); Myron W. Orfield, Jr., "The Exclusionary Rule and Deterrence: An Empirical Study of Chicago Narcotics Officers," 54 *University of Chicago Law Review* 1016 (1987); Gordon Patric, "The Impact of a Court Decision: Aftermath of the *McCollum* Case," 6 *Journal of Public Law* 455 (1957); Traciel V. Reid, "Judicial Policy-Making and Implementation: An Empirical Examination," 41 *Western Political Quarterly* 509 (1988); Harrell R. Rodgers, Jr., and Charles S. Bullock III, *Coercion to Compliance* (Lexington, Mass.: Heath, 1976); Harrell R. Rodgers, Jr., and Charles S. Bullock III, *Law and Social Change: Civil Rights Laws and Their Consequences* (New York: McGraw-Hill, 1972); Frank J. Sorauf, "*Zorach v. Clauson*: The Impact of a Supreme Court Decision," 53 *American Political Science Review* 777 (1959); Stephen Wasby, *The Impact of the United States Supreme Court: Some Perspectives* (Homewood, Ill.: Dorsey Press, 1970); Stephen Wasby, *Small Town Police and the Supreme Court* (Lexington, Mass.: Heath, 1976).

103. 357 U.S. 449 (1958).

104. 371 U.S. 415 (1963).

105. *Jackson* v. *Alabama*, 348 U.S. 888 (1954); *Naim* v. *Naim*, 350 U.S. 891 (1955).

106. Murphy, *Elements of Judicial Strategy*, 193.

107. See Nelson W. Polsby, "Legisla-

tures," in Fred I. Greenstein and Nelson W. Polsby, eds., *Handbook of Political Science*, vol. 5 (Reading, Mass.: Addison-Wesley Publishing, 1975).

108. Richard Davis, *Decisions and Images: The Supreme Court and the Press* (Englewood Cliffs, N.J.: Prentice-Hall, 1994).

109. For evidence that Supreme Court justices follow news coverage of and pay attention to public reaction regarding the Court, its members, and its decisions, see Davis, *Decisions and Images.*

110. Baum, *The Supreme Court*, 3d ed., 103.

111. According to this perspective, the recent move toward appointing appellate court judges to the Court, rather than prominent politicians, is an unfortunate trend.

112. *Plessy* v. *Ferguson*, 163 U.S. 537 (1896).

113. A similar strategy—unanimity to limit the opportunity for defiance—was employed in the Watergate tapes case. *United States.* v. *Nixon*, 418 U.S. 683 (1974). See Woodward and Armstrong, *The Brethren*, 349–55, 366–67.

114. Reprinted in Joel B. Grossman and Richard S. Wells, *Constitutional Law and Judicial Policy Making*, 2d ed., 448–52 (New York: John Wiley and Sons, 1980).

115. Murphy, *Congress and the Court*, 246, fn. excluded.

116. Ibid. at 246.

117. The Burger Court did impose some limits that the Warren Court probably would not have. E.g., *Milliken* v. *Bradley* (418 U.S. 717 [1974]), reversing a federal district court decision to employ an interdistrict desegregation remedy the absence of evidence of an interdistrict violation; *Pasadena Board of Education* v. *Spangler* (427 U.S. 424 [1976]), reversing a federal district court order to require, despite the absence of a finding of intentional segregation, annual readjustment of attendance zones to maintain racial balance and thus prevent resegregation.

118. See, e.g., Curtis J. Berger, "Away from the Court House and into the Field: The Odyssey of a Special Master," 78 *Columbia Law Review* 707 (1978).

119. Most conventional scholars and the bar advocate normative restraints on precisely the sorts of activities that would assist the Court in making accurate predictions about the existence of or potential for a policy consensus and in developing a political consensus

for the Court's policies. Such activities would include publicity or advocacy efforts by the justices, awareness of the interest group composition of litigation, or exchanges of information and views with other government officials. In short, the variety of "extrajudicial activities" that most of the legal community abhor are critical to accurate consensus-building assessments and to successful consensus-building activities.

120. John Hart Ely, "Foreword: On Discovering Fundamental Values," 92 *Harvard Law Review* 5 (1978).

CHAPTER 6

1. "The legitimacy of judicial decrees depends . . . in considerable part on public confidence that the judges are predominantly engaged not in making personal political judgments but in applying a body of law." Archibald Cox, *The Court and the Constitution* 362 (Boston: Houghton Mifflin, 1987). "The democratic integrity of law . . . depends entirely upon the degree to which its processes are legitimate. A judge who announces a decision must be able to demonstrate that he began from recognized legal principles and reasoned in an intellectually coherent and politically neutral way to his result. . . . Those who have tempted the courts to political judging will have gained nothing for themselves but will have destroyed a great and essential institution." Robert H. Bork, *The Tempting of America* 2 (New York: Free Press, 1990).

2. Philip B. Kurland, *Politics, the Constitution and the Warren Court* xxiii–xxiv (Chicago: University of Chicago Press, 1970).

3. Ibid. at xxv.

4. Ibid. at xxv. Kurland then adds, "Let us pray."

5. The *Lochner*-era Court is another.

6. Jeffrey J. Mondak and Shannon Ishiyama Smithey, "The Dynamics of Public Support for the Supreme Court," 59 *Journal of Politics* 1114 (1997).

7. David Adamany and Joel B. Grossman, "Support for the Supreme Court as a National Policymaker," 5 *Law and Policy Quarterly* 405, 406 (1983), fnn. excluded. The primary works advancing the "sacrosanctity" thesis include: Edward S. Corwin, "The Constitution as Instrument and as Symbol," 30 *American Political Sci-*

ence Review 1071 (1936); Jerome Frank, *Law and the Modern Mind* (New York: Coward McCann, 1930); Max Lerner, "Constitution and Court as Symbols," 46 *Yale Law Journal* 1290 (1937); Karl Llewellyn, "The Constitution as an Institution," 34 *Columbia Law Review* 1 (1934).

8. William J. Daniels, "The Supreme Court and Its Publics," 37 *Albany Law Review* 632, 639 (1973).

9. David Easton and Jack Dennis, *Children in the Political System: Origins of Political Legitimacy* (New York: McGraw-Hill, 1969).

10. Ibid. at 278.

11. Gregory A. Caldeira, "Children's Images of the Supreme Court: A Preliminary Mapping," 11 *Law and Society Review* 851 (1977).

12. Ibid. at 864. Caldeira regards the data of Easton and Dennis as largely "methodological artifacts, the result of their uncritical and monistic use of close-ended instrumentation."

13. Walter F. Murphy and Joseph Tanenhaus, "Public Opinion and the Supreme Court: The Goldwater Campaign," 32 *Public Opinion Quarterly* 31, 34–35 (1968), hereinafter referred to as "The Goldwater Campaign."

14. Ibid.

15. Ibid. at 35.

16. John H. Kessel, "Public Perceptions of the Supreme Court," 10 *Midwest Journal of Political Science* 167, 171 (1966).

17. Ibid. at 174.

18. Ibid.

19. Kenneth Dolbeare, "The Public Views the Supreme Court," in Herbert Jacob, ed., *Law, Politics, and the Federal Courts* 194, 199 (Boston: Little, Brown, 1976).

20. Walter F. Murphy and Joseph Tanenhaus, "Public Opinion and the United States Supreme Court: A Preliminary Mapping of Some Prerequisites for Court Legitimation of Regime Change," 2 *Law and Society Review* 357 (1968), hereinafter referred to as "A Preliminary Mapping."

21. Walter Murphy and Joseph Tanenhaus, "Constitutional Courts and Political Representation," in Michael Danielson and Walter Murphy, eds., *Modern American Democracy: Readings* 549 (New York: Holt, Rinehart and Winston, 1969).

22. Kenneth Dolbeare and Phillip E. Hammond, "The Political Party Basis of Attitudes toward the Supreme Court," 37 *Public Opinion Quarterly* 16, 20–21 (1968).

23. Ibid. See also Murphy and Tanenhaus, "The Goldwater Campaign," 35.

24. Dolbeare, "The Public Views the Supreme Court," 199–201.

25. Liane C. Kosaki, "Public Awareness of Supreme Court Decisions" (paper presented at the Annual Meeting of the American Political Science Association, 1991).

26. *Sable Communications* v. *FCC*, 492 U.S. 115 (1989).

27. *Stanford* v. *Kentucky*, 492 U.S. 361 (1989).

28. *Texas* v. *Johnson*, 491 U.S. 397 (1989).

29. *Webster* v. *Reproductive Health Services*, 492 U.S. 490 (1989).

30. Kosaki, "Public Awareness of Supreme Court Decisions," 11. See also Susan R. Burgess, Daniel J. Reagan, and Donald L. Davison, "Reclaiming a Democratic Constitutional Politics: Survey Construction and Public Knowledge," 54 *Review of Politics* 399 (1992). In this survey, respondents were knowledgeable about the abortion issue and could independently articulate arguments for and against their own position (as distinct from their awareness of Supreme Court decisions regarding abortion). The authors criticize existing approaches that merely ask respondents if they know and understand existing Court rulings, which assumes that the Court's decisions are correct and authoritative. By discovering that the public has its own understanding of the Constitution's meaning, they argue, we can reclaim constitutional law as a democratic (rather than an elitist, Court-centered) enterprise.

31. Kosaki, "Public Awareness of Supreme Court Decisions," 8 n. 3.

32. Charles H. Franklin and Liane Kosaki, "Media, Knowledge, and Public Evaluations of the Supreme Court," in Lee Epstein, ed., *Contemplating Courts* (Washington, D.C.: Congressional Quarterly, 1995).

33. Adamany and Grossman, "Support for the Supreme Court," 411.

34. Ibid. at 420.

35. Thomas R. Marshall, *Public Opinion and the Supreme Court* 145 (Boston: Unwin Hyman, 1989).

36. Ibid.

37. The results of this poll are reprinted in

Lee Epstein, Jeffrey A. Segal, Harold J. Spaeth, and Thomas G. Walker, *The Supreme Court Compendium: Data, Decisions, and Developments* 609 (Washington, D.C.: Congressional Quarterly Press, 1994). Justice O'Connor was correctly named by 23 percent of the respondents, Rehnquist by 9 percent, Kennedy 7 percent, Scalia 6 percent, Marshall 5 percent, Blackmun 4 percent, Brennan 3 percent, White 3 percent, and Stevens 1 percent.

38. Reported in Janet A. Flammang, Dennis R. Gordon, Timothy J. Lukes, and Kenneth R. Smorsten, *American Politics in a Changing World* 229 (Pacific Grove, Calif.: Brooks/Cole Publishing Company, 1990).

39. Stephen L. Wasby, *The Supreme Court in the Federal Judicial System*, 4th ed., 357 (Chicago: Nelson-Hall Publishers, 1993), quoting Marcia Coyle, "How Americans View High Court," *National Law Journal* 1 (February 26, 1990).

40. Marshall, *Public Opinion and the Supreme Court*, 137. Regarding the sketchy and superficial media coverage of the Court, see David Grey, *The Supreme Court and the News Media* (Evanston, Ill.: Northwestern University Press, 1968); Ethan Katsh, "The Supreme Court Beat: How Television Covers the U.S. Supreme Court," 67 *Judicature* 6 (1983); Chester Newland, "Press Coverage of the United States Supreme Court," 17 *Western Political Quarterly* 15 (1964); Gerald N. Rosenberg, *The Hollow Hope* 111–16, 229–34 (Chicago: University of Chicago Press, 1991); David Shaw, "Media Coverage of the Courts: Improving but Still Not Adequate," 65 *Judicature* 18 (1981); Elliot E. Slotnick, "Television News and the Supreme Court: A Case Study," 77 *Judicature* 21 (1993); Richard Davis, "Lifting the Shroud: News Media Coverage of the U.S. Supreme Court," 9 *Communications and the Law* 43 (1987); Richard Davis, *Decisions and Images: The Supreme Court and the Press* (Englewood Cliffs, N.J.: Prentice-Hall, 1994).

41. Susan Welch, John Gruhl, Michael Steinman, John Comer, and Jan P. Vermeer, *Understanding American Government*, 4th ed., 87 (Belmont, Calif.: West/Wadsworth, 1997).

42. Ibid.

43. E.g., Gregory Casey, "The Supreme Court and Myth: An Empirical Investigation," 8 *Law and Society Review* 385, 405 (1974); Dolbeare, "The Public Views the Supreme Court"; Kosaki, "Public Awareness of Supreme Court Decisions"; Murphy and Tanenhaus, "Constitutional Courts," 550.

44. Dolbeare and Hammond, "The Political Party Basis of Attitudes toward the Supreme Court."

45. Kessel, "Public Perceptions of the Supreme Court," 190.

46. David Adamany, "Legitimacy, Realigning Elections, and the Supreme Court," 1973 *Wisconsin Law Review* 790 table 5 (1973); Joseph Tanenhaus and Walter F. Murphy, "Patterns of Public Support for the Supreme Court: A Panel Study," 43 *Journal of Politics* 24, 30 (1981).

47. Lloyd A. Free and Hadley Cantril, *The Political Beliefs of Americans*, 192–93 (New Brunswick, N.J.: Rutgers University Press, 1967).

48. The particular question asked was, "Would you be likely to think the right thing had been done in Washington if the action had been taken by the Supreme Court? by the President? by Congress?" Dolbeare, "The Public Views the Supreme Court," 197.

49. Adamany and Grossman, "Support for the Supreme Court as a National Policymaker," 411.

50. Ibid.

51. Marshall, *Public Opinion and the Supreme Court*, 141.

52. All of the following information comes from Marshall's discussion in *Public Opinion and the Supreme Court*, 139–41.

53. In addition to Marshall's discussion (139–41), see Epstein et al., *The Supreme Court Compendium*, 605.

54. For example, see Mondak and Smithey, "The Dynamics of Public Support for the Supreme Court."

55. E.g., Casey, 392–94; Murphy and Tanenhaus, "A Preliminary Mapping," 365; Dolbeare, "The Public Views the Court"; Kessel, "Public Perceptions of the Supreme Court," 174.

56. Gregory Casey, "The Supreme Court and Myth: An Empirical Investigation," 8 *Law and Society Review* 385, 391–93.

57. Larry R. Baas, "The Constitution as Symbol: Patterns of Meaning," 8 *American Politics Quarterly* 237 (1980).

58. Larry R. Baas, "The Constitution as Symbol: The Interpersonal Sources of Meaning of

a Secondary Symbol," 23 *American Journal of Political Science* 101 (1979).

59. Casey, "The Supreme Court and Myth," 393, 397–98.

60. Ibid. at 402, 398–403. Casey is not the only scholar to report this curious result: those who are more attentive to the Court hold a less realistic view of it, subscribing to the myth of judicial neutrality. See Tom R. Tyler and Gregory Mitchell, "Legitimacy and Empowerment of Discretionary Legal Authority: The United States Supreme Court and Abortion Rights," 43 *Duke Law Journal* 703 (1994); James L. Gibson, Gregory A. Caldeira, and Vanessa A. Baird, "On the Legitimacy of National High Courts," 92 *American Political Science Review* 343 (1998).

61. Casey, "The Supreme Court and Myth," 409–10.

62. Gregory A. Caldeira and James L. Gibson, "The Etiology of Public Support for the Supreme Court," 36 *American Journal of Political Science* 635, 640–41 (1992).

63. Ibid.

64. Reported in Adamany, "Legitimacy, Realigning Elections, and the Supreme Court," 811; Richard M. Johnson, *The Dynamics of Compliance: Supreme Court Decision-Making from a New Perspective* 165 (Evanston, Ill.: Northwestern University Press, 1968); Wasby, *The Supreme Court in the Federal Judicial System*, 4th ed., 354.

65. Dolbeare, "The Public Views the Supreme Court," 208; Casey, "The Supreme Court and Myth," 392–93.

66. *National Law Journal* poll reported in Wasby, *The Supreme Court in the Federal Judicial System*, 4th ed., 355.

67. Marshall, *Public Opinion and the Supreme Court*, 139.

68. Murphy and Tanenhaus, "A Preliminary Mapping," 370. See also Robert Lehnen, *American Institutions, Political Opinion, and Public Policy* 138 (Hinsdale, Ill.: Dryden, 1976).

69. Tanenhaus and Murphy, "Patterns of Public Support," 31.

70. Adamany and Grossman, "Support for the Supreme Court as a National Policymaker," 411. As is typically the case, 62 percent could not name *any* decision they liked or disliked.

71. David Adamany, "The Supreme Court," in John B. Gates and Charles A. Johnson, eds.,

The American Courts: A Critical Assessment 19 (Washington, D.C.: Congressional Quarterly Press, 1991).

72. Gregory A. Caldeira, "Neither the Purse nor the Sword: Dynamics of Public Confidence in the Supreme Court," 80 *American Political Science Review* 1209, 1211 (1986).

73. Charles L. Black, Jr. *The People and the Court* (New York: Macmillan, 1960); Robert Dahl, "Decision-Making in a Democracy: The Supreme Court as a National Policy-Maker," 6 *Journal of Public Law* 279 (1957). Alexander Bickel also emphasized the Court's legitimacy-conferring role in *The Least Dangerous Branch* (Indianapolis, Ind.: Bobbs-Merrill 1962).

74. Adamany, "Legitimacy, Realigning Elections, and the Supreme Court"; Marshall, *Public Opinion and the Supreme Court*, 136–56; Murphy and Tanenhaus, "A Preliminary Mapping"; Walter F. Murphy and Joseph Tanenhaus, "Publicity, Public Opinion, and the Court," 84 *Northwestern University Law Review* 985 (1990).

75. Marshall, *Public Opinion and the Supreme Court*, 145–47.

76. Ibid. at 147–52.

77. Ibid. at 155.

78. Rosenberg, *The Hollow Hope.* Canon's contrary belief is that the Court's "cheerleading" *was* effective in the desegregation cases and, more generally, can be effective when it supports change rather than defends the status quo. However, as Canon himself acknowledges, this conclusion is based nearly exclusively on speculation and not on any empirical evidence. Bradley C. Canon, "The Supreme Court as a Cheerleader in Politico-Moral Disputes," 54 *Journal of Politics* 637 (1992).

79. Roy B. Flemming, John Bohte, and B. Dan Wood, "One Voice among Many: The Supreme Court's Influence on Attentiveness to Issues in the United States, 1947–1992," 41 *American Journal of Political Science* 1224 (1997); Valerie J. Hoekstra, "The Supreme Court and Opinion Change: An Experimental Study of the Court's Ability to Change Opinion," 23 *American Politics Quarterly* 109 (1995).

80. Timothy R. Johnson and Andrew D. Martin, "The Public's Conditional Response to Supreme Court Decisions," 92 *American Political Science Review* 299 (1998).

81. 301 U.S. 1 (1937).

82. Gregory A. Caldeira, "Public Opinion and the U.S. Supreme Court: FDR's Court-Packing Plan," 81 *American Political Science Review* 1141, 1149 (1987).

83. Ibid. at 1150.

84. Christopher B. Wlezien and Malcolm L. Goggin, "The Courts, Interest Groups, and Public Opinion about Abortion," 15 *Political Behavior* 381 (1993).

85. Larry R. Baas and Dan Thomas, "The Supreme Court and Policy Legitimation: Experimental Tests," 12 *American Politics Quarterly* 335 (1984).

86. Jeffrey J. Mondak, "Perceived Legitimacy of Supreme Court Decisions: Three Functions of Source Credibility," 12 *Political Behavior* 363 (1990).

87. Jeffrey J. Mondak, "Policy Legitimacy and the Supreme Court: The Sources and Contexts of Legitimation," 47 *Political Research Quarterly* 675, 690 (1994).

88. Charles H. Franklin and Liane C. Kosaki, "Republican Schoolmaster: The U.S. Supreme Court, Public Opinion, and Abortion," 83 *American Political Science Review* 751 (1989).

89. Ibid. at 759. Regarding the *negative* impact of lower federal court action on public opinion, see Benjamin I. Page, Robert Y. Shapiro, and Glenn Dempsey, "What Moves Public Opinion?" 81 *American Political Science Review* 23 (1987).

90. Rosenberg, *The Hollow Hope.*

91. As Caldeira points out, there are considerable methodological difficulties in testing for the Court's impact on public opinion. There may have been no pre- and postdecision surveys conducted regarding the Court's decisions, or the questions may be poorly or inappropriately worded in terms of testing for the Court's decisional impact. There are difficulties as well in controlling for other non-Court influences on public opinion. In addition, the Court does not always provide a "clear and constant stimulus"; its policies are subject to change or may be ambiguous. Finally, aggregate poll data may hide significant shifts among critical constituencies. "Courts and Public Opinion," 305–6.

92. Caldeira, "Neither the Purse nor the Sword," 1212.

93. Herbert Hirsch and Lewis Donohew, "A Note on Black-White Differences in Attitudes Toward the Supreme Court," 49 *Social Science Quarterly* 557 (1968).

94. Murphy and Tanenhaus, "A Preliminary Mapping," 377–80; Murphy, Tanenhaus, and Kastner, *Public Evaluations of Constitutional Courts.*

95. Murphy and Tanenhaus, "Publicity, Public Opinion, and the Court," 1002–4.

96. Jane Mansbridge and Katherine Tate, "Race Trumps Gender: The Thomas Nomination in the Black Community," 24 *PS: Political Science and Politics* 488 (1992); Lee Sigelman and James S. Todd, "Clarence Thomas, Black Pluralism, and Civil Rights Policy," 107 *Political Science Quarterly* 231 (1992); Gregory A. Caldeira and Charles E. Smith, Jr., "Campaigning for the Supreme Court: The Dynamics of Public Opinion on the Thomas Nomination," 58 *Journal of Politics* 655 (1996).

97. Roger Handberg and William S. Maddox, "Public Support for the Supreme Court in the 1970s," 10 *American Politics Quarterly* 333 (1982); Lee Sigelman, "Black and White Differences in Attitudes toward the Supreme Court: A Replication in the 1970s," 60 *Social Science Quarterly* 113 (1979).

98. James L. Gibson and Gregory A. Caldeira, "Blacks and the United States Supreme Court: Models of Diffuse Support," 54 *Journal of Politics* 1120, 1128–32 (1992).

99. Dolbeare and Hammond, "The Political Party Basis of Attitudes toward the Supreme Court"; Dean Jaros and Robert Roper, "The Supreme Court, Myth, Diffuse Support, Specific Support, and Legitimacy," 8 *American Politics Quarterly* 85 (1980); Kessel, "Public Perceptions of the Supreme Court"; Murphy and Tanenhaus, "The Goldwater Campaign"; Murphy and Tanenhaus, "A Preliminary Mapping"; Murphy, Tanenhaus, and Kastner, *Public Evaluations of Constitutional Courts*, 45–51; Gregory Casey, "Popular Perceptions of Supreme Court Rulings," 4 *American Politics Quarterly* 3, 25–29 (1976); Tanenhaus and Murphy "Patterns of Public Support." For a review of the evidence, see Caldeira, "Courts and Public Opinion," 319–26.

100. Dolbeare and Hammond, "The Political Party Basis of Attitudes toward the Supreme Court," 21–22. See also Hadley Cantril, *Public Opinion, 1935–1946* 148–51 (Princeton: Princeton University Press, 1951).

101. Dolbeare and Hammond, "The Political Party Basis of Attitudes toward the Supreme Court," 29–30.

102. Murphy, Tanenhaus, and Kastner, *Public Evaluations of Constitutional Courts.*

103. Ibid. at 50.

104. Caldeira and Gibson borrow Easton's definition of diffuse support: "a reservoir of favorable attitudes or good will that helps members to accept or tolerate outputs to which they are opposed or the effects of which they see as damaging to their wants." "The Etiology of Public Support for the Supreme Court," 63, citing David Easton, *A Systems Analysis of Political Life* 273 (New York: Wiley, 1965).

105. Caldeira and Gibson define specific support as consisting of "a set of attitudes toward an institution based upon the fulfillment of demands for particular policies or actions." "The Etiology of Public Support for the Supreme Court," 637. They argue that most studies claiming to study diffuse support are in fact measuring specific support. Adamany and Grossman, "Support for the Supreme Court"; Jaros and Roper, "The Supreme Court, Myth, Diffuse Support, Specific Support, and Legitimacy"; Kessel "Public Perceptions of the Supreme Court"; Murphy and Tanenhaus, "The Goldwater Campaign"; Murphy and Tanenhaus, "A Preliminary Mapping."

106. Reported in Caldeira, "Courts and Public Opinion," 322.

107. Daniels, "The Supreme Court and Its Publics," 658.

108. Caldeira and Gibson, "The Etiology of Public Support for the Supreme Court," 643.

109. Ibid. at 643–45.

110. Caldeira, "Neither the Purse nor the Sword."

111. Ibid. at 1223.

112. In their study of the New Jersey Supreme Court, Lehne and Reynolds did not find any change in public approval following a period of increased judicial activism and controversy. Richard Lehne and John Reynolds, "The Impact of Judicial Activism on Public Opinion," 22 *American Journal of Political Science* 896 (1978).

113. Caldeira, "Neither the Purse nor the Sword," 1222.

114. David G. Barnum, *The Supreme Court and American Democracy* 92–93, 281 (New York: St. Martin's Press, 1993).

115. In Marshall's study, the Court upheld 76 percent of federal statutes reviewed by the Court between 1935 and 1986, but only 49 percent of state and local laws. *Public Opinion and the Supreme Court*, 83–85.

116. Caldeira, "Neither the Purse nor the Sword," 1223.

117. Ibid. at 1223–24. See also Tanenhaus and Murphy, "Patterns of Public Support."

118. Caldeira and Smith, "Campaigning for the Supreme Court," 676.

119. Caldeira, "Neither the Purse nor the Sword," 1210.

120. Ibid.; Tanenhaus and Murphy, "Patterns of Public Support."

121. Casey, "The Supreme Court and Myth."

122. Caldeira and Gibson, "The Etiology of Public Support for the Supreme Court."

123. Ibid.

124. Most importantly, see Bradley C. Canon, "Courts and Policy: Compliance, Implementation, and Impact," in John B. Gates and Charles A. Johnson, eds. *The American Courts: A Critical Assessment* 435 (Washington, D.C.: Congressional Quarterly Press, 1991); and Rosenberg, *The Hollow Hope.* A more complete listing of judicial impact studies has been provided in the endnotes to chapters 3 and 5.

125. As Martin Shapiro noted with regard to a number of Warren and Burger Court policies, "Few American politicians . . . would care to run on a platform of desegregation, pornography, abortion, and the 'coddling' of criminals." Martin M. Shapiro, "The Supreme Court: From Warren to Burger," in Anthony King, ed., *The New American Political System* 181 (Washington, D.C.: American Enterprise Institute, 1978).

126. David G. Barnum, "The Supreme Court and Public Opinion: Judicial Decision-Making in the Post-New Deal Period," 47 *Journal of Politics* 652 (1985).

127. Ibid. See also Barnum, *The Supreme Court and American Democracy*, 283.

128. William Mishler and Reginald S. Sheehan, "The Supreme Court as a Countermajoritarian Institution? The Impact of Public Opinion on Supreme Court Decisions," 87 *American Political Science Review* 87, 97 (1993). After 1981, the Court failed to follow its earlier pattern; it did not reflect or respond to the public's resurgent liberalism and, instead, became

more conservative. As discussed in chapter 4, this was due in part to the Senate's failure to challenge or reject the conservative appointments of Reagan and Bush.

129. Thomas R. Marshall and Joseph Ignagni, "Supreme Court and Public Support for Rights Claims," 78 *Judicature* 146, 148 (1994).

130. James A. Stimson, Michael B. Mackuen, and Robert S. Erikson, "Dynamic Representation," 89 *American Political Science Review* 543, 555 (1995).

131. Marshall, *Public Opinion and the Supreme Court*, 78. See Caldeira's criticism of Marshall's "data and conceptualization" in "Courts and Public Opinion," 315, and in his book review in the *American Political Science Review* 84 (1989): 663–64.

132. Alan Monroe, "Consistency between Public Preferences and National Policy Decisions," 7 *American Politics Quarterly* 3 (1979); Benjamin I. Page and Robert Y. Shapiro, "Effects of Public Opinion on Policy," 77 *American Political Science Review* 175 (1983).

133. Marshall, *Public Opinion and the Supreme Court*, 80.

134. Mishler and Sheehan argue that the Court's majoritarianism is due both to the politicized appointment process (i.e., the "Dahl-Funston thesis") and to the Court directly and independently responding to public opinion shifts. "The Supreme Court as a Countermajoritarian Institution?" However, Norpoth and Segal persuasively refute the latter argument; instead, they argue, the Court's majoritarianism is a function solely of the appointment process. Helmut Norpoth and Jeffrey A. Segal, "Popular Influence on Supreme Court Decisions," 88 *American Political Science Review* 711 (1994). For more recent studies arguing that the Court does in fact respond directly to public opinion (though not greatly, immediately, or uniformly for all issues and all justices), see William Mishler and Reginald S. Sheehan, "Popular influence on Supreme Court Decisions: A Response to Helmut Norpoth and Jeffrey A. Segal," 88 *American Political Science Review* 716 (1994); Michael W. Link, "Tracking Public Mood in the Supreme Court: Cross-Time Analysis of Criminal Procedure and Civil Rights Cases," 48 *Political Research Quarterly* 61 (1995); Roy B. Flemming and B. Dan Wood, "The Public and the Supreme Court: Individual Justice Responsiveness to American Policy Moods," 41 *American Journal of Political Science* 468 (1997); and Stimson et al., "Dynamic Representation," finding limited support for both of these "pathways" of public-opinion influence.

135. Marshall, *Public Opinion and the Supreme Court*, 82–83.

136. Ibid. at 83–85.

137. When relevant poll data existed, federal law was consistent with public opinion 72 percent of the time, compared to only 58 percent of the time for state/local laws. Ibid. at 83, 85.

138. Ibid. at chap. 7.

139. Ibid. at 181.

140. Ibid. at 192. See also Barry Friedman, "Dialogue and Judicial Review," 91 *Michigan Law Review* 577 (1993); Thomas R. Marshall, "Public Opinion and the Rehnquist Court," 74 *Judicature* 322 (1991); Steven A. Shull, Dennis W. Gleiber, and David Garland, "Ideological Congruence between the General Public and Government Institutions: The Case of Civil Rights" (paper presented at the 1991 Annual Meeting of the Western Political Science Association) (finding little congruence between ideological preferences on civil rights and civil rights policy, *except for* the Supreme Court and the general public).

141. Barnum, *The Supreme Court in American Democracy*, 280.

142. Marshall, *Public Opinion and the Supreme Court*, 192.

143. Marshall, *The Supreme Court and Public Opinion*; Casey, "Popular Perceptions of Supreme Court Rulings"; Dolbeare and Hammond, "The Political Party Basis of Attitudes toward the Supreme Court"; Caldeira, "Neither the Purse nor the Sword"; Murphy and Tanenhaus, "A Preliminary Mapping"; Tanenhaus and Murphy, "Patterns of Public Support"; Murphy, Tanenhaus, and Kastner *Public Evaluations of Constitutional Courts*. Gibson, Caldeira, and Baird argue that the Court is able to build public support and legitimacy, not by satisfying a national majority but "by developing support among a succession of minorities. . . . If different areas of policymaking please different constituents, then legitimacy is attainable through the cumulation of satisfied minorities." "On the Legitimacy of National High Courts," 356.

144. Adamany and Grossman, "Support for the Supreme Court as a National Policymaker"; Shapiro, "The Supreme Court: From Warren to Burger."

145. E.g., Mark Silverstein and Benjamin Ginsberg, "The Supreme Court and the New Politics of Judicial Power," 102 *Political Science Quarterly* 371 (1987). Bork agrees, though disapproves of the relationship. *The Tempting of America*, 77.

146. Adamany, "Legitimacy, Realigning Elections, and the Supreme Court"; Caldeira, "Neither the Purse nor the Sword"; Dolbeare and Hammond, "The Political Party Basis of Attitudes toward the Supreme Court."

147. Adamany and Grossman, "Legitimacy, Realigning Elections, and the Supreme Court"; Murphy, Tanenhaus, and Kastner, *Public Evaluations of Constitutional Courts*, 55–58; John Roche, "Judicial Self-Restraint," 49 *American Political Science Review* 762 (1955); Shapiro, "The Supreme Court: From Warren to Burger."

148. Roche, "Judicial Self-Restraint"; Adamany, "Legitimacy, Realigning Elections, and the Supreme Court"; Caldeira and Gibson, 660–61.

149. Barnum, "The Supreme Court and Public Opinion"; Shapiro, "The Supreme Court: From Warren to Burger."

150. Casey, "The Supreme Court and Myth"; Marshall, *The Supreme Court and Public Opinion*. However, as previously reported, Caldeira did find that when the Court overturned federal laws, this contributed to a decline in public confidence in the Court. "Neither the Purse nor the Sword.")

151. 341 U.S. 494 (1951).

152. Dolbeare and Hammond, "The Political Party Basis of Attitudes toward the Supreme Court," 21–22.

153. Similar reasons for why the Court needs to monitor public opinion are provided in Stimson et al., "Dynamic Representation," 555.

154. The recent trend away from appointing distinguished and highly experienced politicans to the Court may weaken the Court's capacity in this regard.

155. For evidence that Supreme Court justices are attentive to media coverage of the Court and its decisions, see David, *Decisions and Images*.

156. Adamany and Grossman, "Support for the Court as a National Policymaker."

157. Thurman Arnold, "Professor Hart's Theology," 73 *Harvard Law Review* 1298 (1960); William O. Douglas, "Stare Decisis," 49 *Columbia Law Review* 735 (1949); Alpheus T. Mason, "Myth and Reality in Supreme Court Decisions," 48 *Virginia Law Review* 1385 (1962); Arthur S. Miller, "Some Pervasive Myths about the United States Supreme Court," 10 *St. Louis University Law Journal* 153 (1965); Arthur S. Miller and Alan W. Scheflin, "The Power of the Supreme Court in the Age of the Positive State: A Preliminary Excursus, Part One: On Candor and the Court, or, Why Bamboozle the Natives," 1967 *Duke Law Journal* 273 (1967); Arthur S. Miller and Ronald F. Howell, "The Myth of Neutrality in Constitutional Adjudication," 27 *University of Chicago Law Review* 661 (1960).

158. Casey, "The Supreme Court and Myth," 410.

159. Martin M. Shapiro, "The Supreme Court and Constitutional Adjudication: Of Politics and Neutral Principles," 31 *George Washington Law Review* 587 (1963).

160. Ibid. at 589–90. Professor Levinson has pointed out to me that Shapiro's 1963 characterization of law professors as "cheerleaders for the Court" may no longer be true, with "alienated refugees from the sixties" being a more apt characterization today. However, the new generation of law professors, most particularly Critical Legal Studies scholars, does not advance the legitimacy crisis thesis. In fact, I think most would welcome such a crisis. Nonetheless, the assertion of a strong connection between the Court's apolitical orientation and its ongoing legitimacy and power is still frequently made by professors (e.g., Bork and Ely) who, I believe, share a profound admiration and concern for the Court.

161. Caldeira, "Children's Images of the Supreme Court," 868.

162. See chapter 1.

163. Caldeira, "Children's Images of the Supreme Court," 868.

164. Ibid.

165. Paul Brest "The Fundamental Rights Controversy: The Essential Contradictions of Normative Constitutional Scholarship," 90 *Yale Law Journal* 1063, 1106 (1981).

166. Michael Perry, *The Constitution, The*

Courts, and Human Rights: An Inquiry into the Legitimacy of Constitutional Policymaking by the Judiciary 102 (New Haven: Yale University Press, 1982).

167. Ibid. at 112–13.

168. Ibid. at 113–14.

169. As noted in chapter 3, what is curious is why Perry then grants Congress any role at all on such issues, such as his suggestion that it use its power to silence the Court via jurisdictional control.

CHAPTER 7

1. Alexander Bickel, *The Least Dangerous Branch: The Supreme Court at the Bar of Politics* (Indianapolis, Ind.: Bobbs-Merrill, 1962); Jesse H. Choper, *Judicial Review and the National Political Process: A Functional Reconsideration of the Role of the Supreme Court* (Chicago: University of Chicago Press, 1980).

I initially thought that Robert Bork might belong in this category. See Robert H. Bork, *The Tempting of America: The Political Seduction of the Law* 139–41 (New York: Free Press, 1990). For example, he does refer to the American political system as "Madisonian," in that it seeks to accommodate the conflicting principles of self-government and minority and individual rights. However, his view of American democracy is quite conventional since, in practical operation, his interpretive theory of "original understanding" does not often allow the majority will to be overridden. (E.g., "The Constitution . . . holds that we govern ourselves democratically, except on those occasions, few in number though crucially important, when the Constitution places a topic beyond the reach of majorities" [p. 153]).

2. Cass R. Sunstein, "Interest Groups in American Public Law," 38 *Stanford Law Review* 29 (1985).

3. Erwin Chemerinsky, "Foreword: The Vanishing Constitution," 103 *Harvard Law Review* 44 (1989).

4. Bruce Ackerman, *We the People: Foundations* (Cambridge: Harvard University Press, 1991). Ackerman's replacement—"dualist" democracy—is not without its problems, however. His revisionist account of American democracy asserts that there exists a dual or two-track system of lawmaking. "Normal" law-

making takes place on the "lower" track; it consists of those daily decisions made by government officials who are held accountable through periodic elections. Public interest will typically be low during these long periods, and representatives will be subjected to pressure from the more politically active and self-interested among us. However, those officials cannot violate the fundamental principles previously established during periods of "higher lawmaking," in which an aroused and active public passionately debates, institutions struggle, and then We the People approve momentous constitutional change. The people collectively enact our fundamental principles, after which (and under which) our representative institutions carry on the daily business of government. Ackerman finds only three periods of higher lawmaking—the Founding, Reconstruction, and the New Deal. While Ackerman's account of American democracy is superior to the simplistic monistic-majoritarian view, his view of its history as consisting almost entirely of "statutory valleys" and only a few "constitutional peaks" is overly rigid and unpersuasive. As Terrance Sandalow correctly notes, "Constitutional change, as the post-adoption history of the fourteenth amendment demonstrates, is the product of a far more fluid, complex process than Ackerman's conception of 'higher lawmaking' captures. The distinction he draws between 'constitutional politics' and 'normal politics' dichotomizes phenomena more appropriately represented as points along a continuum." Terrance Sandalow, "Abstract Democracy: A Review of Ackerman's *We the People*," 9 *Constitutional Commentary* 309, 324 (1992). Michael McConnell's alternative interpretation of constitutional moments in American history also illustrates the vagueness and manipulability of Ackerman's criteria for each type of lawmaking. "The Forgotten Constitutional Moment," 11 *Constitutional Commentary* 115 (1994).

Ackerman's theory of American democracy seems to me to give too much importance to constitutional moments and too little importance to what he refers to as "normal" politics; furthermore, it does not replace nor significantly add to two satisfactory theories of democratic politics and political change that already exist: pluralist theory and the theory of realigning elections.

5. John Hart Ely, *Democracy and Distrust: A Theory of Judicial Review* 7 (Cambridge: Harvard University Press, 1980).

6. Choper, *Judicial Review and the National Political Process*, 4.

7. Bickel, *The Least Dangerous Branch*, 16–17.

8. Ely, *Democracy and Distrust*, 4–5.

9. Choper, *Judicial Review and the National Political Process*, 6.

10. Michael J. Perry, *The Constitution, the Courts, and Human Rights: An Inquiry into the Legitimacy of Constitutional Policymaking by Judiciary* (New Haven: Yale University Press, 1982).

11. Ely, *Democracy and Distrust*.

12. Raoul Berger, *Government by Judiciary: The Transformation of the Fourteenth Amendment* (Cambridge: Harvard University Press, 1977).

13. Martin M. Shapiro, *Freedom of Speech: The Supreme Court and Judicial Review* 17 (Englewood Cliffs, N.J.: Prentice-Hall, 1966).

14. Ibid. at 25.

15. Robert A. Dahl, *A Preface to Democratic Theory* 125–31 (Chicago: University of Chicago Press, 1956).

16. Ibid. at 125.

17. For a good sampling of this voluminous literature, see Angus Campbell, Philip E. Converse, Warren E. Miller, and Donald E. Stokes, *The American Voter* (New York: Wiley, 1960); Philip E. Converse, "The Nature of Belief Systems in Mass Publics," in David E. Apter, ed., *Ideology and Discontent* 206 (New York: Free Press, 1964); Robert S. Erickson, Norman R. Luttbeg, and Kent L. Tedin, *American Public Opinion: Its Origins, Content, and Impact*, 4th ed. (New York: Macmillan, 1991); Lloyd A. Free and Hadley Cantril, *The Political Beliefs of Americans: A Study of Public Opinion* (New Brunswick, N.J.: Rutgers University Press, 1967); V.O. Key, Jr., *Public Opinion and American Democracy* (New York: Knopf, 1961); Robert E. Lane, *Political Ideology* (New York: Free Press, 1962); William Mayer, *The Changing American Mind: How and Why American Public Opinion Changed between 1960 and 1988* (Ann Arbor: University of Michigan Press, 1992); Herbert McCloskey and John Zaller, *The American Ethos: Public Attitudes toward Capitalism and Democracy* (Cambridge: Harvard University Press, 1984); W. Russell Neuman, *The Paradox of Mass Politics: Knowledge and Opinion in the American Electorate* (Cambridge: Harvard University Press, 1986); Norman H. Nie, Sidney Verba, and John R. Petrocik, *The Changing American Voter* (Cambridge: Harvard University Press, 1976); Robert Nisbet, "Popular Opinion versus Public Opinion," 41 *Public Interest* 167 (1975); Benjamin I. Page and Robert Y. Shapiro, *The Rational Public: Fifty Years of Trends in Americans' Policy Preferences* (Chicago: University of Chicago Press, 1992); Eric R. A. N. Smith, *The Unchanging American Voter* (Berkeley: University of California Press, 1989); James A. Stimson, *Public Opinion in America: Moods, Cycles, and Swings* (Boulder, Colo.: Westview Press, 1991); Jerry L. Yeric and John R. Todd, *Public Opinion: The Visible Politics*, 2d ed. (Itasca, Ill.: Peacock, 1989).

18. Paul Allen Beck, *Party Politics in America*, 8th ed. (New York: Longman, 1997); Cornelius P. Cotter and Bernard Hennessy, *Politics without Power: The National Party Committees* (New York: Atherton, 1964); Pendleton Herring, *The Politics of Democracy*, 2d ed. (New York: W. W. Norton and Co., 1965); William J. Keefe, *Parties, Politics, and Public Policy in America* (Washington, D.C.: Congressional Quarterly Press, 1991); V. O. Key, Jr., *Politics, Parties, and Pressure Groups*, 5th ed. (New York: Thomas Y. Crowell, 1964); V. O. Key, Jr., *Southern Politics in State and Nation* (New York: Knopf, 1949); Everett Carll Ladd, Jr., "Party Reform and the Public Interest," in A. James Reichley, ed., *Elections American Style* (Washington, D.C.: Brookings Institution Press, 1987); Clinton Rossiter, *Parties and Politics in America* (Ithaca: Cornell University Press, 1960); E. E. Schattschneider, *Party Government* (New York: Holt, Rinehart and Winston, 1942).

19. David Broder, *The Party's Over* (New York: Harper and Rowe, 1971); Walter Dean Burnham, *The Current Crisis in American Politics* (New York: Oxford University Press, 1982); Joseph Cooper and Louis Maisel, *Political Parties: Development and Decay* (Beverly Hills, Calif.: Sage Publications, 1978); William J. Crotty and Gary C. Jacobson, *American Parties in Decline* (Boston: Little, Brown, 1980); Leon Epstein, *Political Parties in the American Mold* (Madison: University of Wisconsin Press, 1986); John Haskell, *Fundamentally Flawed: Reforming Presidential Primaries* (Lanham, Md.: Rowman and Littlefield Publishers, 1996); L. Sandy Maisel, *The Parties Respond: Developments in the American Party System*, 2d ed. (Boulder, Colo.: Westview Press, 1994); Sidney M. Milkis, *The President*

and the Parties (New York: Oxford University Press, 1993); Helmut Norpoth and Jerrold Rusk, "Partisan Dealignment in the American Electorate," 76 *American Political Science Review* (1982); Nelson W. Polsby, *Consequences of Party Reform* (New York: Oxford University Press, 1983); Larry J. Sabato, *The Rise of Political Consultants* (New York: Basic Books, 1981); Byron Shafer, ed., *Beyond Realignment? Interpreting American Electoral Eras* (Madison: University of Wisconsin Press, 1991); Martin P. Wattenberg, *The Decline of American Political Parties, 1952–1988*, rev. ed. (Cambridge: Harvard University Press, 1990). For the alternate view that parties are not in serious decline, see Xandra Kayden and Eddie Mahe, Jr., *The Party Goes On: The Persistence of the Two-Party System in the United States* (New York: Basic Books, 1985); Gerald M. Pomper, *Party Renewal in America* (New York: Praeger, 1981); Larry J. Sabato, *The Party's Just Begun* (Glenview, Ill.: Scott, Foresman, 1988).

20. Jeffrey M. Berry, *The Interest Group Society*, 3d ed. (New York: Longman, 1997); Allan J. Cigler and Burdett A. Loomis, eds., *Interest Group Politics*, 4th ed. (Washington, D.C.: Congressional Quarterly Press, 1994); Mark P. Petracca, ed., *The Politics of Interests: Interest Groups Transformed* (Boulder, Colo.: Westview Press, 1992); Kay Lehman Schlozman and John T. Tierney, *Organized Interests and American Democracy* (New York: HarperCollins, 1981); Jack Walker, *Mobilizing Interest Groups in America* (Ann Arbor: University of Michigan Press, 1991).

21. Robert A. Dahl, *The New American Political (Dis)Order* (Berkeley: Institute of Governmental Studies Press, 1994).

22. For example, Bill Clinton won the presidency in both 1992 and 1996 without winning a majority of the popular vote. Additionally, the popular-vote winner lost the electoral vote count and, thus, the election in three presidential races—in 1824, 1876, and 1888.

23. Paul R. Abramson and John H. Aldrich, "The Decline of Electoral Participation in America," 76 *American Political Science Review* 502 (1982); Walter Dean Burnham, "The Turnout Problem," in A. James Reichley, ed., *Elections American Style* (Washington, D.C.: Brookings Institution, 1987); Everett Carll Ladd, Jr., *Where Have All the Voters Gone?* (New York: Norton, 1977); Frances Fox Piven and Richard Cloward, *Why Americans Don't Vote*

(New York: Pantheon, 1988); Howard L. Reiter, "Why Is Turnout Down?" 43 *Public Opinion Quarterly* 297 (1979); Steven J. Rosenstone and John Mark Hansen, *Mobilization, Participation, and Democracy in America* (New York: Macmillan, 1993); Ruy A. Teixeira, *The Disappearing American Voter* (Washington, D.C.: Brookings Institution, 1992); Ruy A. Teixeira, *Why Americans Don't Vote: Turnout Decline in the United States, 1960–1984* (Westport, Conn.: Greenwood Press, 1987); Raymond E. Wolfinger and Steven J. Rosenstone, *Who Votes?* (New Haven: Yale University Press, 1980).

24. Susan Welch John Gruhl, Michael Steinman, John Comer, and Jan P. Vermeer, *Understanding American Government*, 4th ed., 177 (Belmont, Calif.: West/Wadsworth, 1997); Robert Kuttner, "Why Americans Don't Vote," *New Republic* 19 (September 7, 1987).

25. Benjamin Ginsberg and Martin Shefter, *Politics by Other Means: The Declining Importance of Elections in America* 1 (New York: Basic Books, 1990).

26. Regarding the incumbency advantage, see John R. Alford and David W. Brady, "Personal and Partisan Advantage in U.S. Congressional Elections, 1846–1986," in Lawrence C. Dodd and Bruce I. Oppenheimer, eds., *Congress Reconsidered*, 4th ed., 153 (Washington, D.C.: Congressional Quarterly Press, 1989); John R. Alford and John R. Hibbing, "Increased Incumbency Advantage in the House," 43 *Journal of Politics* 1042 (1981); John A. Ferejohn, "On the Decline of Competition in Congressional Elections," 71 *American Political Science Review* 166 (1977); Morris P. Fiorina, "The Case of the Vanishing Marginals: The Bureaucracy Did It," 71 *American Political Science Review* 171 (1977); Morris Fiorina, *Congress: Keystone of the Washington Establishment*, 2d ed. (New Haven: Yale University Press, 1989); James C. Garand and Donald A. Gross, "Change in the Vote Margins for Congressional Elections: A Specification of Historical Trends," 78 *American Political Science Review* 17 (1984); Gary King and Andrew Gelman, "Systemic Consequences of Incumbency Advantage in U.S. House Elections," 35 *American Journal of Political Science* 110 (1991); David R. Mayhew, "Congressional Elections: The Case of The Vanishing Marginals," 6 *Polity* 295 (1974).

27. Ginsberg and Shefter, *Politics by Other Means*, 35. See also Benjamin Ginsberg and

Alan Stone, eds., *Do Elections Matter?* (Armonk, N.Y.: M. E. Sharpe, 1986). A different sort of critique emphasizes the pressures and consequent dangers of "the permanent election campaign." See Anthony King, *Running Scared: The Victory of Campaigning over Governing in America* (New York: Free Press, 1997).

28. Bruce Cain, John Ferejohn, and Morris Fiorina, *The Personal Vote: Constituency Service and Electoral Independence* (Cambridge: Harvard University Press, 1987); Richard F. Fenno, *Home Style: House Members and Their Districts* (Boston: Little, Brown, 1978); Fiorina, *Congress: Keystone of the Washington Establishment*, 2d ed.

29. Of course, this criticism is quite unfair since that is simply not how congressional elections are structured. No member of Congress is elected by "the nation." Each is elected to represent an individual district or state, and constituents give very high marks to their own representatives' performance in this regard.

30. Mark Bisnow, *In the Shadow of the Dome: Chronicles of a Capitol Hill Aide* (New York: William Morrow, 1990); Harrison W. Fox and Susan W. Hammond, *Congressional Staffs: The Invisible Force in American Lawmaking* (New York: Free Press, 1977); Michael J. Malbin, *Unelected Representatives: Congressional Staff and the Future of Representative Government* (New York: Basic Books, 1980); Michael J. Malbin, "Delegation, Deliberation, and the New Role of Congressional Staff," in Thomas E. Mann and Norman J. Ornstein, eds., *The New Congress* (Washington, D.C.: American Enterprise Institute, 1981).

31. Sarah A. Binder and Steven S. Smith, *Politics or Principle? Filibustering in the United States Senate* (Washington, D.C.: Brookings Institution Press, 1996). An increasingly common procedure is the "Senate hold." Rather than actually filibustering, a senator may place a "hold" on a bill, thereby requesting to be informed when the bill reaches the floor and implicitly threatening to filibuster when it does. Holds have been referred to as "silent filibusters." See Bill Dauster, "It's Not *Mr. Smith Goes to Washington*," *Washington Monthly* 34 (November 1996).

32. Herbert Alexander, *Financing Politics* (Washington, D.C.: Congressional Quarterly Press, 1992); Dan Clawson, Alan Neustadtl, and Denise Scott, *Money Talks: Corporate PACs and Political Influence* (New York: Basic Books, 1992); Richard Hall and Frank Wayman, "Buying Time: Moneyed Interests and the Mobilization of Bias in Congressional Committees," 84 *American Political Science Review* 797 (1990); Laura Langbein, "Money and Access," 48 *Journal of Politics* 1052 (1986); Gary C. Jacobson, "Parties and PACs in Congressional Elections," in Lawrence C. Dodd and Bruce I. Oppenheimer, eds., *Congress Reconsidered*, 6th ed. (Washington, D.C.: Congressional Quarterly Press, 1996); David B. Magleby and Candice J. Nelson, *The Money Chase: Congressional Campaign Finance Reform* (Washington, D.C.: Brookings Institution, 1990); Michael J. Malbin, ed., *Money and Politics in the United States* (Washington, D.C.: American Enterprise Institute, 1984); Larry J. Sabato, *PAC Power: Inside the World of Political Action Committees* (New York: Norton, 1984); Jean Reith Schroedel, "Campaign Contributions and Legislative Outcomes," 39 *Western Political Quarterly* 371 (1986); Frank J. Sorauf, *Money in American Elections* (Boston: Little, Brown, 1988); Frank J. Sorauf, *Inside Campaign Finance: Myths and Realities* (New Haven: Yale University Press, 1992); Philip M. Stern, *The Best Congress Money Can Buy* (New York: Pantheon, 1988).

33. For recent and more in-depth analysis of Congress, see R. Douglas Arnold, *The Logic of Congressional Action* (New Haven: Yale University Press, 1990); Roger H. Davidson, ed., *The Postreform Congress* (New York: St. Martin's Press, 1991); Roger H. Davidson and Walter J. Oleszek, *Congress and Its Members*, 5th ed. (Washington, D.C.: Congressional Quarterly Press, 1996); Lawrence C. Dodd and Bruce I. Oppenheimer, *Congress Reconsidered*, 6th ed. (Washington, D.C.: Congressional Quarterly Press, 1996); Linda Fowler and Robert McClure, *Political Ambition: Who Decides to Run for Congress?* (New Haven: Yale University Press, 1989); Allen D. Hertzke and Ronald M. Peters, Jr., eds., *The Atomistic Congress* (Armonk, N.Y.: M. E. Sharpe, 1992); Gary C. Jacobson, *The Politics of Congressional Elections*, 4th ed. (New York: Longman, 1997); Burdett Loomis, *The New American Politician* (New York: Basic Books, 1988); Thomas E. Mann and Norman J. Ornstein, *The New Congress* (Washington, D.C.: American Enterprise Institute, 1981); Leroy N. Rieselbach, *Congressional Reform: The Changing Modern Congress*

(Washington, D.C.: Congressional Quarterly Press, 1993); Barbara Sinclair, *The Transformation of the U.S. Senate* (Baltimore: Johns Hopkins University Press, 1989); Barbara Sinclair, *Unorthodox Lawmaking: New Legislative Processes in the U.S. Congress* (Washington, D.C.: Congressional Quarterly Press 1997); Steven Smith, *The American Congress*, 2d ed. (Boston: Houghton Mifflin, 1995); James A. Thurber and Roger H. Davidson, *Remaking Congress: Change and Stability in the 1990s* (Washington, D.C.: Congressional Quarterly Press, 1995).

34. Bruce Buchanan, *The Citizen's Presidency* (Washington, D.C.: Congressional Quarterly Press, 1986); Bruce Buchanan, *Renewing Presidential Politics* (Lanham, Md.: Rowman and Littlefield Publishers, 1996); Jeffrey E. Cohen, *Presidential Responsiveness and Public Policy Making* (Ann Arbor: University of Michigan Press 1997); George Edwards, *The Public Presidency* (New York: St. Martin's Press, 1983); Paul Brace and Barbara Hinckley, *Follow the Leader: Opinion Polls and the Modern Presidents* (Boulder, Colo.: Basic Books, 1993); Samuel Kernell, *Going Public: New Strategies of Presidential Leadership*, 3d ed. (Washington, D.C.: Congressional Quarterly Press, 1997); Theodore J. Lowi, *The Personal President: Power Invested, Promise Unfulfilled* (Ithaca, N.Y.: Cornell University Press, 1985); Edward Kearney, ed., *Dimensions of the Modern Presidency* (St. Louis, Mo.: Forum Press, 1981); Nelson Polsby and Aaron Wildavsky, *Presidential Elections: Contemporary Strategies of American Electoral Politics*, 9th ed. (Chatham, N.J.: Chatham House, 1995); Jeffrey K. Tulis, *The Rhetorical Presidency* (Princeton: Princeton University Press, 1987).

35. Theodore J. Lowi and Benjamin Ginsberg, *American Government: Freedom and Power*, 3d ed., 229 (New York: W. W. Norton, 1994). See also Arthur M. Schlesinger, Jr., *The Imperial Presidency* (Boston: Houghton Mifflin, 1973).

36. Robert A. Dahl, "Myth of the Presidential Mandate," 105 *Political Science Quarterly* 355 (1990).

37. Ibid. at 364–65; Thomas Ferguson and Joel Rogers, "The Myth of America's Turn to the Right," in Allan J. Cigler and Burdett A. Loomis, eds., *American Politics: Classic and Contemporary Readings* 198 (Boston: Houghton Mifflin, 1989).

38. Harold M. Barger, *The Impossible Presidency* (Glenview, Ill.: Scott, Foresman, 1984); Larry Berman, *The New American Presidency* (New York: HarperCollins, 1987); James MacGregor Burns, *The Power to Lead: The Crisis of the American Presidency* (New York: Simon and Schuster, 1984); Bert A. Rockman, *The Leadership Question* (New York: Praeger, 1984); Thomas E. Cronin, *Inventing the Presidency* (Lawrence: University Press of Kansas, 1989); Jeff Fishel, *Presidents and Promises* (Washington, D.C.: Congressional Quarterly Press, 1986); Richard E. Neustadt, *Presidential Power and the Modern Presidents* (New York: Free Press, 1990); Richard Rose, *The Postmodern President*, 2d ed. (Chatham, N.J.: Chatham House Publishers, 1991); Aaron Wildavsky, *The Beleaguered Presidency* (New Brunswick, N.J.: Transaction Books, 1991).; James A. Thurber, ed., *Rivals for Power* (Washington, D.C.: Congressional Quarterly Press, 1996); Charles O. Jones, *The Presidency in a Separated System* (Washington D.C.: Brookings Institution Press, 1994).

39. These limitations on presidential power are much greater in domestic as compared to foreign policymaking.

40. Lowi and Ginsberg, *American Government*, 257.

41. John P. Burke, *The Institutional Presidency* (Baltimore: Johns Hopkins University Press, 1992); Thomas E. Cronin, "The Swelling of the Presidency: Can Anyone Reverse the Tide?" in Peter Woll, ed., *American Government: Readings and Cases*, 8th ed. (Boston: Little Brown, 1984); Arnold J. Miltsner, ed., *Politics and the Oval Office* (San Francisco: Institute for Contemporary Studies, 1981); Terry Moe, "The Political Presidency," in John Chubb and Paul E. Peterson, eds., *The New Direction in American Politics* (Washington, D.C.: Brookings Institution Press, 1985); Bradley Patterson, *The Ring of Power: The White House Staff and Its Expanding Role* (New York: Basic Books, 1988).

42. Thomas R. Marshall, *Public Opinion and the Supreme Court* (Boston: Unwin Hyman, 1989).

43. Choper, *Judicial Review and the National Political Process*, 25.

44. Bickel, *The Least Dangerous Branch*, 17.

45. Both Simon and Barnard argue that in organizations, the typical form of the authority relationship between hierarchical superi-

ors and their subordinates is one in which the superior takes care to issue only those orders that subordinates are likely to obey. Such commands can be said to lie within the subordinates' "zone of acceptance" (Simon) or "zone of indifference" (Barnard)—that range of commands which are automatically obeyed, rather than consciously evaluated by the recipient for their correctness or acceptability. Chester I. Barnard, *The Functions of the Executive* (Cambridge: Harvard University Press, 1938); Herbert A. Simon, *Administrative Behavior*, 3d ed. (New York: Free Press, 1976).

46. Choper, *Judicial Review and the National Political Process*, 38.

47. Bickel, *The Least Dangerous Branch*, 18.

48. Ibid.

49. Ibid. at 19. For Choper's similar response, see *Judicial Review and the National Political Process*, 44–45.

50. Choper, *Judicial Review and the National Political Process*, 26. Subsequent page references are given parenthetically in text.

51. Some neutralist scholars who have provided similar analysis, include Ely, *Democracy and Distrust*; John Agresto, *The Supreme Court and Constitutional Democracy* (Ithaca: Cornell University Press, 1984); and Perry, *The Constitution, the Courts, and Human Rights* (although he believes that congressional control of the Court's appellate jurisdiction *is* effective).

52. Robert A. Dahl, Pluralist Democracy in the United States 455–56 (Chicago: Rand McNally, 1967). Similarly, and more generally, John Gibbons notes that "[a] major difficulty with identifying enforcement of majority will . . . is the impossibility, in the real world, of determining that will at any moment in time, in any social organization larger than a family." John J. Gibbons, "Keynote Address: Constitutional Adjudication and Democratic Theory" (symposium) 56 *New York University Law Review* 260 (1981).

53. Dahl, *Pluralist Democracy in the United States*, 132.

54. Douglass Cater, *Power in Washington* (New York: Vintage Books, 1964); J. Leiper Freeman, *The Political Process* (New York: Random House, 1965). See also Hugh Heclo, "Issue Networks and the Executive Establishment," in Anthony King, ed., *The New American*

Political System 87 (Washington, D.C.: American Enterprise Institute, 1979).

55. Choper, *Judicial Review and the National Political Process*, 48.

56. As discussed in chapter 5, Congress does in fact respond frequently and in a variety of ways to Supreme Court decisions.

57. See especially Gerald N. Rosenberg, "Judicial Independence and the Reality of Political Power," 54 *Review of Politics* 369 (1992).

58. Gerald N. Rosenberg, *The Hollow Hope: Can Courts Bring about Social Change?* (Chicago: University of Chicago Press, 1991).

59. Choper, *Judicial Review and the National Political Process*, 58.

60. Ibid.

61. Bickel, *The Least Dangerous Branch*, 19.

62. The neutralists argue that the Court's statutory review role is not problematic, as its interpretations can be corrected through ordinary legislation. Correcting its constitutional interpretations, on the other hand, necessitates the use of the amendment process, requiring much more than a legislative act or simply majority support. However, this both underestimates the difficulties involved in overturning the Court's statutory interpretations—mobilizing and translating sufficient opposition into legislative action—and exaggerates the difficulties in affecting or altering the Court's constitutional policies (as discussed in chapters 4 and 5). The distinction is thus more theoretical than real.

63. Bickel, *The Least Dangerous Branch*, 18.

64. Ely, *Democracy and Distrust*, 4.

65. Martin M. Shapiro, *Law and Politics in the Supreme Court* 46 (New York: Macmillan, 1964).

66. Ibid. at 46. For a similar argument, see Chemerinsky, "The Vanishing Constitution," 77, 87.

67. Those critically responsible for the development and defense of pluralist theory include: Arthur F. Bentley, *The Process of Government* (Chicago: University of Chicago Press, 1908); Dahl, *A Preface to Democratic Theory*; Dahl, *Pluralist Democracy in the United States*; Robert A. Dahl, *Who Governs?* (New Haven: Yale University Press, 1961); Robert A. Dahl and Charles E. Lindblom, *Politics, Economics, and Welfare* (New York: Harper, 1953); Herring, *The Politics of Democracy*; Nelson W.

Polsby, *Community Power and Political Theory*, 2d ed. (New Haven: Yale University Press, 1980); David B. Truman, *The Governmental Process*, 2d ed. (New York: Alfred A. Knopf, 1971).

68. *The Federalist, No. 10*, at 77 (James Madison) (New York: New American Library, 1961).

69. Ibid. at 77–79.

70. Of course, the Framers' preoccupation with majorities was also a logical product of the Framers' own vulnerable minority status as members of the intellectual and economic elite. For an exposition of this view, see Charles A. Beard, *An Economic Interpretation of the Constitution of the United States* (New York: Macmillan Publishing Co., 1913). For an opposing view, see Robert E. Brown, *Charles Beard and the Constitution: A Critical Analysis of "An Economic Interpretation of the Constitution"* (Princeton: Princeton University Press, 1956); John P. Roche, "The Founding Fathers: A Reform Caucus in Action," 55 *American Political Science Review* 799 (1961).

71. "If a faction consists of less than a majority, relief is supplied by the republican principle, which enables the majority to defeat its sinister views by regular vote." *The Federalist No. 10*, 80.

72. Ibid. at 81. Empirical evidence supports this view that direct democracy lends itself to majority tyranny. Gamble's study of "antiminority" civil rights initiatives and referendums found that they "experience extraordinary electoral success." Barbara S. Gamble, "Putting Civil Rights to a Popular Vote," 41 *American Journal of Political Science* 245 (1997).

73. The effect of a republic, as compared to a pure democracy, is "to refine and enlarge the public views by passing them through the medium of a chosen body of citizens, whose wisdom may best discern the true interest of their country and whose patriotism and love of justice will be least likely to sacrifice it to temporary or partial considerations." *The Federalist No. 10*, 82.

74. Ibid. at 82–84.

75. A Bill of Rights was not, however, part of the original constitutional plan. The reason was not because the Framers did not wish to protect individual rights and liberties. Rather, such a listing of those rights was seen as unnecessary. Instead, structural fragmenta-tion was seen as quite sufficient to protect a broad range of individual liberties. See Roche, "The Founding Fathers." See also Leonard W. Levy, "The Original Constitution as a Bill of Rights," 9 *Constitutional Commentary* 163 (1992).

76. Martin Landau, "Redundancy, Rationality, and the Problem of Duplication and Overlap," 29 *Public Administration Review* 346 (1969).

77. Dahl, *Pluralist Democracy in the United States*, 327–28.

78. Ibid. at 329.

79. Ibid. at 328–29.

80. Ibid. at 329.

81. Dahl, "Myth of the Presidential Mandate."

82. See also Nelson Polsby, "Presidential Cabinet Making: Lessons for the Political System," 93 *Political Science Quarterly* 15 (1978). Polsby argues that legitimacy is not conferred in the United States only upon the president, our single national leader, every four years, thus delegitimizing all other leaders (as Nixon believed). In contrast to this plebiscitary model, he presents the more accurate "Federalist" model, in which the legitimacy of political leaders and their decisions is conferred continuously and in diverse ways.

83. In the early part of his career, Dahl seemed to be a defender of American democracy and other capitalist-democratic systems. E.g., see *A Preface to Democratic Theory, Pluralist Democracy in the United States, Who Governs?* Dahl has since become more of a critic of such democracies, expressing egalitarian concerns and what might be termed socialist sympathies. E.g., see *Democracy, Liberty, and Equality* (New York: Oxford University Press, 1986); *Dilemmas of Pluralist Democracy* (New Haven: Yale University Press, 1982); "On Removing Certain Impediments to Democracy in the United States," 92 *Political Science Quarterly* 1 (1977); "What Is Political Equality? A Response" 26 *Dissent* 363 (1979).

84. Peter Bachrach, *The Theory of Democratic Elitism* (Boston: Little, Brown, 1967); Peter Bachrach and Morton S. Baratz, "Decisions and Nondecisions: An Analytical Framework," 57 *American Political Science Review* 632 (1963); Peter Bachrach and Morton S. Baratz, "The Two Faces of Power," 56 *American Political Science Review* 947 (1962); William E. Connolly,

ed., *The Bias of Pluralism* (New York: Atherton Press, 1969); G. William Domhoff, *Who Rules America Now?* (Englewood Cliffs, N.J.: Prentice-Hall, 1983); Thomas R. Dye, *Who's Running America?* (Englewood Cliffs, N.J.: Prentice-Hall, 1990); Floyd Hunter, *Community Power Structure* (Chapel Hill: University of North Carolina Press, 1953); Steven Lukes, *Power: A Radical View* (London: Macmillan, 1974); C. Wright Mills, *The Power Elite* (New York: Oxford University Press, 1956). More moderate critics of pluralist theory include: Charles Lindblom, *Politics and Markets* (New York: Basic Books, 1977); Theodore J. Lowi, *The End of Liberalism*, 2d ed. (New York: W. W. Norton, 1979); Grant McConnell, *Private Power and American Politics* (New York: Alfred A. Knopf, 1966); E. E. Schattschneider, *The Semi-Sovereign People* (New York: Holt, Rinehart and Winston, 1960). For a thorough treatment of the different meanings and criticisms of pluralism, see Polsby, *Community Power and Political Theory*, 2d ed.

85. Schattschneider, *The Semi-Sovereign People*, 35.

86. Clement E. Vose, *Caucasians Only: The Supreme Court, the NAACP, and the Restrictive Covenant Cases* (Berkeley: University of California Press, 1959); David R. Manwaring, *Render unto Caesar: The Flag Salute Controversy* (Chicago: University of Chicago Press, 1962).

87. Research regarding what *motivates* interest groups to litigate is limited, but suggests that there are a variety of different motivating factors, including but not limited to policy opposition from other groups and institutions. See Lee Epstein's discussion in "Courts and Interest Groups," in John B. Gates and Charles A. Johnson, eds. *The American Courts: A Critical Assessment* 343–45 (Washington, D.C.: Congressional Quarterly Press, 1991).

88. Epstein, "Courts and Interest Groups," 335, 350–54. See also Lawrence Baum, *The Supreme Court*, 3d ed., 79–88 (Washington, D.C.: Congressional Quarterly Press, 1989); Susan Behuniak-Long, "Friendly Fire: Amici Curiae and *Webster* v. *Reproductive Health Services*," 74 *Judicature* 261 (1991); Robert Bradley and Paul Gardner, "Underdogs, Upperdogs, and the Use of the Amicus Brief: Trends and Explanations," 10 *Justice System Journal* 78 (1985); Gregory A. Caldeira and John R. Wright, "Amici Curiae before the Supreme Court: Who Partici-

pates, When, and How Much?" 52 *Journal of Politics* 782 (1990); Karen O'Connor and Lee Epstein, "An Appraisal of Hakman's 'Folklore,'" 16 *Law and Society Review* 701 (1982); Karen O'Connor and Lee Epstein, *Public Interest Law Groups* (Westport, Conn.: Greenwood Press, 1989).

89. Epstein, "Courts and Interest Groups," 358.

90. This was Cortner's thesis in Richard C. Cortner, "Strategies and Tactics of Litigants in Constitutional Cases," 17 *Journal of Public Law* 287 (1968). In response, see the sources listed above, as well as Lee Epstein, *Conservatives in Court* (Knoxville: University of Tennessee Press, 1985); Karen O'Connor and Lee Epstein, "The Rise of Conservative Interest Group Litigation," 45 *Journal of Politics* 479 (1983).

91. Epstein, "Courts and Interest Groups," 354, citing the analysis of Kay Lehman Schlozman and John T. Tierney, "Washington Pressure Group Activity in a Decade of Change," 45 *Journal of Politics* 351 (1983).

92. Epstein, "Courts and Interest Groups," 354.

93. Caldeira and Wright, "Amici Curiae before the Supreme Court," 802–3. Subsequent page reference will be given parenthetically in the text.

94. Epstein, "Courts and Interest Groups," 354.

95. Ibid.

96. Reginald S. Sheehan, "Governmental Litigants, Underdogs, and Civil Liberties: A Reassessment of a Trend in Supreme Court Decisionmaking," 45 *Western Political Quarterly* 27 (1992); Reginald S. Sheehan, William Mishler, and Donald R. Songer, "Ideology, Status, and the Differential Success of Direct Parties before the Supreme Court," 86 *American Political Science Review* 464 (1992); S. Sidney Ulmer, "Governmental Litigants, Underdogs, and Civil Liberties in the Supreme Court: 1903–1968 Terms," 47 *Journal of Politics* 899 (1985). See also Kevin T. McGuire and Gregory A. Caldeira, "Lawyers, Organized Interests, and the Law of Obscenity: Agenda Setting in the Supreme Court," 87 *American Political Science Review* 717 (1993), regarding the success of libertarian groups.

97. Stanton Wheeler, Bliss Cartwright, Robert Kagan, and Lawrence Friedman, "Do

the 'Haves' Come Out Ahead? Winning and Losing in State Supreme Courts, 1870–1970," 21 *Law and Society Review* 403 (1987).

98. Donald R. Songer and Reginald S. Sheehan, "Who Wins on Appeal? Upperdogs and Underdogs in the United States Courts of Appeals," 36 *American Journal of Political Science* 235 (1992).

99. Manwaring, *Render unto Caesar.*

100. Vose, *Caucasians Only;* Richard Kluger, *Simple Justice* (New York: Knopf, 1976).

101. Michael Meltsner, *Cruel and Unusual: The Supreme Court and Capital Punishment* (New York: Random House, 1973).

102. Susan E. Lawrence, *The Poor in Court* (Princeton: Princeton University Press, 1990).

103. James A. Stimson Michael B. Mackuen, and Robert S. Erikson, "Dynamic Representation," 89 *American Political Science Review* 543, 558 (1995).

104. Similarly, after Reagan's election, environmental groups were forced to return to the courts to insure protection for past political bargains as represented by laws still in force such as the Clean Air Act. Reagan's "mandate" to weaken pollution control efforts or at least to make government regulation more sensitive to the costs imposed on business was one that quite legitimately was tested politically, and the courts played an important role here.

105. John Roche's point that such opposition is rare and that the Court consequently is given "considerable room for maneuver" is of course well taken. He argues that the Court's power

> is a consequence of that fragmentation of political power which is normal in the United States. . . . For complex social and institutional reasons, there are few issues in the United States on which cohesive majorities exist. If, for example, the Court strikes down a controversial decision of the Federal Power Commission, it will be supported by a substantial bloc of congressmen; if it supports the FPC's decision, it will also receive considerable congressional support. . . . Either way it decides the case, there is no possibility that Congress will exact any vengeance on the Court.

Yet Roche does acknowledge that "when monolithic majorities do exist on issues, the Court is likely to resort to judicial self-restraint." "Judicial Self-Restraint," 771.

CHAPTER 8

1. Alexander Bickel, *The Least Dangerous Branch: The Supreme Court at the Bar of Politics* 40 (Indianapolis, Ind.: Bobbs-Merrill, 1962).

2. John Hart Ely, *Democracy and Distrust: A Theory of Judicial Review* (Cambridge: Harvard University Press, 1980).

3. Jesse H. Choper, *Judicial Review and the National Political Process: A Functional Reconsideration of the Role of the Supreme Court* (Chicago: University of Chicago Press, 1980).

4. Bickel, *The Least Dangerous Branch.*

5. Michael Perry, *The Constitution, the Courts, and Human Rights: An Inquiry into the Legitimacy of Constitutional Policymaking by the Judiciary* (New Haven: Yale University Press, 1982.)

6. Laurence H. Tribe, *American Constitutional Law,* 2d ed. (Mineaola, N.Y.: Foundation Press, 1988).

7. Ely is an exception. He is profoundly skeptical of the moral superiority of judges. However, he *is* convinced of their superiority (and that of lawyers generally) with regard to issues of participation and fair treatment. *Democracy and Distrust.*

8. S. Sidney Ulmer, "Government Litigants, Underdogs, and Civil Liberties in the Supreme Court: 1903–1968 Terms," 47 *Journal of Politics* 899 (1985). Included in Ulmer's category of underdog litigants are African Americans, African American organizations, labor unions and their members, aliens, criminal defendants, subversives, and subversive organizations.

9. Reginald S. Sheehan, "Governmental Litigants, Underdogs, and Civil Liberties: A Reassessment of a Trend in Supreme Court Decisionmaking," 45 *Western Political Quarterly* 27, 31–32 (1992).

10. This is where the Skeptics err. As discussed in chapter 3, proponents of provisional review recognize judicial subjectivity and the possibility of judicial error and accordingly welcome political checks on judicial decisionmaking. However, they still insist that the Court's special role or mission is to derive from the Constitution its substantive moral content, and they insist that the justices are better equipped than legislators to do so.

Thus, rather than being one more step in the policy process that has value in and of itself, the Skeptics insist that the Court's contribution must be the elucidation of given moral principles.

11. See my discussion in "The Virtues of 'Value Clarity' in Constitutional Decisionmaking," 55 *Ohio State Law Journal* 1079 (1994).

12. McCloskey has made a similar point. Robert G. McCloskey, *The American Supreme Court* (Chicago: University of Chicago Press, 1960).

13. 491 U.S. 397 (1989).

14. 494 U.S. 872 (1990).

15. Grey would also welcome a "downsizing" of the judicial role: "The truth is that there is just enough of a case for the legitimacy of supplemental judicial review to convince those of us who already believe that, on the whole, the practice produces somewhat better results than would occur in its absence. This modest precedential defense at least does not oversell the product by presupposing, with little justification, that our political life would be both very different and very much worse than it is were it not for judicial review." Thomas C. Grey, "The Constitution as Scripture," 37 *Stanford Law Review* 1, 20 (1984).

16. Nelson W. Polsby, "Legislatures," in Fred I. Greenstein and Nelson W. Polsby, eds., *Handbook of Political Science*, vol. 5 (Reading, Mass.: Addison-Wesley Publishing, 1975).

17. Robert A. Dahl, *A Preface to Democratic Theory* 132 (Chicago: University of Chicago Press, 1956).

18. According to the ideal model of responsible party government, parties take clear and contrasting positions on issues and, through party discipline, force their members to adopt those positions and vote according to them if elected. Thus, when a majority votes a party into power, it has direct, clear, and specific implications for government policy.

19. This brief section was first published in Peretti, "The Virtues of 'Value Clarity'."

20. V. O. Key, *The Responsible Electorate* 2 (Cambridge: Harvard University Press, 1966).

21. See Martin M. Shapiro, *Freedom of Speech: The Supreme Court and Judicial Review* chap. 1 (Englewood Cliffs, N.J.: Prentice-Hall, 1966).

22. The Court's use of its various (and quite flexible) justiciability doctrines—standing, ripeness, mootness, political questions—constitutes a primary tool for doing so, i.e., for selectively and prudently intervening in ongoing political disputes.

23. The Framers expected that minority tyranny would not be a problem, as the majority could always outvote or outmuscle any minority. "If a faction consists of less than a majority, relief is supplied by the republican principle, which enables the majority to defeat its sinister views by regular vote." *The Federalist No. 10* (James Madison) (New York: New American Library ed., 1961). Given the numerous obstacles to majority organization and power, however, minority tyranny is not an uncommon occurrence in American politics.

24. Richard B. Stewart, "The Reformation of American Administrative Law," 88 *Harvard Law Review* 1669 (1978).

25. For example, *Adarand Constructors, Inc. v. Pena*, 515 U.S. 200 (1995).

26. However, the Court can use its case selection discretion to choose which "stories" best suit its policy objectives. For example, to advance its desire for greater fairness in the criminal justice system and greater protection for criminal suspects, the Warren Court would select cases in which police abuse was particularly severe and outrageous. The Burger Court, on the other hand, was more likely to select cases in which the crime was particularly heinous, guilt irrefutable, and police misconduct relatively minor. This served its policy goal of cutting back on some of those protections extended to the accused by the Warren Court.

27. Robert H. Mnookin, *In the Interest of Children: Advocacy, Law Reform, and Public Policy* (New York: W. H. Freeman and Co., 1985).

28. 431 U.S. 816 (1977).

29. David L. Chambers and Michael S. Wald, "*Smith* v. *Offer*," in Mnookin, *In the Interest of Children*.

30. Ibid. at 147.

31. Ibid. at 116.

32. Stephen D. Sugarman, "*Roe* v. *Norton*: Coerced Maternal Cooperation," in Mnookin, *In the Interest of Children*.

33. 443 U.S. 622 (1979).

34. Robert H. Mnookin, "*Bellotti* v. *Baird*: A

Hard Case," in Mnookin, ed., *In the Interest of Children*.

35. As the authors note, this is to be expected given the type of decision facing judges. If they find that a pregnant minor *is* mature, she is permitted to make her own decision regarding an abortion. If a pregnant minor is found to be too immature even to make a decision as to whether to abort, it is highly unlikely that a judge would then force that immature minor to give birth and raise the child.

36. See my discussion in "Restoring the Balance of Power: The Struggle for Control of the Supreme Court," 20 *Hastings Constitutional Law Quarterly* 69 (1992).

37. For a fuller discussion, see Peretti, "The Virtues of 'Value Clarity.' "

38. Mark Silverstein and Benjamin Ginsberg, "The Supreme Court and the New Politics of Judicial Power," 102 *Political Science Quarterly* 371 (1987).

39. Ibid. at 387.

40. As noted in chapter 4, when asked why he wished to serve on the Court, Bork replied that it would be an "intellectual feast." *Nomination of Robert H. Bork to be Associate Justice of the Supreme Court of the United States: Hearings before the Senate Committee on the Judiciary*, 100th Congress, 1st session, 511 (1987).

41. See Alexander Bickel, *The Supreme Court and the Idea of Progress* (New Haven: Yale University Press, 1978).

42. Bruce Ackerman makes the same point in *We the People: Foundations* (Cambridge: Harvard University Press, 1991).

43. See Mary Ann Glendon, *Abortion and Divorce in Western Law* (Cambridge: Harvard University Press, 1987).

44. Ibid. at 34.

45. Ibid.

46. E.g., *Webster* v. *Reproductive Health Services*, 492 U.S. 490 (1989); *Planned Parenthood of Southeastern Pennsylvania* v. *Casey*, 505 U.S. 833 (1992).

47. Robert H. Bork, *The Tempting of America* 171 (New York: Free Press, 1990).

48. Ibid. at 171–76.

49. For example, see Richard A. Brisbin, Jr., "Slaying the Dragon: Segal, Spaeth and the Function of Law in Supreme Court Decision Making," 40 *American Journal of Political Science* 1004, 1013–15 (1996).

50. This argument is also advanced by Susan R. Burgess, *Contest for Constitutional Authority: The Abortion and War Powers Debates* (Lawrence: University Press of Kansas, 1992); Susan R. Burgess, Daniel J. Reagan, and Donald L. Davison, "Reclaiming a Democratic Constitutional Politics: Survey Construction and Public Knowledge," 54 *Review of Politics* 399 (1992).

51. Owen Fiss, "Objectivity and Interpretation," 34 *Stanford Law Review* 739 (1982).

52. Richard Rorty, "Nineteenth-Century Idealism and Twentieth-Century Textualism," in *Consequences of Pragmatism* 139 (Minneapolis: University of Minnesota Press, 1982); quoted in Sanford Levinson, "Law as Literature," 60 *Texas Law Review* 373 (1982).

53. Fiss, "Objectivity and Interpretation," 763.

54. This is the characterization Fisher advances. See Louis Fisher, *American Constitutional Law*, 2d ed. (New York: McGraw-Hill Publishing Co., 1994); Louis Fisher, *Constitutional Dialogues: Interpretation as Political Process* (Princeton: Princeton University Press, 1988); Louis Fisher and Neal Devins, *Political Dynamics of Constitutional Law* (St. Paul, Minn.: West Publishing, 1992).

BIBLIOGRAPHY

●●

Abraham, Henry J. *Justices and Presidents: A Political History of Appointments to the Supreme Court.* 2d ed. New York: Oxford University Press, 1985.

———. *Justices and Presidents: A Political History of Appointments to the Supreme Court,* 3d ed. New York: Oxford University Press, 1992.

Abraham, Henry J.; Bell, Griffin, B.; Grassley, Charles E.; Hickok, Eugene W., Jr.: Kern, Judge John W. III; Markham, Stephen J.; and Reynolds, William Bradford. *Judicial Selection: Merit, Ideology, and Politics.* Washington, D.C.: National Legal Center for the Public Interest, 1990.

Abramson, Paul R., and Aldrich, John H. "The Decline of Electoral Participation in America." 76 *American Political Science Review* 502 (1982).

Ackerman, Bruce. "Beyond *Carolene Products.*" 98 *Harvard Law Review* 713 (1985).

———. *We the People: Foundations.* Cambridge: Harvard University Press, 1991.

———. *We the People: Transformations.* Cambridge: Harvard University Press, 1998.

Adamany, David W. "Legitimacy, Realigning Elections, and the Supreme Court." 1973 *Wisconsin Law Review* 790 (1973).

———. "The Party Variable in Judges' Voting: Conceptual Notes and a Case Study." 63 *American Political Science Review* 59 (1969).

———. "The Supreme Court." In Gates, John B., and Johnson, Charles A., eds. *The American Courts: A Critical Assessment.* Washington, D.C.: Congressional Quarterly Press, 1991.

Adamany, David W., and Grossman, Joel B. "Support for the Supreme Court as a National Policymaker." 5 *Law and Policy Quarterly* 405 (1983).

Agresto, John. *The Supreme Court and Constitutional Democracy.* Ithaca: Cornell University Press, 1984.

Alexander, Herbert. *Financing Politics.* Washington, D.C.: Congressional Quarterly Press, 1992.

Alexander, Larry A. "Painting without the Numbers: Noninterpretive Judicial Review." 8 *University of Dayton Law Review* 447 (1983).

Alford, John R., and Brady, David W. "Personal and Partisan Advantage in U.S. Congressional Elections, 1846–1986." In Dodd, Lawrence C., and Oppenheimer, Bruce I., eds. *Congress Reconsidered.* 4th ed. Washington, D.C.: Congressional Quarterly Press, 1989.

Alford, John R., and Hibbing, John R. "Increased Incumbency Advantage in the House." 43 *Journal of Politics* 1042 (1981).

Aliotta, Jilda. "Combining Judges' Attributes and Case Characteristics: An Alternative Approach to Explaining Supreme Court Decisionmaking." 71 *Judicature* 277 (1988).

Allison, Garland. "Delay in Senate Confirmation of Federal Judicial Nominees." 80 *Judicature* 8 (1996).

Alsop, Joseph, and Catledge, Turner. *The 168 Days.* Garden City, N.Y.: Doubleday, Doran and Co., 1938.

Alumbaugh, Steve, and Rowland, C. K. "The Links between Platform-Based Appointment Criteria and Trial Judges' Abortion Judgments." 74 *Judicature* 153 (1990).

Amar, Akhil Reed. *The Bill of Rights.* New Haven: Yale University Press, 1998.

Arkes, Hadley. *Beyond the Constitution.* Princeton: Princeton University Press, 1990.

Armstrong, Virginia, and Johnson, Charles A. "Certiorari Decisionmaking by the Warren and Burger Courts: Is Cue Theory Time Bound?" 15 *Polity* 141 (1982).

Arnold, R. Douglas. *The Logic of Congressional Action.* New Haven: Yale University Press, 1990.

Arnold, Thurman. "Professor Hart's Theology." 73 *Harvard Law Review* 1298 (1960).

Asaro, Andrea. "The Judicial Portrayal of the Physician in Abortion and Sterilization Decisions." 6 *Harvard Women's Law Journal* 51 (1983).

Baas, Larry B. "The Constitution as Symbol: The Interpersonal Sources of Meaning of a Secondary Symbol." 23 *American Journal of Political Science* 101 (1979).

————. "The Constitution as Symbol: Patterns of Meaning." 8 *American Politics Quarterly* 237 (1980).

Baas, Larry B., and Thomas, Dan. "The Supreme Court and Policy Legitimation: Experimental Tests." 12 *American Politics Quarterly* 335 (1984).

Bachrach, Peter. *The Theory of Democratic Elitism.* Boston: Little, Brown, 1967.

Bachrach, Peter, and Baratz, Morton S. "Decisions and Nondecisions: An Analytical Framework." 57 *American Political Science Review* 632 (1963).

————. "The Two Faces of Power." 56 *American Political Science Review* 947 (1962).

Balkin, J. M. "Tradition, Betrayal, and the Politics of Deconstruction." 11 *Cardozo Law Review* 1613 (1990).

Ball, Milner S. "Don't Die, Don Quixote: A Response and Alternative to Tushnet, Bobbitt, and the Revised Texas Version of Constitutional Law." 59 *Texas Law Review* 789 (1981).

————. "Judicial Protection of Powerless Minorities." 59 *Iowa Law Review* 1059 (1974).

Barber, Sotirios A. *On What the Constitution Means.* Baltimore: Johns Hopkins University Press, 1984.

Barger, Harold M. *The Impossible Presidency.* Glenview, Ill.: Scott, Foresman, 1984.

Barker, Lucius. "Third Parties in Litigation: A Systematic View of the Judicial Function." 29 *Journal of Politics* 41 (1967).

Barnard, Chester I. *The Functions of the Executive.* Cambridge: Harvard University Press, 1938.

Barnum, David G. *The Supreme Court and American Democracy.* New York: St. Martin's Press, 1993.

————. "The Supreme Court and Public Opinion: Judicial Decision-Making in the Post–New Deal Period." 47 *Journal of Politics* 652 (1985).

Barrow, Deborah J.; Zuk, Gary; and Gryski, Gerard S. *The Federal Judiciary and Institutional Change.* Ann Arbor: University of Michigan Press, 1996.

Baum, Lawrence. *American Courts.* 4th ed. Boston: Houghton Mifflin Company, 1998.

————. "Case Selection and Decisionmaking in the U.S. Supreme Court." 27 *Law and Society Review* 443 (1993).

————. "Explaining the Burger Court's Support for Civil Liberties." 20 *Political Science Quarterly* 21 (1987).

————. "Implementation of Judicial Decisions: An Organizational Analysis." 4 *American Politics Quarterly* 86 (1976).

————. "Judicial Demand—Screening and Decisions on the Merits: A Second Look." 7 *American Politics Quarterly* 109 (1979).

————. "Measuring Policy Change in the U.S. Supreme Court." 82 *American Political Science Review* 905 (1988).

————. "Membership Change and Collective Voting Change in the United States Supreme Court." 54 *Journal of Politics* 3 (1992).

————. "Policy Goals in Judicial Gatekeeping: A Proximity Model of Discretionary Jurisdiction." 21 *American Journal of Political Science* 13 (1977).

————. *The Puzzle of Judicial Behavior.* Ann Arbor: University of Michigan Press, 1997.

————. *The Supreme Court.* 3d ed. Washington, D.C.: Congressional Quarterly Press, 1989.

————. *The Supreme Court.* 6th ed. Washington, D.C.: Congressional Quarterly Press, 1998.

————. "What Judges Want: Judges' Goals and Judicial Behavior." 47 *Political Research Quarterly* 749 (1994).

Beard, Charles A. *An Economic Interpretation of the Constitution of the United States.* New York: Macmillan Publishing Co., 1913.

Beck, Paul Allen. *Party Politics in America.* 8th ed. New York: Longman, 1997.

Becker, Theodore L., and Feeley, Malcolm, eds. *The Impact of Supreme Court Decisions.* 2d ed. New York: Oxford University Press, 1973.

Behuniak-Long, Susan. "Friendly Fire: Amici Curiae and *Webster* v. *Reproductive Health Services.*" 74 *Judicature* 261 (1991).

Beiser, Edward N. "Lawyers Judge the Warren Court." 7 *Law and Society Review* 133 (1972).

Bennett, Robert W. "Abortion and Judicial Review: Of Burdens and Benefits, Hard Cases and Some Bad Law." 75 *Northwestern University Law Review* 978 (1981).

————. "'Mere' Rationality in Constitutional Law: Judicial Review and Democratic Theory." 67 *California Law Review* 1049 (1979).

Bentley, Arthur F. *The Process of Government.* Chicago: University of Chicago Press, 1908.

Berger, Curtis J. "Away from the Court House and into the Field: The Odyssey of a Special Master." 78 *Columbia Law Review* 707 (1978).

Berger, Raoul. "Ely's 'Theory of Judicial Review.'" 42 *Ohio State Law Journal* 87 (1981).

————. "Government by Judiciary: John Hart Ely's 'Invitation.'" 54 *Indiana Law Journal* 277 (1979).

————. *Government by Judiciary: The Transformation of the Fourteenth Amendment.* Cambridge: Harvard University Press, 1977.

————. "The Imperial Court." *New York Times Magazine* 40 (October 8, 1977).

————. "Incorporation of the Bill of Rights in the Fourteenth Amendment: A Nine-Lived Cat." 42 *Ohio State Law Journal* 435 (1981).

Berle, Adolf. *The Three Faces of Power.* New York: Harcourt, Brace and World, 1967.

Berman, Larry. *The New American Presidency.* New York: HarperCollins, 1987.

Berry, Jeffrey M. *The Interest Group Society.* 3d ed. New York: Longman, 1997.

Bickel, Alexander M. *The Least Dangerous Branch: The Supreme Court at the Bar of Politics.* Indianapolis, Ind.: Bobbs-Merrill, 1962.

————. "Mr. Taft Rehabilitates the Court." 79 *Yale Law Journal* 1 (1969).

————. *Politics and the Warren Court.* New York: Harper and Rowe, 1965.

————. *The Supreme Court and the Idea of Progress.* New Haven: Yale University Press, 1978.

Binder, Sarah A., and Smith, Steven S. *Politics or Principle? Filibustering in the United States Senate.* Washington, D.C.: Brookings Institution Press, 1996.

Birkby, Robert H., and Murphy, Walter F. "Interest Group Conflict in the Judicial Arena: The First Amendment and Group Access to the Courts." 42 *Texas Law Review* 1018 (1964).

Biskupic, Joan. "Thomas' Victory Puts Icing on the Reagan-Bush Court." 49 *Congressional Quarterly* 3026 (October 19, 1991).

Bisnow, Mark. *In the Shadow of the Dome: Chronicles of a Capitol Hill Aide.* New York: William Morrow, 1990.

Black, Charles L., Jr. *Decision According to Law.* New York: Norton, 1981.

————. "A Note on Senatorial Consideration of Supreme Court Nominees." 79 *Yale Law Journal* 657 (1970).

————. *The People and the Court.* New York: Macmillan, 1960.

————. *Structure and Relationship in Constitutional Law.* Baton Rouge: Louisiana State University Press, 1969.

————. "The Unfinished Business of the Warren Court." 46 *Washington Law Review* 3 (1970).

Bobbitt, Philip. *Constitutional Fate: Theory of the Constitution.* New York: Oxford University Press, 1982.

Bolick, Clint. *Unfinished Business: A Civil Rights Strategy for America's Third Century.* San Francisco: Pacific Research Institute for Public Policy, 1990.

Bond, Jon, and Johnson, Charles A. "Implementing a Permissive Policy: Hospital Abortion Services after *Roe* v. *Wade.*" 26 *American Journal of Political Science* 1 (1982).

Bork, Robert H. "The Full Court Press: The Drive for Control of the Courts." *American Enterprise* 58 (1990).

————. "Neutral Principles and Some First Amendment Problems." 47 *Indiana Law Journal* 1 (1971).

————. *The Tempting of America: The Political Seduction of the Law.* New York: Free Press, 1990.

Boucher, Robert, and Segal, Jeffrey. "Supreme Court Justices as Strategic Decision Makers: Aggressive Grants and Defensive Denials on the Vinson Court." 57 *Journal of Politics* 824 (1995).

Bradley, Robert, and Gardner, Paul. "Underdogs, Upperdogs, and the Use of the Amicus Brief: Trends and Explanations." 10 *Justice System Journal* 78 (1985).

Bradley, Robert, and Ulmer, S. Sidney. "An Examination of Voting Behavior in the Supreme Court of Illinois, 1971–1975." *Southern Illinois University Law Journal* 245 (1980).

Brace, Paul, and Hinckley, Barbara. *Follow the Leader: Opinion Polls and the Modern Presidents.* Boulder, Colo.: Basic Books, 1993.

Breckenridge, Adam Carlyle. *Congress against the Court.* Lincoln: University of Nebraska Press, 1970.

Brennan, William J., Jr. "The Constitution of the United States: Contemporary Ratification." 27 *South Texas Law Journal* 433 (1986).

Brenner, Saul. "The Chief Justice's Self-Assignment of Majority Opinions in Salient Cases." 30 *Social Science Journal* 143 (1993).

————. "Fluidity on the Supreme Court, 1956–1967." 26 *American Journal of Political Science* 388 (1982).

————. "Fluidity on the United States Supreme Court: A Re-examination." 24 *American Journal of Political Science* 526 (1980).

————. "Ideological Voting on the Vinson Court: A Comparison of the Original Vote on the Merits with the Final Vote." 21 *Polity* 102 (1989).

————. "Issue Specialization as a Variable in Opinion Assignment on the U.S. Supreme Court." 46 *Journal of Politics* 1217 (1984).

————. "The New Certiorari Game." 41 *Journal of Politics* 649 (1979).

Brenner, Saul, and Arrington, Theodore S. "Unanimous Decision Making on the U.S. Supreme Court: Case Stimuli and Judicial Attitudes." 9 *Political Behavior* 75 (1987).

Brenner, Saul; Hagle, Timothy M.; and Spaeth, Harold J. "The Defection of the Marginal Justice on the Warren Court." 42 *Western Political Quarterly* 409 (1989).

———. "Increasing the Size of the Minimum Winning Coalitions on the Warren Court." 23 *Polity* 309 (1990).

Brenner, Saul, and Krol, John F. "Strategies in Certiorari Voting on the United States Supreme Court." 51 *Journal of Politics* 828 (1989).

Brenner, Saul, and Spaeth, Harold J. "Issue Specialization in Majority Opinion Assignment on the Burger Court." 39 *Western Political Quarterly* 520 (1986).

———. "Majority Opinion Assignments and the Maintenance of the Original Coalition on the Warren Court." 32 *American Journal of Political Science* 72 (1988).

———. *Stare Indecisis: The Alteration of Precedent on the Supreme Court, 1946–1992.* Cambridge: Cambridge University Press, 1995.

Brenner, Saul, and Stier, Marc. "Retesting Segal and Spaeth's *Stare Decisis* Model." 40 *American Journal of Political Science* 1036 (1996).

Brest, Paul. "Congress as Constitutional Decisionmaker and Its Power to Counter Judicial Doctrine." 21 *Georgia Law Review* 57 (1987).

———. "The Fundamental Rights Controversy: The Essential Contradictions of Normative Constitutional Scholarship." 90 *Yale Law Journal* 1063 (1981).

———. "Interpretation and Interest." 34 *Stanford Law Review* 765 (1982).

———. "The Misconceived Quest for the Original Understanding." 60 *Boston University Law Review* 204 (1980).

———. "The Substance of Process." 42 *Ohio State Law Journal* 131 (1981).

Brigham, John. *Constitutional Language: An Interpretation of Judicial Decision.* Westport, Conn.: Greenwood Press, 1978.

Brisbin, Richard A., Jr. "Slaying the Dragon: Segal, Spaeth and the Function of Law in Supreme Court Decision Making." 40 *American Journal of Political Science* 1004 (1996).

Broder, David. *The Party's Over.* New York: Harper and Rowe, 1971.

Bronner, Ethan. *Battle for Justice: How the Bork Nomination Shook America.* New York: Norton, 1989.

Brown, Robert E. *Charles Beard and the Constitution: A Critical Analysis of "An Economic Interpretation of the Constitution."* Princeton: Princeton University Press, 1956.

Buchanan, Bruce. *The Citizen's Presidency.* Washington, D.C.: Congressional Quarterly Press, 1986.

———. *Renewing Presidential Politics.* Lanham, Md.: Rowman and Littlefield Publishers, 1996.

Bullock Charles S. III, and Lamb, Charles M. "Toward a Theory of Civil Rights Implementation." 2 *Policy Perspectives* 376 (1982).

Burgess, Susan R. *Contest For Constitutional Authority: The Abortion and War Powers Debates.* Lawrence: University Press of Kansas, 1992.

Burgess, Susan R.; Reagan, Daniel J.; and Davison, Donald L. "Reclaiming a Democratic Constitutional Politics: Survey Construction and Public Knowledge." 54 *Review of Politics* 399 (1992).

Burke, John P. *The Institutional Presidency.* Baltimore, Md.: Johns Hopkins University Press, 1992.

Burnham, Walter Dean. *Critical Elections and the Mainsprings of American Politics.* New York: Norton, 1980.

———. *The Current Crisis in American Politics.* New York: Oxford University Press, 1982.

Burnham, Walter Dean. "The Turnout Problem." In Reichley, A. James, ed. *Elections American Style.* Washington, D.C.: Brookings Institution, 1987.

Burns, James MacGregor. *The Power to Lead: The Crisis of the American Presidency.* New York: Simon and Schuster, 1984.

Burris, William J. *The Senate Rejects a Judge: A Study of the John J. Parker Case.* Chapel Hill: University of North Carolina Press, 1962.

Burt, Robert A. *The Constitution in Conflict.* Cambridge: Harvard University Press, 1992.

Cain, Bruce; Ferejohn, John; and Fiorina, Morris. *The Personal Vote: Constituency Service and Electoral Independence.* Cambridge: Harvard University Press, 1987.

Calabresi, Guido. "Foreword: Antidiscrimination and Constitutional Accountability (What the Bork-Brennan Debate Ignores)." 105 *Harvard Law Review* 80 (1991).

Caldeira, Gregory A. "Children's Images of the Supreme Court: A Preliminary Mapping." 11 *Law and Society Review* 851 (1977).

―――. "Commentary on Senate Confirmation of Supreme Court Justices: The Roles of Organized and Unorganized Interests." 77 *Kentucky Law Journal* 531 (1988–89).

―――. "Courts and Public Opinion." In Gates, John B., and Johnson, Charles A., eds. *The American Courts: A Critical Assessment.* Washington, D.C.: Congressional Quarterly Press, 1991.

―――. "Neither the Purse nor the Sword: Dynamics of Public Confidence in the Supreme Court." 80 *American Political Science Review* 1209 (1986).

―――. "Public Opinion and the U.S. Supreme Court: FDR's Court-Packing Plan." 81 *American Political Science Review* 1141 (1987).

―――. Review of *Public Opinion and the Supreme Court*, by Thomas Marshall. 84 *American Political Science Review* 663 (1989).

Caldeira, Gregory A., and Gibson, James L. "The Etiology of Public Support for the Supreme Court." 36 *American Journal of Political Science* 635 (1992).

Caldeira, Gregory A., and Smith, Charles E., Jr. "Campaigning for the Supreme Court: The Dynamics of Public Opinion on the Thomas Nomination." 58 *Journal of Politics* 655 (1996).

Caldeira, Gregory A., and Wright, John R. "Amici Curiae before the Supreme Court: Who Participates, When, and How Much?" 52 *Journal of Politics* 782 (1990).

―――. "Organized Interests and Agenda Setting in the U.S. Supreme Court." 82 *American Political Science Review* 1109 (1988).

Cameron, Charles M.; Cover, Albert D.; and Segal, Jeffrey A. "Senate Voting on Supreme Court Nominees: A Neoinstitutional Model." 84 *American Political Science Review* 525 (1990).

―――. "Supreme Court Nominations and the Rational Presidency." Paper presented at the Annual Meeting of the American Political Science Association, 1990.

Campbell, Angus; Converse, Philip E.; Miller, Warren E.; and Stokes, Donald E. *The American Voter.* New York: Wiley, 1960.

Canon, Bradley C. "Courts and Policy: Compliance, Implementation, and Impact." In Gates, John B., and Johnson, Charles A., eds. *The American Courts: A Critical Assessment.* Washington, D.C.: Congressional Quarterly Press, 1991.

―――. "The Supreme Court as a Cheerleader in Politico-Moral Disputes." 54 *Journal of Politics* 637 (1992).

―――. "Testing the Effectiveness of Civil Liberties Policies at the State and Federal Levels: The Case of the Exclusionary Rule." 5 *American Politics Quarterly* 57 (1977).

Canon, Bradley C., and Ulmer, S. Sidney. "The Supreme Court and Critical Elections: A Dissent." 70 *American Political Science Review* 1215 (1976).

Cantril, Hadley. *Public Opinion, 1935–1946.* Princeton: Princeton University Press, 1951.

Caplan, Lincoln, *The Tenth Justice.* New York: Knopf, 1987.

Carp, Robert A., and Rowland, C. K. *Policymaking and Politics in the Federal District Courts.* Knoxville: University of Tennessee Press, 1983.

Carp, Robert A.; Songer, Donald; Rowland, C. K.; Stidham, Ronald; and Richey-Tracy, Lisa. "The Voting Behavior of Judges Appointed by President Bush." 76 *Judicature* 298 (1993).

Carp, Robert A., and Stidham, Ronald. *Judicial Process in America.* Washington, D.C.: Congressional Quarterly Press, 1990.

Carter, Lief H. *Contemporary Constitutional Lawmaking: The Supreme Court and the Art of Politics.* New York: Pergamon Press, 1985.

———. *Reason In Law.* 5th ed. New York: Longman, 1998.

Carter, Stephen L. *The Confirmation Mess.* New York: Basic Books, 1995.

Casey, Gregory. "Popular Perceptions of Supreme Court Rulings." 4 *American Politics Quarterly* 3 (1976).

———. "The Supreme Court and Myth: An Empirical Investigation." 8 *Law and Society Review* 385 (1974).

Casper, Jonathan D. "The Supreme Court and National Policy Making." 70 *American Political Science Review* 50 (1976).

Cater, Douglass. *Power in Washington.* New York: Vintage Books, 1964.

Cavanagh, Ralph, and Sarat, Austin. "Thinking about Courts: Toward and beyond a Jurisprudence of Judicial Competence." 14 *Law and Society Review* 371 (1980).

Chambers, David L., and Wald, Michael S. "*Smith* v. *Offer.*" In Mnookin, Robert H., ed. *In the Interest of Children.* New York: W. H. Freeman and Co., 1985.

Chemerinsky, Erwin. "The Constitution Is Not 'Hard Law': The Bork Rejection and the Future of Constitutional Jurisprudence." 6 *Constitutional Commentary* 29 (1989).

———. "Foreword: The Vanishing Constitution." 103 *Harvard Law Review* 44 (1989).

Choper, Jesse H. "Consequences of Supreme Court Decisions Upholding Individual Constitutional Rights." 83 *Michigan Law Review* 1 (1984).

———. *Judicial Review and the National Political Process: A Functional Reconsideration of the Role of the Supreme Court.* Chicago: University of Chicago Press, 1980.

Cigler, Allan J., and Loomis, Burdett A., eds. *Interest Group Politics.* 4th ed. Washington, D.C.: Congressional Quarterly Press, 1994.

Clawson, Dan; Neustadtl, Alan; and Scott, Denise. *Money Talks: Corporate PACs and Political Influence.* New York: Basic Books, 1992.

Clinton, Robert Lowry. *Marbury v. Madison and Judicial Review.* Lawrence: University of Kansas Press, 1989.

Cohen Jeffrey E. *Presidential Responsiveness and Public Policy Making.* Ann Arbor: University of Michigan Press, 1997.

Comiskey, Michael. "Can the Senate Examine the Constitutional Philosophies of Supreme Court Nominees?" 26 *PS: Political Science and Politics* 495 (1993).

"Confirmation Controversy: The Selection of a Supreme Court Justice." Symposium. 84 *Northwestern University Law Review* 832 (1990).

Congressional Limits on Federal Court Jurisdiction. 27 *Villanova Law Review* 893 (1982).

Conkle, Daniel. "Nonoriginalist Constitutional Rights and the Problem of Judicial Finality." 13 *Hastings Constitutional Law Quarterly* 9 (1985).

Connolly, William E., ed. *The Bias of Pluralism.* New York: Atherton Press, 1969.

"Constitutional Adjudication and Democratic Theory." Symposium. 56 *New York University Law Review* 259 (1981).

Converse, Philip E. "The Nature of Belief Systems in Mass Publics." In Apter, David E., ed. *Ideology and Discontent.* New York: Free Press, 1964.

Cooper, Joseph, and Maisel, Louis. *Political Parties: Development and Decay.* Beverly Hills, Calif.: Sage Publications, 1978.

Cortner, Richard C. "Strategies and Tactics of Litigants in Constitutional Cases." 17 *Journal of Public Law* 287 (1968).

———. *The Supreme Court and Civil Liberties Policy.* Palo Alto, Calif.: Mayfield, 1975.

Corwin, Edward S. "The Constitution as Instrument and as Symbol." 30 *American Political Science Review* 1071 (1936).

Cotter, Cornelius P., and Hennessy, Bernard. *Politics without Power: The National Party Committees.* New York: Atherton, 1964.

Cover, Robert M. "The Origins of Judicial Activism in the Protection of Minorities." 91 *Yale Law Journal* 1287 (1982).

Cox, Archibald. *The Court and the Constitution.* Boston: Houghton Mifflin, 1987.

———. *The Role of the Supreme Court in American Government.* New York: Oxford University Press, 1976.

———. *The Warren Court: Constitutional Decision as an Instrument of Reform.* Cambridge: Harvard University Press, 1968.

Coyle, Marcia. "How Americans View High Court." *National Law Journal* (February 26, 1990).

Craven, J. Braxton. "Paen to Pragmatism." 50 *North Carolina Law Review* 977 (1972).

"Critical Legal Studies Symposium." 36 *Stanford Law Review* 1 (1984).

Cronin, Thomas E. *Inventing the Presidency.* Lawrence: University Press of Kansas, 1989.

———. "The Swelling of the Presidency: Can Anyone Reverse the Tide?" In Woll, Peter, ed. *American Government: Readings and Cases.* 8th ed. Boston: Little, Brown, 1984.

Crotty, William J., and Jacobson, Gary C. *American Parties in Decline.* Boston: Little, Brown, 1980.

Dahl, Robert A. "Decision-Making in a Democracy: The Supreme Court as a National Policy-Maker." 6 *Journal of Public Law* 279 (1957).

———. *Democracy, Liberty, and Equality.* New York: Oxford University Press, 1986.

———. *Dilemmas of Pluralist Democracy.* New Haven: Yale University Press, 1982.

———. "Myth of the Presidential Mandate." 105 *Political Science Quarterly* 355 (1990).

———. *The New American Political (Dis)Order.* Berkeley, Calif.: Institute of Governmental Studies Press, 1994.

———. "On Removing Certain Impediments to Democracy in the United States." 92 *Political Science Quarterly* 1 (1977).

———. *Pluralist Democracy in the United States.* Chicago: Rand McNally, 1967.

———. *A Preface to Democratic Theory.* Chicago: University of Chicago Press, 1956.

———. "What Is Political Equality? A Response." 26 *Dissent* 363 (1979).

———. *Who Governs?* New Haven: Yale University Press, 1961.

Dahl, Robert A., and Lindblom, Charles E. *Politics, Economics, and Welfare.* New York: Harper, 1953.

Danelski, David J. "Ideology as a Ground for the Rejection of the Bork Nomination." 84 *Northwestern University Law Review* (1990).

————. "The Influence of the Chief Justice in the Decisional Process of the Supreme Court." In Goldman, Sheldon, and Sarat, Austin, eds. *American Court Systems: Readings in Judicial Process and Behavior.* San Francisco: W. H. Freeman and Co., 1978.

————. *A Supreme Court Justice Is Appointed.* New York: Random House, 1964.

————. "Values as Variables in Judicial Decision-Making: Notes toward a Theory." 19 *Vanderbilt Law Review* 721 (1966).

Daniels, William J. "The Supreme Court and Its Publics." 37 *Albany Law Review* 632 (1973).

Dauster, Bill. "It's Not *Mr. Smith Goes to Washington.*" *Washington Monthly* 34 (November 1996).

David, James Allan, and Smith, Tom W. *General Social Survey, 1973–1988.* Chicago: National Opinion Research Center, 1988.

Davidson, Roger H., ed. *The Postreform Congress.* New York: St. Martin's Press, 1991.

Davidson, Roger H., and Oleszek, Walter J. *Congress and its Members.* 5th ed. Washington, D.C.: Congressional Quarterly Press, 1996.

Davis, Richard. *Decisions and Images: The Supreme Court and the Press.* Englewood Cliffs, N.J.: Prentice-Hall, 1994.

————. "Lifting the Shroud: News Media Coverage of the U.S. Supreme Court." 9 *Communications and the Law* 43 (1987).

Davis, Sue. "Power on the Court: Chief Justice Rehnquist's Opinion Assignments." 74 *Judicature* 66 (1990).

————. "President Carter's Selection Reforms and Judicial Policymaking." 14 *American Politics Quarterly* 328 (1986).

————. "The Supreme Court: Rehnquist's or Reagan's?" 44 *Western Political Quarterly* 87 (1991).

Dimond, Paul R. "Provisional Review: An Exploratory Essay on an Alternative Form of Judicial Review." 12 *Hastings Constitutional Law Quarterly* 201 (1985).

————. *The Supreme Court and Judicial Choice: The Role of Provisional Review in a Democracy.* Ann Arbor: University of Michigan Press, 1989.

Dodd, Lawrence C., and Oppenheimer, Bruce I. *Congress Reconsidered.* 6th ed. Washington, D.C.: Congressional Quarterly Press, 1996.

Dolbeare, Kenneth. "The Public Views the Supreme Court." In Jacob, Herbert, ed. *Law, Politics, and the Federal Courts.* Boston: Little, Brown, 1976.

Dolbeare, Kenneth M., and Hammond, Phillip E. "The Political Party Basis of Attitudes Toward the Supreme Court." 37 *Public Opinion Quarterly* 16 (1968).

————. *The School Prayer Decisions: From Court Policy to Local Practice.* Chicago: University of Chicago Press, 1971.

Domhoff, G. William. *Who Rules America Now?* Englewood Cliffs, N.J.: Prentice-Hall, 1983.

Douglas, William O. "Stare Decisis." 49 *Columbia Law Review* 735 (1949).

Dubois, Philip. "The Illusion of Judicial Consensus Revisited: Partisan Conflict on an Intermediate State Court of Appeals." 32 *American Journal of Political Science* 946 (1988).

Ducat, Craig R., and Dudley, Robert L. "Dimensions Underlying Economic Policy Making in the Early and Later Burger Courts." 49 *Journal of Politics* 521 (1987).

————. "Federal District Judges and Presidential Power during the Postwar Era." 51 *Journal of Politics* 98 (1989).

Dudley, Robert L., and Ducat, Craig R. "The Burger Court and Economic Liberalism." 39 *Western Political Quarterly* 236 (1986).

Dworkin, Ronald M. "The Forum of Principle." 56 *New York University Law Review* 469 (1981).

Dworkin, Ronald M. *Law's Empire*. Cambridge: Harvard University Press, Belknap Press, 1986.

———. *Taking Rights Seriously*. London: Duckworth, 1977.

Dye, Thomas R. *Who's Running America?* Englewood Cliffs, N.J.: Prentice-Hall, 1990.

Easton, David. *A Systems Analysis of Political Life*. New York: Wiley, 1965.

Easton, David, and Dennis, Jack. *Children in the Political System: Origins of Political Legitimacy*. New York: McGraw-Hill, 1969.

Eaton, William. *Who Killed the Constitution?* Washington, D.C.: Regnery Gateway, 1988.

Edwards, George. *The Public Presidency*. New York: St. Martin's Press, 1983.

Ely, John Hart. "Another Such Victory: Constitutional Theory and Practice in a World Where Courts Are No Different from Legislatures." 77 *Virginia Law Review* 833 (1991).

———. "The Constitutionality of Reverse Racial Discrimination." 41 *University of Chicago Law Review* 723 (1974).

———. *Democracy and Distrust: A Theory of Judicial Review*. Cambridge: Harvard University Press, 1980.

———. "Foreword: On Discovering Fundamental Values." 92 *Harvard Law Review* 5 (1978).

———. "The Wages of Crying Wolf: A Comment on *Roe* v. *Wade*." 82 *Yale Law Journal* 920 (1973).

Ennis, Bruce L. "Effective Amicus Briefs." 33 *Catholic Unviersity Law Review* 603 (1984).

Epstein, Lee. *Conservatives in Court*. Knoxville: University of Tennessee Press, 1985.

———. "Courts and Interest Groups." In Gates, John B., and Johnson, Charles A., eds. *The American Courts: A Critical Assessment*. Washington, D.C.: Congressional Quarterly Press, 1991.

Epstein, Lee, and Knight, Jack. *The Choices Justices Make*. Washington, D.C.: Congressional Quarterly Press, 1998.

Epstein, Lee, and Kobylka, Joseph. *The Supreme Court and Legal Change*. Chapel Hill: University of North Carolina Press, 1993.

Epstein, Lee, and Rowland, C. K. "Debunking the Myth of Interest Group Invincibility in the Courts." 85 *American Political Science Review* 205 (1991).

———. "Interest Groups in the Courts: Do Groups Fare Better?" In Cigler, Allan J., and Loomis, Burdett A., eds. *Interest Group Politics*, 2d ed. Washington, D.C.: Congressional Quarterly Press, 1986.

Epstein, Lee; Walker, Thomas G.; and Dixon, William J. "The Supreme Court and Criminal Justice Disputes: A Neo-Institutional Perspective." 33 *American Journal of Political Science* 825 (1989).

Epstein, Lee; Segal, Jeffrey A.; Spaeth, Harold J.; and Walker, Thomas G. *The Supreme Court Compendium: Data, Decisions, and Developments*. Washington, D.C.: Congressional Quarterly Press, 1994.

Epstein, Leon. *Political Parties in the American Mold*. Madison: University of Wisconsin Press, 1986.

Epstein, Richard A. "Substantive Due Process by Any Other Name: The Abortion Cases." 1973 *Supreme Court Review* 159 (1973).

———. *Takings: Private Property and the Power of Eminent Domain*. Cambridge: Harvard University Press, 1985.

———. "Toward a Revitalization of the Contract Clause." 51 *University of Chicago Law Review* 703 (1984).

Erickson, Robert S.; Luttbeg, Norman R.; and Tedin, Kent L. *American Public Opinion: Its Origins, Content, and Impact*. 4th ed. New York: Macmillan, 1991.

Eskridge, William N., Jr. "Overriding Supreme Court Statutory Interpretation Decisions." 101 *Yale Law Journal* 331 (1991).

"Essays on the Supreme Court Appointment Process." Symposium. 101 *Harvard Law Review* 1146 (1988).

Estreicher, Samuel. "Platonic Guardians of Democracy: John Hart Ely's Role for the Supreme Court in the Constitution's Open Texture." 56 *New York University Law Review* 547 (1981).

Fair, Daryl. "An Experimental Application of Scalogram Analysis to State Supreme Court Decisions." 1967 *Wisconsin Law Review* 449 (1967).

The Federalist Papers. New York: New American Library, 1961.

Feeley, Malcolm. "Another Look at the 'Party Variable' in Judicial Decision-Making: An Analysis of the Michigan Supreme Court." 4 *Polity* 91 (1971).

Feig, Douglas G. "Expenditures in the American States: The Impact of Court-Ordered Reapportionment." 6 *American Politics Quarterly* 309 (1978).

Fein, Bruce. "A Circumscribed Senate Confirmation Role." 102 *Harvard Law Review* 672 (1989).

Felice, John D., and Weisberg, Herbert F. "The Changing Importance of Ideology, Party, and Region in Confirmation of Supreme Court Nominees, 1953–1988." 77 *Kentucky Law Journal* 509 (1989).

Fenno, Richard F. *Home Style: House Members and Their Districts.* Boston: Little, Brown, 1978.

Ferejohn, John A. "On the Decline of Competition in Congressional Elections." 71 *American Political Science Review* 166 (1977).

Ferguson, Thomas, and Rogers, Joel. "The Myth of America's Turn to the Right." In Cigler, Allan J., and Loomis, Burdett A., eds. *American Politics: Classic and Contemporary Readings.* Boston: Houghton Mifflin, 1989.

Fiorina, Morris P. "The Case of the Vanishing Marginals: The Bureaucracy Did It." 71 *American Political Science Review* 171 (1977).

———. *Congress: Keystone of the Washington Establishment.* 2d ed. New Haven: Yale University Press, 1989.

Fish, Peter G. "*Red Jacket* Revisited: The Case That Unraveled John J. Parker's Supreme Court Appointment." 5 *Law and History Review* 1 (1987).

———. "Spite Nominations to the United States Supreme Court: Herbert Hoover, Owen J. Roberts, and the Politics of Presidential Vengeance in Retrospect." 77 *Kentucky Law Journal* 545 (1989).

Fish, Stanley. "Fish v. Fiss." 36 *Stanford Law Review* 1325 (1984).

Fishel, Jeff. *Presidents and Promises.* Washington, D.C.: Congressional Quarterly Press, 1986.

Fisher, Louis. *American Constitutional Law.* 2d ed. New York: McGraw-Hill Publishing Co., 1994.

———. "Congress and the Fourth Amendment." 21 *Georgia Law Review* 107 (1986).

———. *Constitutional Dialogues: Interpretation as Political Process.* Princeton: Princeton University Press, 1988.

———. "Constitutional Interpretation by Members of Congress." 63 *North Carolina Law Review* 707 (1985).

Fisher, Louis, and Devins, Neal. *Political Dynamics of Constitutional Law.* St. Paul, Minn.: West Publishing Co., 1992.

Fiss, Owen. "Foreword: The Forms of Justice." 93 *Harvard Law Review* 1 (1979).

———. "Objectivity and Interpretation." 34 *Stanford Law Review* 739 (1982).

Flammang, Janet A.; Gordon, Dennis R.; Lukes, Timothy J.; and Smorsten, Kenneth R. *American Politics in a Changing World.* Pacific Grove, Calif.: Brooks/Cole Publishing Co., 1990.

Flemming, Roy B.; Bohte, John; and Wood, B. Dan. "One Voice among Many: The Supreme Court's Influence on Attentiveness to Issues in the United States, 1947–1992." 41 *American Journal of Political Science* 1224 (1997).

Flemming, Roy B., and Wood, B. Dan. "The Public and the Supreme Court: Individual Justice Responsiveness to American Policy Moods." 41 *American Journal of Political Science* 468 (1997).

Fowler, W. Gary. "A Comparison of Initial Recommendation Procedures: Judicial Selection under Reagan and Carter." 1 *Yale Law and Policy Review* 299 (1983).

Fowler, Linda, and McClure, Robert. *Political Ambition: Who Decides to Run for Congress?* New Haven: Yale University Press, 1989.

Fox, Harrison W., and Hammond, Susan W. *Congressional Staffs: The Invisible Force in American Lawmaking.* New York: Free Press, 1977.

Frank, Jerome. *Law and the Modern Mind.* New York: Coward McCann, 1930.

Frank, John P. "The Appointment of Supreme Court Justices: Prestige, Principles, and Politics." 1941 *Wisconsin Law Review* 343 (1941).

Franklin, Charles H., and Kosaki, Liane C. "Media, Knowledge, and Public Evaluations of the Supreme Court." In Epstein, Lee, ed. *Contemplating Courts.* Washington, D.C.: Congressional Quarterly Press, 1995.

———. "Republican Schoolmaster: The U.S. Supreme Court, Public Opinion, and Abortion." 83 *American Political Science Review* 751 (1989).

Free, Lloyd A., and Cantril, Hadley. *The Political Beliefs of Americans: A Study of Public Opinion.* New Brunswick, N.J.: Rutgers University Press, 1967.

Freeman, Alan. "Truth and Mystification in Legal Scholarship." 90 *Yale Law Journal* 1229 (1981).

Freeman, J. Leiper. *The Political Process.* New York: Random House, 1965.

Friedman, Barry. "Dialogue and Judicial Review." 91 *Michigan Law Review* 577 (1993).

Friedman, Leon, and Israel, Fred L., eds. *The Justices of the United States Supreme Court, 1789–1969: Their Lives and Major Opinions.* 4 vols. New York: Chelsea House, 1969.

Friedman, Richard D. "Balance Favoring Restraint." 9 *Cardozo Law Review* 15 (1987).

———. "The Transformation in Senate Response to Supreme Court Nominations: From Reconstruction to the Taft Administration and Beyond." 5 *Cardozo Law Review* 1 (1983).

———. "Tribal Myths: Ideology and the Confirmation of Supreme Court Nominations." 95 *Yale Law Journal* 1283 (1986).

Funston, Richard. "The Supreme Court and Critical Elections." 69 *American Political Science Review* 795 (1975).

Gabel, Peter. Review of *Taking Rights Seriously,* by Ronald Dworkin. 91 *Harvard Law Review* 302 (1977).

Gamble, Barbara S. "Putting Civil Rights to a Popular Vote." 41 *American Journal of Political Science* 245 (1997).

Garand, James C., and Gross, Donald A. "Change in the Vote Margins for Congressional Elections: A Specification of Historical Trends." 78 *American Political Science Review* 17 (1984).

Gates, John B. *The Supreme Court and Partisan Realignment: A Macro- and Microlevel Perspective.* Boulder, Colo.: Westview Press, 1992.

Gates, John B., and Cohen, Jeffrey E. "Presidents, Justices, and Racial Equality Cases, 1954–1984." 10 *Political Behavior* 22 (1988).

Gates, John B., and Johnson, Charles A., eds. *The American Courts: A Critical Assessment.* Washington, D.C.: Congressional Quarterly Press, 1991.

Gauch, James E. "The Intended Role of the Senate in Supreme Court Appointments." 56 *University of Chicago Law Review* 337 (1989).

"Gender, Race, and the Politics of Supreme Court Appointments." Symposium. 65 *Southern California Law Review* 1279 (1992).

George, Tracey E., and Epstein, Lee. "On the Nature of Supreme Court Decision Making." 86 *American Political Science Review* 323 (1992).

Gerber, Scott Douglas. *To Secure These Rights.* New York: New York University Press, 1995.

Gerber, Scott D., and Park, Keeok. "The Quixotic Search for Consensus on the U.S. Supreme Court: A Cross-Judicial Empirical Analysis of the Rehnquist Court Justices." 91 *American Political Science Review* 390 (1997).

Gerety, Thomas. "Doing without Privacy." 42 *Ohio State Law Journal* 143 (1981).

Gibbons, John J. "Keynote Address: Constitutional Adjudication and Democratic Theory." Symposium. 56 *New York University Law Review* 260 (1981).

Gibson, James L. "Decision Making in Appellate Courts." In Gates, John B., and Johnson, Charles A., eds. *The American Courts: A Critical Assessment.* Washington, D.C.: Congressional Quarterly Press, 1991.

———. "Environmental Constraints on the Behavior of Judges: A Representational Model of Judicial Decision Making." 14 *Law and Society Review* 343 (1980).

———. "From Simplicity to Complexity: The Development of Theory in the Study of Judicial Behavior." 5 *Political Behavior* 7 (1983).

———. "Judges' Role Orientations, Attitudes, and Decisions: An Interactive Model." 72 *American Political Science Review* 911 (1978).

Gibson, James L., and Caldeira, Gregory A. "Blacks and the United States Supreme Court: Models of Diffuse Support." 54 *Journal of Politics* 1120 (1992).

Gibson, James L.; Caldeira, Gregory A.; and Baird, Vanessa A. "On the Legitimacy of National High Courts." 92 *American Political Science Review* 343 (1998).

Giles, Michael, and Gatlin, Douglas. "Mass Level Compliance with Public Policy: The Case of School Desegregation." 42 *Journal of Politics* 711 (1980).

Ginsberg, Benjamin, and Shefter, Martin. *Politics by Other Means: The Declining Importance of Elections in America.* New York: Basic Books, 1990.

Ginsberg, Benjamin, and Stone, Alan, eds. *Do Elections Matter?* Armonk, N.Y.: M. E. Sharpe, Inc., 1986.

Glazer, Nathan. "Towards an Imperial Judiciary?" 41 *Public Interest* 104 (1975).

Glendon, Mary Ann. *Abortion and Divorce in Western Law.* Cambridge: Harvard University Press, 1987.

Goldman, Sheldon. "The Bush Imprint on the Judiciary: Carrying on a Tradition." 74 *Judicature* 294 (1991).

———. "Bush's Judicial Legacy: The Final Imprint." 76 *Judicature* 282 (1993).

———. "Carter's Judicial Appointments: A Lasting Legacy." 64 *Judicature* 344 (1981).

———. "Conflict on the U.S. Courts of Appeals, 1965–1971: A Quantitative Analysis." 42 *University of Cincinnati Law Review* 635 (1973).

———. *Constitutional Law: Cases and Essays.* 2d ed. New York: HarperCollins Publishers, 1991.

Goldman, Sheldon. "Federal Judicial Recruitment." In Gates, John B., and Johnson, Charles A., eds. *The American Courts: A Critical Assessment.* Washington, D.C.: Congressional Quarterly Press, 1991.

————. "Judicial Appointments and the Presidential Agenda." In Brace, Paul; Harrington, Christine B.; and King, Gary, eds. *The Presidency in American Politics.* New York: New York University Press, 1989.

————. "Judicial Appointments to the United States Courts of Appeals." 1967 *Wisconsin Law Review* 186 (1967).

————. "Judicial Selection under Clinton: A Midterm Examination." 78 *Judicature* 276 (1995).

————. *Picking Federal Judges: Lower Court Selection from Roosevelt through Reagan.* New Haven: Yale University Press, 1997.

————. "Reaganizing the Judiciary: The First Term Appointments." 68 *Judicature* 313 (1985).

————. "Reagan's Second Term Judicial Appointments: The Battle at Midway." 70 *Judicature* 324 (1987).

————. "Voting Behavior in the United States Courts of Appeals, 1961–1964." 60 *American Political Science Review* 374 (1966).

————. "Voting Behavior on the U.S. Court of Appeals Revisited." 69 *American Political Science Review* 491 (1975).

Goldman, Sheldon, and Sarat, Austin, eds. *American Court Systems.* 2d ed. New York: Longman, 1989.

Goldman, Sheldon, and Saronson, Matthew D. "Clinton's Nontraditional Judges: Creating a More Representative Bench." 78 *Judicature* 68 (1994).

Goldman, Sheldon, and Slotnick, Elliot. "Clinton's First Term Judiciary: Many Bridges to Cross." 80 *Judicature* 254 (1997).

Goldstein, Joseph. *The Intelligible Constitution: The Supreme Court's Obligation to Maintain the Constitution as Something We the People Can Understand.* New York: Oxford University Press, 1992.

Goldstein, Leslie Friedman. *In Defense of the Text.* Lanham, Md.: Rowman and Littlefield, Publishers, 1991.

————. "Indeterminacy and Constitutional Theory: A Critique of CLS and Its Fellow-Travelers." Paper delivered at the Western Political Science Association meeting, San Francisco, 1988.

Gordon, Robert. "New Developments in Legal Theory." In Kairys, David, ed. *The Politics of Law: A Progressive Critique.* New York: Pantheon Books, 1982.

Gottschall, Jon. "Carter's Judicial Appointments: The Influence of Affirmative Action and Merit Selection on Voting on the U.S. Courts of Appeals." 67 *Judicature* 164 (1983).

————. "Reagan's Appointments to the U.S. Courts of Appeals: The Continuation of a Judicial Revolution." 70 *Judicature* 48 (1986).

Graglia, Lino. *Disaster by Decree: The Supreme Court Decisions on Race and the Schools.* Ithaca: Cornell University Press, 1976.

Graham, Fred. "Blackmun May Prove a Surprise to Nixon." *New York Times* (April 19, 1970), 10.

Grano, Joseph D. *Confessions, Truth, and the Law.* Ann Arbor: University of Michigan Press, 1993.

————. "Ely's Theory of Judicial Review: Preserving the Significance of the Political Process." 42 *Ohio State Law Journal* 167 (1981).

————. "Judicial Review and a Written Constitution in a Democratic Society." 28 *Wayne Law Review* 1 (1981).

Grasso, Kenneth L., and Castillo, Cicelia Rodriguez, eds. *Liberty under Law: American Constitutionalism, Yesterday, Today and Tomorrow.* 2d ed. Lanham, Md.: Rowman and Littlefield Publishers, 1997.

Greenawalt, Kent. "The Enduring Significance of Neutral Principles." 78 *Columbia Law Review* 982 (1978).

Grey, David. *The Supreme Court and the News Media.* Evanston, Ill.: Northwestern University Press, 1968.

Grey, Thomas C. "The Constitution as Scripture." 37 *Stanford Law Review* 1 (1984).

————. "Do We Have an Unwritten Constitution?" 27 *Stanford Law Review* 703 (1975).

Grossman, Joel B. *Lawyers and Judges.* New York: Wiley, 1965.

Grossman, Joel B., and Tanenhaus, Joseph, eds. *Frontiers of Judicial Research.* New York: Wiley, 1969.

Grossman, Joel B., and Wasby, Stephen L. "The Senate and Supreme Court Nominations: Some Reflections." 1972 *Duke Law Journal* 557 (1972).

Grossman, Joel B., and Wells, Richard S. *Constitutional Law and Judicial Policy Making.* 2d ed. New York: John Wiley and Sons, 1980.

Gryski, Gerard, and Main, Eleanor. "Social Backgrounds as Predictors of Votes on State Courts of Last Resort: The Case of Sex Discrimination." 39 *Western Political Quarterly* 528 (1986).

Hagle, Timothy M. "Strategic Retirements: A Political Model of Turnover on the United States Supreme Court." 15 *Political Behavior* 25 (1993).

Hagle, Timothy M., and Spaeth, Harold J. "The Business Decisions of the Burger Court: The Emergence of a New Ideology." 54 *Journal of Politics* 120 (1992).

————. "Ideological Patterns in the Justices' Voting in the Burger Court's Business Cases." 55 *Journal of Politics* 492 (1993).

————. "Voting Fluidity and the Attitudinal Model of Supreme Court Decision Making." 44 *Western Political Quarterly* 119 (1991).

Hakman, Nathan. "Lobbying the Supreme Court: An Appraisal of Political Science 'Folklore.'" 35 *Fordham Law Review* 15 (1966).

————. "The Supreme Court's Political Environment: The Processing of Non-Commercial Litigation." In Grossman, Joel B., and Tanenhaus, Joseph, eds. *Frontiers of Judicial Research.* New York: Wiley, 1969.

Hall, Melinda. "An Examination of Voting Behavior in the Louisiana Supreme Court." 71 *Judicature* 40 (1987).

Hall, Richard, and Wayman, Frank. "Buying Time: Moneyed Interests and the Mobilization of Bias in Congressional Committees." 84 *American Political Science Review* 797 (1990).

Halper, Thomas. "Senate Rejection of Supreme Court Nominees." 22 *Drake Law Review* 102 (1972).

Hand, Learned. *The Bill of Rights.* Cambridge: Harvard University Press, 1958.

Handberg, Roger, and Berg, Larry L. *The Supreme Court and Congress.* New York: Free Press, 1971.

Handberg, Roger, and Hill, Harold F., Jr. "Court Curbing, Court Reversals, and Judicial Review: The Supreme Court versus Congress." 14 *Law and Society Review* 309 (1980).

Handberg, Roger, and Maddox, William S. "Public Support for the Supreme Court in the 1970s." 10 *American Politics Quarterly* 333 (1982).

Hansen, Susan B. "State Implementation of Supreme Court Decisions: Abortion Rates since *Roe* v. *Wade.*" 42 *Journal of Politics* 372 (1980).

Hanson, Roger, and Crew, Robert. "The Policy Impact of Reapportionment." 8 *Law and Society Review* 69 (1973).

Harris, Joseph P. *The Advice and Consent of the Senate.* Berkeley, Calif.: University of California Press, 1953.

Hart, Henry M., Jr. "Foreword: The Time Chart of the Justices." 73 *Harvard Law Review* 84 (1959).

Hartley, Roger E., and Holmes, Lisa M. "Increasing Senate Scrutiny of Lower Federal Court Nominees." 80 *Judicature* 274 (1997).

Haskell, John. *Fundamentally Flawed: Reforming Presidential Primaries.* Lanham, Md.: Rowman and Littlefield Publishers, 1996.

Haynie, Stacia L. "Leadership and Consensus on the U.S. Supreme Court." 54 *Journal of Politics* 1158 (1992).

Heck, Edward V., and Shull, Steven A. "Policy Preferences of Justices and Presidents: The Case of Civil Rights." 4 *Law and Policy Quarterly* 327 (1982).

Heclo, Hugh. "Issue Networks and the Executive Establishment." In King, Anthony, ed. *The New American Political System.* Washington, D.C.: American Enterprise Institute, 1979.

Henkin, Louis. "Privacy and Autonomy." 74 *Columbia Law Review* 1410 (1974).

Henschen, Beth M. "Congressional Response to the Statutory Interpretations of the Supreme Court." 11 *American Politics Quarterly* 441 (1983).

————"Statutory Interpretations of the Supreme Court: Congressional Response." 11 *American Politics Quarterly* 441 (1983).

Hensley, Thomas R., and Smith, Christopher E. "Membership Change and Voting Change: An Analysis of the Rehnquist Court's 1986–1991 Terms." 48 *Political Research Quarterly* 837 (1995).

Herring, Pendleton. *The Politics of Democracy.* 2d ed. New York: W. W. Norton and Co., 1965.

Hertzke, Allen D., and Peters, Ronald M., Jr., eds. *The Atomistic Congress.* Armonk, N.Y.: M. E. Sharpe, 1992.

Hess, Robert D., and Torney, Judith V. *The Development of Political Attitudes in Children.* Chicago: Aldine Publishing Co., 1967.

Hirsch, Herbert, and Donohew, Lewis. "A Note on Black-White Differences in Attitudes toward the Supreme Court." 49 *Social Science Quarterly* 557 (1968).

Hoekstra, Valerie J. "The Supreme Court and Opinion Change: An Experimental Study of the Court's Ability to Change Opinion." 23 *American Politics Quarterly* 109 (1995).

Hoffman, Daniel N. *Our Elusive Constitution.* Albany: State University of New York Press, 1997.

Horowitz, Donald L. *The Courts and Social Policy.* Washington, D.C.: Brookings Institution Press, 1977.

Howard, J. Woodford. *Courts of Appeals in the Federal Judicial System: A Study of the Second, Fifth, and District of Columbia Circuits.* Princeton: Princeton University Press, 1981.

————. "On the Fluidity of Judicial Choice." 52 *American Political Science Review* 43 (1968).

————. "Role Perceptions and Behavior on Three U.S. Courts of Appeals." 39 *Journal of Politics* 916 (1977).

Hughes, Charles Evans. *Addresses of Charles Evans Hughes.* New York: Putnam's, 1916.

Hulbary, William E., and Walker, Thomas G. "The Supreme Court Selection Process: Presidential Motivations and Judicial Performance." 33 *Western Political Quarterly* 185 (1980).

Hunter, Floyd. *Community Power Structure.* Chapel Hill: University of North Carolina Press, 1953.

Hutchinson, Allan C., ed. *Critical Legal Studies.* Lanham, Md.: Rowman and Littlefield Publishers, 1989.

Ignagni, Joseph A. "U.S. Supreme Court Decision-Making and the Free Exercise Clause." 55 *Review of Politics* 511 (1993).

Ignagni, Joseph, and Meernik, James. "Explaining Congressional Attempts to Reverse Supreme Court Decisions." 47 *Political Research Quarterly* 353 (1994).

"Interpretation Symposium." 58, nos. 1 and 2, *Southern California Law Review* 1 (1985).

"Interrogations in New Haven: The Impact of *Miranda.*" 49 *Yale Law Journal* 1519 (1967).

Ivers, Gregg, and O'Connor, Karen. "Friends as Foes: The Amicus Curiae Participation and Effectiveness of the American Civil Liberties Union and Americans for Effective Law Enforcement in Criminal Cases, 1969–1982." 9 *Law and Policy* 161 (1987).

Jackson, Robert H. *The Struggle for Judicial Supremacy: A Study of a Crisis in American Power Politics.* New York: A. A. Knopf, 1941.

Jacobsohn, Gary. *The Supreme Court and the Decline of Constitutional Aspiration.* Totowa, N.J.: Rowman and Littlefield, 1986.

Jacobson, Gary C. "Parties and PACs in Congressional Elections." In Dodd, Lawrence C., and Oppenheimer, Bruce I., eds. *Congress Reconsidered.* 6th ed. Washington, D.C.: Congressional Quarterly Press, 1996.

———. *The Politics of Congressional Elections.* 4th ed. New York: HarperCollins, 1997.

Jahnige, Thomas P. "Critical Elections and Social Change: Toward a Dynamic Explanation of National Party Competition in the United States." 3 *Polity* 465 (1971).

Jaros, Dean, and Roper, Robert. "The Supreme Court, Myth, Diffuse Support, Specific Support, and Legitimacy." 8 *American Politics Quarterly* 85 (1980).

Johnson, Charles A. "Personnel Change and Policy Change in the U.S. Supreme Court." 62 *Social Science Quarterly* 751 (1981).

Johnson, Charles A., and Canon, Bradley C. *Judicial Policies: Implementation and Impact.* Washington, D.C.: Congressional Quarterly Press, 1984.

Johnson, Phillip. "Do You Sincerely Want to Be Radical?" 36 *Stanford Law Review* 247 (1984).

Johnson, Richard M. *The Dynamics of Compliance: Supreme Court Decision-Making from a New Perspective.* Evanston, Ill.: Northwestern University Press, 1967.

Johnson, Timothy R., and Martin, Andrew D. "The Public's Conditional Response to Supreme Court Decisions." 92 *American Political Science Review* 299 (1998).

Johnston, Richard E. "Supreme Court Voting Behavior: A Comparison of the Warren and Burger Courts." In Peabody, Robert L., ed. *Cases in American Politics.* New York: Praeger, 1976.

Jones, Charles O. *The Presidency in a Separated System.* Washington, D.C.: Brookings Institution Press, 1994.

"Judicially Managed Institutional Reform." Symposium. 32 *Alabama Law Review* 267 (1981).

"Judicial Review and the Constitution—The Text and Beyond." Symposium. 8 *University of Dayton Law Review* 443 (1983).

Kagan, Robert A., Infelise, Bobby D., and Detlefsen, Robert R. "American State Supreme Court Justices, 1900–1970." 1984 *American Bar Foundation Research Journal* 371 (1984).

Kahn, Ronald. *The Supreme Court and Constitutional Theory, 1953–1993.* Lawrence: University Press of Kansas, 1994.

Kairys, David. *The Politics of Law: A Progressive Critique.* 3d ed. Boulder, Colo.: Basic Books 1998.

Karst, Kenneth L. *Belonging to America.* New Haven: Yale University Press, 1989.

———. "Foreword: Equal Citizenship under the Fourteenth Amendment." 91 *Harvard Law Review* 1 (1977).

Karst, Kenneth L., and Horowitz, Harold W. "The *Bakke* Opinions and Equal Protection Doctrine." 14 *Harvard Civil Rights–Civil Liberties Law Review* 7 (1979).

Katsh, Ethan. "The Supreme Court Beat: How Television Covers the U.S. Supreme Court." 67 *Judicature* 6 (1983).

Kay, Richard S. "Adherence to the Original Intentions in Constitutional Adjudication: Three Objections and Responses." 82 *Northwestern University Law Review* 226 (1988).

Kayden, Xandra, and Mahe, Eddie, Jr. *The Party Goes On: The Persistence of the Two-Party System in the United States.* New York: Basic Books, 1985.

Kearney, Edward, ed. *Dimensions of the Modern Presidency.* St. Louis, Mo.: Forum Press, 1981.

Keefe, William J. *Parties, Politics, and Public Policy in America.* Washington, D.C.: Congressional Quarterly Press, 1991.

Kelman, Mark. "Interpretive Construction in the Substantive Criminal Law." 33 *Stanford Law Review* 591 (1981).

Kennedy, Duncan. "Cost-Reduction Theory as Legitimation." 90 *Yale Law Journal* 1275 (1981).

———. "Form and Substance in Private Law Adjudication." 95 *Harvard Law Review* 1685 (1976).

Kennedy, Duncan, and Klane, Karl E. "A Bibliography of Critical Legal Studies." 94 *Yale Law Journal* 461 (1984).

Kens, Paul. *Judicial Power and Reform Politics.* Lawrence: University Press of Kansas, 1992.

Kernell, Samuel. *Going Public: New Strategies of Presidential Leadership.* 3d ed. Washington, D.C.: Congressional Quarterly Press, 1997.

Kessel, John H. "Public Perceptions of the Supreme Court." 10 *Midwest Journal of Political Science* 167 (1966).

Key, V. O., Jr. *Politics, Parties, and Pressure Groups.* 5th ed. New York: Thomas Y. Crowell, 1964.

———. *Public Opinion and American Democracy.* New York: Knopf, 1961.

———. *The Responsible Electorate.* Cambridge: Harvard University Press, 1966.

———. *Southern Politics in State and Nation.* New York: Knopf, 1949.

———. "A Theory of Critical Elections." 17 *Journal of Politics* 4 (1955).

Keynes, Edward. *The Court versus Congress: Prayer, Busing, and Abortion.* Durham, N.C.: Duke University Press, 1989.

King, Anthony. *Running Scared: The Victory of Campaigning over Governing in America.* New York: Free Press, 1997.

King, Gary, and Gelman, Andrew. "Systemic Consequences of Incumbency Advantage in U.S. House Elections." 35 *American Journal of Political Science* 110 (1991).

Kluger, Richard. *Simple Justice.* New York: Knopf, 1976.

Knight, Jack, and Epstein, Lee. "The Norm of *Stare Decisis.*" 40 *American Journal of Political Science* 1018 (1996).

Kobylka, Joseph F. *The Politics of Obscenity: Group Litigation in a Time of Legal Change.* Westport, Conn.: Greenwood Press, 1991.

Kort, Fred. "Content Analysis of Judicial Opinions and Rules of Law." In Schubert, Glendon, ed. *Judicial Decision-Making*. New York: Free Press, 1963.

———. "Quantitative Analysis of Fact-Patterns in Cases and Their Impact on Judicial Decisions." 79 *Harvard Law Review* 1595 (1966).

Kosaki, Liane C. "Public Awareness of Supreme Court Decisions." Paper presented at the Annual Meeting of the American Political Science Association, 1991.

Kovacic, William E. "The Reagan Judiciary and Environmental Policy: The Impact of Appointments to the Federal Courts of Appeals." 18 *Boston College Environmental Affairs Law Review* 669 (1991).

———. "Reagan's Judicial Appointees and Antitrust in the 1990s." 60 *Fordham Law Review* 49 (1991).

Krislov, Samuel. "The Amicus Curiae Brief: From Friendship to Advocacy." 72 *Yale Law Journal* 694 (1963).

———. Review of *The Hollow Hope*, by Gerald Rosenberg. 9 *Constitutional Commentary* 367 (1992).

Krol, John F., and Brenner, Saul. "Strategies in Certiorari Voting on the United States Supreme Court: A Reevaluation." 43 *Western Political Quarterly* 335 (1990).

Kurland, Philip B. "The Appointment and Disappointment of Supreme Court Justices." 1972 *Law and Social Order* 183 (1972).

———. *Politics, the Constitution, and the Warren Court*. Chicago: University of Chicago Press, 1970.

Kuttner, Robert. "Why Americans Don't Vote." *New Republic* 19 (September 7, 1987).

Ladd, Everett Carll, Jr. "Party Reform and the Public Interest." In Reichley, A. James, ed. *Elections American Style*. Washington, D.C.: Brookings Institution Press, 1987.

———. *Where Have All the Voters Gone?* New York: Norton, 1977.

Lamb, Charles. "Warren Burger and the Insanity Defense: Judicial Philosophy and Voting Behavior on a U.S. Court of Appeals." 24 *American University Law Review* 91 (1974).

Landau, Martin. "Redundancy, Rationality, and the Problem of Duplication and Overlap." 29 *Public Administration Review* 346 (1969).

Lane, Robert E. *Political Ideology*. New York: Free Press, 1962.

Langbein, Laura. "Money and Access." 48 *Journal of Politics* 1052 (1986).

Larisa, Joseph. "Popular Mythology: The Framers' Intent, the Constitution and Ideological Review of Supreme Court Nominees." 69 *Boston College Law Review* 1989.

"Law and Literature." Symposium. 60 *Texas Law Review* (1982).

Law, Sylvia. "Rethinking Sex and the Constitution." 132 *University of Pennsylvania Law Review* 955 (1984).

Lawrence, Susan E. *The Poor in Court*. Princeton: Princeton University Press, 1990.

Laycock, Douglas. "Taking Constitutions Seriously: A Theory of Judicial Power." 59 *Texas Law Review* 343 (1981).

Leedes, Gary C. "A Critique of Illegitimate Noninterpretivism." 8 *University of Dayton Law Review* 533 (1983).

———. "The Supreme Court Mess." 57 *Texas Law Review* 1361 (1979).

Lehne, Richard, and Reynolds, John. "The Impact of Judicial Activism on Public Opinion." 22 *American Journal of Political Science* 896 (1978).

Lehnen, Robert. *American Institutions, Political Opinion, and Public Policy*. Hinsdale, Ill.: Dryden, 1976.

Lerner, Max. "Constitution and Court as Symbols." 46 *Yale Law Journal* 1290 (1937).

Leuchtenberg, William E. *The Supreme Court Reborn.* New York: Oxford University Press, 1995.

Levinson, Sanford. "The Constitution in American Civil Religion." 1979 *Supreme Court Review* 123 (1979).

———. "Law as Literature." 60 *Texas Law Review* 373 (1982).

———. "The Turn toward Functionalism in Constitutional Theory." 8 *University of Dayton Law Review* 567 (1983).

Levinson, Sanford, and Mailloux, Steven, eds. *Interpreting Law and Literature: A Hermeneutic Reader.* Evanston, Ill.: Northwestern University Press, 1988.

Levy, Leonard W. "The Original Constitution as a Bill of Rights." 9 *Constitutional Commentary* 163 (1992).

———. *Original Intent and the Framers' Constitution.* New York: Macmillan, 1988.

Lewis, Anthony. "The Supreme Court and Its Critics." 45 *Minnesota Law Review* 305 (1961).

———. "A Talk with Warren on Crime, the Court, the Country." *New York Times Magazine* (October 19, 1969), 128.

Lindblom, Charles. *Politics and Markets.* New York: Basic Books, 1977.

Lindgren, Janet S. "Beyond Cases: Reconsidering Judicial Review." 1983 *Wisconsin Law Review* 583 (1983).

Link, Michael W. "Tracking Public Mood in the Supreme Court: Cross-Time Analysis of Criminal Procedure and Civil Rights Cases." 48 *Political Research Quarterly* 61 (1995).

Lively, Donald. "The Supreme Court Appointment Process: In Search of Constitutional Roles and Responsibilities." 59 *Southern California Law Review* 563 (1986).

Llewellyn, Karl. "The Constitution as an Institution." 34 *Columbia Law Review* 1 (1934).

———. "A Realistic Jurisprudence—The Next Step." 30 *Columbia Law Review* 431 (1930).

———. "Some Realism about Realism—Responding to Dean Pound." 44 *Harvard Law Review* 1222 (1931).

Loomis, Burdett. *The New American Politician.* New York: Basic Books, 1988.

Lowi, Theodore J. *The End of Liberalism.* 2d ed. New York: W. W. Norton, 1979.

———. *The Personal President: Power Invested, Promise Unfulfilled.* Ithaca: Cornell University Press, 1985.

Lowi, Theodore J., and Ginsberg, Benjamin. *American Government: Freedom and Power.* 3d ed. New York: W. W. Norton, 1994.

Lukes, Steven. *Power: A Radical View.* London: Macmillan, 1974.

Lusky, Louis. *By What Right? A Commentary on the Supreme Court's Power to Revise the Constitution.* Charlottesville, Va.: Michie Co., 1975.

Lytle, Clifford M. *The Warren Court and Its Critics.* Tucson: University of Arizona Press, 1968.

Macedo, Stephen. *The New Right v. the Constitution.* Washington, D.C.: Cato Institute, 1987.

MacKinnon, Catharine. "*Roe* v. *Wade*: A Study in Male Ideology." In Garfield, Jay L., and Hennessey, Patricia, eds. *Abortion: Moral and Legal Perspectives.* Amherst: University of Massachusetts Press, 1984.

Madison, Christopher. "A Class Apart." *National Journal* 564 (March 9, 1991).

Magleby, David B., and Nelson, Candice J. *The Money Chase: Congressional Campaign Finance Reform.* Washington, D.C.: Brookings Institution Press, 1990.

Maisel, L. Sandy. *The Parties Respond: Developments in the American Party System.* 2d ed. Boulder, Colo.: Westview Press, 1994.

Malbin, Michael J. "Delegation, Deliberation, and the New Role of Congressional Staff." In Mann, Thomas E., and Ornstein, Norman J., eds. *The New Congress.* Washington, D.C.: American Enterprise Institute, 1981.

Malbin, Michael J., ed. *Unelected Representatives: Congressional Staff and the Future of Representative Government.* New York: Basic Books, 1980.

———. *Money and Politics in the United States.* Washington, D.C.: American Enterprise Institute, 1984.

Maltese, John Anthony. *The Selling of Supreme Court Nominees.* Baltimore: Johns Hopkins University Press, 1995.

Maltz, Earl. "Murder in the Cathedral: The Supreme Court as Moral Prophet." 8 *University of Dayton Law Review* 623 (1983).

———. "Some New Thoughts on an Old Problem—The Role of the Intent of the Framers in Constitutional Theory." 63 *Boston University Law Review* 811 (1983).

Maltzman, Forrest, and Wahlbeck, Paul J. "May It Please the Chief? Opinion Assignments in the Rehnquist Court." 40 *American Journal of Political Science* 421 (1996).

———. "Strategic Policy Considerations and Voting Fluidity on the Burger Court." 90 *American Political Science Review* 581 (1996).

Mann, Thomas E., and Ornstein, Norman J. *The New Congress.* Washington, D.C.: American Enterprise Institute, 1981.

Mansbridge, Jane, and Tate, Katherine. "Race Trumps Gender: The Thomas Nomination in the Black Community." 24 *PS: Political Science and Politics* 488 (1992).

Manwaring, David R. *Render unto Caesar: The Flag Salute Controversy.* Chicago: University of Chicago Press, 1962.

Marshall, Thomas R. "Public Opinion and the Rehnquist Court." 74 *Judicature* 322 (1991).

———. *Public Opinion and the Supreme Court.* Boston: Unwin Hyman, 1989.

———. "Symbolic versus Policy Representation on the U.S. Supreme Court." 55 *Journal of Politics* 140 (1993).

Marshall, Thomas R., and Ignagni, Joseph. "Supreme Court and Public Support for Rights Claims." 78 *Judicature* 146 (1994).

Mason, Alpheus T. "Myth and Reality in Supreme Court Decisions." 48 *Virginia Law Review* 1385 (1962).

———. *The Supreme Court: Vehicle of Revealed Truth or Power Group?* Boston: Boston University Press, 1953.

Massaro, John. *Supremely Political: The Role of Ideology and Presidential Management in Unsuccessful Supreme Court Nominations.* Albany: State University of New York Press, 1990.

Massey, Calvin R. "The Duty of Keeping Political Power Separated." 20 *Hastings Constitutional Law Quarterly* 1 (1992).

Mayer, William. *The Changing American Mind: How and Why American Public Opinion Changed between 1960 and 1988.* Ann Arbor: University of Michigan Press, 1992.

Mayhew, David R. "Congressional Elections: The Case of the Vanishing Marginals." 6 *Polity* 295 (1974).

McCloskey, Herbert, and Zaller, John. *The American Ethos: Public Attitudes toward Capitalism and Democracy.* Cambridge: Harvard University Press, 1984.

McCloskey, Robert G. *The American Supreme Court.* Chicago: University of Chicago Press, 1960.

———. "Economic Due Process and the Supreme Court: An Exhumation and Reburial." 1962 *Supreme Court Review* 34 (1962).

———. *The Modern Supreme Court.* Cambridge: Harvard University Press, 1972.

McConnell, Grant. *Private Power and American Politics.* New York: Alfred A. Knopf, 1966.

McConnell, Michael W. "The Forgotten Constitutional Moment." 11 *Constitutional Commentary* 115 (1994).

McConnell, A. Mitchell, Jr. "Haynsworth and Carswell: A New Senate Standard of Excellence." 59 *Kentucky Law Journal* 7 (1970).

McCubbins, Matthew D., and Schwartz, Thomas. "Congress, the Courts, and Public Policy: Consequences of the One Man, One Vote Rule." 32 *American Journal of Political Science* 388 (1988).

McDowell, Gary L., ed. *Taking the Constitution Seriously*. Dubuque, Iowa: Kendall/Hunt Publishing, 1981.

McFeeley, Neil D. *Appointment of Judges*. Austin: University of Texas Press, 1987.

McGuire, Kevin T. "Obscenity, Libertarian Values and Decision Making in the Supreme Court." 18 *American Politics Quarterly* 47 (1990).

McGuire, Kevin T., and Caldeira, Gregory A. "Lawyers, Organized Interests, and the Law of Obscenity: Agenda Setting in the Supreme Court." 87 *American Political Science Review* 717 (1993).

McGuire, Kevin T., and Palmer, Barbara. "Issue Fluidity on the U.S. Supreme Court." 89 *American Political Science Review* 691 (1995).

McHargue, Daniel S. "Factors Influencing the Selection and Appointment of Members of the United States Supreme Court, 1789–1932." Ph.D. diss., University of California, Los Angeles, 1949.

———. "President Taft's Appointments to the Court." 12 *Journal of Politics* 478 (1950).

Meernik, James, and Ignagni, Joseph. "Congressional Attacks on Supreme Court Rulings Involving Unconstitutional State Laws." 48 *Political Research Quarterly* 43 (1995).

———. "Judicial Review and Coordinate Construction of the Constitution." 41 *American Journal of Political Science* 447 (1997).

Meese, Edwin III. "The Supreme Court of the United States: Bulwark of a Limited Constitution." 27 *South Texas Law Journal* 455 (1986).

Melone, Albert. "The Senate's Confirmation Role in Supreme Court Nominations and the Politics of Ideology versus Impartiality." 75 *Judicature* 68 (1991).

Meltsner, Michael. *Cruel and Unusual: The Supreme Court and Capital Punishment*. New York: Random House, 1973.

Michelman, Frank I. "Bringing the Law to Life: A Plea for Disenchantment." 74 *Cornell Law Review* 256 (1989).

———. "Law's Republic." 97 *Yale Law Journal* 1493 (1988).

Mikva, Abner J., and Bleich, Jeff. "When Congress Overrules the Court." 79 *California Law Review* 729 (1991).

Milkis, Sidney M. *The President and the Parties*. New York: Oxford University Press, 1993.

Miller, Arthur S. "Some Pervasive Myths about the United States Supreme Court." 10 *St. Louis University Law Journal* 153 (1965).

———. *Toward Increased Judicial Activism: The Political Role of the Supreme Court*. Westport, Conn.: Greenwood Press, 1982.

Miller, Arthur S., and Howell, Ronald F. "The Myth of Neutrality in Constitutional Adjudication." 27 *University of Chicago Law Review* 661 (1960).

Miller, Arthur S., and Scheflin, Alan W. "The Power of the Supreme Court in the Age of the Positive State: A Preliminary Excursus, Part One: On Candor and the Court, or, Why Bamboozle the Natives?" 1967 *Duke Law Journal* 273 (1967).

Miller, Mark C. "Congress and the Constitution: A Tale of Two Committees." 3 *Constitutional Law Journal* 317 (1993).

———. "Courts, Agencies, and Congressional Committees: A Neo-Institutional Perspective." 55 *Review of Politics* 471 (1993).

Mills, C. Wright. *The Power Elite*. New York: Oxford University Press, 1956.

Miltsner, Arnold J., ed. *Politics and the Oval Office*. San Francisco: Institute for Contemporary Studies, 1981.

Mishler, William, and Sheehan, Reginald S. "Policy Legitimacy and the Supreme Court: The Sources and Contexts of Legitimation." 47 *Political Research Quarterly* 675 (1994).

——. "Popular Influence on Supreme Court Decisions: A Response to Helmut Norpoth and Jeffrey A. Segal." 88 *American Political Science Review* 716 (1994).

——. "Public Opinion, the Attitudinal Model, and Supreme Court Decision Making: A Micro-Analytic Perspective." 58 *Journal of Politics* 169 (1996).

——. "The Supreme Court as a Countermajoritarian Institution? The Impact of Public Opinion on Supreme Court Decisions." 87 *American Political Science Review* 87 (1993).

Mnookin, Robert H. "*Bellotti* v. *Baird*: A Hard Case." In Mnookin, Robert H., ed. *In the Interest of Children*. New York: W. H. Freeman and Company, 1985.

——, ed. *In the Interest of Children: Advocacy, Law Reform, and Public Policy*. New York: W. H. Freeman and Company, 1985.

Moe, Terry. "The Politicized Presidency." In Chubb, John, and Peterson, Paul E., eds. *The New Direction in American Politics*. Washington, D.C.: Brookings Institution Press, 1985.

Mondak, Jeffrey J. "Perceived Legitimacy of Supreme Court Decisions: Three Functions of Source Credibility." 12 *Political Behavior* 363 (1990).

——. "Policy Legitimacy and the Supreme Court: The Sources and Contexts of Legitimation." 47 *Political Research Quarterly* 675 (1994).

Mondak, Jeffrey J., and Smithey, Shannon Ishiyama. "The Dynamics of Public Support for the Supreme Court." 59 *Journal of Politics* 1114 (1997).

Monroe, Alan. "Consistency between Public Preferences and National Policy Decisions." 7 *American Politics Quarterly* 3 (1979).

Morgan, Richard E. *Disabling America: The "Rights Industry" in Our Time*. New York: Basic Books, 1984.

Muir, William K., Jr. *Legislature: California's School for Politics*. Chicago: University of Chicago Press, 1982.

——. *Prayer in the Public Schools: Law and Attitude Change*. Chicago: University of Chicago Press, 1967.

Munzer, Stephen R., and Nickel, James W. "Does the Constitution Mean What It Always Meant?" 77 *Columbia Law Review* 1029 (1977).

Murphy, Walter F. *Congress and the Court*. Chicago: University of Chicago Press, 1962.

——. "Constitutional Interpretation: The Art of the Historian, Magician, or Statesman?" 87 *Yale Law Journal* 1752 (1978).

——. *Elements of Judicial Strategy*. Chicago: University of Chicago Press, 1964.

——. "Lower Court Checks on Supreme Court Power." 53 *American Political Science Review* 1017 (1959).

——. "Reagan's Judicial Strategy." In Berman, Larry, ed. *Looking Back on the Reagan Presidency*. Baltimore: Johns Hopkins University Press, 1990.

Murphy, Walter F., and Tanenhaus, Joseph. "Constitutional Courts and Political Representation." In Danielson, Michael, and Murphy, Walter, eds. *Modern American Democracy: Readings*. New York: Holt, Rinehart and Winston, 1969.

——. "Publicity, Public Opinion, and the Court." 84 *Northwestern University Law Review* 985 (1990).

——. "Public Opinion and the Supreme Court: The Goldwater Campaign." 32 *Public Opinion Quarterly* 31 (1968).

Murphy, Walter F., and Tanenhaus, Joseph. "Public Opinion and the United States Supreme Court: A Preliminary Mapping of Some Prerequisites for Court Legitimation of Regime Change." 2 *Law and Society Review* 357 (1968).

Murphy, Walter; Tanenhaus, Joseph; and Kastner, Daniel. *Public Evaluations of Constitutional Courts: Alternative Explanations.* Beverly Hills: Sage Publications, 1973.

Nagel, Robert F. *Constitutional Cultures: The Mentality and Consequences of Judicial Review.* Berkeley: University of California Press, 1989.

Nagel, Stuart S. "Court-Curbing Periods in American History." 18 *Vanderbilt Law Review* 925 (1965).

————. "Ethnic Affiliations and Judicial Propensities." 24 *Journal of Politics* 92 (1962).

————. "Multiple Correlation of Judicial Backgrounds and Decisions." 2 *Florida State University Law Review* 258 (1974).

————. "Off-the-Bench Judicial Attitudes." In Schubert, Glendon, ed. *Judicial Decision-Making.* New York: Free Press, 1964.

————. "Political Party Affiliation and Judges' Decisions." 55 *American Political Science Review* 92 (1961).

Nedelsky, Jennifer. *Private Property and the Limits of American Constitutionalism: The Madisonian Framework and Its Legacy.* Chicago: University of Chicago Press, 1990.

Neubauer, David W. *Judicial Process: Law, Courts, and Politics in the United States.* 1st ed. Pacific Grove, Calif.: Brooks/Cole Publishing Co., 1991.

————. *Judicial Process: Law, Courts, and Politics in the United States.* 2d ed. New York: Harcourt Brace, 1997.

Neuman, W. Russell. *The Paradox of Mass Politics: Knowledge and Opinion in the American Electorate.* Cambridge: Harvard University Press, 1986.

Neustadt, Richard E. *Presidential Power and the Modern Presidents.* New York: Free Press, 1990.

Newland, Chester. "Press Coverage of the United States Supreme Court." 17 *Western Political Quarterly* 15 (1964).

Nie, Norman H.; Verba, Sidney; and Petrocik, John R. *The Changing American Voter.* Cambridge: Harvard University Press, 1976.

Nisbet, Robert. "Popular Opinion versus Public Opinion." 41 *Public Interest* 167 (1975).

Nomination of Robert H. Bork to be Associate Justice of the Supreme Court of the United States: Hearings before the Senate Committee on the Judiciary, 100th Congress, 1st session, 1987.

Noonan, John. "The Root and Branch of *Roe* v. *Wade.*" 63 *Nebraska Law Review* 668 (1984).

Norpoth, Helmut, and Rusk, Jerrold. "Partisan Dealignment in the American Electorate." 76 *American Political Science Review* (1982).

Norpoth, Helmut, and Segal, Jeffrey A. "Popular Influence on Supreme Court Decisions: Comment." 88 *American Political Science Review* 711 (1994).

O'Brien, David M. *Constitutional Law and Politics.* New York: W. W. Norton, 1991.

————. *Judicial Roulette: Report of the Twentieth Century Fund Task Force on Judicial Selection.* Background paper. New York: Priority Press Publications, 1988.

————. "The Politics of Professionalism: President Gerald R. Ford's Appointment of Justice John Paul Stevens." 21 *Presidential Studies Quarterly* 103 (1991).

————. "The Reagan Judges: His Most Enduring Legacy?" In Jones, Charles O., ed. *The Reagan Legacy: Promise and Performance.* Chatham, N.J.: Chatham House Publishers, 1988.

————. *Storm Center: The Supreme Court in American Politics.* 4th ed. New York: W. W. Norton, 1996.

————. *Supreme Court Watch—1992.* New York: Norton, 1992.

O'Connor Karen. "The Amicus Curiae Role of the U.S. Solicitor General in Supreme Court Litigation." 66 *Judicature* 256 (1983).

―――. *Women's Organizations' Use of the Courts.* Lexington, Mass.: Lexington Books, 1980.

O'Connor, Karen, and Epstein, Lee. "An Appraisal of Hakman's 'Folklore.'" 16 *Law and Society Review* 701 (1982).

―――. "Court Rules and Workload: A Case Study of Rules Governing Amicus Curiae Participation." 8 *Justice System Journal* 35 (1983).

―――. *Public Interest Law Groups.* Westport, Conn.: Greenwood Press, 1989.

―――. "The Rise of Conservative Interest Group Litigation." 45 *Journal of Politics* 479 (1983).

Olson, Susan M. *Clients and Lawyers—Serving the Rights of Disabled People.* Westport, Conn.: Greenwood Press, 1984.

―――. "Interest-Group Litigation in Federal District Court: Beyond the Political Disadvantage Theory." 52 *Journal of Politics* 854 (1990).

Orfield, Myron W., Jr. "The Exclusionary Rule and Deterrence: An Empirical Study of Chicago Narcotics Officers." 54 *University of Chicago Law Review* 1016 (1987).

Overby, L. Marvin; Henschen, Beth M.; Walsh, Michael H.; and Strauss, Julie. "Courting Constituents: An Analysis of the Senate Confirmation Vote on Justice Clarence Thomas." 86 *American Political Science Review* 997 (1992).

Pacelle, Richard L., Jr. *The Transformation of the Supreme Court's Agenda: From the New Deal to the Reagan Administration.* Boulder, Colo.: Westview Press, 1991.

Page, Benjamin I., and Shapiro, Robert Y. "Effects of Public Opinion on Policy." 77 *American Political Science Review* 175 (1983).

―――. *The Rational Public: Fifty Years of Trends in Americans' Policy Preferences.* Chicago: University of Chicago Press, 1992.

Page, Benjamin I.; Shapiro, Robert Y.; and Dempsey, Glenn. "What Moves Public Opinion?" 81 *American Political Science Review* 23 (1987).

Palmer, Jan. "An Econometric Analysis of the U.S. Supreme Court's Certiorari Decisions." 39 *Public Choice* 387 (1982).

―――. "Senate Confirmation of Appointments to the U.S. Supreme Court." 41 *Review of Social Economy* 152 (1983).

Parker, Richard Davies. "The Past of Constitutional Theory—And Its Future." 42 *Ohio State Law Journal* 223 (1981).

Pascal, Richard A. "The Continuing Colloquy: Congress and the Finality of the Supreme Court." 8 *Journal of Law and Politics* 143 (1991).

Patric, Gordon. "The Impact of a Court Decision: Aftermath of the *McCollum* Case." 6 *Journal of Public Law* 455 (1957).

Patterson, Bradley. *The Ring of Power: The White House Staff and Its Expanding Role.* New York: Basic Books, 1988.

Peretti, Terri Jennings. "Restoring the Balance of Power: The Struggle for Control of the Supreme Court." 20 *Hastings Constitutional Law Quarterly* 69 (1992).

―――. "The Virtues of 'Value Clarity' in Constitutional Decisionmaking." 55 *Ohio State Law Journal* 1079 (1994).

Perry, H. W., Jr. "Agenda Setting and Case Selection." In Gates, John B., and Johnson, Charles A., eds. *The American Courts: A Critical Assessment.* Washington, D.C.: Congressional Quarterly Press, 1991.

―――. *Deciding to Decide: Agenda Setting in the United States Supreme Court.* Cambridge: Harvard University Press, 1991.

Perry, Michael J. "Abortion, the Public Morals, and the Police Power: The Ethical Function of Substantive Due Process." 23 *UCLA Law Review* 689 (1976).

———. "The Authority of Text, Tradition, and Reason: A Theory of Constitutional 'Interpretation.'" 58 *Southern California Law Review* 551 (1985).

———. *The Constitution, the Courts, and Human Rights: An Inquiry into the Legitimacy of Constitutional Policymaking by the Judiciary.* New Haven: Yale University Press, 1982.

———. "Substantive Due Process Revisited: Reflections on (and beyond) Recent Cases." 71 *Northwestern University Law Review* 417 (1977).

Pertschuk, Michael, and Schaetzel, Wendy. *The People Rising: The Campaign against the Bork Nomination.* New York: Thunder's Mouth Press, 1989.

Petracca, Mark P., ed. *The Politics of Interests: Interest Groups Transformed.* Boulder, Colo.: Westview Press, 1992.

Pfeffer, Leo. "Amici in Church-State Litigation." 44 *Law and Contemporary Problems* 83 (1981).

Piven, Frances Fox, and Cloward, Richard. *Why Americans Don't Vote.* New York: Pantheon, 1988.

Polsby, Nelson W. *Community Power and Political Theory.* 2d ed. New Haven: Yale University Press, 1980.

———. *Consequences of Party Reform.* New York: Oxford University Press, 1983.

———. "Legislatures." In Greenstein, Fred I., and Polsby, Nelson W., eds. *Handbook of Political Science.* Vol. 5. Reading, Mass.: Addison-Wesley Publishing, 1975.

———. "Presidential Cabinet Making: Lessons for the Political System." 93 *Political Science Quarterly* 15 (1978).

Polsby, Nelson, and Wildavsky, Aaron. *Presidential Elections: Contemporary Strategies of American Electoral Politics.* 9th ed. Chatham, N.J.: Chatham House Publishers, 1995.

Pomper, Gerald M. *Party Renewal in America.* New York: Praeger, 1981.

Posner, Richard A. "This Magic Movement." *New Republic* 32 (April 6, 1998).

———. "What Am I? A Potted Plant?" *New Republic* 23 (September 28, 1987).

Post, Robert, ed. *Law and the Order of Culture.* Berkeley, Calif.: University of California Press, 1991.

Powell, H. Jefferson. "The Original Understanding of Original Intent." 98 *Harvard Law Review* 886 (1985).

Powell, Justice Lewis. "*Carolene Products* Revisited." 82 *Columbia Law Review* 1087 (1982).

Pritchett, C. Herman. *Congress versus the Supreme Court, 1857–1960.* Minneapolis, Ind.: University of Minnesota Press, 1962.

———. *The Roosevelt Court: A Study in Judicial Politics and Values, 1937–1947.* New York: Macmillan, 1948.

Provine, Doris Marie. *Case Selection in the United States Supreme Court.* Chicago: University of Chicago Press, 1980.

———. "Deciding What to Decide: How the Supreme Court Sets Its Agenda." 64 *Judicature* 320 (1981).

Puro, Steven. "The Role of Amicus Curiae in the United States Supreme Court, 1920–1966." Ph.D. diss., State University of New York at Buffalo, 1971.

———. "The United States as Amicus Curiae." In Ulmer, S. Sidney, ed. *Courts, Law and Judicial Processes.* New York: Free Press, 1981.

Rabkin, Jeremy. *Judicial Compulsions: How Public Law Distorts Public Policy.* New York: Basic Books, 1989.

Rakove, Jack N. *Original Meanings.* New York: Knopf, 1995.

Rathjen, Gregory J., and Spaeth, Harold J. "Access to the Federal Courts: An Analysis of Burger Court Policy Making." 23 *American Journal of Political Science* 360 (1979).

———. "Denial of Access and Ideological Preferences: An Analysis of the Voting Behavior of the Burger Court Justices, 1969–1976." 36 *Western Political Quarterly* 71 (1983).

Redish, Martin H. *The Constitution as Political Structure.* New York: Oxford University Press, 1995.

Rehnquist, William H. "The Notion of a Living Constitution." 54 *Texas Law Review* 693 (1976).

———. "Presidential Appointments to the Supreme Court." 2 *Constitutional Commentary* 319 (1985).

———. "Ruing Fixed Opinions." *New York Times* (February 22, 1988), 20.

———. *The Supreme Court: How It Was, How It Is.* New York: Morrow, 1987.

Reid, Traciel V. "Judicial Policy-Making and Implementation: An Empirical Examination." 41 *Western Political Quarterly* 509 (1988).

Reiter, Howard L. "Why Is Turnout Down?" 43 *Public Opinion Quarterly* 297 (1979).

Reynolds, William Bradford. "The Confirmation Process: Too Much Advice and Too Little Consent." 75 *Judicature* 80 (1991).

Richards, David A. J. *Conscience and the Constitution.* Princeton: Princeton University Press, 1993.

———. *The Moral Criticism of Law.* Encino, Calif.: Dickenson Publishing, 1977.

———. "Moral Philosophy and the Search for Fundamental Values in Constitutional Law." 42 *Ohio State Law Journal* 319 (1981).

———. "Rules, Policies and Neutral Principles: The Search for Legitimacy in Common Law and Constitutional Adjudication." 11 *Georgia Law Review* 1069 (1977).

———. "Sexual Autonomy and the Constitutional Right to Privacy: A Case Study in Human Rights and the Unwritten Constitution." 30 *Hastings Law Journal* 957 (1979).

———. "Unnatural Acts and the Constitutional Right to Privacy: A Moral Theory." 45 *Fordham Law Review* 1281 (1977).

Rieselbach, Leroy N. *Congressional Reform: The Changing Modern Congress.* Washington, D.C.: Congressional Quarterly Press, 1993.

Roche, John P. "The Founding Fathers: A Reform Caucus in Action." 55 *American Political Science Review* 799 (1961).

———. "Judicial Self-Restraint." 49 *American Political Science Review* 762 (1955).

Rockman, Bert A. *The Leadership Question.* New York: Praeger, 1984.

Rodgers, Harrell R., Jr., and Bullock, Charles S. III. *Coercion to Compliance.* Lexington, Mass.: Heath, 1976.

———. *Law and Social Change: Civil Rights Laws and Their Consequences.* New York: McGraw-Hill, 1972.

Rohde, David W. "Policy Goals, Strategic Choice, and Majority Opinion Assignments in the U.S. Supreme Court." 16 *American Journal of Political Science* 652 (1972).

Rohde, David W., and Spaeth, Harold J. "Ideology, Strategy and Supreme Court Decisions: William Rehnquist as Chief Justice." 72 *Judicature* 247 (1989).

———. *Supreme Court Decision Making.* San Francisco: W. H. Freeman, 1976.

Rose, Richard, *The Postmodern President.* 2d ed. Chatham, N.J.: Chatham House Publishers, 1991.

Rosenberg, Gerald N. *The Hollow Hope: Can Courts Bring about Social Change?* Chicago: University of Chicago Press, 1991.

Rosenberg, Gerald N. "Judicial Independence and the Reality of Political Power." 54 *Review of Politics* 369 (1992).

Rosenstone, Steven J., and Hansen, John Mark. *Mobilization, Participation, and Democracy in America.* New York: Macmillan, 1993.

Rossiter, Clinton. *Parties and Politics in America.* Ithaca: Cornell University Press, 1960.

"'Round and 'Round the Bramble Bush: From Legal Realism to Critical Legal Scholarship." 95 *Harvard Law Review* 1669 (1982).

Rowland, C. K., and Carp, Robert A. *Political Appointments and Political Jurisprudence in the Federal District Courts.* Lawrence: University Press of Kansas, 1992.

———. *Politics and Judgment in Federal District Courts.* Lawrence: University of Kansas Press, 1996.

———. "The Relative Effects of Maturation, Time Period, and Appointment President on District Judges' Policy Choices: A Cohort Analysis." 5 *Political Behavior* 109 (1983).

Rowland, C. K.; Carp, Robert A.; and Songer, Donald. "Presidential Effects on Criminal Justice Policy in the Lower Federal Courts: The Reagan Judges." 22 *Law and Society Review* 191 (1988).

Rowland, C. K.; Carp, Robert A.; and Stidham, Ronald. "Judges' Policy Choices and the Value Basis of Judicial Appointments: A Comparison of Support for Criminal Defendants among Nixon, Johnson, and Kennedy Appointees to the Federal District Courts." 46 *Journal of Politics* 886 (1984).

Rowland, C. K., and Todd, Bridget Jeffery. "Where You Stand Depends on Who Sits: Platform Promises and Judicial Gatekeeping in the Federal District Courts." 53 *Journal of Politics* 175 (1991).

Ruckman, P. S., Jr. "The Supreme Court, Critical Nominations, and the Senate Confirmation Process." 55 *Journal of Politics* 793 (1993).

Sabato, Larry J. *PAC Power: Inside the World of Political Action Committees.* New York: Norton, 1984.

———. *The Party's Just Begun.* Glenview, Ill.: Scott, Foresman, 1988.

———. *The Rise of Political Consultants.* New York: Basic Books, 1981.

Sager, Lawrence G. "Rights Skepticism and Process-Based Responses." 56 *New York University Law Review* 417 (1981).

Salokar, Rebecca Mae. *The Solicitor General: The Politics of Law.* Philadelphia, Penn.: Temple University Press, 1992.

Sandalow, Terrance. "Abstract Democracy: A Review of Ackerman's *We the People*." 9 *Constitutional Commentary* 309 (1992).

———. "Constitutional Interpretation." 79 *Michigan Law Review* 1033 (1981).

———. "Judicial Protection of Minorities." 75 *Michigan Law Review* 1162 (1977).

Saphire, Richard B. "The Search for Legitimacy in Constitutional Theory: What Price Purity?" 42 *Ohio State Law Journal* 335 (1981).

Savage, David G. *Turning Right: The Making of the Rehnquist Supreme Court.* New York: John Wiley and Sons, 1992.

Schattschneider, E. E. *Party Government.* New York: Holt, Rinehart and Winston, 1942.

———. *The Responsible Electorate.* Cambridge: Harvard University Press, 1966.

———. *The Semi-Sovereign People.* New York: Holt, Rinehart and Winston, 1960.

Schauer, Frederick. "Deliberating about Deliberation." 90 *Michigan Law Review* 1187 (1992).

———. "Easy Cases." 58 *Southern California Law Review* 399 (1985).

Scheb John M. II; Bowen, Terry; and Anderson, Gary. "Ideology, Role Orientations, and Behavior in the State Courts of Last Resort." 19 *American Politics Quarterly* 324 (1991).

Scheb, John M. II, and Ungs, Thomas D. "Competing Orientations to the Judicial Role: The Case of Tennessee Judges." 54 *Tennessee Law Review* 391 (1987).

Schlesinger, Arthur M., Jr. *The Imperial Presidency.* Boston: Houghton Mifflin, 1973.

Schlozman, Kay Lehman, and Tierney, John T. *Organized Interests and American Democracy.* New York: HarperCollins, 1981.

———. "Washington Pressure Group Activity in a Decade of Change." 45 *Journal of Politics* 351 (1983).

Schmidhauser, John R. *Judges and Justices: The Federal Appellate Judiciary.* Boston: Little, Brown, 1979.

———. "Judicial Behavior and the Sectional Crisis of 1837–1860." 23 *Journal of Politics* 615 (1961).

———. "The Justices of the Supreme Court: A Collective Portrait." 3 *Midwest Journal of Political Science* 1 (1959).

———. "*Stare Decisis*, Dissent, and the Background of the Justices of the Supreme Court of the United States." 14 *University of Toronto Law Journal* 194 (1962).

———. *The Supreme Court: Its Politics, Personalities, and Procedures.* New York: Holt, Rinehart and Winston, 1960.

Schmidhauser, John R., and Berg, Larry L. *The Supreme Court and Congress.* New York: Free Press, 1972.

Schroedel, Jean Reith. "Campaign Contributions and Legislative Outcomes." 39 *Western Political Quarterly* 371 (1986).

Schubert, Glendon. "The Certiorari Game." In Schubert, Glendon, ed. *Judicial Behavior: A Reader in Theory and Research.* Chicago: Rand McNally, 1964.

———. *The Judicial Mind.* Evanston, Ill.: Northwestern University Press, 1965.

———. *The Judicial Mind Revisited: Psychometric Analysis of Supreme Court Ideology.* New York: Oxford Press, 1974.

———. "The 1960–1961 Term of the Supreme Court: A Psychological Analysis." 56 *American Political Science Review* 90 (1962).

———. "Policy without Law: An Extension of the Certiorari Game." 14 *Stanford Law Review* 224 (1962).

———. *Quantitative Analysis of Judicial Behavior.* Glencoe, Ill.: Free Press, 1959.

Schubert, Glendon, ed. *Judicial Decision-Making.* New York: Free Press, 1963.

Schultz, David A., and Smith, Christopher E. *The Jurisprudential Vision of Justice Antonin Scalia.* Lanham, Md.: Rowman and Littlefield Publishers, 1996.

Schwartz, Bernard. *Decision: How the Supreme Court Decides Cases.* New York: Oxford University Press, 1996.

Schwartz, Herman. *Packing the Courts: The Conservative Campaign to Rewrite the Constitution.* New York: Charles Scribner's Sons, 1988.

Scigliano, Robert. *The Supreme Court and the Presidency.* New York: Free Press, 1971.

Scott, Christy. "Constitutional Moments and Crackpot Revolutions." 25 *Connecticut Law Review* 967 (1993).

Segal, Jeffrey A. "Amicus Curiae Briefs by the Solicitor General during the Warren and Burger Courts." 41 *Western Political Quarterly* 135 (1988).

———. "Courts, Executives, and Legislatures." In Gates, John B., and Johnson, Charles A., eds. *The American Courts: A Critical Assessment.* Washington, D.C.: Congressional Quarterly Press, 1991.

Segal, Jeffrey A. "Judicial-Executive Interactions: The Effect of Presidential Ideology." State University of New York at Stony Brook, 1989. Photocopy.

―――. "Predicting Supreme Court Cases Probabilistically: The Search and Seizure Cases, 1962–1981." 78 *American Political Science Review* 891 (1984).

―――. "Senate Confirmation of Supreme Court Justices: Partisan and Institutional Politics." 49 *Journal of Politics* 998 (1987).

―――. "Supreme Court Justices as Human Decision Makers: An Individual-Level Analysis of the Search and Seizure Cases." 48 *Journal of Politics* 938 (1986).

―――. "Supreme Court Support for the Solicitor General: The Effect of Presidential Appointments." 43 *Western Political Quarterly* 137 (1990).

Segal, Jeffrey A.; Cameron, Charles M.; and Cover, Albert D. "A Spatial Model of Roll Call Voting: Senators, Constituents, Presidents, and Interest Groups in Supreme Court Confirmations." 36 *American Journal of Political Science* 96 (1992).

Segal, Jeffrey A., and Cover, Albert. D. "Ideological Values and the Votes of U.S. Supreme Court Justices." 83 *American Political Science Review* 557 (1989).

Segal, Jeffrey A.; Cover, Albert D.; and Cameron, Charles M. "The Role of Ideology in Senate Confirmation of Supreme Court Justices." 77 *Kentucky Law Journal* 485 (1988–89).

Segal, Jeffrey A.; Epstein, Lee; Cameron, Charles M.; and Spaeth, Harold J. "Ideological Values and the Votes of U.S. Supreme Court Justices Revisited." 57 *Journal of Politics* 812 (1995).

Segal, Jeffrey A., and Reedy, Cheryl D. "The Supreme Court and Sex Discrimination: The Role of the Solicitor General." 41 *Western Political Quarterly* 553 (1988).

Segal, Jeffrey A., and Spaeth, Harold J. "Decisional Trends on the Warren and Burger Courts: Results from the Supreme Court Data Base Project." 73 *Judicature* 103 (1989).

―――. "If a Supreme Court Vacancy Occurs, Will the Senate Confirm a Reagan Nominee?" 69 *Judicature* 187 (1986).

―――. "The Influence of *Stare Decisis* on the Votes of United States Supreme Court Justices." 40 *American Journal of Political Science* 971 (1996).

―――. "Norms, Dragons, and *Stare Decisis*: A Response." 40 *American Journal of Political Science* 1064 (1996).

―――. *The Supreme Court and the Attitudinal Model.* New York: Cambridge University Press, 1993.

Segal, Jennifer A. "The Decision Making of Clinton's Nontraditional Judicial Appointees." 80 *Judicature* 279 (1997).

Shafer, Byron, ed. *Beyond Realignment? Interpreting American Electoral Eras.* Madison: University of Wisconsin Press, 1991.

Shapiro, Martin M. "The Constitution and Economic Rights." In Harmon, M. Judd, ed. *Essays on the Constitution of the United States.* Port Washington, N.Y.: Kennikat Press, 1978.

―――. *Freedom of Speech: The Supreme Court and Judicial Review.* Englewood Cliffs, N.J.: Prentice-Hall, 1966.

―――. "Interest Groups and Supreme Court Appointments." 84 *Northwestern University Law Review* 935 (1990).

―――. *Law and Politics in the Supreme Court.* New York: Macmillan, 1964.

―――. "Stability and Change in Judicial Decisionmaking: Incrementalism or *Stare Decisis*?" 2 *Law in Transition Quarterly* 134 (1965).

―――. "The Supreme Court and Constitutional Adjudication: Of Politics and Neutral Principles." 31 *George Washington Law Review* 587 (1963).

————. "The Supreme Court: From Warren to Burger." In King, Anthony, ed. *The New American Political System*. Washington, D.C.: American Enterprise Institute, 1978.

Shaw, David. "Media Coverage of the Courts: Improving but Still Not Adequate." 65 *Judicature* 18 (1981).

Sheehan, Reginald S. "Governmental Litigants, Underdogs, and Civil Liberties: A Reassessment of a Trend in Supreme Court Decisionmaking." 45 *Western Political Quarterly* 27 (1992).

Sheehan, Reginald S.; Mishler, William; and Songer, Donald R. "Ideology, Status, and the Differential Success of Direct Parties before the Supreme Court." 86 *American Political Science Review* 464 (1992).

Sherry, Suzanna. "Civic Virtue and the Feminine Voice in Constitutional Adjudication." 72 *University of Virginia Law Review* 543 (1986).

————. "The Ghost of Liberalism Past." 105 *Harvard Law Review* 918 (1992).

Shull, Steven A.; Gleiber, Dennis W.; and Garland, David. "Ideological Congruence between the General Public and Government Institutions: The Case of Civil Rights." Paper presented at the Annual Meeting of the Western Political Science Association, 1991.

Siegan, Bernard H. *Economic Liberties and the Constitution*. Chicago: University of Chicago Press, 1981.

————. *The Supreme Court's Constitution: An Inquiry into Judicial Review and Its Impact on Society*. New Brunswick, N.J.: Transaction Books, 1987.

Sigelman, Lee. "Black and White Differences in Attitudes toward the Supreme Court: A Replication in the 1970s." 60 *Social Science Quarterly* 113 (1979).

Sigelman, Lee, and Todd, James S. "Clarence Thomas, Black Pluralism, and Civil Rights Policy." 107 *Political Science Quarterly* 231 (1992).

Silverstein, Mark. *Judicious Choices: The New Politics of Supreme Court Confirmations*. New York: W. W. Norton, 1994.

————. "The People, the Senate and the Court: The Democratization of the Judicial Confirmation System." 9 *Constitutional Commentary* 41 (1992).

Silverstein, Mark, and Ginsberg, Benjamin. "The Supreme Court and the New Politics of Judicial Power." 102 *Political Science Quarterly* 371 (1987).

Silverstein, Mark, and Haltom, William. "Can There Be a Theory of Supreme Court Confirmations?" Paper presented at the Annual Meeting of the Western Political Science Association, 1990.

Simon, Herbert A. *Administrative Behavior*. 3d ed. New York: Free Press, 1976.

Simon, Larry G. "The Authority of the Framers of the Constitution: Can Originalist Interpretation Be Justified?" 73 *California Law Review* 1482 (1985).

Simson, Gary J. "Taking the Court Seriously: A Proposed Approach to Senate Confirmation of Supreme Court Nominees." 7 *Constitutional Commentary* 283 (1990).

Sinclair, Barbara. *The Transformation of the U.S. Senate*. Baltimore: Johns Hopkins University Press, 1989.

————. *Unorthodox Lawmaking: New Legislative Processes in the U.S. Congress*. Washington, D.C.: Congressional Quarterly Press, 1997.

Slotnick, Elliot E. "The ABA Standing Committee on Federal Judiciary: A Contemporary Assessment." 66 *Judicature* 349 (1983).

————. "The Chief Justice and Self-Assignment of Majority Opinions." 31 *Western Political Quarterly* 219 (1978).

————. "Federal Judicial Recruitment and Selection Research: A Review Essay." 71 *Judicature* 317 (1988).

Slotnick, Elliot E. "Television News and the Supreme Court: A Case Study." 77 *Judicature* 21 (1993).

———. "Who Speaks for the Court? Majority Opinion Assignment from Taft to Burger." 23 *American Journal of Political Science* 60 (1979).

Smith, Christopher E. *Critical Judicial Nominations and Political Change: The Impact of Clarence Thomas.* Westport, Conn.: Praeger Publishers, 1993.

———. *The Rehnquist Court and Criminal Punishment.* Hamden, Conn.: Garland Publishing, 1997.

———. "The Supreme Court's Emerging Majority: Restraining the High Court or Transforming Its Role? 24 *Akron Law Review* 393 (1990).

Smith, Christopher E.; Baugh, Joyce A.; and Hensley, Thomas R. "The First-Term Performance of Justice Stephen Breyer." 79 *Judicature* 74 (1995).

Smith, Christopher E.; Baugh, Joyce Ann; Hensley, Thomas R.; and Johnson, Scott Patrick. "The First-Term Performance of Justice Ruth Bader Ginsburg." 78 *Judicature* 74 (1994).

Smith, Christopher E., and Beuger, Kimberly A. "Clouds in the Crystal Ball: Presidential Expectations and the Unpredictable Behavior of Supreme Court Appointees." 27 *Akron Law Review* 115 (1993).

Smith, Christopher E., and Hensley, Thomas R. "Assessing the Conservatism of the Rehnquist Court." 76 *Judicature* 83 (1993).

———. "Unfulfilled Aspirations: The Court-Packing Efforts of Presidents Reagan and Bush." 57 *Albany Law Review* 1111 (1994).

Smith, Christopher E., and Johnson, Scott Patrick. "The First-Term Performance of Justice Clarence Thomas." 76 *Judicature* 172 (1993).

Smith, Eric R. A. N. *The Unchanging American Voter.* Berkeley: University of California Press, 1989.

Smith, Rogers M. *Liberalism and American Constitutional Law.* Cambridge: Harvard University Press, 1985.

Smith, Steven. *The American Congress.* 2d ed. Boston: Houghton Mifflin, 1995.

Solomon, Rayman. "The Politics of Appointment and the Federal Courts' Role in Regulating America: U.S. Courts of Appeals Judgeships from T.R. to F.D.R." 2 *American Bar Foundation Research Journal* 285 (1984).

Solomine, Michael E., and Walker, James L. "The Next Word: Congressional Response to Supreme Court Statutory Decisions." 65 *Temple Law Quarterly* 425 (1992).

Songer, Donald R. "Concern for Policy Outputs as a Cue for Supreme Court Decisions of Certiorari." 41 *Journal of Politics* 1185 (1979).

———. "Consensual and Nonconsensual Decisions in Unanimous Opinions of the United States Courts of Appeals." 26 *American Journal of Political Science* 225 (1982).

———. "The Policy Consequences of Senate Involvement in the Selection of Judges in the United States Courts of Appeal." 35 *Western Political Quarterly* 107 (1982).

———. "The Relevance of Policy Values for the Confirmation of Supreme Court Nominees." 13 *Law and Society Review* 927 (1979).

Songer, Donald R., and Davis, Sue. "The Impact of Party and Region on Voting Decisions in the United States Courts of Appeals, 1955–1986." 43 *Western Political Quarterly* 317 (1990).

Songer, Donald R., and Lindquist, Stephanie A. "Not the Whole Story: The Impact of Justices' Values on Supreme Court Decision Making." 40 *American Journal of Political Science* 1049 (1996).

Songer, Donald R., and Sheehan, Reginald S. "Interest Group Success in the Courts: Amicus Participation in the Supreme Court." 46 *Political Research Quarterly* 339 (1993).

―――. "Who Wins on Appeal? Upperdogs and Underdogs in the United States Courts of Appeals." 36 *American Journal of Political Science* 235 (1992).

Sorauf, Frank J. *Inside Campaign Finance: Myths and Realities.* New Haven: Yale University Press, 1992.

―――. *Money in American Elections.* Boston: Little, Brown, 1988.

―――. "*Zorach* v. *Clauson*: The Impact of a Supreme Court Decision." 53 *American Political Science Review* 777 (1959).

Spaeth, Harold J. "An Analysis of Judicial Attitudes in the Labor Relations Decisions of the Warren Court." 25 *Journal of Politics* 290 (1963).

―――. "An Approach to the Study of Attitudinal Differences as an Aspect of Judicial Behavior." 5 *Midwest Journal of Political Science* 165 (1961).

―――. "Consensus in the Unanimous Decisions of the U.S. Supreme Court." 72 *Judicature* 274 (1989).

―――. "Distributive Justice: Majority Opinion Assignments in the Burger Court." 67 *Judicature* 299 (1984).

―――. "The Judicial Restraint of Mr. Justice Frankfurter—Myth or Reality?" 8 *American Journal of Political Science* 22 (1964).

―――. *Supreme Court Policy Making: Explanation and Prediction.* San Francisco: W. H. Freeman and Co., 1979.

―――. "Warren Court Attitudes toward Business: The 'B' Scale." In Schubert, Glendon, ed. *Judicial Decision-Making.* New York: Free Press, 1963.

Spaeth, Harold J., and Altfield, Michael F. "Influence Relationships within the Supreme Court: A Comparison of the Warren and Burger Courts." 38 *Western Political Quarterly* 70 (1985).

Spaeth, Harold J., and Brenner, Saul, eds. *Studies in U.S. Supreme Court Behavior.* New York: Garland, 1990.

Spaeth, Harold J., and Teger, Stuart H. "Activism and Restraint: A Cloak for the Justices' Policy Preferences." In Halpern, Stephen C., and Lamb, Charles M., eds. *Supreme Court Activism and Restraint.* Lexington, Mass.: D. C. Heath, 1982.

Sprague, John D. *Voting Patterns of the United States Supreme Court.* Indianapolis, Ind.: Bobbs-Merrill, 1968.

Squire, Peverill. "Politics and Personal Factors in Retirement from the United States Supreme Court." 10 *Political Behavior* 180 (1988).

Stern, Philip M. *The Best Congress Money Can Buy.* New York: Pantheon, 1988.

Stern, Robert L. "The Commerce Clause and the National Economy, 1933–1946." 59 *Harvard Law Review* 645 (1946).

Stewart, Richard B. "The Reformation of American Administrative Law." 88 *Harvard Law Review* 1669 (1978).

Stidham, Ronald, and Carp, Robert A. "Judges, Presidents, and Policy Choices: Exploring the Linkages." 68 *Social Science Quarterly* 395 (1987).

―――. "Support for Labor and Economic Regulation among Reagan and Carter Appointees to the Federal Courts." 26 *Social Science Journal* 433 (1989).

Stidham, Ronald; Carp, Robert A.; and Rowland, C. K. "Patterns of Presidential Influence on the Federal District Courts: An Analysis of the Appointment Process." 14 *Presidential Studies Quarterly* 548 (1984).

Stidham, Ronald; Carp, Robert A.; and Songer, Donald. "The Voting Behavior of President Clinton's Judicial Appointees." 80 *Judicature* 16 (1996).

Stidham, Ronald; Carp, Robert; Songer, Donald; and Surratt, Donean. "The Impact of Major Structural Reform on Judicial Decisionmaking: A Case Study of the U.S. Fifth Circuit." 45 *Western Political Quarterly* 143 (1992).

Stimson, James A. *Public Opinion in America: Moods, Cycles, and Swings.* Boulder, Colo.: Westview Press, 1991.

Stimson, James A.; MacKuen, Michael B.; and Erikson, Robert S. "Dynamic Representation." 89 *American Political Science Review* 543 (1995).

Stooky, John, and Watson, George. "The Bork Hearings: Rocks and Roles." 71 *Judicature* 194 (1988).

Strauss, David A., and Sunstein, Cass R. "The Senate, the Constitution, and the Confirmation Process." 101 *Yale Law Journal* 1491 (1992).

Stumpf, Harry. "Congressional Response to Supreme Court Rulings: The Interaction of Law and Politics." 14 *Journal of Public Law* 377 (1965).

———. "The Political Efficacy of Judicial Symbolism." 19 *Western Political Quarterly* 293 (1966).

Sugarman, Stephen D. "*Roe* v. *Norton*: Coerced Maternal Cooperation." In Mnookin, Robert H., ed. *In the Interest of Children.* New York: W. H. Freeman, 1985.

Sulfridge, Wayne. "Ideology as a Factor in Senate Consideration of Supreme Court Nominations." 42 *Journal of Politics* 560 (1980).

Sundquist, James L. *Dynamics of the Party System: Alignment and Realignment of Political Parties in the United States.* Rev. ed. Washington, D.C.: Brookings Institution Press, 1983.

Sunstein, Cass R. "Beyond the Republican Revival." 97 *Yale Law Journal* 1539 (1988).

———. "Interest Groups in American Public Law." 38 *Stanford Law Review* 29 (1985).

———. *Legal Reasoning and Political Conflict.* New York: Oxford University Press, 1996.

———. *The Partial Constitution.* Cambridge: Harvard University Press, 1993.

"The Supreme Court, 1994 Term." 109 *Harvard Law Review* 340 (1995).

Swindler, William. "The Politics of 'Advice and Consent.'" 56 *American Bar Association Journal* 533 (1970).

"Symposium on Critical Legal Studies." 6 *Cardozo Law Review* 691 (1985).

Tanenhaus, Joseph. "The Cumulative Scaling of Judicial Decisions." 79 *Harvard Law Review* 1583 (1966).

———. "Supreme Court Attitudes toward Federal Administrative Agencies, 1947–1956— An Application of Social Science Methods to the Study of the Judicial Process." 14 *Vanderbilt Law Review* 482 (1961).

Tanenhaus, Joseph, and Murphy, Walter F. "Patterns of Public Support for the Supreme Court: A Panel Study." 43 *Journal of Politics* 24 (1981).

Tanenhaus, Joseph; Schick, Marvin; Muraskin, Matthew; and Rosen, Daniel. "The Supreme Court's Certiorari Jurisdiction: Cue Theory." In Schubert, Glendon, ed. *Judicial Decision Making.* New York: Free Press, 1963.

Tarr, G. Alan, and Porter, Mary Cornelia. *State Supreme Courts in State and Nation.* New Haven: Yale University Press, 1988.

Tate, C. Neal. "Personal Attribute Models of the Voting Behavior of U.S. Supreme Court Justices' Liberalism in Civil Liberties and Economics Decisions, 1946–1978." 75 *American Political Science Review* 355 (1981).

Tate, C. Neal, and Handberg, Roger. "Time Binding and Theory Building in Personal Attribute Models of Supreme Court Voting Behavior, 1916–1988." 35 *American Journal of Political Science* 460 (1991).

Taylor, Telford. Review of *The Constitution, the Courts, and Human Rights: An Inquiry into the Legitimacy of Constitutional Policymaking by the Judiciary*, by Michael J. Perry. 5 *Cardozo Law Review* 223 (1983).

Teger, Stuart H., and Kosinski, Douglas. "The Cue Theory of Supreme Court Certiorari Jurisdiction: A Reconsideration." 42 *Journal of Politics* 834 (1980).

Teixeira, Ruy A. *The Disappearing American Voter*. Washington, D.C.: Brookings Institution Press, 1992.

———. *Why Americans Don't Vote: Turnout Decline in the United States, 1960–1984*. Westport, Conn.: Greenwood Press, 1987.

Thayer, James Bradley. *John Marshall*. Boston: Houghton Mifflin, 1901.

Thurber, James A., ed. *Rivals for Power*. Washington, D.C.: Congressional Quarterly Press, 1996.

Thurber, James A., and Davidson, Roger H. *Remaking Congress: Change and Stability in the 1990s*. Washington, D.C.: Congressional Quarterly Press, 1995.

Toma, Eugenia Froedge. "Congressional Influence and the Supreme Court: The Budget as a Signaling Device." 20 *Journal of Legal Studies* 131 (1991).

Tomasi, Timothy B., and Velona, Jess A. "All the President's Men? A Study of Ronald Reagan's Appointments to the U.S. Courts of Appeals." 87 *Columbia Law Review* 766 (1987).

Totenberg, Nina. "Behind the Marble, Beneath the Robes." 60 *New York Times Magazine* (March 16, 1975).

———. "The Confirmation Process and the Public: To Know or Not to Know." 101 *Harvard Law Review* 1213 (1988).

Tribe, Laurence H. *American Constitutional Law*. 1st ed. Mineola, N.Y.: Foundation Press, 1978.

———. *American Constitutional Law*. 2d ed. Mineola, N.Y.: Foundation Press, 1988.

———. *God Save This Honorable Court*. New York: Random House, 1985.

———. "The Puzzling Persistence of Process-Based Constitutional Theories." 89 *Yale Law Journal* 1063 (1980).

———. "Structural Due Process." 10 *Harvard Civil Rights–Civil Liberties Law Review* 193 (1975).

Tribe, Laurence H., and Dorf, Michael C. *On Reading the Constitution*. Cambridge: Harvard University Press, 1991.

Truman, David B. *The Governmental Process*, 2d ed. New York: Alfred A. Knopf, 1971.

Tulis, Jeffrey K. *The Rhetorical Presidency*. Princeton: Princeton University Press, 1987.

Tushnet, Mark. "Darkness on the Edge of Town: The Contributions of John Hart Ely to Constitutional Theory." 89 *Yale Law Journal* 1037 (1980).

———. "Following the Rules Laid Down: A Critique of Interpretivism and Neutral Principles." 96 *Harvard Law Review* 781 (1983).

———. "Legal Realism, Structural Review, and Prophecy." 8 *University of Dayton Law Review* 809 (1983).

———. *The NAACP's Legal Strategy against Segregated Education, 1925–1950*. Chapel Hill: University of North Carolina, 1987.

———. *Red, White, and Blue: A Critical Analysis of Constitutional Law*. Cambridge: Harvard University Press, 1988.

Tyler, Tom R., and Mitchell, Gregory. "Legitimacy and Empowerment of Discretionary Legal Authority: The United States Supreme Court and Abortion Rights." 43 *Duke Law Journal* 703 (1994).

Ulmer, S. Sidney. "The Analysis of Behavior Patterns on the United States Supreme Court." 22 *Journal of Politics* 629 (1960).

Ulmer, S. Sidney. "Conflict with Supreme Court Precedent and the Granting of Plenary Review." 45 *Journal of Politics* 474 (1983).

———. *Courts as Small and Not So Small Groups.* New York: General Learning Press, 1971.

———. "The Decision to Grant Certiorari as an Indicator to Decision 'On the Merits.'" 4 *Polity* 429 (1972).

———. "Dissent Behavior and the Social Background of Supreme Court Justices." 32 *Journal of Politics* 580 (1970).

———. "Earl Warren and the *Brown* Decision." 33 *Journal of Politics* 689 (1971).

———. "Government Litigants, Underdogs, and Civil Liberties in the Supreme Court: 1903–1968 Terms." 47 *Journal of Politics* 899 (1985).

———. "The Political Party Variable in the Michigan Supreme Court." 11 *Journal of Public Law* 352 (1962).

———. "Scaling Judicial Cases: A Methodological Note." 4 *American Behavioral Scientist* 31 (1961).

———. "Selecting Cases for Supreme Court Review: An Underdog Model." 72 *American Political Science Review* 902 (1978).

———. "Social Background as an Indicator to the Votes of Supreme Court Justices in Criminal Cases." 17 *Midwest Journal of Political Science* 622 (1973).

———. "Supreme Court Behavior and Civil Rights." 13 *Western Political Quarterly* 288 (1960).

———. "Supreme Court Justices as Strict and Not-So-Strict Constructionists: Some Implications." 8 *Law and Society Review* 13 (1973).

———. "The Supreme Court's Certiorari Decisions: Conflict as a Predictive Variable." 78 *American Political Science Review* 901 (1984).

———. "Toward a Theory of Sub-Group Formation in the United States Supreme Court." 27 *Journal of Politics* 133 (1965).

———. "The Use of Power on the Supreme Court: The Opinion Assignments of Earl Warren, 1953–1960." 30 *Journal of Public Law* 49 (1970).

Ulmer, S. Sidney; Hintze, William; and Kirklosky, Louise. "The Decision to Grant or Deny Certiorari: Further Consideration of Cue Theory." 6 *Law and Society Review* 637 (1972).

Unger, Roberto Mangabeira. "The Critical Legal Studies Movement." 96 *Harvard Law Review* 561 (1983).

———. *The Critical Legal Studies Movement.* Cambridge: Harvard University Press, 1986.

———. *Law in Modern Society: Toward a Criticism of Social Theory.* New York: Free Press, 1976.

Van Alstyne, William. "A Graphic Review of the Free Speech Clause." 70 *California Law Review* 107 (1982).

Vines, Kenneth N. "Federal District Judges and Race Relations Cases in the South." 26 *Journal of Politics* 338 (1964).

Vose, Clement E. *Caucasians Only: The Supreme Court, the NAACP, and the Restrictive Covenant Cases.* Berkeley: University of California Press, 1959.

———. "Litigation as a Form of Pressure Group Activity." 319 *Annals of the American Academy of Political and Social Science* 20 (1958).

———. "National Consumers' League and the Brandeis Brief." 1 *Midwest Journal of Political Science* 178 (1957).

Wahlbeck, Paul J. "The Life of the Law: Judicial Politics and Legal Change." 59 *Journal of Politics* 778 (1997).

Walker, Jack. *Mobilizing Interest Groups in America.* Ann Arbor: University of Michigan Press, 1991.

Walker, Thomas G., and Epstein, Lee. *The Supreme Court of the United States.* New York: St. Martin's Press, 1993.

Walker, Thomas G.; Epstein, Lee; and Dixon, William J. "On the Mysterious Demise of Consensual Norms in the United States Supreme Court." 50 *Journal of Politics* 361 (1988).

Wallace, J. Clifford. "Interpreting the Constitution: The Case for Judicial Restraint." 71 *Judicature* 83 (1987).

———. "The Jurisprudence of Judicial Restraint: A Return to the Moorings." 50 *George Washington Law Review* 1 (1981).

Warren, Charles. *The Supreme Court in United States History.* 2 vols. Boston: Little, Brown, 1937.

Warren, Elizabeth. *The Legacy of Judicial Policy-Making*—Gautreaux v. Chicago Housing Authority: *The Decision and Its Impact.* Lanham, Md.: University Press of America, 1988.

Wasby, Stephen L. *The Impact of the United States Supreme Court: Some Perspectives.* Homewood, Ill.: Dorsey Press, 1970.

———. "Justice Harry A. Blackmun: Transformation from Minnesota Twin to Independent Voice." In Lamb, Charles M., and Halpern, Stephen C., eds. *The Burger Court: Political and Judicial Profiles.* Urbana: University of Illinois Press 1991.

———. *Small Town Police and the Supreme Court.* Lexington, Mass.: Heath, 1976.

———. *The Supreme Court in the Federal Judicial System.* 3d ed. Chicago: Nelson-Hall Publishers, 1988.

———. *The Supreme Court in the Federal Judicial System.* 4th ed. Chicago: Nelson-Hall Publishers, 1993.

Watson, George L., and Stookey, John A. *Shaping America: The Politics of Supreme Court Appointments.* New York: HarperCollins, 1995.

Watson, Richard. "The Defeat of Judge Parker: A Study in Pressure Groups and Politics." 50 *Mississippi Valley Historical Review* 213 (1963–64).

Wattenberg, Martin P. *The Decline of American Political Parties, 1952–1988.* Rev. ed. Cambridge: Harvard University Press, 1990.

Wechsler, Herbert. "Toward Neutral Principles of Constitutional Law." 73 *Harvard Law Review* 1 (1959).

Welch, Susan; Gruhl, John; Steinman, Michael; Comer, John; and Vermeer, Jan P. *Understanding American Government.* 4th ed. Belmont, Calif.: West/Wadsworth, 1997.

Wellington, Harry H. "Common Law Rules and Constitutional Double Standards: Some Notes on Adjudication." 83 *Yale Law Journal* 221 (1973).

———. "History and Morals in Constitutional Adjudication." 97 *Harvard Law Review* 326 (1983).

———. "The Importance of Being Elegant." 42 *Ohio State Law Journal* 427 (1981).

———. *Interpreting the Constitution: The Supreme Court and the Process of Adjudication.* New Haven: Yale University Press, 1991.

———. "The Nature of Judicial Review." 91 *Yale Law Journal* 486 (1982).

Wenner, Lettie M. *The Environmental Decade in Court.* Bloomington: Indiana University Press, 1982.

Wenner, Lettie, and Ostberg, Cynthia. "Restraint in Environmental Cases by Reagan-Bush Judicial Appointees." 77 *Judicature* 217 (1994).

"What's the Alternative? A Roundtable on the Confirmation Process." 78 *American Bar Association Journal* 41 (1992).

Wheeler, Stanton; Cartwright, Bliss; Kagan, Robert; and Friedman, Lawrence. "Do the 'Haves' Come Out Ahead? Winning and Losing in State Supreme Courts, 1870–1970," 21 *Law and Society Review* 403 (1987).

White, G. Edward. "The Evolution of Reasoned Elaboration: Jurisprudential Criticism and Social Change." 59 *Virginia Law Review* 279 (1973).

Wildavsky, Aaron. *The Beleaguered Presidency.* New Brunswick, N.J.: Transaction Books, 1991.

Wilkinson, J. Harvey, and White, G. Edward. "Constitutional Protection for Personal Lifestyles." 62 *Cornell Law Review* 563 (1977).

Witt, Elder. *A Different Justice: Reagan and the Supreme Court.* Washington, D.C.: Congressional Quarterly Press, 1986.

Wlezien, Christopher B., and Goggin, Malcolm L. "The Courts, Interest Groups, and Public Opinion about Abortion." 15 *Political Behavior* 381 (1993).

Wold, John. "Political Orientations, Social Backgrounds, and Role Perceptions of State Supreme Court Judges." 27 *Western Political Quarterly* 239 (1974).

Wolfe, Christopher. *How to Read the Constitution.* Lanham, Md.: Rowman and Littlefield Publishers, 1996.

———. *Judicial Activism: Bulwark of Freedom or Precarious Security?* 2d ed. Lanham, Md.: Rowman and Littlefield Publishers, 1997.

Wolfinger, Raymond E., and Rosenstone, Steven J. *Who Votes?* New Haven: Yale University Press, 1980.

Woodward, Bob, and Armstrong, Scott. *The Brethren: Inside the Supreme Court.* New York: Avon Books, 1979.

Wright, J. Skelly. "Professor Bickel, the Scholarly Tradition, and the Supreme Court." 84 *Harvard Law Review* 769 (1971).

Yeric, Jerry L., and Todd, John R. *Public Opinion: The Visible Politics.* 2d ed. Itasca, Ill.: Peacock, 1989.

TABLE OF CASES

INDEX

● ●